Find Gold in
Windows Vista™

Find Gold in
Windows Vista™

by Dan Gookin

1807
WILEY
2007

Wiley Publishing, Inc.

Find Gold in Windows Vista™
Published by
Wiley Publishing, Inc.
111 River Street
Hoboken, NJ 07030-5774

www.wiley.com

Copyright © 2007 by Wiley Publishing, Inc., Indianapolis, Indiana

Published by Wiley Publishing, Inc., Indianapolis, Indiana

Published simultaneously in Canada

For general information on our other products and services, please contact our Customer Care Department within the U.S. at 800-762-2974, outside the U.S. at 317-572-3993, or fax 317-572-4002.

For technical support, please visit www.wiley.com/techsupport.

Wiley also publishes its books in a variety of electronic formats. Some content that appears in print may not be available in electronic books.

Library of Congress Control Number: 2007926006

ISBN: 978-0-470-04692-0

Manufactured in the United States of America

10 9 8 7 6 5 4 3 2 1

WILEY

About the Author

Dan Gookin has been writing about technology for over 20 years. He's contributed articles to numerous high-tech magazines and written over 110 books on personal computers, many of them accurate.

Dan combines his love of writing with his gizmo fascination to create books that are informative, entertaining, and not boring. Having sold more than 14 million titles translated into over 30 languages, Dan can attest that his method of crafting computer tomes seems to work.

Perhaps his most famous title is the original *DOS For Dummies,* published in 1991. It became the world's fastest-selling computer book, at one time moving more copies per week than the New York Times #1 bestseller (though as a reference, it could not be listed on the NYT Bestseller list). From that book spawned the entire line of *For Dummies* books, which remains a publishing phenomenon to this day.

Dan's most popular titles include *Word 2007 for Dummies, Laptops for Dummies,* and *PCs For Dummies.* He also maintains the vast and helpful Web page, www.wambooli.com.

Dan holds a degree in Communications/Visual Arts from the University of California, San Diego. Presently he lives in the Pacific Northwest, where he enjoys spending time with his sons in the gentle woods of Idaho.

Publisher's Acknowledgments

Some of the people who helped bring this book to market include the following:

Acquisitions, Editorial, and Media Development

Sr. Project Editor: Mark Enochs

Executive Editor: Greg Croy

Copy Editor: Becky Whitney

Technical Editor: James F. Kelly

Editorial Manager: Leah Cameron

Media Development Manager: Laura VanWinkle

Editorial Assistant: Amanda Foxworth

Sr. Editorial Assistant: Cherie Case

Composition Services

Project Coordinator: Lynsey Osborn

Layout and Graphics: Lissa Auciello-Brogan, Carrie A. Foster, Melanee Prendergast, Ronald Terry

Design: Lissa Auciello-Brogan

Proofreaders: Christy Pingleton, Jeannie Smith

Indexer: Sherry Massey

Anniversary Logo Design: Richard Pacifico

Publishing and Editorial for General User Technology

Richard Swadley, Vice President and Executive Group Publisher

Andy Cummings, Vice President and Publisher

Mary Bednarek, Executive Acquisitions Director

Mary C. Corder, Editorial Director

Composition Services

Gerry Fahey, Vice President of Production Services

Debbie Stailey, Director of Composition Services

Table of Contents

S

T

U

W

Introduction

This book is unlike any other Windows book you've ever read.

Or, if you've never read a Windows book, this book is unlike any Windows book you've never read — including that book Home Depot sells, but that's really a book on Windows *treatments* and has nothing to do with computers.

Howdy!

Find Gold in Windows Vista is a reference book. The topic is Windows Vista, the most recent version of the Windows operating system to rise from the slab at Castle Microsoft.

This book covers Windows Vista in a unique fashion, one that will have you finding the gold in no time. *Gold* in this case means *value,* not the yellow, flaky substance that Humphrey, Tim, and Walter were looking for in the Sierra Madré.

Yes, this book is both informative and entertaining. That's just the way I write. I can't help it. Yet this book's lighthearted nature does not imply that the material here is for beginners or that it's presented in a condescending manner.

This book is for anyone who has ever used Windows. It was written to follow the thinking pattern of the typical Windows user's brain: Twisted. Tortured. Desperate. Sad. Yeah, I can feel that way, too.

You see, the subject here is not about enjoying Windows. It's not about praising Microsoft. It's not about loving your computer. This book is written for you. It's about what you need, and what you want. In the case of a new computer operating system like Windows Vista, what you want is simple. You want to know *where the bodies are buried.* Or, to be more socially acceptable, you want to know where the gold is. And, you want information more specific than "Up thar in them hills." That's the point of this book.

What! No Chapters?

This book has no traditional chapters. Instead, what you could call a chapter is an entry that covers a specific item, feature, program, process, thing to do, or place to go in Windows Vista.

My thinking behind this approach is simple: You probably already know Windows. You've used either Windows XP or Windows 2000 (or one of the sorrier early versions of Window), and you pretty much know what it is you want from a computer. Your problem is finding where they hid your favorite feature in the latest version of Windows.

By making each *thing* in Windows its own entry, I've solved the problem of your having to wade through pages of useless reference material or tutorials to get the tidbit of information you desire. I feel that the result is a true reference book, one that you'll use often as you explore, or, rather, stumble through the new experiences of Windows Vista.

Assumptions

I assume that you're a computer owner. Furthermore, I assume that your PC has Windows Vista as its operating system.

If you did things properly, you bought a new computer with Vista preinstalled, and everything works great! If you've never read one of my books or heeded my sane advice, you upgraded to Windows Vista and you finally understand why some people want to strangle inanimate objects.

This book covers all flavors of Windows Vista. Yet you should note that some programs mentioned here may not appear in your version of Windows Vista. If so, it's noted in the text.

You probably should be on a computer network to benefit from the networking information in this book.

This book explains a few things to do on the Internet, so I have to also assume that your PC has Internet access. I hope that you have high-speed Internet. If not, know that I typed the dial-up Internet information very slowly because you're used to reading at that speed.

How to Use This Book

This book is an alphabetical reference to Windows Vista. Entries cover specific items in Windows: topics, programs, window names, folder names, concepts, tasks, and stuff.

Entry layout

Each entry is divided into six sections. The same sections appear in every entry. After a brief introduction, they appear in this order:

Where's the Gold? This section describes where to find an item, what it does, or how it fits into the big picture.

What to Do with It: You'll find multiple tasks listed in this section. Each task describes how to work through the main entry topic, what can be done, or how to get things done in Windows.

- ✂ Some tasks are explanations, but most involve step-by-step procedures. Follow the steps.

- ✂ The stuff you have to type in is presented in **bold text**. Type it exactly as written.

- ✂ Do not press the Enter key or click the mouse on a button until a step directs you to do so.

- ✂ Some text is `monospaced`, which means that it refers to what you see on the computer screen or perhaps is the name of a file or command.

Watch Your Step! This section contains general warnings and cautionary notes about how the topic can adversely affect what you do or various parts of Windows.

When Things Go Wrong: A troubleshooting section, this part of each entry has information that helps you figure out how to fix things when they run amok.

Gold Rush Nuggets: This section lists some trivial asides or interesting points that just don't fit anywhere else in the entry.

Digging Elsewhere: Each entry concludes with a cross-reference to similar items in Windows or other places worth looking into.

Icons

Three icons are used in this book:

 Clue: Here's a special type of tip, but it's more like a hint. Clues offer more advice than would otherwise seem obvious.

 Eureka: A true gold nugget has been found in the text — something unexpected or a value-added tip that's worthy of a snort o' whiskey.

 Dag Nabbit: Some darn annoying thing may happen that might well ruin your day.

The By The Way Saloon sidebars

Some entries just don't merit the full-on entry treatment. These include some of the many, many aspects of Windows that either aren't often used or perhaps are used so well that there's no point in writing out things in detail.

Yes, this book has an index

Despite this book's alphabetical nature (and I really wanted the publisher to call it an encyclopedia, but apparently the Britannica people threatened to sue), you'll still find a handy index in back. Use it.

For example, when you want to set the PC's clock in Windows, you have to look up the *Time* entry. I could have named it Clock. I could have named it Date and Time. But I named it Time. That's because I knew that I would have an index and it would just probably have entries for Date, Time, Clock, Tick-Tock, Cuckoo, and Big Ben, all of which will point to my *Time* entry.

Behold the Control Panel

A key location in Windows Vista is the Control Panel. Just to make things more complex, you can view the Control Panel in two ways: the traditional, icon-filled window and the Control Panel Home, which is friendlier but takes more steps.

In this book I refer to the traditional, icon-filled Control Panel Classic view window first. Then I mention how to open the same icon for the Control Panel Home. Don't let that throw you, and see *Control Panel* for more information.

A special note about UAC security warnings

Not mentioned in the steps and procedures in this book are the various times when the User Account Control (UAC) security warnings appear. I did that on purpose.

UAC warnings should be heeded. Your reactions to the security warnings should be your own, not those dictated by any other source, including this book. Get in the habit of treating a UAC as unexpected and respond accordingly.

Nothing in this book was written with the intent of harming your computer or causing you to unknowingly do anything to jeopardize your computer's security. As in real life, UAC warnings appear, and you must deal with them. That's why I chose not to include them in any steps you see in the various tasks in each entry. See the entry User Account Control (UAC) for more information.

Where to Start

This computer book is most likely the first one I've ever written (and I've written about 110) that has no "Getting Started" entry — not even something similar! Nope, the entries just start marching off in alphabetical order. In fact, I didn't even write them in alphabetical order! (The first entry I wrote was about the Recycle Bin.)

Start anywhere!

If you're really desperate, consider the Login and Log Off entry. Or, perhaps start at the Start Button and Menu entry or even the Desktop entry. If it has a name in Windows, it has a topic in this book. Somewhere.

Finding More Information

I provide my e-mail address in every book I write. Here it is:

`dgookin@wambooli.com`

That's my real address, and I do try to answer every message I get. I enjoy discussing subjects dealing with this book, but please note that I cannot and will not troubleshoot your PC problems, nor can I answer questions about your computer that aren't related to this book. When you have computer problems or questions, please contact your computer dealer. Thanks.

I also have a Web page:

`http://www.wambooli.com/`

On this page you'll find more information about Windows, PCs, the Internet, plus other helpful topics. Be sure to check it out.

Enjoy what you find in Windows Vista!

Dan Gookin

Access Control

Windows Vista has significantly pumped up file security, especially when compared to previous versions of Windows. Each file now sports an *owner,* or someone who has ultimate control over the file. Each user on the computer has his own set of access rights to various files. Furthermore, each user belongs to a group, which has its own set of rights and privileges for modifying files. The whole enchilada — users, access rights, and permissions attached to each file — is called *access control* in Windows. It's something you probably can ignore most of the time — until you need it.

WHERE'S THE GOLD?

Permissions are stored with every file in Windows. To see who has which type of access, you must display a file's Properties dialog box, like this:

1. Right-click a file's icon.

2. Choose Properties from the pop-up menu.

3. In the file's Properties dialog box, click the Security tab.

The Security tab lists two important items: a list of users or groups who have access to the file or have been specifically denied access and the list of things each user or group can do with the file. The second list is composed of *permissions.* Together, these items comprise the access control for the file.

Windows stores the Users and Groups information in the Computer Management console. Here's how to find the information:

1. Open the Computer Management console.

    You can open the console by right-clicking the Computer icon on the desktop

Users and groups   Selected user or group

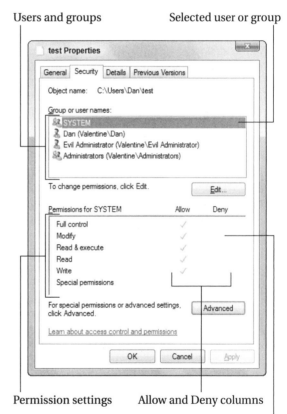

Permission settings   Allow and Deny columns

Permissions for the selected user

and choosing the Manage command from the pop-up menu. Or, you can summon the Run dialog box (press Win+R), type **mmc compmgmt.msc**, and press Enter.

2. On the left side of the Computer Management console, open System Tools and then Local Users and Groups.

3. Select the Users folder.

   In the center of the console window, you see a list of all users with accounts on the computer, including perhaps some disabled or inactive accounts, like Guest or Administrator. (*See also* Administrator, Guest.)

4. Select the Groups folder.

   The various groups are listed in the center of the window, along with a description of each one.

5. Close the Computer Management console when you're done gawkin'.

Groups provide Windows with a way of assigning privileges and rights to various tasks and processes that occur within Windows without having to go back and re-create a slate of permissions for each task. When a user is a member of a group, that user shares the same permissions and has the same access and security settings as other users or programs assigned to that group.

What to Do with It

Access control is something you probably don't want to mess with on a regular basis. Windows is good about setting permissions and granting access to those who need it. Only when special circumstances arise is it necessary to mess with a file's security settings.

Check your user settings

To see the groups your user account belongs to, which affects your security settings, do this:

1. Open the Computer Management window.

2. Open the `System Tools\Local Users and Groups\Users` folder.

3. In the Users folder, double-click to open your account.

4. In your account's Properties dialog box, click the Member Of tab.

You see all the groups you belong to listed in the dialog box. Administrators, for example, are members of the Administrators group. Standard accounts are members of the Users group.

Close all open windows when you're done poking around.

Check the groups

To see the powers and abilities bestowed on groups, follow these steps:

1. Open the Computer Management window.

2. Choose the Groups folder under `System Tools\Local Users and Groups`.

   A list of different groups is displayed. Most of them are empty; many of them exist for special circumstances or for backward compatibility with older versions of Windows.

3. Double-click to open a group.

The group's Properties dialog box lists group members, which can include users in addition to the computer itself or specific programs or tasks.

It's possible, although not really necessary, for one user account to belong to several groups; an account's security settings match whatever highest privilege is available to it.

Close all open windows when you're done messing things up.

Set folder access

You can grant or limit who on your computer has access to which folders. Normally, the Public folder is the only folder shared with all users (who have password-protected accounts). And, Administrator accounts often share their folders, but you can change all that.

Follow these steps to specify which accounts have which level of access to a folder:

1. Press Win+E to open Windows Explorer.

2. Navigate to the folder where you want to change permissions.

3. Press Alt+⇧ to open the folder's parent folder.

   Sometimes this trick works, and sometimes it doesn't. When it doesn't, you need to navigate to your folder (refer to Step 2) by opening the Computer window and then Drive C, and then opening subfolders until you find your folder's parent window.

4. Right-click the folder's icon.

5. Choose Properties from the pop-up menu.

6. In the folder's Properties dialog box, click the Sharing tab.

   When the Sharing tab isn't available, the folder cannot be shared and, therefore, permissions for the folder need not be set. You're done.

7. Click the Advanced Sharing button.

   The Advanced Sharing dialog box appears.

8. Click the Permissions button.

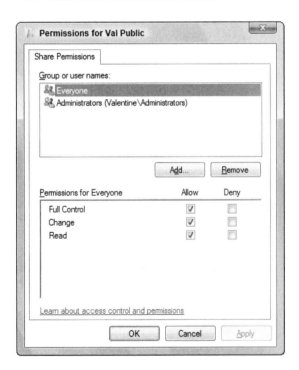

9. Optionally, remove people from the list of allowed users:

a. Click to select the user name or group name.

b. Click the Remove button.

c. Repeat substeps A and B until the list is pruned of undesirables.

10. Optionally, add new users:

a. Click the Add button.

b. In the bottom text box, type the name of the user account to add.

c. Click the Check Name button to confirm the name.

d. If the name isn't found, the Name Not Found dialog box shows up. Choose Remove "name" from Selection, and then click the Cancel button.

e. Use the Advanced button to search for names: Click Advanced, and then, in the Select Users or Groups dialog box, click the Find Now button to display a list of users. Choose the user from the list that's displayed.

f. Click OK after you've chosen the users to add.

11. Optionally, set permissions for each user:

There are three levels of access:

✗ **Full Control:** Gives the user the ability to read, create, modify, and delete files in the folder.

✗ **Change:** Gives the user the ability to read and modify files in the folder.

✗ **Read:** Gives the user read-only access.

You can choose to allow or deny each level of access for each user:

a. Click to select the user or group.

b. Set the access level for that user: Full Control, Change, or Read.

c. Repeat substeps A and B for each user.

12. Click OK to close the Permissions dialog box.

13. Click OK to close the Advanced Sharing dialog box.

14. Click OK to close the folder's Properties dialog box.

Change a file's security access

Windows gives out file permissions as best as it sees fit. You can change those permissions, but really the only way to do so is to utterly obliterate the current permissions and then start over assigning permissions to users and groups as you see fit.

Obviously, this task is a complex, technical process. Follow these steps only when it's imperative that you change a file's security settings!

1. Right-click the icon representing the file that won't obey you.

2. In the file's Properties dialog box, click the Security tab.

3. Click the Advanced button.

An Advanced Security Settings dialog box musters forth.

4. Choose the user you want to disinherit.

5. Click the Edit button.

An *even more* Advanced dialog box appears.

6. Deselect the check box labeled Include Inheritable Permissions from This Object's Parent.

7. Click the Remove button to confirm.

Now you've done it! No one has access to the file, so you have to add yourself back into the list.

8. Click the Add button.

The Select User or Group dialog box appears.

9. Type your account name in the bottom-most text box in the Select User or Group dialog box.

10. Click the Check Names button.

If you don't get it right, pop up the Start button's menu to confirm your account name. This step is one you shouldn't miss!

11. Click OK to add the name.

12. In the Permission Entry dialog box, choose the permissions for the user or group.

For my own account, and the SYSTEM account, I select the Full Control check box in the Allow column. For other accounts, I might be picky.

13. Click the OK button.

14. Optionally, consider adding other names: Repeat Steps 8 through 13 for other accounts or groups to have access to the file.

I recommend adding SYSTEM to the list and giving SYSTEM full control.

15. Click OK to dismiss the *even more* Advanced dialog box.

16. Click OK to dismiss the Advanced Security dialog box.

In the file's Properties dialog box, you see that only your account has access to the file and that it has full access.

17. Click OK.

Change the file owner

You cannot mess with a file in Windows Vista that you do not own. Back in the old days, for example, you could remove a file from the Windows folder or replace it with a better one — *if* you knew what you were doing. But files outside your User Account folder are not "owned" by you. Still, you can mess with the files, if you're sneaky and you follow these steps:

1. Right-click the icon for the file you want to totally own.

2. Choose Properties from the pop-up menu.

3. In the file's Properties dialog box, click the Security tab.

4. Click the Advanced button.

5. In the Advanced Security dialog box, click the Owner tab.

6. Click the Edit button.

7. Choose the owner from the list in the bottom of the dialog box.

When the owner you want isn't listed, do this:

a. Click the Other Users or Groups button.

b. In the Select User or Group dialog box, type the user name in the bottom part of the dialog box.

c. Click the Check Name button.

This substep sets the name properly for Windows.

d. Click OK.

8. Click the OK button.

9. Click OK at the information dialog box thingy.

It says that you cannot change the file's permissions until after you close all open dialog box windows.

10. Click OK to close the Advanced Security dialog box.

11. Click OK to close the file's Properties dialog box.

Watch Your Step!

Generally speaking, it's a good idea *never* to mess with things you don't understand in a computer, especially with regard to security. My guess is that you can successfully use your Windows Vista computer every day until Windows Optimus Prime (or whatever) comes out in a few years and not once have to mess with any of this stuff.

Obviously, you need administrator access to pull off these tricks. *See also* Administrator.

You cannot change the permissions of a file unless you own it.

When Things Go Wrong

Restoring a file's previous version may save you from certain peril when you utterly screw up permissions or ownership. *See also* Previous Versions.

Then again, perhaps the only true way to recover a file you fouled is to restore a copy of that file from a recent backup. *See also* Backup.

Gold Rush Nuggets

Access control also refers to those traffic lights you find at on-ramps for busy freeways — two cars per green.

Digging Elsewhere

Encryption, Public Folder, Share Stuff on the Network, User Accounts

Add Hardware

A relic from ancient computer times is the Add Hardware Wizard. Once upon a time, adding new hardware to a computer was a true ordeal. Whether it was a printer, scanner, digital camera, modem, or mouse, adding the hardware required more than just plugging the thing in. You had software to add and settings in Windows to make, plus a seemingly endless series of starts and restarts. Thankfully, that era is long gone, but the Add Hardware Wizard remains.

The Add Hardware Wizard isn't needed. Instead, refer to the directions that came with your new hardware. Sometimes, all you need to do is connect the device and it works. At other times, you may need to install software from a CD or DVD first and then add the hardware. The instruction booklet that came with the new hardware should awkwardly attempt to explain it.

When you need it, the Add Hardware Wizard can be started from an icon in the classic Control Panel. (Oddly, there's no equivalent you can use from the Control Panel Home.) You can manually run the Add Hardware Wizard by typing **hdwwiz** into the Run dialog box. (*See* Run.)

You can use the Add Hardware Wizard in one of two ways. First, start the wizard as described earlier in this entry. Second, after clicking the Next button, you need to choose one or the other approach:

⚒ **Search For and Install the Hardware Automatically:** This option directs Windows to look for new hardware and add it. This option is the best, so try it first.

⚒ **Install the Hardware That I Manually Select from a List:** This option is good when Windows becomes intolerably slow in installing hardware. I recommend using it only when you know a lot about the hardware you're installing or when the hardware's instruction manual directs you to do this.

Note that you do not need to use the Add Hardware Wizard to add most internal items in the console. These items include more memory, a disk drive, or any expansion cards.

About the only thing that truly must be installed manually anymore is an external modem. See Modem for more information.

Address Bar

The Address bar answers the oft-asked question "Where the heck?" — as in "Which folder am I viewing?" or "Which Web page is this?" The Address bar can also be used to change locations, by typing a new address or choosing an address from its history list. After you unlock its secrets, you'll find happy hour at the Address bar quite an enjoyable experience.

WHERE'S THE GOLD?

As a navigational tool, the Address bar sits atop both the Windows Explorer and Internet Explorer windows. Atop the Windows Explorer window, the Address bar is used to determine which folder's contents are displayed in the window. Not only does the Address bar show the *pathname* to the folder, but the pathname can also be manipulated to navigate elsewhere on the disk or network.

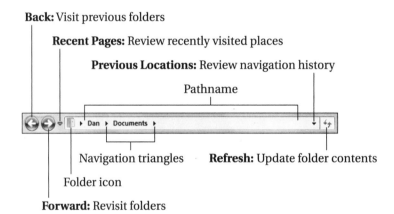

Back: Visit previous folders

Recent Pages: Review recently visited places

Previous Locations: Review navigation history

Pathname

Navigation triangles   **Refresh:** Update folder contents

Folder icon

Forward: Revisit folders

Internet Explorer uses the Address bar to display the full address of the current Web page. You can also use the Address bar to type a new address. Note that in Internet Explorer, the Address bar grows an extra button, named Stop, which halts the loading of a Web page.

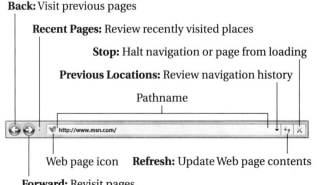

Back: Visit previous pages

Recent Pages: Review recently visited places

Stop: Halt navigation or page from loading

Previous Locations: Review navigation history

Pathname

Web page icon   **Refresh:** Update Web page contents

Forward: Revisit pages

You may also find the Address bar as a toolbar on the Taskbar. In this mode, the Address bar is used to either type Web page addresses or pathnames or visit folders on your computer's disk system or the network.

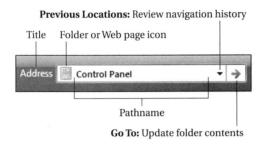

Previous Locations: Review navigation history

Title   Folder or Web page icon

Pathname

Go To: Update folder contents

As you type, you may see a list of items matching what you typed so far. Feel free to choose any item from the list, either with the mouse or by using the down-arrow key on the keyboard. *See also* AutoComplete.

Edit a Web page address

Web page addresses that appear in the Address bar can be edited just as any text is edited in Windows.

Clue   Use the mouse to select all or part of the address, type new text to replace old text, or use the Delete or Backspace key to modify the address.

Type or edit a pathname

Typing a pathname in the Windows Explorer Address bar requires that you switch from navigation mode to editing mode:

1. Click the folder icon on the far left side of the pathname.

2. Edit the pathname or type a new one.

As you type the pathname, a drop-down list of available paths appears. The more you type, the narrower the list of paths becomes. At some

What to Do with It

The Address bar can be your handiest tool or the option you choose to ignore most often. It's necessary for typing Web page addresses, but for navigating folders it can be eschewed in favor of the folder tree on the left side of the Windows Explorer window. Even so, I believe you'll discover that for navigating a disk system, the Address bar can be one handy tool.

Type a Web page address

Typing a Web page address is cinchy: Just type the address. Press the Enter key to fetch that page from the Web.

point, it's just easier to use the down-arrow key to highlight the pathname you want and then press the Enter key to display that folder's contents.

Retrieve a previous address

Any Web page address or pathname you typed earlier can be retrieved from the Previous Locations list:

1. Click the Previous Locations button.

   Or, press the F4 key on the keyboard.

2. Choose an item from the list.

Pressing F4 switches the Windows Explorer Address bar into editing mode. Refer to the preceding section.

When you're choosing a Web site address while using Windows Explorer, a new Internet Explorer window opens. Conversely, when you're choosing a folder while using Internet Explorer, a new Windows Explorer window opens. (See the warning in the "Watch Your Step!" section.)

Navigate to another folder on the hard drive

Using the Address bar to help navigate the forest of folders on your PC's hard drive is simple — much better than the traditional folder tree method.

Each triangle in the pathname serves as a menu button. Click that button to browse to other folders at the same level as the folder to the left, as shown with the Program Files folder.

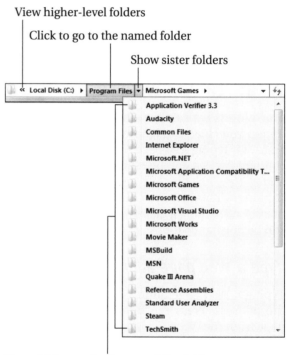

View higher-level folders

Click to go to the named folder

Show sister folders

Sister folders to the Program Files folder

Each folder name in the path also serves as a button; click the folder name to view the contents of that folder.

Click the leftmost arrow or double chevron to start navigating at a top-level folder.

Type common folder names in the Address bar

You can type any of the following folder names in the Windows Explorer Address bar:

Computer	Favorites	Pictures
Contacts	Games	Recycle Bin
Control Panel	Music	Videos

Type the name, press Enter, and then see that folder's contents.

Add the Address bar to the Taskbar

To place a bonus Address bar on the Taskbar, heed these steps:

1. Right-click a blank part of the Taskbar.
2. Choose Toolbars➪Address from the shortcut menu.

To make the Address bar wider, unlock the Taskbar.

To remove the "Address" title, unlock the Taskbar, and then right-click Address. Choose the Show Title command from the pop-up menu.

To remove the Address bar from the Taskbar, repeat the preceding steps and deselect Address.

Use the Address bar to make a shortcut

Eureka You can make a shortcut to any folder or a Web page by dragging its icon from the Address bar. This action creates a Web page or folder shortcut icon wherever you release the mouse.

Clue Obviously, this trick works best when the Web page or folder window isn't maximized to fill the screen.

For example, to save a shortcut to a Web page, drag the icon to the left of the Web page's address (in the Address bar) from the Internet Explorer window out to the desktop or to a folder window.

Watch Your Step!

Some Web page addresses are case sensitive. When the proper page doesn't load, double-check your typing and ensure that you're matching upper- and lowercase letters.

Web page addresses use forward slashes as separators. With pathnames, backslashes are preferred, although forward slashes can be used in many cases.

When you're browsing a Web page and you choose a pathname from the Recent Locations list, a User Account Control appears, informing you that the Web site wants to open local content. It's okay to proceed because you chose the location yourself.

Anything you type into an Address bar that isn't recognized causes Windows to search the Internet for a Web site matching what you type. Click the Back button when such behavior doesn't match your intentions.

When Things Go Wrong

Clicking a folder icon in the Address bar switches from navigation mode (with the triangles) to editing mode. There's no easy way to switch back, although I click the Back button and then the Forward button, which seems to restore things nicely.

Click the Stop button when you enter the wrong Web page address.

Gold Rush Nuggets

The Address bar was born with Mosaic, the first popular program for browsing the World Wide Web, back in 1993.

The Address bar for working with files in Windows made its debut with Windows 98.

The icon associated with a Web page, appearing to the left of its address in the Address bar, is the *favicon*, which is short for *fav*orites *icon*.

In quite a few cases, you can dispense with the `http://www` part of a Web page address.

The final slash mark (/) on a Web page address is also optional (although the Web browser software adds it automatically).

The double less-than symbol, <<, at the start of a path indicates that the folder name you see on the far left isn't the highest-level folder available. Click the << button to see higher-level folders.

Digging Elsewhere

Pathnames, Toolbars

Administrative Tools

Nestled deep in the bosom of the Control Panel is an icon named Administrative Tools. Opening that icon reveals a host of additional icons, each of which is designed to assist you with managing various aspects of your computer. Or, on rare occasions, you may need to wade into the administrative waters to fix some problem or adjust a setting. But most of the time, the Administrative Tools icon can be freely and safely ignored.

To view the Administrative Tools window, open the Administrative Tools icon in the Control Panel. From the Control Panel Home, choose System and Maintenance, and then scroll down to choose Administrative Tools.

The Administrative Tools window lists icons representing various tools you can use to modify Windows or places you can go to observe things that Windows is doing.

Administrative Tools icon

Each icon represents a different part of Windows or some specific administrative tool:

Computer Management: In addition to the obvious task "manage your computer," an icon that lets you monitor system events, configure hard drives, and monitor system performance; also gives you access to the Task Scheduler and Device Manager.

Data Sources (ODBC): A database management tool used to move information between programs. ODBC stands for Open Database Connectivity, which is an $800 answer in *Double Jeopardy*.

Event Viewer: A tool used to review system logs, including security and error messages generated by the computer and various loaded applications.

iSCSI Initiator: A program that monitors network storage devices. ISCSI, or Internet Small Computer System Interface, has been ruled too technical to qualify as an answer in any *Jeopardy!* round.

Local Security Policy: A console that controls aspects of network and user security.

Memory Diagnostics Tool: A utility that checks your computer's RAM.

Print Management: A console that lets you manage printers connected to your PC as well as network printers that your computer is using.

Reliability and Performance Monitor: A handy tool that monitors your PC's microprocessor, memory, hard drive, network, and resource performance, complete with nifty displays and graphics. Woo!

Services: A console that lets you examine or modify the various services, or tiny programs, that run about and do various things to keep your computer running.

System Configuration: Allows you to customize how Windows starts, as well as which programs and services run at startup; better known in previous versions of Windows as the MS Config program.

Task Scheduler: A place where you can schedule various programs to run or activities to take place at specific times or intervals.

Windows Firewall with Advanced Security: A console that allows you to view and change specific settings for the Windows Firewall program.

Some icons are programs, but most are Microsoft Management Console (MMC) plug-ins, which use the same type of interface to display information.

To see an example of the MMC, open the Computer Management icon in the Administrative Tools window. The Computer Management tool uses an MMC to display its information. A folder tree helps to organize information. The center pane of the window displays specific settings that can be adjusted. The pane on the right lists various commands.

If you're seriously interested in exploring the Administrative Tools, I recommend finding a book specific to the subject. Most of them are designed for folks administrating large networks, so don't expect buried treasure. But when you're curious, that's the type of book you need. (I haven't looked over the lot yet, so I cannot recommend a specific book.)

Click to select

Snap-in name

Microsoft Management Console (MMC)

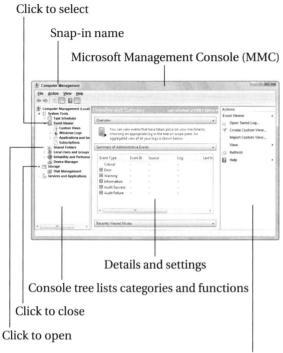

Details and settings

Console tree lists categories and functions

Click to close

Click to open

Action pane shows commands and options

Administrative Tools. I don't recommend changing anything "just to see what it does." That's a bad idea. Instead, take advantage of the help that Windows offers — which is quite extensive.

When you open a setting or option in one of the many security MMCs, click the Explain tab to get a rational rundown of what the setting controls and how the options work.

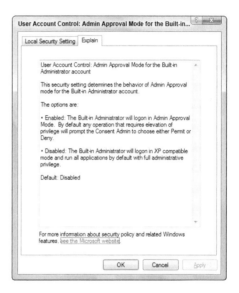

What to Do with It

My advice is not to do anything with Administrative Tools unless you're directed to do something from tech support, an article on a Web page or magazine, or a book. Otherwise, here's a smattering of things to mess with for general purposes.

Discover what the setting really means

Plenty of help is available for when you plan to go spelunking through the caves and caverns of the

Look up a specific service

Microsoft gives the name *service* to those many tiny programs that serve (get it?) a specific purpose inside the computer. Many services are running, and many more are disabled and not needed under every circumstance. To display the lot, heed these steps:

1. Open the Administrative Tools icon in the Control Panel.

2. Open the Services icon.

The services are listed like a detailed folder entry, beginning with the service's official name and also containing a brief description.

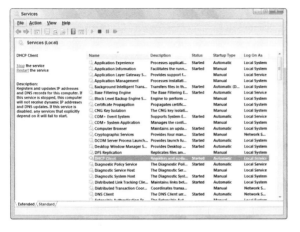

Check the Event Viewer

Anytime anything happens in Windows, a record is made. Those records are stored in log files, categorized by the type of event: an error, a warning, success, or just plain old information.

Most events occurring in Windows are uneventful. But occasionally, you must check the logs for troubleshooting or for optimizing the system.

When you need to do that, bring up the Event Viewer:

1. Open the Administrative Tools icon in the Control Panel.

2. Open the Event Viewer icon.

The *Event Viewer* is an MMC that organizes the various messages and logs that Windows creates. For example, to view the Windows Security log, open Windows Logs on the left side of the Event Viewer MMC, and then select Security. The list of security events appears in the center of the window, listed by date and time. To view a specific event, double-click to open it.

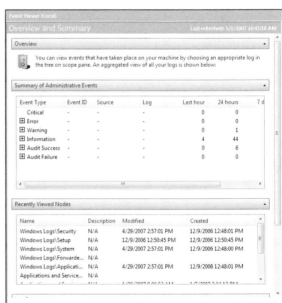

Watch Your Step!

Holy smokes, are there plenty of pratfalls in the Administrative Tools! It seems that most power users and wannabes have a craving about knowing the "secrets" of Windows. I would tread lightly.

I do not recommend enabling or disabling any security policy or service without knowing what you're doing. Unless you're willing to risk access to your computer, don't goof around!

When Things Go Wrong

System Restore, my friend, System Restore. *See* System Restore.

 Not every version of Windows Vista sports the same number or type of Administrative Tools. Don't be alarmed if a certain tool isn't available.

Gold Rush Nuggets

Microsoft updated the Administrative Tools in Windows Vista specifically to keep the most powerful programs to control a PC in one central location.

The MMC was introduced with Windows 2000.

You can open a *blank* MMC by using the Run command: Press Win+R to summon the Run dialog box, type **mmc.exe**, and press the Enter key. Although that task is boring in and of itself, you can select recent consoles to load from the File menu or choose File⇨Open to browse for consoles, most of which are found in the \Windows\System32 folder.

Digging Elsewhere

Control Panel, System Restore

Administrator

Administrator refers to two things: an account on all Windows Vista computers — the main account that has control over the system — and a type of user account, the highest account available over the Standard and Guest accounts. *See* Standard User for more information.

WHERE'S THE GOLD?

The Administrator account is most often the only account you have, if you're an individual who first set up Windows Vista on your computer. If so, your account — no matter what its name — is the administrator.

Administrator *access* simply means that changes you make can affect the entire computer system. Such changes include installing software, which is installed on all accounts on the same computer, as well as making any changes to the computer that affect all users. That, plus a few maintenance and recovery issues, is all that separates the administrator-level account from a Standard account.

What to Do with It

Microsoft recommends that you use the Administrator account only when you're making changes that apply to everyone using the computer, such as installing software or configuring network access. Otherwise, you should set up and use a Standard account. *See* Standard User.

Confirm that you're an administrator

To confirm that you have an Administrator account, pop up the Start button's menu and click your account's picture in the upper right corner. That's the handy shortcut to open the User Accounts window. By your account's name, you should see the type listed, such as Administrator.

Check other users' status

When you have an Administrator account, you can view all other accounts on the computer to see which other users are administrators or on Standard or Guest accounts. Do this:

1. Open the Control Panel's User Accounts icon.

   If you're using the Control Panel Home, choose User Accounts and Family Safety and then choose User Accounts.

2. Click the link labeled Manage Another Account.

3. Click the Continue button if you see a User Access Control warning.

4. View or change the other accounts.

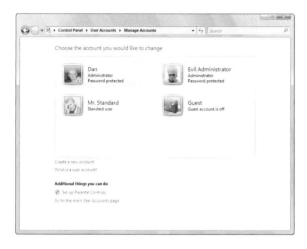

Promote or demote an administrator

As an administrator, you can apply administrator access to any account, or you can remove that privilege. Continue after the first three steps of the preceding section:

4. Click to choose a user's account.

5. Click the link labeled Change the Account Type.

6. Choose either Standard User or Administrator.

7. Click the Change Account Type button.

Recover a lost administrator password

 I strongly recommend that you password-protect your Administrator account, specifically by using a strong password.

If you forget the Administrator account password, you can do two things:

First, use the Password Reset Disk; *see* Password Reset Disk.

Second, if another Administrator account is on the same computer, you can use that account to change the other Administrator account's password (or the password on any user account):

1. Open the User Accounts icon in the Control Panel.

From the Control Panel Home, choose User Accounts and Family Safety and then choose User Accounts.

2. Click the link labeled Manage Another Account.

3. Click to select the other administrator's account.

4. Choose either Change the Password to assign a new password or Remove the Password to allow the user access — and, hopefully, to assign her a new password.

When you have no password reset disk and no other Administrator accounts are on the computer, you're basically screwed. That's one of those rare instances where you must reinstall Windows to create another administrator-level account.

Activate the secret Administrator account

Okay: I lied. There is, in fact, an account named Administrator on your PC. It's a secret account, one that's most likely disabled. (That means you still cannot use it to rescue a password.)

To enable the account, obey these steps:

1. Open the Control Panel's Administrative Tools icon.

   From the Control Panel Home, choose System and Maintenance and then scroll down to choose Administrative Tools.

2. Open the Computer Management icon.

3. On the left side of the Computer Management console, open Local Users and Groups.

4. Select the Users folder.

5. Right-click the Administrator account, on the right side of the console.

6. Choose Properties from the shortcut menu.

7. In the Administrator Properties dialog box, deselect the check mark by the item labeled Account Is Disabled.

8. Click OK.

The secret Administrator account is now active, and it appears when you log in to Windows. The account still needs a password, of course. To disable it, repeat the preceding steps; I don't recommend removing the account.

Watch Your Step!

At least one account on the computer must be named Administrator. Windows doesn't let you remove the last or only administrator-level account, nor are you allowed to demote that account to a Standard account.

When using Windows Vista at a large organization, you may find it automatically configured so that you have a Standard account and Administrator is another account to which you do not have access.

When Things Go Wrong

When the option to run a program as administrator is unavailable, it means that the particular program has been blocked from administrator privilege — and probably for good reason.

Gold Rush Nuggets

They say that the Administrator account is similar to the root account on a Unix system. This comparison is valid, although the root account in Unix has far more privileges and more freedom than the Administrator command as initially configured in Windows Vista.

Digging Elsewhere

Guest, Password Reset Disk, Standard User, User Accounts

All Programs Menu

The theory goes that every single program ever installed on your computer, as well as the many programs that come with Windows, can be found on the All Programs menu. It's the one handy spot for starting any program you need.

When the All Programs menu is active, it appears on the left side of the Start menu. Otherwise, all you see is the text *All Programs* in the lower left part of the Start button's menu.

To view the All Programs menu, click All Programs on the Start menu. You can also just point the mouse at All Programs, and the menu appears, replacing the contents of the Start button menu's left side.

The All Programs menu follows a *hierarchical* structure, with important programs appearing first and secondary programs dished up on submenus.

On the top level, the All Programs menu lists the programs used most often.

Submenus hold other programs or represent program categories, such as Games or Microsoft Office or sometimes the name of the software developer. The submenus display more programs to run, or they may contain more submenus for another layer of organization.

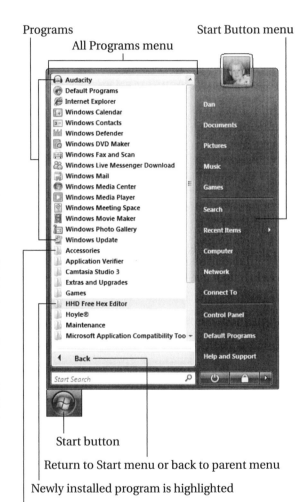

Programs

All Programs menu

Start Button menu

Start button

Return to Start menu or back to parent menu

Newly installed program is highlighted

Submenus

Clue Windows Vista has *two* All Programs lists. One is a *local* list, containing programs specific to your account. The other is a *master* list, which is shared by all users. The program shortcuts and menus you see on your screen are produced by combining both lists.

What to Do with It

The All Programs menu is just one of several places you can go in order to start programs on your computer. I consider it the main place to go because, in theory, just about every program installed on your computer can be run from the All Programs menu.

Run a program

Just about any program can be run from the All Programs menu. Here's the general way things go:

1. Click the Start button.
2. Choose All Programs.
3. If your program is visible, click to select it, and the program starts. Otherwise:
4. Scroll down through the list to look for your program, and then go back to Step 3 — or:
5. Open a submenu folder to see whether your program is there and, if so, go back to Step 3.

Click a submenu once to open it and again to close it.

To close the All Programs menu, click the Back button.

Edit the All Programs menu

The All Programs menu is *your* menu. You're free to customize it as you see fit, by adding, removing, or combining submenus or shuffling the programs around to best suit your needs.

Clue The All Programs menu is really a series of shortcut icons and program folders on the hard drive. Those shortcuts appear as program entries on the All Programs menu, and the folders appear as submenus. Because of the relationship between the menu items and the shortcuts and folders, you can easily edit the All Programs menu. Of course, it helps to have a basic understanding of how Windows manipulates files to do the best job. *See* Copy, Cut, and Paste Files; Delete; Rename.

Edit your account programs

To edit only those items on the All Programs menu that are unique to your account, right-click the All Programs menu and choose the Open command. A Windows Explorer window opens, showing the contents of the Start Menu folder for your account. One folder is visible: Programs. Open that folder.

Any shortcut icons you see in the Programs window represent programs specific to the All Programs menu shown for your account. Some folders may be visible too; opening them details any submenus, and the shortcut icons there are also specific to your account.

Refer to other sections in this entry for information on how to edit the program shortcuts that are specific to your account.

Edit all account programs

To edit the items on the All Programs menu, which appears in every user account on your computer, right-click the All Programs menu and choose the Open All Users command. A Windows Explorer window opens to show you the Start Menu folder, which lists program shortcuts and folders that appear on the All Programs menu for each user on the PC.

Organize the All Programs menu

Installation programs tend to install new programs in *dis*organized ways. To keep them organized, I recommend creating menus based on the categories of software you use. For example, the following submenus can help you organize the All Programs menu by software category:

- ✂ Education
- ✂ Entertainment
- ✂ Financial
- ✂ Games
- ✂ Graphics
- ✂ Internet
- ✂ Productivity
- ✂ Utilities

Submenus within these categories can help organize things even further, perhaps by program name or developer or even subcategories.

Creating these or similar menus is covered in the next section.

Add a new menu

Creating a new menu for the All Programs menu is done by making a new folder in the proper place.

To make a new folder for all users on the computer, open the Programs folder by following the instructions in the earlier section "Edit all account programs."

To make a new folder for only your account, open the Programs folder by following the instructions in the earlier section "Edit your account programs."

To create the menu, simply add a folder:

1. Click the Organize button on the toolbar.

2. Choose New Folder from the menu.

3. Type the new folder's name and press Enter.

The folder's name becomes the new menu name. If you're creating the folder for all accounts, every account on the PC sees the new submenu.

Cut, prune, and graft

Windows Vista has no strict rules regarding how the All Programs menu is organized. If, for example, you want to move the WordPad program from the Accessories menu to the main menu, you're free to do so.

Moving programs around on menus is done by using that file's Cut and Paste commands:

1. Locate the program shortcut you want to move.

   Say that you want to move the Calculator from the Accessories window to the main window. If so, open the Accessories folder inside the Programs folder.

2. Click to select the program to move.

   In the example, click to select the Calculator shortcut.

3. Press Ctrl+X to cut it.

   Or, from the Organize button's menu, choose Cut.

4. Return to the Programs menu.

   Click the Back button or choose Programs from the Address bar.

5. Press Ctrl+V to paste.

The icon is moved. Likewise, you can move graphics programs from various folders into a general Graphics menu folder.

Moving an entire folder is referred to as *pruning* and *grafting*. The steps are the same as for moving a single program shortcut, but when you move a folder, you're also moving the folder's entire contents.

Remove a menu or an item

Windows doesn't automatically remove empty folders from the All Programs menu, but you can! When a folder is empty, delete it:

1. Click to select the folder.

2. Press the Delete key on the keyboard.

3. Optionally, click Yes to confirm the deletion.

Rename a menu or an item

Renaming a menu or program shortcut works just like renaming a file:

1. Click to select the folder or program shortcut.

2. Press the F2 key on the keyboard or, from the Organize button's menu, choose the Rename command.

3. Type the new name.

4. Press Enter to accept the new name.

See Rename for various file- and folder-naming rules and regulations.

Watch Your Step!

When changes are made to the All Programs menu for everyone, everyone witnesses those changes.

When Things Go Wrong

To immediately undo a file moving (cut and paste), deleting, or renaming operation, press the Ctrl+Z key combination. That's the Undo command's keyboard shortcut, and it undoes whatever you just did. It only works for the last thing you did, though, so be careful!

Eureka
You can restore deleted program shortcuts and folders from the Recycle Bin. *See* Recycle Bin.

Gold Rush Nuggets

The All Programs menu is an ancestor of the original Program Manager, from very early versions of the Windows operating system.

Not *every* program dwells on the All Programs menu. Some internal programs are unavailable, plus a few select utilities and tools in Windows that aren't found on the All Programs menu.

The All Programs menu for your account secretly dwells on the hard drive in the hidden AppData folder, found in your account's User Profile folder. The path is

```
..\AppData\Roaming\Microsoft\Windows\
Start Menu\Programs
```

Likewise, the All Programs menu, which is shared by all users, is found in this folder:

```
\ProgramData\Microsoft\Windows\Start
Menu\Programs
```

Digging Elsewhere

Delete, Files, Folders, Rename, Shortcuts, Start Button and Menu

Antivirus

I t seems like good news always comes with the bad. Computers provide a great way to get things done and exercise creativity, but it didn't take long before someone developed a program that intended to do evil instead of good. Those nasty programs are given the names *virus, Trojan horse,* and *worm.* They're all categorized as *malware,* and it's a sad part of computing life in the early 21st century that you must actively fight against these threats.

WHERE'S THE GOLD?

You won't find an antivirus utility in Windows Vista. Although your computer may have come with an antivirus program, it's not a Windows program, not like Windows Defender or the Windows Firewall.

To help ward off viruses, you can do two things: First, you can buy and install antivirus software. That's the best way to protect your computer.

Second, you can be vigilant. Windows Vista provides plenty of security tools to help you become aware of when something isn't acting right in your PC. But before that happens, you need to monitor what it is that you do with your computer, especially on the Internet and specifically with e-mail.

I do not have any favorite antivirus programs to recommend. The most popular one is Norton AntiVirus, followed by McAfee. But I've also heard nice things about Kaspersky.

What to Do with It

The best antivirus programs run in the background, guarding the PC but not bothering you much. Only when something nasty happens are you told about it, and even then the warning should come after the antivirus program has protected your computer.

Choose your mode of operation

Antivirus programs generally have two modes of operation. In one mode, the program scans the memory and files on disk for signs of infection. In the other mode, the program sits in memory and watches computer activity — specifically, any new programs that are installed. When suspect activity occurs, the antivirus program checks the activity to see whether it shows signs of infection. If it does, the activity is stopped and you're made aware of the situation.

One problem with the second mode I mention is that it can slow down your computing. Having antivirus software monitor everything you do consumes resources on your computer. A better approach is to configure the antivirus software to monitor only those programs you download from the Internet and your e-mail attachments.

Unless your computer is constantly under attack or is out in a public place, that's about all you need for antivirus protection.

Update antivirus signatures

A virus is identified by its *signature,* or special piece of programming code within the virus itself. Because the Bad Guys keep producing more viruses, the antivirus people need to keep updating their signature databases to help keep up the fight.

Every so often, ensure that your antivirus software gets a new batch of signature files. These signatures are generally downloaded over the Internet by your antivirus software as it runs, or they might be downloaded on a schedule.

To ensure that you keep getting new signatures, you should wisely renew your antivirus program's subscription every year. Yes, this costs money, but your computer and your data are worth it.

Disable antivirus software while you install new programs

Because viruses and other nasty programs like to install themselves in your computer, most antivirus programs guard against *any* program being installed in your PC. Therefore, you have to disable or suspend the antivirus program whenever you install new programs.

You can disable antivirus software in different ways, but the most common way is to right-click the antivirus software's teeny icon in the

Notification Area. Choose the Suspend, Disable, or Stop command from the pop-up menu. Then install your software. Then restart Windows to ensure that the antivirus software is reenabled and continues protecting your PC.

Scan for viruses

Your antivirus software should have a mode where you can manually scan both memory and files on the disk drives for signs of infection. You may even find two modes of operation: a quick scan and a more thorough scan.

There's no need to scan for viruses every day, unless your PC is highly prone to infection. Otherwise, a quick scan whenever you suspect something is okay. A full scan every month or so works well.

Determine when your PC is infected

Some signs that your computer has a virus include

- ✗ Overall sluggishness
- ✗ Lots of disk activity when you're not doing anything in particular
- ✗ Lots of modem activity when you're not doing anything in particular
- ✗ Unknown or random programs starting and stopping
- ✗ Nasty messages
- ✗ Random restarts and freezes
- ✗ An inability to navigate the Internet

Having any or all of these signs doesn't mean that your computer has a virus, but when you notice them, you should pull out some other tools and check. Using Software Explorer in Windows Defender can help locate rogue programs running on your PC. *See also* Windows Defender.

Watch Your Step!

I no longer recommend those free antivirus programs that you can download from the Internet. Instead, do yourself and your computer investment a favor and *buy* antivirus software. Pay the subscription fee. Renew it every year. Your computer is worth it.

Most viruses are effective not because of their programming but because of *social engineering*. In other words, you (the human) are fooled into doing something that you know you shouldn't do because the Bad Guys have figured out a way to make you drop your defenses.

You can fight viruses without using antivirus software. Simply heed this advice:

- ✗ Do not open an e-mail attachment that you were not expecting.

- ✗ Do not download a program from the Internet when you cannot trust the source. Specifically avoid downloading files from porn sites, from sites full of cheat codes for games, or from "hacker" sites.

- ✗ Never start your computer by using a floppy disk, also known as a *boot floppy*. Do not let others do this, either.

- ✗ Avoid installing a "cool game" or watching a video from a CD-R. Technically, that's piracy (theft!), and the odds are good that the swag is infected.

- ✗ Keep Windows updated. *See* Updates.

- ✗ Use a firewall. *See* Firewall.

Although these suggestions will help keep your computer safe, they will not do the job of removing a virus if your computer becomes infected; only an antivirus program can do that.

When Things Go Wrong

Antivirus programs generally do not detect or remove spyware. Even though spyware can be just as nasty and awful as computer viruses, it's just not within the scope of most antivirus software programs to deal with spyware. Therefore, you must bolster your antivirus software with anti-spyware software. Fortunately, Windows comes with such a program: Windows Defender.

Even if you don't update your antivirus subscription, the antivirus program continues to protect your computer. The only problem is that newer viruses aren't detected by the antivirus program until you pay for a new subscription and download those new antivirus signatures.

Gold Rush Nuggets

It's often said that the Windows platform has more than 100,000 viruses and nasty programs eager to attack it, whereas the Macintosh computer has practically none. In the late 1980s, however, computer viruses began targeting Macintosh and PC systems equally. Things can change.

The computer nerds love to refer to viruses by the general term *malware* — essentially, evil software. And, although specifically there are viruses and worms and Trojan horses, I think that the generic term *virus* can be used to describe them all. You can quibble over the meaning of *virus* versus *worm* at your next computer geek cocktail party.

Digging Elsewhere

Firewall, Windows Defender

AutoComplete

The AutoComplete function creates some confusion. What it does is assist you in filling in forms on various Web pages. When AutoComplete is active, the forms are filled in automatically; text shortcuts are displayed as you type, to save time. AutoComplete is not, however, the feature that displays previously visited Web pages in the Address bar. That's the *History* command. Both AutoComplete and History help you save time by doing some of the typing for you.

WHERE'S THE GOLD?

You control AutoComplete from the Internet Options dialog box:

1. Open the Internet Options dialog box.

You can summon the dialog box by opening the Internet Options icon in the Control Panel or from within Internet Explorer by choosing Internet Options from the Tools toolbar button.

2. Click the Content tab.

AutoComplete is the second item from the bottom.

3. Click the Settings button in the AutoComplete area.

In the AutoComplete Settings dialog box, you can enable or disable individual places where AutoComplete comes into play.

You may have also encountered AutoComplete when you first filled in a form or entered a password on a Web page. In that case, a question mark dialog box appears, asking whether you want Internet Explorer to remember information for that page.

What to Do with It

AutoComplete works automatically, although you should note that some Web pages may not activate AutoComplete. When security is an issue, AutoComplete may not work automatically. That's a good annoyance.

Use AutoComplete

When you're visiting a Web page, AutoComplete makes itself known by displaying a drop-down menu of items previously typed in a form. Use the mouse or the down-arrow key to select an item and keep going.

On pages with long forms, note that selecting the first item may fill in the rest of the form for you automatically. That's the beauty of AutoComplete.

Clear the AutoComplete information

To purge your computer of information that AutoComplete remembers, obey these directions:

1. Open the Internet Options dialog box.

2. Click the General tab (if needed).

3. Click the Delete button in the Browsing History area.

4. Click the Delete Forms button to remove any form data remembered by AutoComplete.

5. Click the Yes button to confirm.

6. Click the Delete Passwords button to remove any passwords remembered by AutoComplete.

7. Click the Yes button to confirm.

8. Click OK.

The Delete Browsing History dialog box is where you can not only remove AutoComplete information but also purge other items stored by Internet Explorer, such as the Web page History list.

Turn off AutoComplete

To disable AutoComplete, deselect all check marks in the AutoComplete Settings dialog box.

Watch Your Step!

You have to pay attention to two issues with AutoComplete:

✗ Sometimes, AutoComplete automatically fills in a Web page form but does so incorrectly. Always ensure that you double-check the information that AutoComplete types.

✗ Also, AutoComplete forces you to be lazy with your Internet account names and passwords. I highly recommend keeping a second copy of your passwords elsewhere, just in case you forget or because a Web page may change and AutoComplete will "forget" the password for you.

Remember that AutoComplete isn't the same as the Web browser's History feature. The Web page addresses you see in the Address bar drop-down list are kept in the History feature, not in AutoComplete. *See also* History.

When Things Go Wrong

To recover AutoComplete information after accidentally deleting it, use System Restore.

 AutoComplete doesn't work on certain secure Web sites.

Gold Rush Nuggets

Versions of AutoComplete are available in most Web browsers, such as Firefox and Opera. Obviously, controlling those applications' versions of AutoComplete is different from following the directions offered here.

Digging Elsewhere

History, Internet Explorer, Passwords, System Restore

AutoPlay

The Windows AutoPlay feature appears whenever you add new media to your computer system. You're most likely to see the familiar AutoPlay dialog box quizzing you about what to do with new media whenever you insert a CD or DVD or attach a USB flash drive or media card. When you don't see the dialog box, AutoPlay has been configured to automatically handle, or *play,* the media per your directions. Likewise, you can configure AutoPlay to never bug you. So, it's really more of an AutoPlayNoPlay command.

WHERE'S THE GOLD?

AutoPlay is one of the few elements in Windows Vista that isn't buried away in some obscure corner of the computer. The dialog box appears whenever you add media to your computer. The choices that are presented, which depend on what Windows finds on the media, can be any of the following:

- ✂ Burn audio CD
- ✂ Burn DVD data disc
- ✂ Burn files to disc
- ✂ Import pictures
- ✂ Install or run program
- ✂ Open folder to view files
- ✂ Play audio CD
- ✂ Play DVD
- ✂ Play videos
- ✂ Rip music from CD
- ✂ Run enhanced content

- ✂ Speed up my system
- ✂ View pictures

Additional information may appear, depending on which software is installed on your computer.

To make the AutoPlay dialog box work, choose from the list which action you want to take.

When a check box is available, you can select it to assert that AutoPlay should always take the action you select for that type of media. Or, you can simply close the dialog box to take no action.

You use the AutoPlay icon in the Control Panel to modify AutoPlay behavior.

AutoPlay icon

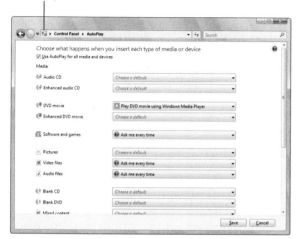

The AutoPlay dialog box lists various types of media or media content and allows you to choose preset options for each media type.

Two additional options are available:

⤬ **Take no action:** Disables AutoPlay for the device or type of media.

⤬ **Ask me every time:** Re-enables the AutoPlay dialog box to be displayed whenever the media or disk type is inserted.

What to Do with It

AutoPlay is designed to be a *helpful* feature, by assisting you with what to do when new media is inserted or attached to your computer. You can set options based on what you find useful or annoying — which is a refreshing switch from most things the computer does.

Choose what to do

After you insert a CD, DVD, or other type of media, the AutoPlay dialog box appears. Choose whichever task relates to what you want to do with the disk; for example:

⤬ Choose Open Folder to view files to simply work with the media, like any disk.

⤬ Choose Burn Files to Disc to write data to a CD or DVD.

⤬ Choose Rip Music from CD to copy music to your computer.

⤬ Choose Install or Run Program to run the setup or install program on a CD.

Or, simply close the dialog box to dismiss it.

Set up AutoPlay for a digital camera's media card

After inserting the camera's card, choose the option Import Pictures to use the Windows Photo Gallery for your image management. Or, when you prefer to manage your own images, choose Open Folder to View Files.

Eureka If you have specific image organization software, that program's option may appear on the AutoPlay list. If so, choose it as the action you always want to take when inserting your camera's media.

Set specific AutoPlay options

Use the AutoPlay dialog box to configure specific actions to always take when a certain type of media is inserted:

1. Open the Control Panel.

2. Open the AutoPlay icon.

3. Click the menu button next to the media type or contents.

   For example, Blank CD.

4. Choose an action from the button's menu.

   This action directs Windows behavior when that type of media is inserted.

5. Repeat Steps 3 and 4 for common types of media you use.

6. Click the Save button when you're done.

Disable AutoPlay

When you tire of seeing AutoPlay pop up, you can disable it. For example, if you prefer not to have a musical CD or movie DVD play when it's inserted, simply make the proper change to that media type's AutoPlay options; in the steps from the previous section, choose the action Take No Action in Step 4.

Reactivate AutoPlay

When you change your mind about not taking any action when inserting a specific media type, you can reset things to the way they were. Open the AutoPlay icon in the Control Panel and locate the media type you want to change. Instead of selecting Take No Action for that media, choose Ask Me Every Time or some other option. Then click the Save button.

Force the AutoPlay dialog box to appear

You can force the AutoPlay dialog box to appear whenever any media is inserted, by pressing and holding the Shift key. This action overrides any other AutoPlay settings you may have made.

Use Windows ReadyBoost

An option that appears in the AutoPlay dialog box when you add special high-speed, USB flash memory storage is to use Windows ReadyBoost to help speed up your computer system. When you choose that option, Windows sets aside a certain amount of storage on the removable media for use in improving system performance. Here's how it works:

1. Attach a high-speed USB media card or flash drive to your PC.

2. In the AutoPlay dialog box, choose the option Speed Up My System.

   The AutoPlay dialog box goes away and the device's Properties dialog box appears, with the ReadyBoost tab selected. The dialog box explains how much memory on the device will be used by Windows.

3. Click OK.

Windows automatically uses the device to help improve system performance.

Remember to properly remove the device when you're done. *See* Safely Remove.

Watch Your Step!

Most installation CDs and DVDs assume that you have AutoPlay on, which is how they automatically run their setup or install programs. If you disable this feature or choose another option, you must manually install the programs. That's relatively easy: Select the disc's icon in the My Computer window and click the AutoPlay button on the toolbar.

AutoPlay behaves differently when a media program is open in Windows. For example, if you're running Media Player or Media Center and you insert a musical CD or a movie DVD, AutoPlay is sidestepped and the media is played inside Media Player automatically.

When Things Go Wrong

The AutoPlay dialog box may appear unexpectedly, especially when you configure AutoPlay either not to appear or for a specific action to take place. It happens when Windows examines the media and doesn't come up with a proper guess about the media's content.

AutoPlay can be disabled or limited as part of your PC's security policy, such as when you're using the PC in a large office or other organization.

 Clue The check box directing AutoPlay to "always do this action" may go missing from the AutoPlay dialog box. It happens because several types of media are available on the disc or media.

Gold Rush Nuggets

Windows looks for a file named AUTORUN.INF on any media you insert. If that file is found, it's opened and its contents read, directing Windows about what to do next.

You can manually run a disc's AUTORUN.INF file by right-clicking the disc's icon in the My Computer window and choosing the Open AutoPlay command from the pop-up menu.

Folders can be configured to better display certain types of media, such as pictures or music. *See* Folders.

Digging Elsewhere

Computer, Discs (CDs and DVDs)

Backup

Perhaps the most ancient of all computer utilities is Backup. Even if the program itself isn't ancient, the concept is: Keep a copy of your computer files in a safe location. That copy is a *backup* copy, available in case anything happens to the originals. Obviously, having that backup copy is important. But equally as obvious, few computer users ever back up their data. Some sadly accept it as a consequence of the digital age that when you lose your files — all that music and video and especially all those digital pictures — they're gone forever. That's sad. Sadder still is that I've been writing about backing up information for over 20 years and nothing has changed!

WHERE'S THE GOLD?

The main place to find Backup, as well as its companion, Restore, is in the Backup and Restore Center. To display the Backup and Restore Center, open the Control Panel's Backup and Restore Center icon. From the Control Panel Home, choose Back Up Your Computer, beneath the System and Maintenance heading.

The Backup and Restore Center is where you begin the backup or restore process. It's the central location for both backing up and restoring files.

In addition to the Backup and Restore Center, you have the Backup Status and Configuration window. You can open it from the Start button's menu by choosing All Programs⇨Accessories⇨ System Tools⇨Backup Status and Configuration.

Note that Windows Backup may not be available with all versions of Windows Vista.

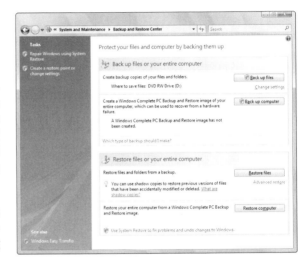

What to Do with It

Creating a safety copy of your files is one of the most important things you'll never do with your computer. If you've read this far, congratulations.

Configure and run your first file backup

The first thing you need to do is configure the Backup program to start a regular backup schedule. As part of that configuration, you back up your files. Here's how to do that:

1. Open the Backup and Restore Center.

2. In the Backup area (at the top), choose Change Settings.

   The Backup Status and Configuration window appears.

3. Click the big button near the bottom, Change Backup Settings.

4. Choose where to back up.

   I recommend a network drive or an external disk drive — something roomy that's not inside your computer. I'm not discounting the CD/DVD option, but using an external drive ensures that scheduled backups happen automatically.

5. Click the Next button.

6. Keep all files selected in the next window, and click the Next button.

7. Set the frequency for the automatic backup.

8. Ensure that the CD/DVD disc is ready or that the external drive is online and ready.

9. Click the button labeled Save Settings and Start Backup.

10. Switch to the Backup Files window.

It should be the only blinking button on the Taskbar.

11. Click OK.

12. If you're using a CD or DVD, format the disc.

13. Sit back and watch; it takes awhile.

   This is one reason why some folks favor automatic, unattended backups.

14. Click the Close button when the backup is done.

15. Close the various Backup program windows.

16. Eject the CD or DVD (if necessary), label it, and put it in a safe place.

Check Automatic Backup success

To confirm that a backup has taken place and been successful, you must open the Task Scheduler window (*see* Task Scheduler). Look for the entry in the category Task Scheduler Library, Microsoft, Windows, Windows Backup.

Back up the entire computer

To back up everything on your computer — all files, programs, Windows, and everything — do this:

1. Summon the Backup and Restore Center.

2. Click the Back Up Computer button.

3. Choose to back up to an external hard drive or a DVD drive.

4. Click the Next button.

On the next screen, take note of how many DVDs the backup requires. Yes, it's quite a few. Ensure that you have that many DVDs ready.

5. Click the Start Backup button.

When backing up to a DVD, you have to remove and insert a new disc every so often to keep up with the tremendous volume of information.

 I don't recommend doing a full computer backup that often, if at all. It's better to back up only your files (in the User Profile folder). Then, if disaster strikes, you can reinstall Windows (or use a System Recover disc from your PC's manufacturer), reinstall your applications, and then restore your own files from a backup. That's how I work things.

Disable Automatic Backup

Automatic backups are wonderful for folks who take backing up seriously and who have either an external or a network hard drive available for backup files. Otherwise, you probably want to do away with automatic backups and just manually back up your files. Here's how to disable the Automatic Backup feature:

1. Summon the Backup Status and Configuration window.

2. Click the Turn Off button.

3. Close the Backup Status and Configuration window.

 With Automatic Backup turned off, you must remember to manually back up your computer every so often.

Perform a manual backup

To back up your files manually, follow these steps:

1. In the Backup and Restore Center, click the Back Up Files button.

2. If necessary, Switch to the Back Up Files window and insert the DVD you used for the previous backup.

3. Click the Close button when the backup is done.

4. Remove the DVD, ensure that it's properly labeled, and store it in a safe place.

Restore files

To retrieve one or more files or folders from a backup, follow these steps:

1. Ensure that the most recent backup disc is available in the DVD drive, attached to the PC, or available on the network.

2. Open the Backup and Restore Center.

3. Click the Restore Files button.

4. Click the Next button.

5. Click the Add Files button.

6. Use the Browse window to locate files or folders to recover from the backup; select the file or files and click the Add button.

7. Repeat Steps 4 and 5 as necessary.

8. Click the Next button.

9. Choose the option In the Following Location only if you want to recover an older version of a file without overwriting the original.

See also Previous Versions.

10. Click the Start Restore button.

11. Click the Finish button.

 Put the DVD back into its safe location when you're done restoring files.

Watch Your Step!

The more important and irreplaceable your stuff is, the better you should get off your butt and back it up.

Windows Backup cannot back up specific files or folders. It can back up only general files from your account or the entire computer.

Windows Backup does not back up files in the Recycle Bin.

You cannot back up to the same hard drive that you're backing up. (For example, you can't back up the entire contents of the C: drive to the C: drive.) You cannot back up to a USB flash drive.

You need to be there when Windows performs an automatic backup to a DVD drive and more than one DVD is needed.

When Things Go Wrong

Windows alerts you when you need to insert the proper DVD for a backup or restore operation. Be on the alert for a pop-up warning bubble from the Notification Area or a blinking button on the Taskbar. Click the bubble or blinking Taskbar button to continue.

Gold Rush Nuggets

Better backup programs exist for your PC, stuff that makes Windows Backup seem restricted and awkward. Alternatives to consider are Norton Ghost, EMC Retrospect, and Roxio Backup MyPC.

Digging Elsewhere

Files, System Restore, User Profile Folder

BitLocker

Windows features the special, high-encryption tool *BitLocker,* which goes well beyond basic file encryption (*see* Encryption). In fact, BitLocker is designed to encrypt — and encrypt well — all the information on an entire hard drive.

BitLocker works by encrypting all the data on your hard drive — everything. Scramble. Scramble. Scramble. The information stays encrypted until you log in to your password-protected account. Then the information is decrypted and made available.

The idea behind BitLocker is that it renders the hard drive utterly useless to anyone who doesn't have a password-protected account on the computer.

Sadly, setting up and configuring BitLocker involves advanced planning, the proper computer equipment, and an ample length of time. It's a major activity.

First, you cannot install BitLocker on just any PC hard drive. The hard drive must be divided into separate pieces, or *partitions*. For most of us, that requires having a full hard drive backup, uninstalling Windows, repartitioning the hard drive (which requires special software), reinstalling Windows, and then restoring all your files, data, and programs. I don't know about you, but for me that seriously does not sound like a good time.

After completing the drastic chore of rejiggering the PC's hard drive, you may discover that your computer lacks a Trusted Platform Module (TPM) chip. BitLocker relies on the special TPM computer security chip for its unscrambling chores. Now you can get by without a TPM chip by using a USB flash or key ring drive. But, honestly!

If you're still eager to walk down the BitLocker path, you can find the BitLocker program lurking in the Control Panel: Open the BitLocker icon. Or, from the Control Panel Home, choose Security and then BitLocker Drive Encryption. (Note that BitLocker isn't available in all Windows Vista releases.)

The main BitLocker window tells you immediately whether you can convert your PC's hard drive to the BitLocker format. Odds are that you cannot. Furthermore, my guess is that your computer lacks the TPM chip, which isn't really an impediment to using BitLocker, but it's another reason to leave this baby in the bath water.

See also Encryption, which is probably a better way to protect your files. You might also find the Access Control entry useful, for security reasons.

Calendar

One of the many tiny programs (often called *applets*) included with Windows is the Windows Calendar scheduling tool. Because Microsoft prepends the word *Windows* to all its tiny programs, I just call the thing Calendar.

The Windows Calendar is part of a suite of programs designed to manage personal information inside your computer. In many cases, these programs are all-in-one personal information managers, or PIMs. In fact, you may have such a program on the computer that works in conjunction with your cellphone or a PDA or handheld computer.

Windows Calendar works with the Contacts folder as well as with your e-mail program to coordinate your life — if you want it to.

To set an appointment, click the New Appointment button. Fill in the date and time and details in the Appointment part of the Calendar window (on the right). Note that you can color-code your appointments, by designating certain colors to certain types of appointments — red for work, pink for home, blue for your social organization, and so on.

Note that you can have the computer remind you of appointments by using the Reminder menu. Select a time before the appointment that you want the computer to annoy you. And, keep in mind that the reminder works only when the computer is on and you're near the thing to see the reminder.

To pull in attendees, click the Attendees button, which connects the Calendar program with the Contacts list. (*See* Contacts.)

You can move or copy appointments by using the Edit menu's Move or Cut commands; select an event to move or copy, then go to the new day and choose Edit⇨Paste to paste the event to the new time. (*See also* Copy, Cut, and Paste Data.)

Windows Calendar also lets you create a to-do list of tasks. Click the New Task list to create a task.

You can also publish your calendar to share it with others, although for this to be most effective, you must have "space" on the Internet as a destination. (Space can be a Web site or a shared folder on some network server.)

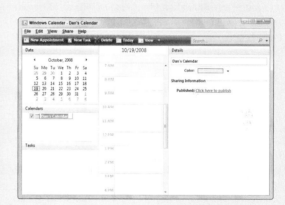

Character Map

One of those old-time Windows tools that we computer geeks love is the Character Map. It's a simple little program — a *utility* or *tool* — that provides visual access to all the characters available in a font. It's the way we know-it-alls can stick those strange characters into text. As such, I suppose that I would be wise to shut up about it and not divulge the secret. But, naaa.

The Character Map dwells on the Start button's menu: Choose All Programs⇨Accessories⇨SystemTools⇨ Character Map. Why such a handy program is considered a system tool is beyond me. It's really a text creation tool.

To use the Character Map, first select a font from the drop-down menu on top. The font you choose then has all its various characters splayed out in a grid. First come the standard symbols and characters, the so-called *Latin* character set. By scrolling down, you soon see accented characters, and then oddball characters from other languages, and then symbols and a whole assortment of goodies.

To use a character, click to select it, and then click the Select button. That places the character into the Characters to Copy text box. You can continue to do this to build a character string. Click the Copy button to place the single character or string of text into the Clipboard. From the Clipboard, you can then paste the special text into any document or program in Windows that accepts pasted text. (*See* Copy, Cut, and Paste Data.)

For characters you use often, note the Keystroke item, in the lower right corner of the Character Map window. The keystroke that's listed can be used in any program that allows keyboard input. The key to using the keystroke is to press and hold the Alt key and then type the numbers listed on the numeric keypad. Release the Alt key to see the character. For example, Alt+0174 is the registered trademark symbol, ®. (If this technique doesn't work at first, try turning on the Num Lock key.)

Check for Disk Errors (Check Disk)

The Check Disk program has been around for eons, dating back to the early days of the DOS operating system. Although many users attribute magical powers to Check Disk, what it does is very simple: Check Disk scans a disk drive to ensure that it has no obvious errors. You can do a detailed scan or a quick scan. If errors are found, Check Disk tries to fix them, although it cannot fix everything.

WHERE'S THE GOLD?

The Check Disk command is found lurking in a disk drive's Properties dialog box. Here's the path to take to find this jewel:

1. Open the Computer window.

2. Right-click a disk drive or storage media icon.

   Check Disk does not work on CDs or DVDs.

3. Choose Properties from the pop-up menu.

4. In the disk drive's Properties dialog box, click the Tools tab.

5. Click the Check Now button to run Check Disk.

The Check Disk interface isn't that impressive, nor is it spectacular to watch while it does its job.

What to Do with It

You don't need to run Check Disk often. I recommend running it only when you're having disk drive troubles or when Windows recommends that you use it to ensure that a disk drive is functioning properly.

Fully check a disk

Check Disk checks only one disk or media at a time. To check a disk, follow these steps:

1. Start Check Disk for a given drive.

2. Place a check mark by the Automatically Fix File System Errors option.

    Fixing disk problems is Check Disk's first priority.

3. Optionally, place a check mark by the Scan for and Attempt Recovery of Bad Sectors option.

4. Click the Start button.

5. Sit back and watch.

6. Read the summary.

7. Click the Close button.

8. Click OK to close the disk's Properties dialog box, and, optionally, close the Computer window or choose another disk to check.

Schedule a disk check

Check Disk doesn't run on a disk drive that's busy. Rather than attempt to run it (and potentially screw something up), you're given the option of scheduling Check Disk for later.

Click the Schedule Disk Check button. Windows automatically schedules Check Disk for the next time you restart Windows.

Watch Your Step!

Choosing the Surface Scan option gives the disk a good binary scrubbing but also adds to the length of time that Check Disk takes to do its task.

The Check Disk program is not magic. Too many PC users feel that running Check Disk will instantly solve all computer ills and fix problems not even remotely associated with the hard drive. Running Check Disk too often does nothing for your computer. When your PC has problems, you need to troubleshoot them. Check Disk may be a part of that, but it's not the miraculous solution to all problems.

When Things Go Wrong

Check Disk tries its best, but it cannot fix certain disk problems. You can try other disk utilities, including third-party programs, such as Norton Disk Doctor. But these types of programs may not address the issue of a failing hard drive.

When the number of bad sectors on a hard drive grows and grows, it's a sign that the disk is about to die. The best thing to do is back up all your files, install a new disk, and then restore your files. *See* Backup.

Gold Rush Nuggets

Modern hard drives use S.M.A.R.T. (Self-Monitoring And Reporting Technology) to instantly repair hard drive errors. This technology may be implemented by your PC manufacturer or dealer.

The original DOS Check Disk program was named CHKDSK. It mostly checked a disk but also collected (rescued) orphan files. CHKDSK was replaced by ScanDisk in Windows, which was more effective at working with larger hard drives. And now, with Windows Vista, the thing is named CHKDSK again, which is still a valid command at the command prompt.

Digging Elsewhere

Defrag, Disk Drives

Command Prompt

T he command prompt provides you with a traditional, text-based way to control your computer. Way back when, computers were primarily text devices lacking any true graphics display. The first terminals used on computers were adapted teletype machines — essentially, noisy printers that whacked out one character at a time (and provided the foundation for the Hollywood fantasy that computers make noise when text is displayed). Early computer monitors were also text-only devices, and, therefore, everything the computer did was text based — including the operating system.

Today, the command prompt remains a throwback to the text-based era, but more importantly it provides a handy place for power users to take advantage of the various potent text commands to control their computers.

The command prompt exists as a program on the All Programs menu. To run it, pop up the Start button menu and then choose All Programs⇨Accessories⇨ Command Prompt. The Command Prompt window appears, showing a text-based interface for using your computer.

Control menu

Command

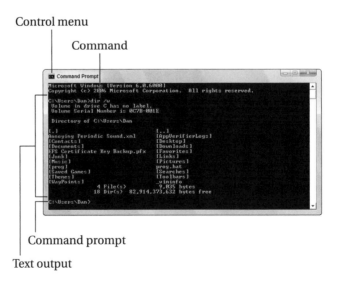

Command prompt

Text output

The Command Prompt program is named CMD.EXE. You can start a Command Prompt window by typing **cmd** in the Run dialog box. *See* Run.

You can have as many Command Prompt windows open as Windows itself can stand.

What to Do with It

Although you may not achieve that cryptic level of PC sophistication, sometimes you may need to use the command prompt to carry out some task or procedure.

Open a Command Prompt window

To open a Command Prompt window, choose All Programs➪Accessories➪Command Prompt, or double-click any Command Prompt icon or shortcut icon to open it.

Close the Command Prompt window

You can close the Command Prompt window by clicking its red X (Close) button in the upper right corner, just like in any other window.

The DOS command to close a window is EXIT. Type **exit** at the command prompt and press the Enter key, and the window closes.

Configure the Command Prompt window

The Command Prompt window can be customized, primarily in a visual way. The key is found in the window's Properties dialog box.

(These are the *window's* properties, not the properties of the Command Prompt program.) Do this:

1. Click the Command Prompt window's Control menu button.

2. Choose Properties from the menu.

3. Click the Options tab (if necessary).

   The Options tab lists commands for using the text cursor and command history and for editing. I find none of these options interesting or worth changing from their standard settings.

4. Click the Font tab.

   The Font tab lets you set which font to use for displaying the command prompt's text. Note that the font size affects the window's proportions, as you can see in the Preview window.

5. Click the Layout tab.

   The Layout tab controls the window's size and position. Back in the old days, the IBM PC's monitor showed 80 columns of text in 25 rows, which is how the Command Prompt window is configured. You can change these proportions by using the dialog box gizmos. The *buffer* refers to visual information (text that's displayed), which you can scroll through to view a transcript of your Command Prompt session.

6. Click the Colors tab.

   On the Colors tab, you can set the text, background, and colors for the Command Prompt window.

7. Click the OK button to lock in your choices.

The changes you make are recalled for any new Command Prompt window you open (except for an administrator Command Prompt window).

Type a command

Commands are typed at the command prompt, which is that little bit of text in front of the blinking text cursor.

Type the commands by using the keyboard, just as you type any text in Windows. Use the Backspace key to back up and erase. You can also use the Windows text-editing key commands to move the cursor, but not to select text. *See* Text Editing.

No command obeys you until you press the Enter key. Pressing Enter sends the command off to be interpreted and acted upon.

Here are some sample commands you can type if you're curious:

CLS   Clears the screen.

DIR   Displays a list of files.

VER   Displays the Windows Command Prompt version.

VOL   Displays the disk drive's volume name.

Commands can be typed in upper- or lowercase. Spelling is important!

To cancel a command or start over again with a new prompt, press Ctrl+C. (C means *cancel* here, not *copy*.)

Eureka To recall a previously typed command, press the up-arrow key.

Run a program

Although you can type DOS commands at the prompt, most of the commands you type run programs. In Windows, you can type the name of any Windows program and run it from the command prompt. It helps to know the command name, of course. But after that, you just type the command and press Enter, and the program runs.

For example, to run the Notepad text editor, type **notepad** at the DOS prompt and press Enter, and the Notepad window opens. (The Command Prompt window remains open but is in the background.)

Here are some other commands you can type:

MSPAINT   Runs the Paint program.

EXPLORER   Opens a Windows Explorer window.

WRITE   Runs WordPad. (Write was WordPad's original name.)

CONTROL   Opens the Control Panel window.

START   Opens another Command Prompt window.

TASKMGR   Starts the Task Manager.

Generally speaking, any command you can type in the Run dialog box can also be typed at the DOS prompt.

Get command prompt help

The command prompt offers help with its commands and such, although you shouldn't expect the type of friendly help you get in Windows. Command prompt help is brief and to the point.

To see a list of all command prompt commands, type **help** and press Enter. The list scrolls by quickly; be sure to use the scroll bar to look at the entire thing.

Help can be found for each individual command by typing the command name followed by a slash and a question mark, as in **sort /?**. Again, the information that's displayed is helpful only when you know what the command does in the first place; the help doesn't show you *how* to use any command.

Copy text from the Command Prompt window

To get text out of the Command Prompt window, you must select it with the mouse and copy it. This isn't as easy as it seems because clicking the mouse in the Command Prompt window is interpreted as a mouse click by whatever DOS program is running. To get the text out, you must do this:

1. From the Control menu, choose Edit➪ Mark.

2. Use the mouse to drag and select a rectangle of text on the screen.

3. Press Enter to select the rectangle of text.

4. Switch to (or open) the program into which you want to paste the text.

5. Press Ctrl+V to paste the text.

The text is pasted one line at a time.

See also Copy, Cut, and Paste Data.

Paste text into the Command Prompt window

Text can be pasted into the Command Prompt window, either to the command prompt itself or into any program running in text mode.

To paste text, first position the cursor (if necessary) to accept the text. The text is pasted as though it's being typed. From the Control menu, choose Edit➪Paste.

Print from the command prompt

In the old days of DOS, you could print a transcript of your DOS command session by pressing the Ctrl+P key combination. Pressing Print Screen actually sent a copy of the DOS text screen to the printer. Or, you could redirect text output to the printer by using various DOS commands. But the Command Prompt window in Windows Vista has been disconnected from the printer. To get printed output, you must either save text to a file, which can then be printed using a text editor, or copy the text from the Command Prompt window into a program window and then print from there.

Start an administrator's command prompt

Some command prompt commands require administrator access. To start the command prompt in Administrator mode, do this:

1. Pop up the Start button's menu.

2. In the Search box, type **command prompt** and press Enter.

3. Right-click the Command Prompt icon.

4. Choose Run As Administrator from the pop-up menu.

Create an administrator's command prompt icon

You can create a shortcut icon that runs the command prompt with elevated privileges. *See* Shortcuts for information on creating a desktop shortcut to the command prompt. Then do this:

1. Right-click the Command Prompt shortcut icon.

2. Choose Properties from the pop-up menu.

3. Click the Shortcut tab in the Properties dialog box.

4. Click the Advanced button.

5. Place a check mark by the option Run As Administrator.

6. Click OK to close the Advanced Properties dialog box.

7. Click OK to close the Properties dialog box.

You might also consider renaming the shortcut icon to Administrator Prompt or something similar.

Watch Your Step!

Unlike in other versions of Windows, you can close a Command Prompt window *while* a program is running. Windows simply closes the window, and anything that the running program was doing is killed off and any unsaved documents remain unsaved. Watch out!

Changing the font or window size may make for a better-looking Command Prompt window, but you should recognize that most DOS commands and programs are geared toward using an 80-column-by-25-row text screen. Some programs may not display properly at other sizes and resolutions.

When you mistype a DOS command, you see this message:

```
'explode' is not recognized as an
internal or external command, opera-
ble program or batch file.
```

Simply try typing the command again.

You cannot paste graphics into the Command Prompt window. Even if you are, for some incredible reason, running an old DOS graphics program, you cannot paste graphics. Use the old graphics program's commands to open or import graphics files.

When Things Go Wrong

Most of the problems at the command prompt are typing problems; check your typing and try again.

Many command prompt programs can be canceled by pressing the Esc key. You can also try Ctrl+C or Ctrl+Break. (The Break and Pause key are the same.)

Gold Rush Nuggets

Once upon a time, the command prompt was the *DOS prompt*, and DOS, not Windows, was the computer's operating system (the *Disk Operating System*). To start Windows, you typed **win** at the DOS prompt. But people wanted multitasking and pretty graphics, so the DOS prompt was demoted to its status as a mere program within Windows.

Power users prefer the command prompt. Using the various text commands is often faster and more effective than attempting to do some things in the Windows graphical interface.

Digging Elsewhere

Pathnames, Run, Start Button and Menu

Compressed Folders

A special type of folder is the Compressed Folder. It's not used like a regular folder is, for organization or separating like files or anything like that. No, a Compressed Folder is a storage bin, an *archive*. It's used to hold files collectively as a single unit. The files are compressed, taking up less disk space. But, more importantly, because the files are compressed and all held in one container, they can be quickly transmitted from one computer to another. This makes the Compressed File a popular way to store and retrieve information from the Internet.

WHERE'S THE GOLD?

Compressed Folders dwell in a folder window along with other files and folders. Essentially, the Compressed Folder is known as a Zip file. (The Compressed Folder has the ZIP filename extension.) Unlike other folders, the Compressed Folder sports its own icon.

Compressed
Folder icon

Opening a Compressed Folder displays its contents, just like any other folder. But the display can be misleading because the files listed in the window still exist in a compressed state. Therefore, opening a Compressed Folder is more of a look-see operation than any type of true file management.

What to Do with It

Making and using a Compressed Folder is part of the archiving chore on your computer. Mostly, you're collecting and archiving information to send as an e-mail attachment. You can also archive older files, although for that task I recommend using regular file compression; *see* File Compression.

Create a new Compressed Folder

To create a new, empty Compressed Folder, do this:

1. Right-click in a folder window.

2. From the pop-up menu, choose New⇨ Compressed (Zipped) Folder.

3. Type a proper name for the folder; press Enter to lock in the name.

For filenaming rules, *see* Rename.

Assign files to a new Compressed Folder

Another way to create a Compressed Folder, especially when you know its contents in advance, is to do this:

1. Select all the files and folders to be placed in the Compressed Folder.

   Remember that you can select files and folders from one only folder window at a time.

2. Right-click one of the selected files.

3. Choose Send To⇨Compressed (Zipped) Folder from the pop-up menu.

   The Compressed Folder shares the name of the first selected file in the list, but you can go to Step 4.

4. Optionally, rename the new Compressed Folder.

Add files and folders to a Compressed Folder

Files can be added to the contents of a Compressed Folder just as they're added to a real folder: Copy and paste, drag and drop, or perform any of the file copying techniques I cover. *See* Copy, Cut, and Paste Files.

The files you copy are instantly compressed when they reside in the Compressed Folder.

Manage files within a Compressed Folder

You have some control over files within a Compressed Folder, but not as much freedom as you do with files in a regular folder. You can

✗ Delete a file just as you delete a file from any folder.

✗ Cut or copy a file.

✗ Open some files.

✗ Preview some files.

You cannot

✗ Rename a file.

✗ Undo a Delete operation.

✗ Access a file deleted from a Compressed Folder in the Recycle Bin.

Extract a file from a Compressed Folder

Removing a file from a Compressed Folder works just like copying a file from any folder: Select the file or files, copy them, and then paste them into a new folder. *See* Copy, Cut, and Paste Files for details.

Files removed from a Compressed Folder are decompressed as they're copied out.

Extract all files from a Compressed Folder

Most often, you want to extract all files from a Compressed Folder at one time. You can do this in a few different ways:

- ✂ Right-click the Compressed Folder icon and choose Extract All from the pop-up menu.

- ✂ Within the Compressed Folder, click the Extract All button on the toolbar.

Either way, the Extract Compressed (Zipped) Folder window opens. Follow these steps:

1. Choose a folder for the files.

   Windows automatically creates a new folder with the same name as the Compressed Folder. That's fine, although you can use the Browse button to choose another folder.

2. Place a check mark by the option Show Extracted Files When Complete.

3. Click the Extract button.

A new folder window opens, revealing the extracted files.

After extracting the files, you can delete the original Compressed Folder. I keep Compressed Folders around (in my Downloads folder) for programs I download, just in case I need to reinstall a program.

Install a program from a downloaded Compressed Folder

Programs are often stored on the Internet in Compressed Folders (also known as Zip files). After downloading a Compressed Folder to your computer, extract all files from it, per the directions in the preceding section.

After the new folder is open, locate the install or setup program and start that program to install your new software.

Watch Your Step!

You cannot browse Compressed Folders, as you can browse other folders. That's because, despite their display in the Windows Explorer window, the files and folders held in a Compressed Folder exist in a compressed state and cannot be accessed until they are extracted from the Compressed Folder.

Some files don't compress well. For example, Compressed Folders themselves cannot be recompressed. Video files, MP3 audio files, JPG, TIFF, and PNG files, and Office 2007 documents do not compress, either. These files can still be stored in a Compressed Folder, but they won't be compressed much.

When Things Go Wrong

Windows may not recognize some Zip file formats, so the icon may appear to be a Compressed Folder when it's actually a special Zip file format. When that happens, you need to obtain either another version of the file (one that's compatible with Windows Vista) or a third-party Zip file management utility. I recommend WinZIP: `www.winzip.com`.

Previous versions of Windows offered password protection for Compressed Folders. This is no longer an option in Windows Vista.

Gold Rush Nuggets

Compressed Folders are essentially Zip files, popularized by the PKZIP utility back in the early 1990s. Before PKZIP, the ARC utility was used to collect and compress files for easy transfer over modems by the online community.

Digging Elsewhere

File Compression, Folders, Windows Explorer

Computer

T he Computer window is the apex of your computer's long-term storage system. In that window, you'll find a list of all your PC's disk drives and any attached storage media. The Computer window remains an ideal spot to start a browsing expedition through all those storage devices, or for generally working with your computer's disk drives.

You have a number of ways to display the Computer window. The most obvious way is to open the Computer icon on the desktop, although that icon may not show up. (*See* Desktop Icons.)

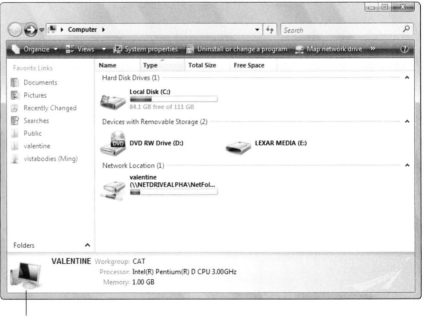

Computer icon

You can also choose the Computer command from the right side of the Start menu, although it may not appear there either.

Finally, from any Windows Explorer window (press Win+E), you can click the leftmost triangle in the Address bar and choose Computer from the drop-down menu. (*See* Address Bar.)

The Computer window lists all available storage devices, typically grouped by type.

What to Do with It

The Computer window is basically a starting place for disk activities and for exploring your computer's storage system. As such, several useful things can be done there.

Change the view

As with other Windows Explorer windows, you can peek at things in the Computer window in a number of different ways.

The Views menu sets the size of the icons. I recommend the Tiles setting because it applies more information to each icon, such as storage capacity and the drive's full name.

Right-click in the window and choose Type from the shortcut menu. The Group By⇨Type item on the Type submenu arranges storage media into categories such as Hard Disk Drives, Devices with Removable Storage, and Network Location.

Browse the storage system

To peruse the information stored on a disk drive or storage medium, double-click to open the given icon. The contents of that drive's root folder are then displayed.

 To open a disk drive in its own window, right-click the icon and choose Explore from the pop-up menu.

Manage the storage devices

The Computer window toolbar is unique in that it contains various buttons that help you lord it over the PC's storage devices. These buttons appear based on items you select in the Computer window.

✗ **AutoPlay:** Automatically run software or perform some activity for a disk. *See* AutoPlay.

✗ **Burn to disk:** Create a CD/DVD. *See* Discs (CDs and DVDs).

✗ **Eject:** Eject the selected disk or media. *See also* Safely Remove.

✗ **Map network drive:** *See* Map a Network Drive.

✗ **Open Control Panel:** *See* Control Panel.

✗ **Properties:** Display the Properties dialog box for the selected disk.

✕ **System Properties:** Display the System Properties dialog box, which provides more control over your computer.

✕ **Uninstall or change a program:** *See* Uninstall Programs.

Watch Your Step!

It's not a *good thing* to mess with any files you didn't create yourself. Although it can be fun to spelunk through a hard drive, avoid changing, deleting, modifying, or randomly opening any icons you find.

When Things Go Wrong

Press the F5 key to refresh the Computer window, updating it to reflect any new additions to the computer's storage system or changes in network drives.

When you choose to group or stack the icons in the Computer window, you're using the Windows Search command to display information. (The window's title bar reflects this.) To return to normal Computer view, use the Back button or simply close the window and reopen a new Computer window.

Gold Rush Nuggets

The Computer window was referred to as the *My Computer* window in all previous releases of Windows. You may still hear some old-timers slip and refer to the Computer window as My Computer. (In the other Vista book I wrote, I mistakenly typed "My Computer" 12 times.)

Digging Elsewhere

Control Panel, Desktop, Folders, User Profile Folder, Windows Explorer

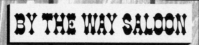
Contacts

No, they're not the things you put on your eyeballs when you don't want to wear glasses. In computerese, contacts are people. Specifically, a *contact* is a database entry that details information about

a person: his name, e-mail address, and physical address, plus other scintillating tidbits that only a computer database would love.

In Windows, you can manage your contacts by using something called Windows Contacts. It's not really a program — it's a folder! Specifically, it's the Contacts folder inside your User Account folder. Not only does the folder window list current contacts, but you can also use toolbar buttons to create more contacts.

(You can also create contacts from within the Windows Mail program.)

To create a contact, open the Contacts folder (found in your User Account folder). Click the New Contact button. Then just fill in the blanks. You don't need to fill in all the blanks: First name, last name, and e-mail address are the minimum number of blanks. Click OK to save the contact.

If you have a photo of the contact, you can add it by choosing the Change Picture command from the Photo icon's menu button. When a contact has a photo, the photo also shows up on the icons when you're viewing the Contacts window.

You can create groups of contacts for mass e-mailings: Choose the New Contact Group button to display a special dialog box. Give the group a name, and then use the Add to Contact Group button to add existing contacts to the group.

To send e-mail to a contact or group, click to select the contact or contacts, and then click the E-Mail button on the toolbar.

The easiest way to add a contact is in the Windows Mail program. When reading a message from someone, choose Tools⇨Add Sender to Contacts. This works especially well when the e-mail sender uses a vCard in his e-mail signature.

Contacts are used by Windows Mail, but also the Windows Calendar program for scheduling or sharing appointments. *See* Calendar.

When you don't use Windows Mail or the Windows Calendar, you can attempt to export your contacts to whichever e-mail or personal information program you use: Choose the Export button on the Contacts window toolbar.

Control Panel

O ne of the most traditional and ancient pieces of Windows is the Control Panel, a central location for making adjustments and changes and for configuring Windows and the PC. I'd write something pithy about the Control Panel here, but my morning coffee hasn't kicked in yet.

WHERE'S THE GOLD?

The Control Panel is accessed by opening the Control Panel icon, often found right on the desktop. If not, you can choose Control Panel from the Start button's menu.

The Control Panel can also be accessed from any Windows Explorer window: Press Win+E on the keyboard to summon the Explorer window, and then, on the Address bar, click the leftmost triangle and choose Control Panel from the menu.

The Control Panel can also be summoned from the Run dialog box: Type **control panel** and press the Enter key. *See* Run.

The Control Panel has two *views,* or ways of accessing information. I prefer Classic view, which presents a window chock-full o' icons, each one representing some part of Windows or your PC (hardware, software, or something that Windows does) that you can control.

The Control Panel Home, which is how Windows naturally configures itself, presents various categories and tasks (shown as links). Although this view is easier to use than the Control Panel's Classic view, especially when you're not familiar with Windows, it does involve more steps to get things done.

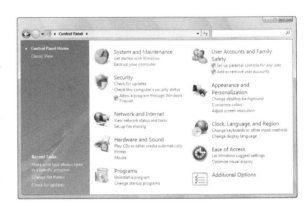

What to Do with It

The Control Panel is merely a portal through which you view various icons or links that control parts of Windows. When you need to make a change to the PC's display, sound system, network, keyboard, or any number of features, you open the Control Panel as the first step.

Switch to Classic view

To use Classic view, click the Classic View link, in the upper left corner of the window.

Switch to Control Panel Home

To switch to the Control Panel Home from Classic view, click the Control Panel Home link, in the upper left corner of the Control Panel window.

View Control Panel icons as a submenu on the Start menu

A quick way to get instant access to any Control Panel icon is to display the Control Panel as a menu on the Start menu. Here's how:

1. Right-click the Start button.

2. Choose Properties from the pop-up menu.

3. Ensure that the Start Menu tab is chosen in the Taskbar and Start Menu Properties dialog box.

4. Click the Customize button.

5. Beneath the Control Panel entry in the list, choose Display As Menu.

6. Click OK, and click OK again to close all open dialog boxes.

When you pop up the Start button menu again, you see that the Control Panel item (on the right) operates as a submenu. From the submenu, you can choose any Control Panel icon.

Watch Your Step!

Many icons in the Control Panel have settings that affect the entire computer. For example, the Network and Device Manager icons open windows that create opportunities for all sorts of mischief when you don't know what you're doing. So, just because some icons present opportunities for fun, such as Sound or Personalization, don't let that be an excuse to run amok.

Not every icon in the Control Panel belongs to Windows. Some icons are placed there by programs or utilities you install yourself.

When Things Go Wrong

When you're given instructions to do something with the Control Panel, ensure that those instructions explain whether you're using the Control Panel Home or Classic view. When you cannot find an icon, chances are that you're using the Control Panel Home and the directions assume that you're using Classic view instead.

Gold Rush Nuggets

The figure shows the Control Panel for Windows 3.1, circa 1992.

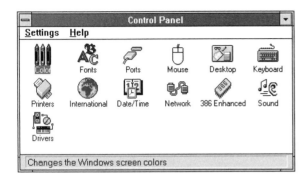

Digging Elsewhere

Computer, Desktop

Cookies

It doesn't take long after you first use the Internet to stumble onto the word *cookies*. If these little data nuggets weren't named after a delicious snack, I don't think anyone would have any problem with them. But for some reason, some people obsess over cookies. There's no reason for it; cookies can be good things.

A *cookie* is basically a small piece of information that a Web page can save on your computer. The information that's saved depends on the Web page; only that specific Web page can access the information again. That way, a Web page can remember, for example, your name, customer number, or shoe size — or perhaps that you have items waiting to be purchased in an electronic shopping cart.

Cookies aren't evil, but they can be used to track where you go on the Internet. For that reason, some Web site cookies are considered spyware. Don't fret over this; the Windows Defender program deals with those types of cookies. *See also* Windows Defender. But the rest — the majority of cookies on the Internet — are good things.

Cookie settings are made in the Internet Options dialog box. You can open that dialog box from Internet Explorer: Choose the Toolbar button's menu and then Internet Options. Or, you can open the Internet Options icon in the Control Panel.

In the Internet Options dialog box, click the Privacy tab. Cookie settings are set by using the slider: Up is the highest, most restrictive level; down is a more casual, cookies-allowed setting.

The way I configure cookies on my computer is to click the Advanced button. I choose to accept all first-party cookies, which allows me to shop and have the Web site remember who I am. But I choose to block all third-party cookies, which means cookies from advertisements on the Web sites I frequent. Then I add a check mark to allow session cookies, which is okay in most cases.

Cookies are designed to expire. Some last only while you're viewing a Web site (*session* cookies), and some die well into the future. Regardless, cookies can be deleted from the Internet Options dialog box.

Here's how:

1. Click the General tab.
2. Click the Delete button.
3. In the Delete Browsing History dialog box, click the Delete Cookies button.
4. Click the Yes button to confirm.

The only drawback here is that some Web sites that now remember who you are will forget who you are after deleting all your cookies.

To ensure that IE is doing its job and eating the proper cookies, you can summon a Privacy Report.

Look for the little Privacy Report icon, dwelling on IE's bottom-most Status bar. (If the Status bar isn't there, from the toolbar's Tools button choose Toolbars⇨Status Bar.) Double-click the Privacy Report icon to see the Privacy Report dialog box, listing suppressed or permitted cookies found by IE. Use the Show menu button to list various Web sites that have had their cookies blocked.

Copy, Cut, and Paste Data

A common feature available in all Windows applications, or just about anywhere that text or graphics can be manipulated, is the ability to copy, cut, and paste. In fact, next to multitasking (running several programs at a time), it's this cut-copy-paste method of sharing information between programs that makes Windows such a powerful and useful operating system.

WHERE'S THE GOLD?

The Copy, Cut, and Paste commands exist to help you copy and move information around not only within a single application but also between
different applications.

- ✗ **The Copy command** places a copy of selected text or graphics into the Windows Clipboard.

- ✗ **The Cut command** deletes selected text or graphics and places a copy in the Windows Clipboard.

- ✗ **The Paste command** places the contents of the Clipboard into a document.

Traditionally, the Copy, Cut, and Paste commands are found on the Edit menu, along with Undo and Clear or Delete. All these Edit menu commands are basic editing techniques, and Undo is the equivalent of the eraser on the end of a pencil (but much more effective and less messy).

When a program lacks an Edit menu, you can try looking for an Edit button on the toolbar. In

Windows Explorer, the Copy, Cut, and Paste commands are on the toolbar's Organize button's menu. In Internet Explorer, the commands are on the toolbar's Page button's menu.

Regardless of whether a menu is available, the keyboard equivalents for these popular commands are shown in this table:

Button	Command	Keyboard Command
📋	Copy	Ctrl+C
✂	Cut	Ctrl+X
📋	Paste	Ctrl+V

You may also have toolbar buttons for Copy, Cut, and Paste, as shown in the table.

What to Do with It

Many folks know about Cut and Copy within a single program; word processing humans use these commands all the time. But few Windows users recognize or take advantage of its ability to copy and paste graphics as well as text — especially between different programs.

Copy text from one place to another

Here's how the concept of copy and paste works with regard to text:

1. Select the text to duplicate.

   See Text Editing for information on selecting text.

2. Choose the Copy command.

3. Move the insertion pointer to where you want to place the text copy.

   Click the mouse to set the insertion pointer in a document.

 You can also switch to another document or program, paste the text into a text input box, or use the Text tool in a graphics application to paste text. *See* Multitasking for information on switching programs.

4. Choose the Paste command.

And there's the text copy, just as though you typed it yourself but without wasting one molecule of typing energy.

Cut and paste text

Cutting and pasting text works just like copying and pasting except that the original text is deleted. In the olden days, this operation was known as a *block move*. Here's how it goes:

1. Select the text to move.

2. Choose the Cut command.

3. Find a location for the text, a destination.

   Set the insertion pointer by clicking the mouse button. You can set the destination in the current document, in a document in another window, or in a graphical application by using its text tool.

4. Choose the Paste command.

Copy and paste graphics

To copy and paste graphics, follow these steps:

1. Click the graphic to select it, or use a selection tool (if available) to lasso the image.

2. Choose the Copy command.

3. Switch to the destination document, or the location where you want to paste the image.

   See Multitasking.

4. Choose the Paste command to create a duplicate of the image.

To cut and paste, simply replace the Copy command in Step 2 with Cut.

Copy a Web page address

Any text in any text box in Windows can be copied or cut or pasted into. A common use of this technique is to copy a Web page address. Here's how:

1. Navigate to the desired Web page.

2. Select the Web page address on the Address bar.

   Sometimes, pressing the F4 key works for this step, and sometimes it doesn't.

3. Press Ctrl+C to copy the address.

After the address is in the Clipboard, you can paste the address anywhere else: on a blog, in a document, or what-have-you.

Preview what's in the Clipboard

Sadly, Windows Vista doesn't come with a tool to view the Clipboard's contents. Windows once came with a Clipboard Viewer and, later, a Clipbook Viewer. That utility is gone from Windows Vista, for some odd reason.

 To see what's in the Clipboard, open the WordPad program. From the Start button's menu, choose All Programs⇨Accessories⇨Word Pad. Then press Ctrl+V to paste. Because WordPad accepts both text and graphics, you should be able to see what's in the Clipboard. (Close WordPad when you're done; there's no need to save.)

Watch Your Step!

The Windows Clipboard holds only one item at a time. Whenever you copy or cut something new, it replaces whatever previously existed in the Clipboard.

An exception to the one-item rule for the Clipboard happens in Microsoft Office; the Office Clipboard can hold up to 12 items.

When Things Go Wrong

When you accidentally cut something instead of copy it, either immediately paste the item back in or press Ctrl+Z, the Undo command, to undo your mistake.

 You can only paste text into an application that accepts text. You can only paste graphics into an application that accepts graphics.

When there is nothing to paste, odds are good that you didn't properly select and copy or cut the information. Try again.

Gold Rush Nuggets

Pressing Ctrl+C for Copy makes sense. And, you can sort of see how an X in Ctrl+X can mean Cut. But Ctrl+V for paste? The answer lies on your keyboard. If you look down, you see the X, C, and V keys all together on the bottom row on the left. Furthermore, the Z key, which is used for Ctrl+Z/Undo, is right down there as well.

Digging Elsewhere

Copy, Cut, and Paste Files; Multitasking

Copy, Cut, and Paste Files

One of your key duties as computer operator is to keep organized the stuff you collect and create. Part of that duty involves using folders to keep similar files together. Part of that duty involves using the Save As dialog box to save files into their proper folders. And, when you mess that up or change your mind later, you rely on the various methods Windows offers to copy and move your files up and down, in and out, back and forth, and all around the PC's disk storage system.

WHERE'S THE GOLD?

Manipulating files is something Windows is very good at. It's so good, in fact, that there are many, *many* ways to copy or move a file hither, thither, and yon. Philosophically, however, I'd like to divide the file manipulation task into three categories: menu, keyboard, and mouse:

- ✂ **By menu:** In the Windows Explorer window, the menu commands dwell on the toolbar's Organize button's menu: Cut, Copy, and Paste. By pressing the F10 key, you can see the traditional Windows Explorer menu bar. On the Edit menu, you find the Cut, Copy, Paste, Copy to Folder, and Move to Folder commands.

- ✂ **By keyboard:** On the keyboard, you can use the standard Windows shortcut keys: Ctrl+C to copy, Ctrl+X to cut, and Ctrl+V to paste.

- ✂ **By mouse:** Contrary to myth, using the mouse to copy and move files isn't the easiest thing. First, you need both folder windows open and visible on the screen: the *source* folder, from whence you're copying, and the *destination* folder, where

the icon is moved or copied. Second, you drag and drop the file, copying or moving it between the two visible windows. Third, you may have to press the Ctrl or Shift key while you drag, to ensure that a file is moved or copied.

What to Do with It

You can manipulate files individually or in groups. Individually, the commands affect only the icon you've selected. Grouping icons together means that you can copy or move them as a unit; *see* Icons to see how to group icons, although the same commands described here are used to manipulate the group.

Copy a file or folder

To copy a file or folder from one folder to another, follow these steps:

1. Open the folder containing the file or folder to copy.

2. Click to select the icon or icons.

   See Icons for information on selecting more than one icon.

3. Press Ctrl+C to copy the icons.

4. Open the folder into which you want to paste the icons.

5. Press Ctrl+V to paste the icons, creating the duplicate files.

See also Shortcuts for ways to make file duplicates without consuming too much disk space.

Move a file or folder

Moving a file works just like copying a file, although the original is deleted. Here's how it's done:

1. Open the folder containing the files or folders to copy.

2. Select the file or folder icons.

3. Press Ctrl+X to cut the icons.

Cut icons appear dimmed, or ghostly, in the window. Nothing has been deleted yet, and won't be until you paste the icons.

4. Open the folder into which you want to paste the icons.

5. Press Ctrl+V to paste the icons, which completes the move operation.

Create a duplicate of a file in the same folder

Copying a file to the same folder is how you create a duplicate copy of the file. It's cinchy: Copy the file and then paste it in the same folder. Rather than overwrite the original or cough up

an error, Windows creates the duplicate file with the text – Copy appended to the filename.

See also Shortcuts for information on creating a shortcut instead of a duplicate.

See Rename for information on giving the duplicate a new name.

Copy a file or folder to another storage device

There's no difference between copying a file to a folder on your PC's hard drive and copying a file to a folder on another storage device, removable disk drive, or other type of media. It all works the same.

The only exception is when you're copying files to a recordable CD or DVD. *See* Discs (CDs and DVDs).

Drag a file to another folder

Clue The key to dragging files to copy them is to have both folder windows visible at the same time. Or, have the source folder open and an icon for the destination folder or disk drive visible. Then you merely "drag and drop" the file or folder icon or icons from the source window to the destination window or icon.

Use the Send To menu

Another way to copy files to popular locations in Windows is to use the Send To menu: Right-click the file and choose Send To from the pop-up menu. On the list, you find shortcuts to popular folders, the CD/DVD drive, and network drives mapped to your PC.

Eureka To use the Send To command with a group of files, press F10 to access the ancient menu bar, and then choose File⇨Send To.

Watch Your Step!

Dag Nabbit When copying or cutting a folder, you're also copying and moving all the files in that folder *plus* any subfolders and all their files and folders.

Windows remembers only one thing at a time in its Clipboard. When you copy or cut a file or folder, you cannot copy or cut other things, including more files or folders, and expect the earlier things to paste. Only the most recent thing that's cut or copied can be pasted.

When you copy a file or folder and an icon with the same name already exists, you're given the option to overwrite that existing icon. If you choose to overwrite the icon, the only way to recover the original icon is by using the Previous Versions tool. *See* Previous Versions. I do not, however, recommend copying over an existing icon in the first place.

When you're dragging an icon between two folders on the same hard drive, Windows figures that you want to move the files, and the icons you drag reflect that concept graphically. To copy the files instead, press and hold the Ctrl key as you drag.

When you're dragging an icon between two folders on different disk drives or media, Windows automatically assumes that you want to copy the files. To override this assumption, press and hold the Shift key as you drag.

When Things Go Wrong

Generally speaking, the Undo command (keyboard shortcut: Ctrl+Z) is your savior when it comes to massively screwing up file operations. As long as you use Undo immediately after the mistake (before doing another file operation), Windows can usually recover.

When the Undo command doesn't cut it, your next refuge is the Previous Versions command for the folder in which you're working. *See* Previous Versions.

When Windows refuses to paste the file or files, you either didn't select anything in the first place or you copied or cut something other than a file before you used the Paste command. Try again.

Gold Rush Nuggets

There's only one way to paste a file, but as I count it, you can copy a file in at least eight ways:

⊗ Ctrl+C

⊗ Organize⇨Copy

⊗ F10, Edit⇨Copy

⊗ F10, Edit⇨Copy to Folder

⊗ F10, File⇨Send To

⊗ Right-click, Copy

⊗ Right-click, Send To

⊗ Drag with the mouse

Digging Elsewhere

Files, Folders, Icons, Rename, Shortcuts, Windows Explorer

Ctrl+Alt+Delete

Certain keystrokes, despite their obscurity, have retained a certain cultural awareness. One of them is Alt+F4, which closes a window. Another is F1, for help. Ranking right up there is Ctrl+Alt+Delete, a key combination that has always held meaning for PC users. It's so famous, in fact, that it has been adopted into popular culture as an alternative way of saying "Halt" or "Go away."

WHERE'S THE GOLD?

Ctrl+Alt+Delete is a keyboard *shortcut,* a combination of keys found on your keyboard. The shortcut consists of either Ctrl (Control) key, either Alt key, plus the Del or Delete key. By the way, it's pronounced "control alt delete."

Any combination of the Ctrl+Alt+Delete key press has the same result in Windows Vista: A special menu is displayed that provides access to various commands, including options for ease of access and shutting down Windows.

What to Do with It

Originally, Ctrl+Alt+Delete was the keyboard command that restarted DOS on a PC. In Windows, depending on the version, Ctrl+Alt+Delete summoned either the Task Manager or the Login dialog box.

Escape from the menu and return to Windows!

To return to your Windows session, click the Cancel button.

Lock the computer

The Lock This Computer option keeps your programs running but temporarily logs you off Windows and returns to your account's Login screen. *See also* Login and Log Off.

Switch users

Switching users works a lot like locking the computer, but rather than see your account's login window, you see the main window for logging in to Windows by using any account.

Log off

Choosing the Log Off option ends your Windows session, closing any open windows and programs and returning you to the main Login screen.

Change your password

Choosing the Change Your Password option summons the User Accounts window, where you can change your password. *See* Passwords.

Summon the Task Manager

You can choose the Task Manager item to display the Windows Task Manager. *See* Task Manager.

The new keyboard shortcut for the Task Manager is Ctrl+Shift+Esc.

Shut down the computer

To shut down the computer from the Ctrl+Alt+Delete menu, click the red power button in the lower right part of the menu. Or, you can click that button's menu and choose Shutdown from the menu. *See* Shutdown Windows.

Restart Windows

To restart Windows, click the menu button on the red power button (in the lower right part of the menu). Choose Restart from the menu. *See* Shutdown Windows.

Put the computer to sleep

To put the computer into sleep mode, choose the Sleep command from the red power button's menu on the Ctrl+Alt+Delete menu. *See* Sleep Mode.

Watch Your Step!

Pressing Ctrl+Alt+Delete at the login screen does not summon the menu.

When Things Go Wrong

Don't fret if the Ctrl+Alt+Delete menu vanishes; it's designed to go away after a spell. If your intent is to hide what you're doing, press Win+L rather than Ctrl+Alt+Delete to lock the computer.

Gold Rush Nuggets

Ctrl+Alt+Delete has been dubbed the *Vulcan nerve pinch*, in reference to *Star Trek's* Mr. Spock, who would dispatch an enemy by lightly grabbing his shoulder. Similar unconsciousness resulted when the Ctrl+Alt+Delete key combination was given to early PCs.

Ctrl+Alt+Delete is also known as the *three-finger salute*.

Contrary to popular myth, Bill Gates did not invent Ctrl+Alt+Delete. The key combination was created at IBM, as a hardware-based "soft" reset. (The original key combination was Ctrl+Alt+Esc, but that was too easy to press accidentally.)

Digging Elsewhere

Keyboard, Login and Log Off, Task Manager

Defrag

Although your computer tries as best it can to store information on disk in nice, clean chunks, occasionally the information becomes fragmented. This isn't necessarily a bad thing; when you split a large file into pieces, or *fragments,* the operating system can more efficiently use disk space. On the downside, the fragmented files take longer to save and longer to open. Having a disk full of fragmented files slows down the system. The solution is defragmentation.

WHERE'S THE GOLD?

The Disk Defragmenter (its official name) program is run automatically in Windows Vista; unlike in previous versions of Windows, you don't need to run the program on your own. Still, why should that stop you?

The desperate way to run Windows disk-defrag program is to type **dfrgui** in the Run dialog box. *See* Run.

A more traditional approach is to use a disk drive's Properties dialog box, by following these steps:

1. Open the Computer window.

2. Right-click a disk drive icon.

3. Choose Properties from the pop-up menu that appears.

4. Click the Tools tab.

   If there's no Tools tab, you can't run the defragmenter program on that type of disk.

5. Click the Defragment Now button.

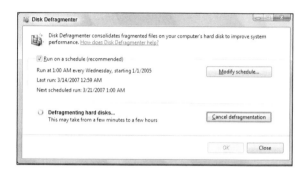

The button isn't exactly correct; it doesn't defragment your hard drive "now," although it does summon the Disk Defragmenter program, in which you can click a second Defragment Now button, which is more serious than the first.

What to Do with It

There's nothing wrong with fragmented files. In fact, Windows fragments files to ensure that disk storage space is used as efficiently as possible. But, every so often, you have to defragment a hard drive. Doing so improves disk performance, which is a good thing.

Defragment a hard drive now

To defragment a hard drive *right now,* summon the Disk Defragmenter program and click the Defragment Now button. Sit and wait.

After defragmenting is done, you can close the Disk Defragmenter window.

 Eureka
The less you do with your computer while it's defragmenting, the less time the operation takes. So, it's best to schedule defragmentation to take place late at night or at a time when you're not using the computer for something else.

Stop defragmentation

It's okay to stop the defragmenter. Simply click the Cancel Defragmentation button in the Disk Defragmenter window. Clicking that button doesn't undo any defragmenting that's already done, but it halts the program from completely defragmenting all your PC's hard drives.

Schedule regular defragmentation

Have the Disk Defragmenter work at a time when your computer is on but you're not using it. Here's how to set up that task:

1. Summon the Disk Defragmenter program.

2. Ensure that there's a check mark by the Run on a Schedule (Recommended) option.

3. Click the Modify Schedule button.

4. Choose how often you want to run Disk Defragmenter.

Weekly or monthly is best; avoid the Daily option.

5. Choose the day to run the program.

6. Choose the time — specifically, a time when the computer will be on but not heavily used.

7. Click OK, and then click Close to dismiss the Disk Defragmenter window.

I'm a fan of keeping my computer on all the time, so I have Disk Defragmenter work away in the middle of the night.

Watch Your Step!

There's no point in overdefragmenting a hard drive. To get the best from the disk defragmentation process, you should do it only every so often — once a week or less often. (Too many people obsess over defragmenting their PC's hard drives.)

When Things Go Wrong

No, the computer isn't stuck. Defragmenting a hard drive can take a while to accomplish. *See* Task Manager to find out how to determine when a program is stuck, or not responding.

Unlike earlier versions of the Disk Defragmenter program, this defragmenter has no pretty display or fun graphics to watch while the disk defragments.

The Disk Defragmenter window indicates when the disk was last successfully defragmented, which is your assurance that the program ran successfully.

The first defragmenter program I recall using was Mace Utilities. One of the best defragmenters available now is Vopt, available from Golden Bow Systems at `http://goldenbow.com`.

Gold Rush Nuggets

Defragmenting has been a proper hard disk maintenance tool ever since hard drives for PCs first became popular, back in the mid-1980s.

Digging Elsewhere

Check for Disk Errors (Check Disk), Disk Drives, Task Scheduler

Delete

As a creation tool, computers just can't be beat: words, pictures, music, video — name the type of art, and a computer can help you do it. But creation is closely paired with its twin, destruction; computers can not only help you create fun and useful things, they can also help you obliterate stuff when you're done.

WHERE'S THE GOLD?

Finding a Delete command depends directly on what it is you want to rid yourself of. Generally speaking, you delete three things: files, folders, and programs. (You can also delete selected text; *see* Text Editing.)

Programs: Deleting programs means uninstalling them. *See* Uninstall Programs.

Files and folders: For deleting files and folders, you can find options in many places:

- ✗ On the keyboard, the Delete key removes any selected files.

- ✗ From the toolbar's Organize button menu, you can choose Delete to remove selected files.

- ✗ You can summon the secret hidden menu bar by pressing the F10 key and then choosing File⭢Delete.

- ✗ Use the mouse to drag the file's icon to the Recycle Bin.

- ✗ Right-click a file, and you can find the Delete command on the pop-up menu that appears.

The Delete command doesn't remove files; it merely shuffles them off to the Recycle Bin, where they sit for a spell to await potential resurrection. *See* Recycle Bin.

There's also a *destructive* delete command, one that removes files without storing them in the Recycle Bin: Pressing Shift+Delete on the keyboard deletes any selected files immediately.

Finally, you can find some third-party tools that not only delete files but also wipe their data clean, unrecoverably erasing the files' information from the hard drive. Such tools don't come with Windows, but you can check out one named Wipe (available from SourceForge):

```
http://wipe.sourceforge.net
```

What to Do with It

The following tasks should sate your destructive urges. These examples use the keyboard shortcuts for the Delete command. Refer to the preceding section for alternative ways to delete stuff, although the keyboard shortcuts are perhaps the most efficient.

Delete a single file or folder

To banish a single file:

1. Select the file or folder.

2. Press the Delete key on the keyboard.

3. If prompted with a Delete File or Delete Folder warning, click the Yes button or press the Y key.

Delete a group of files

To banish a group of files:

1. Select the files slated for destruction.

2. Press the Delete key on the keyboard.

3. Click the Yes button if prompted to confirm the files' banishment.

Permanently delete a file

To delete a file without possibility of recovery from the Recycle Bin, carefully follow these steps:

1. Select the files you want to permanently delete.

2. Press Shift+Delete on the keyboard.

3. Click the Yes button in the Delete File dialog box that appears.

The Delete File dialog box always appears when you're permanently deleting a file.

Deleting files on removable media may permanently delete those files all the time, offering no opportunity for recovery from the Recycle Bin. Don't fret: You're warned before the files are deleted.

Disable the Delete File warning dialog box

You can disable the Delete File warning dialog box by following these steps:

1. Right-click the Recycle Bin icon, found on the desktop.

2. Choose Properties from the pop-up menu that appears.

3. In the Recycle Bin Properties dialog box, click to remove the check mark by the Display Delete Confirmation Dialog option.

4. Click OK.

If your desktop doesn't show the Recycle Bin icon, you need to temporarily make the icon visible, follow the preceding steps, and then hide the icon again. *See* Recycle Bin.

Watch Your Step!

Deleting a folder removes not only the folder but also all the files and folders that dwelleth within that folder. Be careful!

Don't delete programs! To remove software, you must uninstall it. *See* Uninstall Programs.

Don't delete files or folders in the Windows folder or any of its subfolders. In fact, don't delete any file or folder you didn't create yourself.

Another way to delete a file is to overwrite it, by either copying or creating a new file in the same folder with the same name. Overwriting a file pretty much obliterates the original, but you can still recover the file in Windows Vista, thanks to the Previous Versions tool. *See* Previous Versions.

You can use the Delete command on files written to a CD or DVD by using the Live File System. *See* Discs (CDs and DVDs). The files aren't truly deleted, however; they're merely hidden from view. The space used by the files can't be recovered.

When Things Go Wrong

Any file or folder you delete can be restored to its original condition. *See* Recycle Bin for the details.

There's a reason that the Shift+Delete command is called *permanently* deleting: Files deleted with that command can't be easily recovered, if at all.

Some third-party utilities might be able to recover the file. Good luck!

A file can't be deleted when it's *busy* — when some program is using the file or the file is otherwise open. Close all open applications and try deleting the file again.

Gold Rush Nuggets

The computer pioneer Peter Norton built his fortune on the first widespread program that could recover accidentally deleted files. Since that time, most computer operating systems have adopted the Trash / Recycle Bin concept, in which deleted files are stored rather than deleted outright.

Digging Elsewhere

Files, Previous Versions, Recycle Bin, Uninstall Programs

Desktop

I f Windows were a building, the desktop would be the lobby. It's the first thing you see after you log in to Windows, the main interface. You use the desktop, and its features, to help control the computer, run your programs, and keep your stuff organized. And it's to the desktop you return when you're done doing work or goofing off (well, maybe more goofing off than you'll admit to).

WHERE'S THE GOLD?

Of all the goodies in Windows, the desktop is perhaps the least buried. It's *right there* when you start Windows, although occasionally it's obscured by various windows, and sometimes it's covered with icons like freckles on a redhead in summer.

The desktop itself is rather boring. Sure, it can sport icons. It's home to the Taskbar and the Start button, which dwells on the Taskbar. In Windows Vista, the desktop is also home to the Sidebar, which I talk about more in the Sidebar entry.

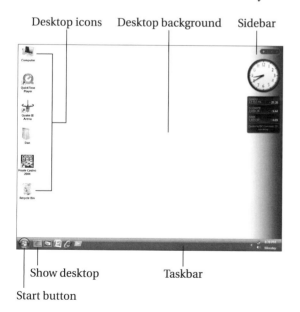

Desktop icons   Desktop background   Sidebar

Show desktop   Taskbar

Start button

What to Do with It

The desktop is more of a way station than a locus for activity in Windows. It's considered the top level in the system hierarchy, above the Computer window, Control Panel, and just about everything else. Despite its lofty position, most of the time the desktop serves merely as an intermediate step between doing one thing and the next.

Display the desktop

To quickly show the desktop, hiding all open windows, press the Win+D key combination.

Clicking the Show Desktop shortcut, found on the Quick Launch bar, also displays the desktop.

Manage the desktop icons

You can show and hide any icon on the desktop, such as shortcut icons placed there when you install new software. Various system icons can also appear on the desktop: Computer, Control Panel, Network, Recycle Bin, and others. *See* Desktop Icons for the details.

Mess around with the Taskbar

The desktop is home to the Taskbar, which is instrumental in Windows for not only harboring the Start button but also switching between programs. *See* Multitasking, Taskbar.

Change the background image

You have your choice for what you see as the desktop's background. It can be a solid color, a pattern, or an image. Here's how to set things up:

1. Right-click the desktop.

2. Choose Personalize from the pop-up menu that appears.

3. In the Personalization window, choose Desktop Background.

4. Use the Picture Location drop-down list to choose a background type:

   Windows Wallpapers: Images that Windows comes with, specifically designed for use as desktop backgrounds.

   Pictures: Images culled from your account's Pictures folder (images you created or saved to disk).

   Sample Pictures: The Windows Wallpapers plus other images that came with Windows.

   Public Pictures: Any images saved in the Public account's Pictures folder.

   Solid Colors: For those who would rather not have a picture or graphical image.

   C:\Users . . . : A pathname to an image downloaded from the Internet.

5. Select a picture or solid color from the list displayed.

6. For pictures, choose a layout: stretched, tiled, or centered.

 Clue As you choose options, you can move the desktop background window around to see how different settings affect the image.

7. Click OK to set the background.

Use an Internet image as the background

You can easily pluck any image from the Internet and use it as the desktop background. It's too easy:

1. Hunt down the image you want to use on the Internet.

   Obviously, the larger the image (or the more appropriate its size in relation to the screen), the better it looks.

2. Right-click the image and choose Set As Background from the shortcut menu that appears.

3. Click Yes in the confirmation dialog box.

4. Show the desktop.

   After all, you want to see the image.

5. (Optional) Run through the steps in the preceding section to adjust the image (which you do in Step 6) as needed.

Only one image from the Internet is stored by Windows at a time for desktop background purposes. If you want to reuse the image, refer to the steps in the preceding section and choose the C:\Users . . . option from Step 4.

Of course, you can always save an image from the Internet to your PC's hard drive, in which case you can use it for not only the desktop background but also other purposes. *See* Internet Explorer.

Extend the desktop to a second monitor

You can extend the desktop to a second monitor, allowing for more desktop space. I sometimes use two monitors on my computers and enjoy being able to view multiple documents at once.

To extend the desktop to a second monitor, you must first ensure that your version of Windows Vista supports that feature. Furthermore, the video adapter in your PC must support a second monitor, or else you need two video adapters installed. After you ensure that you have everything you need, heed these steps:

1. Right-click the desktop.

2. Choose Personalize from the shortcut menu that appears.

3. Click the Display Settings link, at the bottom of the Personalization window.

The Display Settings dialog box confirms that your computer system is capable of supporting two monitors by showing both monitors.

4. Click to select the second monitor.

5. Put a check mark in the box by Extend the Desktop onto This Monitor.

6. Click the Apply button to activate the second monitor.

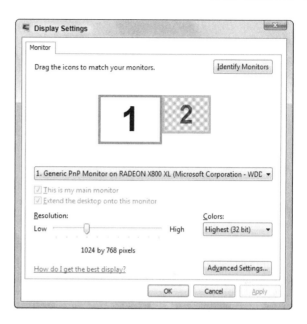

7. Set the second monitor's resolution.

8. Drag the second monitor's icon to position the second monitor properly in relation to the first monitor.

Drag a test window between the two monitors and use it to help you set the proper resolution and orientation of both monitors.

9. Click OK.

Watch Your Step!

Microsoft recommends that you don't use the desktop as a place to create files or put project folders. Instead, create your files and folders in the User Profile folder (*see* User Profile Folder), and put only shortcuts to those items on the desktop (*see* Shortcuts).

Even if you have two monitors, the first monitor remains the main monitor on your PC. Any icons you drag to the second monitor hop back to the first monitor whenever you restart Windows.

 Using two monitors can be a pain, often requiring both hardware and software headaches. The best way to set things up is to get a single video adapter that supports two monitors.

Icons you store on the desktop are secretly kept in the Desktop folder, located in your User Profile folder. Although the layout is different in the Desktop folder, the contents are the same as what you see on the desktop. Changing icons in one place changes them in the other.

When Things Go Wrong

The desktop is hidden any time you maximize a window. It's not gone; it's just lurking behind the open window or windows.

The Show Desktop shortcut icon occasionally gets lost from the Quick Launch bar. Unlike in previous versions of Windows, it's not easy to re-create the icon. But, if you have other accounts on the same computer, you can copy and paste the Show Desktop icon from another account into the Public folder. From there, you can copy it back to your own account's Quick Launch bar.

If the desktop image looks ugly or distorted, the original picture may not be properly sized for use as a desktop image. Try using another image, or perhaps just center the image you're having trouble with.

Gold Rush Nuggets

Have you ever noticed that the desktop resembles a real desktop in no way whatsoever? That's because the term remained, even though the desktop's look has changed over the years. Originally, on some early computers, the desktop was a graphical desktop. It was complete with scissors, a pot of glue, papers, and other desktop items. That metaphor didn't survive, but the term *desktop* did.

The desktop background was once called *wallpaper*. You may still hear old-timers refer to it that way.

Digging Elsewhere

Desktop Icons, Display, Screen Saver, Sidebar, Start Button and Menu, Taskbar, Windows Explorer

Desktop Icons

The Windows operating system has been through several generations and quite a few dramatic changes. Yet, for about a dozen years or so, having certain icons on the desktop has become as predictable as the group of elderly gentlemen who gather around the corner barbershop to solve the world's ills. I call these icons the *desktop icons:* Computer, Account, Network, Recycle Bin, and Control Panel. Any other icons on the desktop are typically shortcuts, although it's possible to have folders and files saved directly to the desktop. (That's not recommended; *see* Desktop.)

The secret to controlling whether the icons appear on the desktop is found in the Desktop Icon Settings dialog box. There, you can dictate which icons appear as well as how they look.

Here's how to open the dialog box:

1. Right-click the desktop and choose Personalize from the pop-up menu.

2. In the Personalization window, click the link labeled Change Desktop Icons in the upper left corner.

Further control is offered from the desktop's shortcut menu, shown by right-clicking the desktop. Specifically, items on the View submenu control how the icons appear.

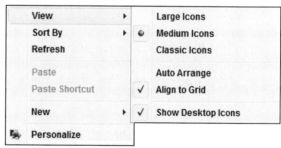

What to Do with It

I know folks who want a clean desktop. I know some who put every dang doodle icon in the world on the desktop. And some, like myself, enjoy a smattering of icons but just can't live without the Computer, Account, or Network icon right there on the desktop.

Add or remove the standard desktop icons

You can stick five standard desktop icons on the desktop — if you desire. They aren't shortcut icons, but are in fact *the real deal*. Therefore, you must officially add or remove them:

1. Summon the Desktop Icon Settings dialog box.

2. To add a standard icon to the desktop, click to put a check mark by the icon.

3. Click the OK button when you're done.

4. Close the Personalization window.

After an icon is on the desktop, you can move it around just like you can move any other icon. However, to remove the icon, you must repeat these steps and remove the check mark in Step 2.

Change the look of the desktop icons

The standard desktop icons need not look like they do on everyone else's computer. You can change them at will. To do so, heed these steps:

1. Summon the Desktop Icon Settings dialog box.

   Refer to Steps 1 and 2 from the preceding section.

2. Click to select an icon in the center of the box.

   Note that the Control Panel icon cannot be changed. Also, there are *two* Recycle Bin icons — one empty and one with something in it.

3. Click the Change Icon button.

   A Change Icon dialog box appears, listing icons in the common icon file `imageres.dll`.

4. Choose a replacement icon from the list or use the Browse button to open other files to hunt for icons.

5. Repeat Steps 2 through 4 to change whatever icons you want.

6. Click the OK button when you're done, and, optionally, close the Personalization window.

 Clue

You can change all the desktop icons at one time by using a theme. *See* Themes.

You can create your own icons, such as an icon picture of yourself for your desktop account (User's Files) icon. *See* Icons.

Hide all desktop icons

Whether you prefer a clean, iconless desktop or just want to temporarily hide all desktop icons (so that you can see your Danica Patrick wallpaper in its full 1280-by-1024-resolution glory), do this:

1. Right-click the desktop.

2. Choose View➪Show Desktop Icons.

Removing the check mark by the Show Desktop Icons command *hides* all desktop icons — the standard icons plus any shortcuts or real icons.

Adding the check mark by the Show Desktop Icons command *reveals* any previously hidden icons.

Change the desktop icon size

As with icons in a folder window, you can set the size of the desktop icons: Large, Medium, or Classic, which I assume is a euphemism for teensy. To change this setting, right-click the desktop and choose the proper size from the View submenu.

Large icons occupy a 96-by-96-pixel grid.

Medium icons occupy the traditional 48-by-48-pixel grid.

Classic icons fit snugly into a 32-by-32-pixel grid.

Line up the desktop icons

Some folks like their desktop icons to be arranged willy-nilly. Others prefer the gridlike perfection of icons in even rows and columns. Either way, you'll benefit from following these steps:

1. Right-click the desktop to summon the shortcut menu.

2. Choose View➪Align to Grid.

Removing the check mark by the Align to Grid option allows you to freely locate any desktop icon anywhere. Adding or keeping the check mark directs Windows to keep the icons in gridlike formation. (Although you're still free to place the icon anywhere on the desktop, it "snaps" to the nearest grid location.)

Set the icon grid size

To control the size of the grid that Windows uses to arrange desktop icons, follow these steps:

1. Right-click the desktop and choose Properties from the pop-up menu.

2. In the Personalization window, choose Window Color and Appearance.

3. Choose the link labeled Open Classic Appearance Properties for More Color Options, near the bottom of the window.

4. In the Appearance Settings dialog box, click the Advanced button.

5. From the Item drop-down list, choose Icon Spacing (Horizontal).

6. Enter a new value in the Size box.

   The size is measured in pixels as the distance, from left to right, between icons on the desktop, as well as in folder windows.

7. From the Item drop-down list, choose Icon Spacing (Vertical).

8. Enter a new size value in the Size box.

Vertical spacing is also measured in pixels, but from top to bottom.

9. Click the OK button to close the Advanced Appearance dialog box.

10. Click OK to close the Appearance Settings dialog box and, optionally, close the Personalization window.

These changes are most visible when you choose to arrange icons by using a grid; see the earlier section "Line up the desktop icons."

Watch Your Step!

Changes you make to the desktop icons affect only your account on the computer. Other users aren't affected.

Many folks assume that all Windows computers sport the same or similar icons. When you get all fancy and use nonstandard or just plain weird icon images for the standard desktop icons, a certain amount of confusion may result.

Changing the icon grid spacing affects the way icons appear in the folder windows as well. This is most visible when viewing Medium icons.

When Things Go Wrong

If the standard icons don't seem to be showing up, refer to the earlier section "Hide all desktop icons," for information on showing desktop icons.

When the desktop icons seem to move around on their own, you most likely have the Auto Arrange option activated. To deactivate it, right-click the desktop and choose View⇨Auto Arrange, which removes the check mark by Auto Arrange.

When you cannot position desktop icons as you like, right-click the desktop and choose View⇨Align to Grid to remove that command's check mark.

To return the desktop icons to their standard appearance, select the appropriate icon in the Desktop Icons Settings dialog box and click the Restore Default button.

Gold Rush Nuggets

In some versions of Windows, the standard icons could not be removed. Sometimes, all icons except for the Recycle Bin could be removed. Windows Vista is the first Windows release that allows all icons to be customized.

The Internet Explorer icon was once considered one of the *immortals*, along with Computer, Recycle Bin, and the old My Documents and Network Neighborhood / My Network Places icons. Just like those icons, Internet Explorer could not be removed from the desktop. I suppose that a lawsuit or two may be responsible for that change, but I could be wrong.

Digging Elsewhere

Desktop, Icons, Themes

Device Manager

The Device Manager is a great tool in Windows for discovering which of your computer's gizmos might be misbehaving, or for making specific adjustments to those same-said gizmos.

WHERE'S THE GOLD?

You can easily start the Device Manager by opening the Device Manager icon in the Control Panel. From the Control Panel Home, choose System and Maintenance, and then click the Device Manager heading.

The Device Manager is also available as an item in the Computer Management window, which you open from the Administrative Tools thingy. *See* Administrative Tools.

The nerdy way to start the Device Manager is to type `mmc.exe devmgmt.msc` in the Run dialog box.

The Device Manager window shows one of those hierarchical tree-structure things listing categories for various devices inside or attached to your computer. Clicking the + (plus sign) button opens a category to reveal either more categories or specific devices.

To see a Properties dialog box for an individual device, double-click the device name inside the Device Manager window.

Device name

Device category   Devices in the computer

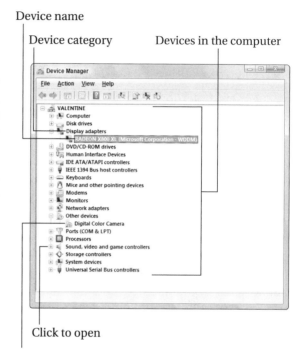

Click to open

Malfunctioning device

What to Do with It

The Device Manager is used primarily for hardware troubleshooting. In fact, it should be the first place you check when you suspect hardware trouble.

Confirm a device name

The Device Manager can help you learn the specific, official, technical name for any gizmo in your computer. For example, your PC's video adapter has a brand name and number. It's difficult to gather that information, sometimes even by looking at the video adapter itself. But the Device Manager knows the name. Here's how to find it:

1. Open the Device Manager.

2. Open the category for the device.

   For example, open Display Adapters for the graphics adapter or Network Adapters for a networking controller or NIC.

The device name is listed under the category. On my computer, for example, the graphics adapter device is named RADEON X800 XL.

Locate a bum device

The Device Manager flags malfunctioning devices with a tiny yellow triangle with an exclamation point in the middle — the international highway symbol for *warning*. The device's category is automatically opened to reveal the bum device.

Device
Manager
icon

Warning
icon

Disabled
Device
icon

To get more information about the device, double-click its name to open its Properties dialog box. In the device's Properties dialog box, on the General tab, the reason for the malfunction is listed in the Device Status area.

Update a device driver

Device driver is a fancy name for the software that controls some hardware gizmos. For example, the video adapter in your PC has a device driver that controls the adapter. It's through that device driver that Windows communicates with the graphics hardware.

Obviously, having an up-to-date device driver is important for performance, as well as security, reasons. To bring a device driver up-to-date, or ensure that the current driver is up-to-date, follow these steps:

1. Open the Device Manager.

2. Open the category for the device you want to update.

3. Double-click the device name to display its Properties dialog box.

4. In the Properties dialog box, click the Driver tab.

5. Click the Update Driver button.

6. When your computer has just had a crash or perhaps someone else was messing with it, you can choose the option Browse My Computer for Driver Software. Most of the time, you should choose the top option, Search Automatically for Updated Driver Software.

Wait while Windows looks for a better driver.

7. If a better driver is found, follow the directions to install or update it; otherwise, click the Close button when your driver is determined to be up-to-date.

Roll back a device driver

Sometimes, installing a new device driver may do more harm than good. This is often the case when software isn't fully tested — although it's rare, it does happen.

The first thing you should try when a driver update goes rotten is System Restore; *see* System Restore. If the driver really affects things for the worst, use System Restore in Safe Mode; *see* Safe Mode.

If you're able, follow the steps in the preceding section, but in Step 5, click the Roll Back Driver button. Heed the directions on the screen to restore the old driver.

Disable a device

You can direct Windows to ignore a device by disabling that device in the Device Manager. This not only prevents Windows from recognizing and using the device but also makes it as though the gizmo wasn't even there. It also provides a quick way to suppress warnings about failing devices.

To disable a device, do this:

1. Open the Device Manager.

2. Open the category for the device you want to disable.

3. Double-click the device name to display the device's Properties dialog box.

4. Click the Drive tab.

5. Click the Disable button.

6. Click Yes to confirm.

7. Click the OK button to close the Properties dialog box.

Disabled devices appear with a tiny circle and downward-pointing arrow by their icons. This is your visual clue that a device has been disabled.

To reenable a device, repeat the preceding steps, but in Step 5, click the Enable button. Follow the directions on the screen.

Watch Your Step!

You don't need to obsess over bringing device drivers up-to-date. The Windows Update service provides your PC with most new drivers automatically when those drivers become available. *See* Updates.

Don't disable working devices. Your computer may not function properly, and it would be difficult to recover from such a mistake.

When Things Go Wrong

Screwing up your system by removing a device driver or disabling a device generally requires a System Restore operation to set things right. If that doesn't work, start the computer as you would to enter Safe mode (*see* Safe Mode), but from the Advanced Boot Options menu, choose to start the computer with the last known good configuration.

Gold Rush Nuggets

The Device Manager was originally a tab in the System Properties dialog box. Windows Vista has promoted it to its own Control Panel icon.

Digging Elsewhere

Help, Safe Mode, System Information

Dialog Box

A special type of window in Windows is a *dialog box*. As its name suggests, it's a window designed to collect information from you, the computer user. The computer is conducting a *dialogue* with you, asking for input, options, or settings or allowing you to have more control over something. Dialog boxes do a lot in Windows, from displaying simple messages to providing more gizmos and doodads than a modern jet cockpit.

WHERE'S THE GOLD?

Dialog boxes pop up all over. There are different types, from the simple warning dialog boxes you see anytime you try to do anything in Windows Vista (*see* User Account Control [UAC]) to complex dialog boxes that control printing or setting a font. Most often, dialog boxes appear when you choose various menu commands.

What to Do with It

Dialog boxes are about communication; you're telling the computer what to do or how to work.

Work a basic dialog box

When a dialog box appears, presenting options or information, you work it like this:

1. Make settings or enter information by manipulating the various dialog box gizmos.

2a. Confirm your changes and dismiss the dialog box by clicking the OK button, or:

2b. Chicken out and cancel any changes, closing the dialog box by clicking the Cancel button, or:

2c. Confirm your changes and keep the dialog box open by clicking the Apply button.

 Using the Apply button can be a boon when you're testing things. By clicking Apply, you can observe changes without leaving the dialog box. That way, you can fine-tune, click Apply, and repeat that cycle until things are perfect. Then click OK.

Manipulate gizmos

Dialog boxes can be as simple as a line of text and an OK button or as complex as the Print dialog box that comes with the latest abomination of Adobe Acrobat. Here's a quick rundown of the gizmos you may find in a dialog box and how they work:

Text box: A one-line, or occasionally larger, square (with scroll bars) into which you type text. Sometimes, a one-line text box comes with a menu button on the right, which lets you quickly recall previously typed items. Also note that all the Windows text-editing commands — including

Copy, Cut, and Paste — are available in any text box.

File name: Document.rtf ▼

Check box: An on–off option; it's set (on) if a check mark is in the box or reset (off) if there's no check mark. Click the mouse in the check box to set or reset the check mark, or, from the keyboard, press the spacebar when the gizmo is highlighted.

☐ Forget settings on exit

Radio button group: Radio buttons come in groups in which only one of the buttons can be selected at a time (like the buttons on old-fashioned car radios). Click with the mouse to set a radio button, or use the arrow keys and spacebar to choose a button.

◉ Radio
○ Soap
○ No soap

Spinner: You enter values in a spinner box, by either typing the value directly or clicking the itty-bitty up and down buttons to the right of the number to *spin* the value up or down.

UACs per minute: 24 ⬍

Drop-down menu/button: It looks like a button, but it's really a menu: Click it, and a drop-down list of options appears. Sometimes, the drop-down menu may simply be a scrolling list of items beneath a text box.

Topping: [Glass & metal shards ▼]

Slider: Sliders are commonly used to set varying degrees of things, such as screen resolution or mouse sensitivity. Often, a slider is accompanied by a text input box for entering a precise value, although that's not always the case.

Chip crispness: Wet paper ───◘─── Plywood

Scrolling list/tree structure: The scrolling list contains items that may employ a combination of gizmos, such as an expanding tree structure, check marks by each item, or a menu button to the right of an item. Sometimes, you just double-click an item to open it and adjust more information.

Stupid things Poindexter will do today:

☐ Smell
☐ Sit on his pen, leaving stain on pants
☐ Talk about his model trains
☐ Nap
☐ Wear matching socks
☑ Spill coffee on his shirt

You can move between gizmos in a dialog box by pressing the Tab key. Press Shift+Tab to move backward. Any item highlighted in the dialog box can also be manipulated by using the keyboard, usually the arrow keys or spacebar. Choose any specific item in a dialog box by pressing the Alt key, and then press the key associated with the underlined letter in the gizmo's name.

Work the tabbed dialog box

Rather than overwhelm you, some dialog boxes use a tabbed interface: Different things that the dialog box does are categorized under various headings that appear on tabs, like tabbed file folders.

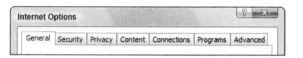

To choose a tab, click its heading with the mouse. Or, press Ctrl+Tab on the keyboard to cycle through the tabs. (Shift+Ctrl+Tab cycles backward.)

Watch Your Step!

When typing text in a dialog box, remember that the Tab key, not Enter, moves you from one element to the next. This key is easy to forget when you're typing and absentmindedly press Enter to end a line of text.

Some settings, especially in the Personalization part of the Control Panel, can render the screen in such an odd way that it's difficult to see or control the computer. To help avoid these settings, use the Apply button rather than OK wherever possible to test your settings.

When Things Go Wrong

Sometimes, the OK button is replaced by some type of verb button, such as the Print button in a Print dialog box.

The Cancel button may also be replaced, typically with a Close button. Unlike OK or Cancel, Close accepts settings but doesn't carry out any action. For example, nothing prints if you click the Close button in a Print dialog box.

Gold Rush Nuggets

Windows has three levels of alert dialog box. An *alert* is an informative dialog box, usually with a simple message (or warning) plus an OK button. The alert levels are Asterisk, Exclamation, and Question. Each alert level also has an accompanying sound that plays. *See* Sounds.

Digging Elsewhere

Open, Printing, Save, Windows

Discs (CDs and DVDs)

In the beginning, there were no disks. And the computer lab was dark and full of tape and Hollerith cards. Then lo came the floppy drive, quickly followed by the hard drive. And so it was good for a long time. Then came the CD, which the PC could use for data or music. But that wasn't enough! People wanted to create CDs! And when the DVD came along, people wanted to write to those! Eventually, the combination CD/DVD drive became standard on the PC. Along with that came the ability to create your own CDs and DVDs. Next to the hard drive, the CD and DVD together are now the second most popular storage media for computer data.

WHERE'S THE GOLD?

Your PC most likely has a combination CD/DVD drive located right squat on the console's face. Or, it may have two CD/DVD drives or separate CD and DVD drives. Either way, the drives eat what I refer to as the "shiny" media: a compact disc (CD) or digital versatile disc (DVD).

On the software side, icons representing any CD/DVD drives you have attached to your PC appear in the Computer window. *See* Computer.

Windows recognizes all types of CDs and DVDs, from discs that contain computer data to media discs, such as musical CDs, movie DVDs, and recordable discs.

Windows Vista is the first version of Windows that fully recognizes all recordable disc formats. They are

CD-R: The basic, standard CD-recording format. There are different CD-Rs for music and data. Generally speaking, the music CD-Rs are of lower quality and shouldn't be used for storing data.

DVD-R: The most compatible DVD recording format.

DVD+R: A faster DVD recording format, but one that's not as compatible with home DVD movie players.

Windows Vista also recognizes the rewritable, or RW, forms for CDs and DVDs. They are

CD-RW: The standard CD recording, erasing, and rewriting format.

DVD-RW: The minus (–) format for DVD recording, erasing, and rewriting. This format is the most compatible RW format for DVDs.

DVD+RW: The plus (+) format for creating DVDs, which is more efficient than the minus format but less compatible.

What to Do with It

CDs and DVDs are designed to be used! They come in handy for installing programs and for data reference. And for sharing data or backing up, nothing beats the PC's most popular form of removable storage media.

Insert a CD or DVD

There are two popular types of CD/DVD drive. One has a sliding tray, into which the disc is laid label up. The second is a slot-drive, into which the disc is inserted label up.

After you insert the disc, the computer reads it. Windows obeys any AutoPlay directions or displays the AutoPlay dialog box — unless you pressed the Shift key while inserting the disc. *See* AutoPlay.

The disc eventually appears in the Computer window and can be browsed or opened. *See* Computer.

Play a DVD movie

DVD movies play after they're inserted into the drive. Windows Media Player, or whichever media player you've installed, fires up, and the movie appears on the screen.

Some movies require a specific codec to play. The program that installs the codec should be on the DVD with the movie. If not, don't play that movie; consider it incompatible with your computer system.

Eureka
I avoid installing codecs myself. I don't like junking up my computer with extra software just to watch a movie. Instead, I just play that DVD in a DVD player attached to a TV set.

Play a musical CD

Music CDs should play after being inserted, using Windows Media Player or some other media software you have installed on your PC.

Eject a CD or DVD

When you're done with a CD or DVD, you can eject it from your computer. Here's how:

1. Open the Computer window.

2. Select the CD or DVD drive's icon.

3. Click the Eject button on the toolbar.

You can also use the Eject button on the CD/DVD drive on the console (if it has one), although note that the disc doesn't eject if it's busy or if files are open and being used. To unbusy the disc, close all open programs and files.

From within the Windows Media Player, eject a disc with the Ctrl+J keyboard command.

Create a CD or DVD with Live File System

The Live File System method for writing to a CD or DVD allows you to write files to the disc one at a time or in batches. This interactive format allows you to eject the disc and then reinsert it to add files later. Live File System is far more interactive than the Mastered format, but it tends to use more disc space, which is its major drawback.

To create a Live File System CD or DVD, follow these steps:

1. Insert the blank CD or DVD into the drive.

   It can be any format: R/RW, +/–.

2. If the AutoPlay dialog box appears, choose the option Burn Files to Disc.

3. In the Burn a Disc dialog box, choose Show Formatting Options.

4. Choose Live File System.

5. Type a name for the disc.

   You can't change the name later, so choose something clever that's short and specific and describes the disk's contents.

6. Click the Next button to complete the process.

After formatting, the disc's window opens, allowing you to copy files to the disk. As long as the disc remains in the drive, you can copy files to it just as you can copy files to any folder or storage media in your PC.

 Eureka Use the Burn button on the Windows Explorer toolbar to copy selected files and folders to the disc.

Copying files to a Live System disc takes longer than using the Mastered format.

When you need to eject the disk, simply eject it per the directions in the preceding section. Reinsert the disc to add more files, which is the beauty of the Live File System format.

When the disc is full, you can't add more files to it.

Create a CD or DVD in the Mastered format

The Mastered format is more of a collect-and-write way to create a CD or DVD. Files are copied to a temporary holding location on the hard drive. (Actually, shortcuts are created.) They sit and wait at that location until you're ready to burn the disc. At that point, all the information is written to the disc at once, and the disc is "closed" so that nothing else can be added.

The advantage of the Mastered format is that it's more efficient than the Live File System; files are written to disc quickly in one fell swoop, and disc space is used more efficiently. The disadvantage is that, unlike the Live System, the Mastered format isn't interactive.

To prepare and use a Mastered-format disc, follow these steps:

1. Insert the blank CD or DVD into the drive.

   It can be a recordable CD of any format: + or –, R or RW.

2. If the AutoPlay dialog box appears, choose the option Burn Files to Disc.

3. Click the Show More button by the Show Formatting Options option in the Burn a Disc dialog box.

4. Choose Mastered.

5. Type a name for the disc.

   You can change the name later.

6. Click the Next button, and you're done.

A window opens for the disc, but it's really the temporary holding bin for files and folders. In fact, files and folders you copy to the folder sport a download flag on their icon, indicating that the file is awaiting a Mastered burn to a CD or DVD.

Folder icon with
a download flag

Before burning the disc, you can remove any files from the disc's folder window to prevent them from being written to the disc. Deleting the temporary files doesn't delete the original. You can use the Delete Temporary Files toolbar button to remove all the files.

When you're ready to create the disc, heed these steps:

1. Open the disc's window.

2. Click the Burn to Disc toolbar button.

3. Rename the disc, if necessary.

4. Set a recording speed.

Eureka

Believe it or not, slower speeds guarantee a more reliable disc. Only if you're in an absolute rush do I recommend burning a disc at the top speed.

5. If necessary, place a check mark by the option Close the Wizard after the Files Have Been Written.

6. Click the Next button.

When the disc is done burning, it's ejected from the drive automatically. You can now use the disc in any computer, but you can't add more files to it.

(You can erase all files on the disc if it's an RW disc; see "Erase an RW disc," later in this chapter.)

Make a music CD

Music CDs are created by music-playing programs, such as Microsoft Media Player or Apple's iTunes. The disc is created in one of two ways.

A *playlist* of songs is created. The playlist can then be written to a CD.

You can copy songs individually to the disc by dragging and dropping them or by using some gizmo that adds songs one at a time.

After choosing the songs that you want to put on the disc, the disc is burned and ejected by the music-playing program. The disc is then ready to use in any computer or CD player. (You can't add any more songs to the disc after it has been created.)

Although you can write music to a CD-RW, it's not always the best idea. First, RW discs cost more than CD-R music discs. Second, the RW format isn't fully compatible with all CD players.

Erase an RW disc

An RW disc, either CD or DVD, can be erased at any time. The whole disc must be erased, and then you can start over, using the disc again.

To erase an RW disc, follow these steps:

1. Insert the disc into the drive.

2. If the AutoPlay dialog box appears, choose the option Open Folder to View Files.

3. In the folder window, click the toolbar button Erase This Disc.

   The Burn to Disc window appears.

4. Ensure that there's a check mark by the option Close This Wizard after the Disc Is Erased.

5. Click the Next button.

The disc is erased and ejected. You can immediately reinsert it to use it again.

Back up to a DVD

You can use recordable DVDs to back up data from your computer. *See* Backup.

Watch Your Step!

Many recordable discs have their type (CD or DVD) and format (+/–, R/RW) stenciled directly on the disc. But some discs lack such information, and it's therefore difficult to determine by looking at which type of disc you have. In those rare instances, I recommend writing on the disc with a Sharpie to record the disk type and format.

Some DVDs are advertised as DL, or Dual Layer. These DVDs store a lot of information but aren't compatible with all DVD players.

Place only copies of files and folders on a recordable CD or DVD. Don't save the originals directly to those discs. You must first save your stuff on the hard drive. Then, after saving to the hard drive, you can copy stuff to a CD or DVD. *See* Copy, Cut, and Paste Files.

Although it may seem like you can delete files from a Live System disc, the files themselves aren't truly deleted. The disc merely *ignores* the data already written to disc, so the information you've erased isn't fully gone and the space it used isn't recovered.

CDs and DVDs are *not* forever. Studies have shown that data recorded to a CD or DVD fades over time, and it fades faster when a label has been affixed to the disc. When using CDs or DVDs for backup or archival purposes, consider replicating the discs every so often.

When Things Go Wrong

When a CD or DVD fails to format or contains errors, toss it out!

Gold Rush Nuggets

Those who predicted that the DVD format would never take off dubbed the acronym Dead, Very Dead.

The battle for successor to the DVD now rages between the HD-DVD and Blu-ray Disc. Of the two, HD-DVD seems to be gaining more ground. Whether it's adopted for wide use on the PC is up in the air. My personal guess is that the CD and DVD will be the last removable spinning media that we'll see for computers — and for music and film.

Digging Elsewhere

Computer, Disk Drives, Windows Explorer

Disk Cleanup

Put away that whisk broom! Set down the cleanser! Cleaning up a disk is nothing like cleaning a credenza. There's no filth to sweep under the carpet. There isn't even a carpet! The disk cleanup operation is more akin to cleaning up the yard after a windstorm. There's stuff to be picked up, walkways and gutters to clean, plus dead things to find and remove. The result is a cleaner yard. For your computer, the result is a hard drive with a lot more free space and less clutter, which tends to slow down disk operations.

WHERE'S THE GOLD?

The Disk Cleanup utility is necessary to not only get rid of the junk you don't need on your PC's hard drive but also to increase hard drive storage.

Disk Cleanup is its own program, so it's easy to run:

- ✗ Click the Start button and choose All Programs⇨Accessories⇨System Tools⇨ Disk Cleanup.

- ✗ From a hard drive's Properties dialog box, click the Disk Cleanup button found on the General tab.

- ✗ In the Run dialog box, type **cleanmgr** and press Enter.

Disk Cleanup is just one of a trilogy of regular hard drive maintenance chores. The other two are checking for errors and defragmenting. I should also mention backup, just because.

What to Do with It

You should run Disk Cleanup every so often, say, at least once a month. Run it more often when

you're a heavy-duty PC user or browse the Internet more than you should.

Clean your files or everyone's files?

When Disk Cleanup first starts, it asks whether you want to clean up only the files for your account or for all accounts on the computer. (You need administrator access to clean all accounts.)

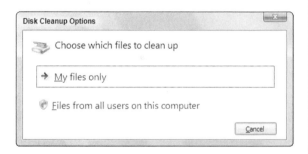

Obviously, choosing the option Files from All Users on This Computer is more thorough, although I recommend alerting other users before you do so.

Choose which items to clean

The Disk Cleanup dialog box presents a scrolling list of items to clean up. Selecting any of them displays, in the Description area in the bottom half of the dialog box, an explanation of what the item is. Despite that, I often find that people enjoy my suggestions on what to do:

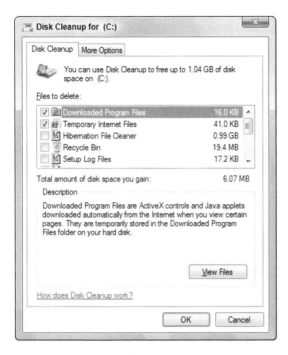

Downloaded Program Files: These files are *not* program files that you downloaded. Instead, they're supplemental updates and add-ons for Internet Explorer. They're *always* safe to remove.

Temporary Internet Files: These files are okay to remove. *See* Web Page Cache for more information.

Hibernation File Cleaner: Don't remove this item if you use the Hibernation command. Otherwise, it's safe.

Recycle Bin: This item is okay to remove, but *see* Recycle Bin first before doing so wantonly.

Setup Log Files: Unless your PC has been having trouble lately *and* you know someone who understands the log files, obliterate them at will!

Temporary Files: These files are okay to remove.

Thumbnails: A *thumbnail* is the little preview picture you see in a folder, representing a graphical image, video, or document. Deleting them causes no harm, but Windows will re-create them all over time and time again.

(Something) Error Reporting: These are all log files and can be used to troubleshoot errors. I have no problem removing them.

Remove unneeded programs

Another way to free disk space, and clean up the crud, is to remove programs you seldom use. To do so, you need to access the Programs and Features icon in the Control Panel, which can also be accessed from the Disk Cleanup dialog box:

1. Start Disk Cleanup.

2. Choose Files from All Users on This Computer.

3. Click the More Options tab in the Disk Cleanup dialog box.

4. In the Programs and Features area, click the Clean Up button.

See Uninstall Programs for more information.

Clean up System Restore

The System Restore utility is handy, but it certainly wastes disk space! To remove some of the slop, follow these steps:

1. Start Disk Cleanup.

2. Choose the Files from All Users on This Computer option.

3. Click the More Options tab.

4. Click the Clean Up button in the System Restore and Shadow Copies area.

5. Click the Delete button.

6. Click OK to banish the Disk Cleanup dialog box.

System Restore keeps oodles of information about your computer on the hard drive. That information is needed when you're having trouble, but otherwise it's just extra space you could use.

Schedule Disk Cleanup automatically

You can have Disk Cleanup run on a predetermined schedule by using the Task Scheduler. You should create a basic task with the `cleanmgr.exe` program. *See* Task Scheduler for the details.

Watch Your Step!

Disk Cleanup is designed only for hard drives. You can't "clean" a CD-R, DVD±R, or RW disc. (Doing so simply wastes disc space.) To clean up a removable USB media drive, just manually delete files or reformat the media.

Don't remove System Restore information if you've had a lot of PC troubles recently or if you upgraded hardware or software within the past several weeks. You want to keep those extra restore points, just in case!

Emptying the Recycle Bin means that you can't recover any recently deleted files. *See* Recycle Bin.

When Things Go Wrong

Disk Cleanup won't save your butt if hard drive space gets woefully shallow. In those cases, your best and only option is to add another hard drive to the system, either internally or through external USB storage.

If you don't see the More Options tab in the Disk Cleanup dialog box, it means that you didn't elect to clean up files for all users. Start Disk Cleanup again.

Gold Rush Nuggets

Years ago, Windows and Microsoft Office were notorious for littering the PC's hard drive with dozens of temporary files. The names of these files all began with the ~ character, which made it easy to find and delete them, but still, it was rather sloppy for a program to create temporary files and then not clean up after itself when it was done.

Digging Elsewhere

Backup, Check for Disk Errors (Check Disk), Defrag, Disk Drives, System Restore, Uninstall Programs

Disk Drives

The computer has two forms of storage: temporary and permanent. Temporary storage is provided by computer memory, or RAM. Long-term storage is the domain of the disk drives, although as computers have evolved, long-term storage takes place on more than simple disks.

Disk drives can be divided into three categories. First, there are hard drives, which provide the best form of long-term storage on PCs. Second come removable discs, such as CDs and DVDs, but also floppy disks and other spinning storage media. Finally, the new boys on the block are the digital storage media, removable USB flash drives, and digital camera storage cards. Yet, despite all the differences, subtle and gross, long-term storage in a computer is still referred to under the generic term *disk drives.*

WHERE'S THE GOLD?

Disk Drives icon

Physically, disk drives are buried in the PC's console. The hard drives are stored internally, with a blinking diode on the console's face the only sign that the hard drive is active and alert.

Removable drives can also be found on the PC's console, as well as attached via the USB or IEEE ports as peripherals. Media cards can also be attached to the console directly or read through a USB media card reader.

In Windows, disk drives dwell in the main Computer window. The window displays all the PC's storage media, including media borrowed from other computers on the network. *See* Computer.

Although the Computer window lists disk drives, it's the Disk Management window that controls them. To summon that window, follow these steps:

1. Open the Control Panel's Administrative Tools icon; from the Control Panel Home, choose System and Maintenance, and then choose Administrative Tools.

2. Double-click to open the Computer Management console.

3. In the Computer Management console, open the Storage item on the left (if necessary).

4. From beneath Storage, choose Disk Management.

What to Do with It

Disk drives are designed for storing information. *See* Files and Folders for details on that level. Beyond that level, you can work with disk drives in a variety of ways, as covered in the sections that follow.

Assign a new disk drive letter

Windows assigns letters to disk drives, A through Z, in pretty much the same order that the drives are found. Drives A: and B:, for ancient reasons, are reserved for floppy drives. Drive C: is always the first hard drive. After that, letters are assigned to internal drives and then to any external drives in the order that they're found by the hardware at boot time.

You can reassign drive letters, however, by using the Disk Management window thusly:

1. Summon the Disk Management window.

2. Right-click a disk drive.

3. Choose Change Drive Letter and Paths from the pop-up menu that appears.

    The Change Drive Letter and Paths dialog box appears.

4. Click the Change button.

5. Choose a new drive letter from the drop-down list.

6. Click OK to set the drive letter.

7. Click Yes to dismiss the warning, if necessary.

To change a drive letter back to the original letter, simply repeat the preceding steps and, in Step 5, choose the original drive letter from the list.

See the section "Watch Your Step!" later in this chapter, for more information.

Mount a disk drive into a folder

Disk drives can be attached (I prefer the word *mounted*) to an empty folder anywhere on your computer disk system. For example, if you want to use an external drive through a folder named Media in your User Profile folder, you can do as follows:

1. Ensure that you have an empty folder to which you can attach the drive.

    If you don't, create a new folder to use as the mount point. Don't put any other icons — files or folders — into that folder!

2. Bring up the Disk Management window.

3. Right-click a disk drive and choose Change Drive Letter and Paths from the pop-up menu that appears.

4. Click the Add button.

5. Use the Browse button to locate your empty folder.

    You can find your User Profile folder by opening drive C: (generally), the Users folder, and then the folder that has your account name.

6. Select the folder, or use the New Folder button to create a new folder within the selected folder.

7. Click OK.

8. Click OK to close the Add Drive Letter or Path dialog box.

Opening the folder now reveals the contents of the disk drive.

To undo this mounting, repeat Steps 1 through 3 in the preceding list, but then click to highlight the folder pathname and click the Remove button. Click the Yes button to confirm.

I've used this technique to mount an external hard drive into my User Account folder scheme. That way, I can store massive media files on another hard drive, yet access them conveniently through my own folder scheme.

It's also possible to have folders in your User Account folder shadow network folders. *See* Folders for more information.

Format a disk

Thanks to the demise of the floppy drive, disk formatting is something that just isn't done that often in the 21st century. Windows still has a Format command, however. And, you can format some removable disks and media cards, although there's no real reason to do so.

To format a disk, open the Computer window. Right-click the disk icon and choose the Format command from the pop-up menu that appears. Thus appears the Format dialog box.

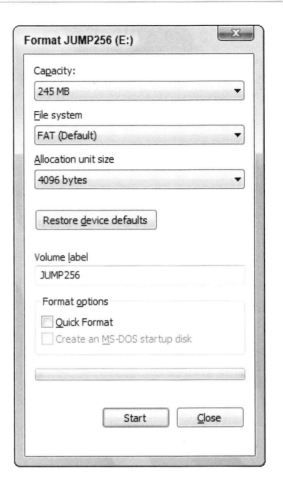

Generally speaking, the options preset in the dialog box are perfect; don't mess with them unless you know what you're doing. Just click the Start button and follow the directions on the screen.

One option worth noting in the Format dialog box is the File System drop-down list. The file system refers to the way the disk is formatted. Presently, you have four file systems to choose from:

FAT (or FAT16): The oldest format, which isn't efficient for large (greater than 2GB) disks, but is very compatible with older PCs and other computers.

FAT32: A better edition of the FAT system, which can store more information than FAT16 yet is still compatible with a large number of computers.

NTFS: The NT File System is the one preferred by Windows Vista. Files on media formatted with NTFS can be compressed and encrypted, but this file system isn't as compatible with other computers.

HPFS: The High Performance File System is also a FAT32 replacement and has nifty features, plus it's more generally compatible with other computers (such as Macs). It lacks the compression and encryption features of NTFS.

Although recordable CDs and DVDs need to be formatted, they don't use the Format command as described here. *See* Discs (CDs and DVDs).

Watch Your Step!

You can't change the drive letter for drive C: or any drive that has Windows on it.

Reassigning the drive letter for a CD or DVD drive means that software installed from that drive, or software that's programmed to access that drive, might continue to look at the old drive letter, not the new one. You can use a Browse button to help the software locate the drive by its new letter.

You can mount a disk drive into only an *empty* folder. Furthermore, that folder must be on an NTFS-formatted disk drive.

Tools are available to unformat a disk you accidentally formatted, but such tools don't come with Windows! Norton Utilities most likely still has accidental format recovery in its chest of tools.

When Things Go Wrong

Disk drive letter changes may not show up until you refresh the Computer window. *See* Refresh.

If a disk fails to format, it's generally a sign that the disk is bad. Throw it away.

Gold Rush Nuggets

Even if your PC doesn't have a floppy drive, drive letter A: is reserved for any floppy drive you may attach. For example, when you add a USB floppy drive to your PC, it pops up in the Computer window as Drive A:.

Digging Elsewhere

Computer, Discs (CDs and DVDs), Map a Network Drive

Disk Space

There's personal space, office space, inner space, and the final frontier. On a computer, *disk space* refers to the amount of room available on a hard drive for storing junk. There are three figures to fuss over:

Total space: The full capacity of the disk

Used space: How much disk space is occupied by Windows, applications, and the stuff you collect or create

Free space: The amount of space left over, available for storing new things; the difference between total space and used space

Disk space calculations are found in the same spot where Windows keeps disk drives: the Computer window. You can open the Computer window from an icon on the desktop, choose Computer from the Start button's menu, or travel to the Computer window from the Address bar in a Windows Explorer window.

What to Do with It

You have several ways to examine disk space figures. The used space value goes up over time, but you can get temporary relief by running the Disk Cleanup program. *See* Disk Cleanup.

Check disk space

To view storage information for a specific disk or media, click to select that media in the Computer window. Storage information appears in the Details pane, at the bottom of the Computer window.

If you don't see the Details pane, click the toolbar's Organize button and choose Layout↪ Details Pane from the menu that appears.

Disk space information isn't available this way for media cards or flash drives.

CD and DVD drives always show 0 (zero) bytes free; because they're read-only media, no extra information can be stored on those discs.

Check disk space graphically

To view a graphical representation of used space on a hard drive, click the Views toolbar button in the Computer window and then choose Tiles from the menu that appears.

Hard drives appear in Tiles view with a graphical thermometer displaying disk space usage.

To get a pie chart representation of disk or media storage, see the following section.

Get specific disk storage figures

This section is written for accountants. To view the actual byte-by-byte storage information for any storage media on your PC, follow these IRS-like steps:

1. Open the Computer window per US Code, Title LXVI, Section 99-A, paragraph 12(c).

2. Right-click a storage media icon according to the clicking directions found in IRS Circular 2002-27R.

3. Choose the Properties command, unless the value from line 27 on Form 87C is greater than your IQ.

4. Observe the totals in the device's Properties dialog box, on the General tab.

5. Click the OK button upon completion, and sign form 27B/6 in triplicate.

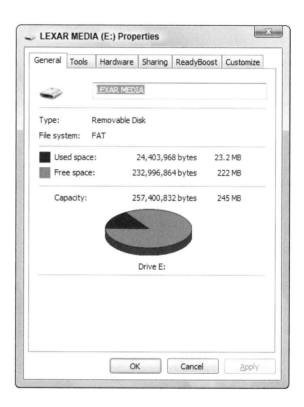

Watch Your Step!

It helps a little bit to understand what a byte is in order to comprehend disk storage:

✗ A *byte* is a single unit of storage in a computer, used to measure both media and memory storage.

✗ A single byte can store one character of information. As an example, it takes 8 bytes to store the word *infinite.*

✗ Approximately 1000 bytes of storage is referred to as a *kilobyte* (K). That's enough storage for a single sheet of typed text. A typical picture on the Internet uses about 60K of storage.

✗ Approximately 1 million bytes of storage is referred to as a *megabyte* (MB). That's enough storage for a single minute of recorded audio sound, or all of William Shakespeare's works in plain text. CD storage is measured in megabytes, as are most digital media cards.

✗ Approximately 1 billion bytes of storage is referred to as a *gigabyte* (GB). Hard drive and DVD storage is measured in gigabytes. You can store about 40 minutes of video or 1,000 good-size photographs in 1 gigabyte.

When Things Go Wrong

Generally speaking, the disk-sizing techniques covered in this chapter report accurate numbers. The numbers include various hidden and system files that aren't normally visible to the computer user.

Some PCs may have their hard drives configured for *quota management,* which means that your account's access to a disk's full storage capacity is limited. This happens mostly at large installations where the IT department has enabled quota management on computer hard drives. Yeah, there's probably nothing you can do about it.

Gold Rush Nuggets

Once upon a time, some wag referred to disk space as *disk memory.* The term is accurate, as far as computer science is concerned, but it's confusing. In fact, many beginners often confuse RAM with disk storage.

Digging Elsewhere

Address Bar, Computer, Disk Cleanup, Disk Drives

Display

The computer shows you an image, a vision produced by its electronic cerebrum. The gizmo that shows you that image is the *monitor.* Pick up the monitor and drop it on your foot, and you'll say something along the lines of "Ouch!" The part of the monitor on which the image appears is the *screen.* The image itself is the *display.* Why three different terms? Because computer nerds demand precision in their lingo. You don't adjust the monitor. You can't adjust the screen. But Windows lets you adjust the display.

WHERE'S THE GOLD?

You have two ways to adjust the computer's display. The first is hardware adjustment, which involves using your thumbs and some buttons that may or may not be obvious on the monitor itself.

The software way to control the PC's monitor is to right-click the desktop and choose Personalize from the shortcut menu that appears. Then, in the Personalization window, choose Display Settings to see the Display Settings dialog box.

What to Do with It

The Display Settings dialog box is about real estate, or how much information can be displayed on the screen at once. For a computer, that's pixels, pixels, pixels.

Set the display resolution

The display resolution determines how much information at a time is visible on the screen. The higher the pixel values, the more information can be displayed — but the information appears smaller on the screen than at lower resolutions.

To set display resolution, obey these steps:

1. Summon the Display Settings dialog box.

2. Use the slider to set screen resolution.

   The resolution is described beneath the slider in horizontal-by-vertical pixels. The preview window also adjusts as you set monitor resolution.

3. Click OK to set the resolution.

Common resolutions are 600 x 800, 1024 x 768, and 1280 x 720. Superwide, or *cinematic*, monitors can take advantage of resolutions such as 1600 x 1200 and 2560 x 1600. Golly!

To make the desktop icons appear larger, *see* Desktop Icons.

Adjust color values

The Colors drop-down list sets the maximum number of colors available at a given display resolution. The value is dependent on the resolution, but ideally, you want to set the number of colors available to the highest value possible, which provides for the most realistic images on the PC.

Values available from the Colors drop-down list in the Display Settings dialog box include Highest (32-bit) and Medium (16-bit). Some display adapters may show more or fewer colors available.

Eureka

Set the resolution first, and then set the maximum number of colors available.

Set the monitor's color tone (Color Management)

One problem that graphical designs have with computers is that no two computer monitors render colors the same way, much less the way the colors actually look when printed. To compensate for this difference, you can calibrate your computer's display by using Windows Color Management. Just follow these steps:

1. In the Display Settings dialog box, click the Advanced Settings button.

2. In the display adapter's Properties dialog box, click the Color Management tab.

3. Click the Color Management button to start the Color Management program.

4. In the Color Management window, choose your monitor from the drop-down list.

5. Place a check mark by the Use My Settings for This Device option.

6. Click the Add button.

7. Choose a profile from the list or use the Browse button to find a profile on the PC's hard drive.

   At this point, it helps to know what you need. Professionals who use and need color management know which profile to select. If you're just messing around, you should probably leave things alone.

8. Click OK.

9. Click the Close button to dismiss the Color Management window.

Adjust the monitor's DPI value

When you're working with graphics, resolution really refers to the DPI (dots per inch) value. Although you set a monitor's resolution by using total horizontal and vertical pixel values, the true resolution being set is DPI.

The typical PC monitor displays 96 pixels, or dots, per inch on the display. (The Macintosh displays 72 DPI, which is better for graphics artists and also explains why things look different on a Mac.)

You can, however, adjust the DPI value for your monitor, setting the number of dots per inch displayed to whatever value you want. Do this:

1. Right-click the desktop.

2. Choose Personalize from the pop-up menu that appears.

3. In the Personalization window, choose the Adjust Font Size (DPI) task (on the left).

4. In the DPI Scaling dialog box, click the Custom DPI button.

5. Use the Custom DPI Scaling dialog box to set the screen's DPI.

   You can choose a percentage or use the mouse to manipulate the graphical ruler.

6. Click OK to set the new DPI scale and (optional) close other dialog boxes and windows.

Sadly, you can't make the scale smaller than 96 DPI, but you can certainly make it larger.

Watch Your Step!

Setting the resolution too high results in a reduced number of colors available. The number of colors you can have at a given resolution is limited by how much memory is available to the video adapter. If you start pushing higher resolutions (and more pixels), less memory is available to display colors.

LCD monitors work best within a limited range of resolutions. Be sure that you set a display resolution compatible with your LCD monitor.

When Things Go Wrong

Generally speaking, when the display suddenly shows a very low resolution, such as 640 x 480, and the colors are gone, it means that Windows has lost the display driver. *See* Device Manager for information on recovery.

A low resolution can also be a sign that you're in Safe mode. *See* Safe Mode.

A fuzzy display, or one with twinkly splotches of color, can often be cured by turning the monitor off and then on again. Otherwise, such things portend that you're using the wrong resolution on an LCD monitor.

Gold Rush Nuggets

A *pixel* is a dot on the screen, an individual point of light.

The early microcomputers had their screen resolution measured in *characters*. The Apple II could display 40 characters in a row and 24 in a column. The first PC displayed 80 characters in a row and 25 in a column.

The first IBM PC graphics adapter, the CGA (Color Graphics Adapter), displayed color in two modes: a high-resolution 640-x-480 two-color mode and a lower resolution 320-x-240 four-color mode. We've come a long way.

Digging Elsewhere

Desktop, Screen Saver, Themes

Encryption

To *encrypt* information is to scramble it in such a way that only those who know how to decrypt the information can access it. By encrypting files or folders, you keep that information safe from prying eyes. In Windows, only the person who encrypted the information can access it. To all others, the information can't be read; an Access Denied warning appears when they try to read the encrypted file or folder.

File encryption isn't available in all versions of Windows Vista.

WHERE'S THE GOLD?

File encryption is attached to the file being encrypted. In a way, it's buried in the file itself because the file's data — the file's text or binary information that comprises an image, spreadsheet, or music video — is scrambled by the encryption process.

The key to viewing the file in an unscrambled state is to have an Encrypted File System (EFS) certificate. This EFS certificate is automatically created when you encrypt files in your own account. Therefore, accessing encrypted files and folders is transparent as far as you're concerned; opening and viewing a file takes place as it does for non-encrypted files. For anyone else, the file's guts can't be accessed.

 Clue In Windows Vista, encrypted files and folders appear in the Windows Explorer window in green text (not black).

What to Do with It

Obviously, encrypting files is a good thing to do for sensitive data. The only way to be more secure is to encrypt an entire disk drive, which you can do by using the Windows BitLocker technology. *See* BitLocker.

Encrypt a file or folder

To encrypt a file or folder, pursue these steps:

1. Right-click the file or folder's icon.

2. Choose Properties from the shortcut menu that appears.

3. On the General tab in the Properties dialog box, click the Advanced button.

4. Put a check mark by the item Encrypt Contents to Secure Data.

5. Click OK, and then click OK again to close the Properties dialog box.

If you're encrypting a single file, you may see an Encryption warning, asking whether to encrypt all files in the folder (which Microsoft recommends) or only the single file. Choose Encrypt This File Only, and then click OK.

Remove encryption

To repeal an encryption, repeat the steps from the preceding section, but in Step 4, remove the check mark.

 Clue Your confirmation that the file is no longer encrypted is that it returns to its regular text color (black instead of green).

Back up your encryption key

The EFS certificate allows Windows to swiftly access and display the contents of encrypted files and folders. It's a good idea to back up the certificate, if only to avoid the incessant pop-up warnings that bother you when you forget. Here's how:

1. Summon the Run dialog box; press Win+R (or *see* Run).

2. Type **mmc certmgr.msc** and press Enter to conjure up the Certification Manager console thing.

3. On the left side of the console, open the Personal folder.

4. Select Certificates on the left side of the console.

5. On the right side of the window, choose the item that says Encrypted File System in the Intended Purposes Column.

   You may need to resize the columns or scroll the window to see the Encrypted File System item.

6. Choose Action⇨All Tasks⇨Export.

   A wizard runs.

7. Click the Next button.

8. Choose Yes, export the private key, and then click the Next button.

9. Ensure that Personal Information Exchange is selected, and then click the Next button.

10. Type a password for the key (twice), and then click the Next button.

    I recommend *not* using the same password that you use to log in to Windows.

11. Enter a filename for the encryption key backup.

12. Use the Browse button to save the file in the Documents folder.

    The file is saved in the Documents folder by default; you can use the Browse button to save it elsewhere.

13. Click the Next button.

14. Click the Finish button.

15. Click OK to dismiss the final dialog box; close the Certification Manager console thing.

So far, you just made a copy of the certificate, which comes in handy when sharing encrypted files. For backing up, you need to complete one more step.

16. Copy the encryption key backup from the Documents folder to a safe place.

Share an encryption key (EFS certificate)

To allow others to access your encrypted files, you must first create a backup of your encryption key, as described in the preceding section. Then follow these steps to import that key into another user's account:

1. Open the key icon.

The Certificate Import Wizard runs.

2. Click the Next button.

3. Click the Next button again.

4. Type the key's password.

5. Put a check mark by the Mark This Key As Exportable option.

6. Click the Next button.

7. Click the Next button again.

8. Click the Finish button.

Manage encryption certificates

Windows provides a central location for managing multiple certificates and encryption keys, which comes in handy if you're using one of those USB encryption dongle-doohickeys. Here's how to manage things:

1. Open the User Accounts icon in the Control Panel.

 The shortcut here is to click your account picture, found atop the Start button menu.

2. Under Tasks (on the left side of the User Accounts window), select Manage Your File Encryption Certificates.

3. Click the Next button.

What you do next depends on what you need. To import a certificate from a smart card, choose Create a New Certificate, click Next, and then choose the Smart Card option on the page that appears.

To back up your certificate, click Next, and then fill in the page's text boxes with the required information.

Watch Your Step!

All files created in an encrypted folder (or copied or moved there) become encrypted.

Copying an encrypted file or folder to a non-NTFS formatted disk or media removes the encryption. (*See* Disk Drives.)

Encrypt the original file, not the shortcut. *See* Shortcuts.

E-mailing the encrypted file decrypts it. This makes sense because you must open the encrypted file to attach it to an e-mail message. Duh.

When Things Go Wrong

If you neglect to use the Browse button to save the encryption key, Windows might place the key in the \Windows\System32 folder.

Back up the encryption key! If anything happens to the original, you can use the backup to access your encrypted files.

If the Encryption option isn't available, the file is most likely sitting on a disk formatted with something other than the NTFS. Either that or your version of Windows doesn't support encryption.

Gold Rush Nuggets

The command line program that controls encryption and decryption and working with the EFS certificates and keys is named CIPHER. Type **cipher /?** at the command prompt for a list of options.

Encryption keys end with the extension .pfx. Here's their icon:

Encryption
Key icon

Digging Elsewhere

BitLocker, Files, Read Only

Favorites

To help you cross the vast and uncharted seas of the Internet, your Web browser (Internet Explorer, or IE) comes with the ability to add the Web pages you visit to a list of *Favorites*. The Favorites list stores Web page addresses, allowing you to revisit a favorite page, a page you want to visit daily, or a page you visited long ago. It's all made possible, and your voyage is made easier, by using the Favorites tool.

WHERE'S THE GOLD?

Favorites are part of IE, stored in a secret area dwelling on the left side of the browser window. To view the area, click the Favorites button on the toolbar, and then click Favorites to see the Favorites list. Or, you can press Alt+C and then Ctrl+I to see the list.

The list of Favorites contains shortcuts to Web pages, plus folders to help you organize the shortcuts. Note that the Favorites area is also home to two other lists in IE: the list of RSS Feeds (*see* RSS) and the History (*see* History).

A special folder in the list of Favorites is the Links folder. Favorites stored in the Links folder can appear on the Links toolbar in IE. *See* Links Bar.

To help you deal with Favorites, IE also has an Add to Favorites button, located just east of the Favorites button on the toolbar. Clicking this button, or pressing the oddball key combination Alt+Z, displays a handy menu of Favorites-related commands.

The Favorites you save or create are stored in your User Account folder, in the aptly named Favorites folder. The Favorites folder simply contains the real Web page shortcuts and folders that are represented in the Favorites list shown in the IE window.

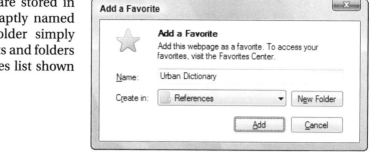

| Favorites button | Add to Favorites button | Favorites folder icon | Open Tab button | Pin button |

What to Do with It

Favorites are places you've been and want to return to on the Web. There's truly no limit to the number of Favorites you can keep, and you can edit and hone the list later, so I encourage liberal use of the Favorites commands and customs.

Add a Favorite

To add the current Web page you're viewing to the Favorites list, press Ctrl+D. I remember this key combination because, in the old days, the mnemonic was *d*rop a bookmark. Sadly, no one has come up with a D-mnemonic for Favorites.

After pressing Ctrl+D, you see a teensy Add a Favorite dialog box.

Do this:

1. **Edit the Web page name or type a shorter name.**

   The name that appears in the Name box is the Web page's title, which may not be the same name you use to refer to the Web page; may be complex or long; or may even be in a different language. Feel free to edit the name.

2. **(Optional) Choose a proper Favorites folder into which you want to place the link.**

   I recommend organizing the Favorites list into folders, just as you can organize information in your User Account folder. Otherwise, you can just create the link in the main Favorites folder.

3. **Click the Add button.**

Editing the name as you add the link, and putting the link into the proper folder, helps save organization time later.

Add the link to the main Favorites folder if — okay, when — you don't know where else it could go.

Remember to add the main page from a Web site. Sometimes, when you're surfing a site, the notion to add the site hits you only after you've been browsing a while. Rather than drop a bookmark, er, add the Favorite for whatever page you happen to be viewing, consider navigating back to the main (or *home*) page and add your Favorite there.

Add a Favorite in a new folder

One way to organize Favorites as you collect them is to take advantage of the New Folder button in the Add a Favorite dialog box. If you click that button, you see a Create a Folder dialog box.

Do this:

1. Type a name for the new folder.

2. Choose the parent folder from the Create In menu.

3. Click the Create button.

As with organizing files into folders, you don't have a limit on folders you can create in the Favorites, although I highly recommend being organized. See "Organize Favorites," later in this chapter.

Folders created in the Links folder become menus on the Links toolbar. *See* Links Bar.

View the Favorites list

To see the list of Favorites, click the Favorites button to display the side panel in Internet Explorer, and then click the Favorites button to ensure that you're looking at the list of Favorites, not the RSS Feeds or History.

The Favorites list keyboard shortcut is Alt+C and then Ctrl+I. Can't Imagine how that's a shortcut for Favorites.

Visit a Favorite

To return to a favorite place on the Web, display the Favorites list, and then click to select a Favorite from the list.

Don't forget that you can open folders in the Favorites list: Click the folder to display its contents, and then choose a favorite from that list.

When you click the Open Tab button to the right of the Favorite, it opens in a tab. Clicking the Open Tab button by a folder opens *all* of that folder's Favorites in a series of tabs in the same IE window.

Edit a Favorite name

You can go into the Favorites list and change the name of any Favorite. For example, the *Wall Street Journal*'s Web site home page is originally titled (on my PC's screen, at least) U.S. Home – WSJ.com. I prefer the title Wall St. Journal, so to edit the thing, I do this:

1. Open the Favorites list.

2. Right-click the Favorite you want to rename.

3. Choose Rename from the shortcut menu that appears.

   The Favorite's name is selected for editing.

4. Type the new name or edit the existing name.

   See Text Editing for the details.

5. Press Enter to lock in the new name.

Change a Favorite address

When a Web site changes its address, you can update the Favorite by editing the address. (Of course, it's often easier to add the Web page again and delete the original, but what the hey.) Do this:

1. Open the list of Favorites.

2. Right-click the Favorite you want to change.

3. Choose Properties from the pop-up menu that appears.

4. Click the Web Document tab.

5. Type (or paste) in the new address.

6. Click OK.

Remove a Favorite

To delete a shortcut from the Favorites list, right-click the link and choose Delete from the pop-up menu that appears.

Organize Favorites

The Favorites list eventually becomes junky and long. I use the length as my key for editing and organizing the list; when the links start to scroll off the bottom of the list, I prune and graft, making good use of the folders to keep things organized.

The key to organizing Favorites is to use the Organize Favorites command, found on the Add to Favorites toolbar button's menu. Choosing that command displays the Organize Favorites dialog box, which works like a mini–Windows Explorer window for managing links and folders.

To move a link into a specific folder, do this:

1. Select the link.

2. Click the Move button.

3. Choose the destination folder from the Browse for Folder window.

4. Click the OK button.

Eureka

I typically organize my links into the following folders:

Blogs	News	Search
Financial	Political	Shopping
Games	Reference	Travel

To create a new folder, follow these steps:

1. Click the New Folder button.

2. Type a name for the new folder.

3. Press Enter to set the name.

As with file folders, use short, descriptive names. The same rules for naming folders applies to Favorites as well as to files. *See* Rename.

To rename a link or folder, obey these steps:

1. Select the link or folder to rename.

2. Click the Rename button or press F2, the shortcut key.

3. Type the new name, obeying the standard file-naming rules.

4. Press Enter to lock in the new name.

To remove a link or folder, proceed thusly:

1. Select the link or folder.

2. Click the Delete button.

I typically delete the preset Microsoft and Windows sites from the Favorites list.

When you're done organizing, click the Close button.

Explode a folder of tabs

One special folder I created for organizing my links, one not mentioned earlier, is my Daily folder. The Daily folder contains links to Web pages I like to visit each morning — often, links that are duplicated elsewhere in the Favorites list. But the true power of the Daily folder comes when I open it into a slew of tabs in IE.

For example, the Daily folder contains links to each site I visit in the morning: news, blogs, puzzles, and other locations I routinely visit. By putting them all in one folder, I can open each link in its own tab by clicking the Open Tab button to the right of the folder in the Favorites list.

Close the Favorites area

To get rid of the Favorites panel on the left side of the window, click the star button.

If you want to keep the Favorites (and Feeds and History) panel open, click the Pin button in the panel's upper right corner. Pinning the Favorites list to the side of the screen resizes the Web browsing window so that you can view a full Web page *and* see the Favorites list at the same time.

Watch Your Step!

Be careful about working the Add a Favorite dialog box too fast! The dialog box remembers which folder you stuck a link in the last time you used the dialog box. Don't assume that any new links you add to the Favorites list are going to the main Favorites folder.

When Things Go Wrong

If a Favorite doesn't seem to show up in the Favorites list, close the IE window and then reopen it. That may fix the problem.

Gold Rush Nuggets

What Microsoft calls Favorites were originally referred to as *bookmarks* in other Web browsers. They still may be called bookmarks on various Web sites, which urge you to "Bookmark our site!"

Digging Elsewhere

Links Bar, Shortcuts

Fax

I'm surprised that there are still fax machines in the world in the 21st century. I realize that they're used in government, real estate, and the medical profession, but with the popularity of e-mail and the PDF file, it seems to me that the fax may soon go the way of the iceman. I hope so, mostly because I believe that faxing in Windows continues to be more difficult than it needs to be.

Faxing works exactly like printing, although the fax machine/printer may be miles away and you use a phone line rather than a USB cable to connect to the printer. Otherwise, it works pretty much the same. That's why you find the fax where Windows keeps its printers: You can fax from any Print dialog box by choosing the Fax option. Otherwise, you need to run the Windows Fax and Scan program, which you can find on the All Programs menu on the Start thing.

The Windows Fax and Scan window looks a lot like an e-mail program, and that's pretty much the gist of it: You can send or receive faxes by using your computer's modem, or you can subscribe to an Internet-based fax service. (You set things up the first time you try to send a fax.)

Sending a fax basically starts in some other program: Word, Publisher, or any program in which you've created a document to fax. Just choose Fax as the printer, and you're thrust into a New Fax window. The document you're trying to send is transformed into a temporary graphics file (a TIF image); faxes send only images, not true text. You can, optionally, choose and fill in a cover page, select an existing contact to send to (see Contacts), and type a brief message. (If you're wondering, you type the recipient's fax number in the To field.) Click the Send button on the toolbar to send the message.

After you send the fax message, it's transferred into the Windows Fax and Scan program and placed in the Outbox folder. Unlike in previous versions of the Windows Fax program (which were quite annoying), the fax is sent immediately.

When a fax comes in, Windows alerts you to the incoming call. The fax is then placed in the Windows Fax and Scan program's Inbox, where you can read and print it.

One important point I need to drive home is that faxes are *graphics*. The fax you receive is essentially a big picture; you can't copy or edit the text on an incoming fax. (If it's text you want, have them send an e-mail message.)

The Windows Fax may not be available in all versions of Windows Vista. That's a good thing: Better programs exist.

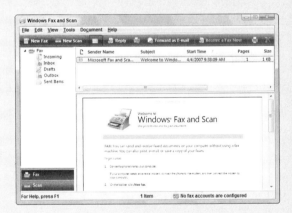

File Compression

Who wouldn't want to lose a little weight? Yep, even those files you have lingering on your hard drive want to. Some of them can bloat to enormous proportions. But forget about binary exercise programs. Files use something called compression.

File compression is the art of squeezing the space and redundancy from computer files without losing any of the file's data. It's possible, by using advanced mathematics and haruspicy, to smoosh a million-byte file to perhaps 130,000 bytes when it's stored on disk. Then, when you access the file, it can be inflated back to its million-byte size with no loss of integrity. (Try that, Congressman!)

Some files are already compressed. TIFF images, MP3 music files, almost all video files, Office 2007 documents — they're already compressed. For other files, such as BMP images and text files, you can apply Windows file compression to the file, making it occupy less disk space.

WHERE'S THE GOLD?

File compression is attached to the file or folder itself, like an attribute (*see* Read Only). The way you can tell that a file or folder is compressed is that its name appears in blue text. Other than the file's new name color , a compressed file or folder works like any other file or folder on your computer (unlike the compressed folder, which has restrictions; *see* Compressed Folders).

The actual compression takes place in the file or folder's Properties dialog box, on the General tab. By clicking the Advanced button, you display the Advanced Attributes dialog box, where the Compress Contents to Save Disk Space setting controls file and folder compression.

You can also find the file compression option in a disk drive's Properties dialog box, if the disk is formatted with NTFS. In the disk's Properties dialog box, at the bottom of the General tab, is the option Compress This Drive to Save Disk Space.

What to Do with It

The File Compression option itself claims that you use compression to save disk space. That's true. But before you use file compression, I seriously recommend considering a second, larger hard drive. Disk compression is a software solution to a hardware problem.

Compress a file or folder

To compress a file for folder, heed these steps:

1. Right-click the file or folder you want to compress.

2. Choose Properties from the pop-up window that appears.

3. In the Properties dialog box, ensure that the General tab is selected.

4. Click the Advanced button.

5. In the Advanced Attributes dialog box, place a check mark in the box by the Compress Contents to Save Disk Space option.

6. Click OK and close other open dialog boxes or windows.

When applying compression to a folder, you're prompted about whether the compression applies to only the selected folder or to all files and subfolders. For my Junk folder, I chose to compress all files and subfolders. (Junk is a good folder to compress because I don't often access its contents; *see* User Profile Folder.)

Decompress a file or folder

Compression can be removed as easily as it's applied: Just repeat the steps from the preceding section and remove the check mark in Step 5.

Compress an entire disk

I don't recommend compressing an entire disk. This practice was popular back in the early 1990s, when software was exploding in size

faster than disk storage could keep up. Disk compression now remains more of an anachronism, and I see little value in it beyond curiosity.

If you feel rebellious and want to compress a disk drive, eschew my advice and do this:

1. Open the Computer window.

2. Right-click the icon representing the disk you want to screw up — I mean, compress.

3. Choose Properties from the pop-up menu that appears.

4. Ensure that the General tab is forward.

5. Put a check mark by the Compress This Drive to Save Disk Space option.

6. Say a small prayer, something about how much you don't want to screw up all the data on your hard drive.

7. Click the OK button and close any other open windows.

There are many problems with compressing an entire disk. First, most of today's disk-consuming files are already compressed, so you don't save anything. Second, and worse, you run into problems if you want to decompress the disk in the future. I rant on this topic in the "When Things Go Wrong" section, later in this chapter.

Watch Your Step!

File compression is a feature of the NTFS disk format. You can't compress files stored on disks and media formatted with FAT or HPFS — at least not without special third-party software. *See* Disk Drives.

Files can be encrypted *or* compressed, but not both.

It's okay to e-mail or give someone else a compressed folder. The process of e-mailing the file or copying the file to another medium automatically decompresses it.

Although you can compress any file or folder, some types of files are already compressed on disk, and, therefore, using Windows file compression on those files offers no benefit. Here's a brief list of files that are already compressed (so file compression doesn't offer much help):

- ✕ Office 2007 documents
- ✕ TIFF, GIF, PNG, and JPG images
- ✕ ZIP files and compressed folders
- ✕ MP3 music files
- ✕ All video file formats

When Things Go Wrong

When the Advanced button doesn't appear in a file's Properties dialog box (on the General tab), the file most likely roosts on a non-NTFS formatted disk. In that case, you can't use Windows file compression.

If you choose to go against my advice and compress an entire disk, you run the possibility of storing so much information on the disk that it can't be decompressed. The only solution to that problem is to buy another hard drive (internal or external), one that's larger than you need, and then copy the contents of the compressed disk to that secondary disk. Yes, that's a pain — which is why I don't recommend compressing a disk in the first place.

Gold Rush Nuggets

Compressed files are automatically decompressed when Windows reads them. This adds a modicum of overhead to the time it takes to open the file, but the overhead isn't noticeable from a human perspective. The files are automatically recompressed when they're saved back to disk.

File compression began with the old ARC utility popularized by PC modem users back in the 1980s. Eventually, ARC evolved into the ZIP utilities still used today for compressed folders. The history of individual file compression, as well as full disk compression, lies with the Stacker program, which was popular back in the late 1980s and early 1990s.

Digging Elsewhere

Compressed Folders, Encryption, Files

Files

A *file* is a computer's storage unit, like those metal sheds that people rent when they can't find room in their garage to shove all their junk. On a computer, files store chunks of information, and that information can be anything — text, a graphical image, a document, raw data, a program, music, video. The file provides a name, creation date, icon, location, and other basic attributes that help you keep and organize your stuff.

WHERE'S THE GOLD?

Files are stored on the computer's long-term storage system, primarily on the PC's internal hard drive. That's the key location for storing files, although files can dwell on any disk drive or storage media attached to the computer.

Files are created mostly by you, the computer operator. Some programs may create files as well, but most of the files you have on your computer were put there when you made something by using a program, or perhaps when you downloaded a file from the Internet or copied a file from elsewhere.

In Windows, files dwell in folders (*see* Folders). The files themselves are represented on-screen as icons (*see* Icons). Each file type — music, document, worksheet, or whatever — sports its own, unique icon. That icon, combined with the file's name and its folder location, helps tell you what the file may contain.

What to Do with It

One major job given to an operating system, such as Microsoft Windows, is managing files.

Even the basic task of opening or saving a file, although it happens in an application, is truly the domain of the operating system.

Manage files

File management is simply the art of organizing or manipulating files. There are several basic file-management tasks, each of which is covered elsewhere in this book:

Backing up: It's a good idea to keep a safety copy of your files and important stuff. *See* Backup.

Compressing: A file can be compressed, making it occupy less disk space. *See* File Compression.

Copying: To copy a file from one folder to another, or from one disk drive to another storage media, you copy and paste the file. *See* Copy, Cut, and Paste Files.

Deleting: You kill off files by using the Delete key on the computer keyboard. *See* Delete.

Duplicating: A file duplicate is simply a copy of a file made in the same folder as the original. *See* Copy, Cut, and Paste Files.

Encrypting: A file's contents can be encrypted for extra security. *See* Encryption.

Making a shortcut: A shortcut is like a file copy operation, but without all the bulk. *See* Shortcuts for more information.

Moving: Copying a file and deleting the original is known as a file *move*. You move a file in Windows by cutting the original file and pasting it elsewhere. *See* Copy, Cut, and Paste Files.

Renaming: You can change a file's name by pressing the F2 key and typing in the new name. But there's more to it than that. *See* Rename.

Selecting: To work with a single file or group of files, the files must be selected. *See* Select Files.

Create a file

Files are created by programs in Windows — typically, the program category known as an *application*. The application helps you craft a document, graphic, movie, or whatever and then save that data from the computer's memory (short-term storage) to a file on disk (long-term storage). For more information, *see* Save.

Open a file

By saving a file on disk, you're allowed the convenience of recalling it later. The file can be modified and saved again, viewed, printed, or not changed. *See* Open.

Preview a file's contents and stuff

Files abide in folders, and in Windows, folder contents are displayed by the Windows Explorer program. In that program, you can click to select a file and gather information about the file from various places around the window.

The Details pane displays useful technical tidbits about the file. To show the Details pane, from the Organize button on the toolbar, choose Layout⇨Details Pane.

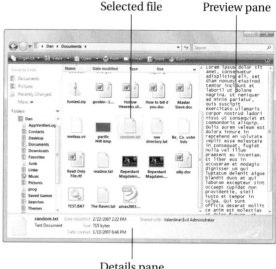

Selected file   Preview pane

Details pane

The Preview pane displays contents for certain types of files. To view the Preview pane, choose Layout⇨Preview Pane from the toolbar's Organize button menu.

Get and change file information

For more detailed information about a file, right-click its icon and choose the Properties command from the pop-up menu that appears. The file's Properties dialog box is displayed, from which you can gather more information or change various settings associated with the file.

Here's a breakdown of the tabs you may find in a file's Properties dialog box:

Custom: A tab not found in every file's Properties dialog box; lets you create and apply custom attributes to a file.

Details: Extra information saved with the file; usually file creation, modification, and content details. Some files, such as those documents produced by Microsoft Office applications, have more information than other files.

General: Information about the file's name, size, location, creation and modification dates, attributes, and which program opens the file.

Previous Versions: A history list of the file as it has been modified or changed since its original creation. Used for file recovery. *See* Previous Versions.

Security: Settings that determine who owns the file and which users can access its contents. *See* User Account Control (UAC).

Reveal filename extensions

The final part of a filename consists of a period (or dot) followed by a three- or four-character filename *extension*. The extension is important in Windows because it tells the operating system the file type. Therefore, you have good reason not to show filename extensions, which is how Windows behaves normally. If you want to see filename extensions, follow these steps:

1. Open the Control Panel's Folder Options icon or, from the Control Panel Home,

click Appearance and Personalization, and then click Folder Options.

2. Click the View tab in the Folder Options dialog box.

3. In the scrolling list, remove the check mark by the option Hide Extensions for Known File Types.

4. Click OK and (optional) close the Control Panel window.

Windows warns you if you accidentally try to change a filename extension. Unless you know what you're doing, I don't recommend changing a filename extension.

Add file tags

A *file tag* is simply an extra bit of text you can apply to a file. You can use the tags to describe file details, which helps you categorize files and can also aid in making the Windows Search command more effective.

You can add tags to files in the Details pane, found in the Windows Explorer window. You can also add them to the Details or Custom tabs in a file's Properties dialog box.

To add a tag, in the Details pane, locate the item titled *Tag*. Click to the left of that title and type the tag text, such as **Christmas vacation 2008**.

You can also add a tag by summoning the file's Properties dialog box and editing the Tag field on the Details tab.

Tag text shows up when you're viewing files in Details view in Windows Explorer. The Tags column may be to the left; summon the Tags column by right-clicking any column heading in Details view and then choosing Tags from the list that appears.

Remove personal information from a file

More information is good when you're trying to organize or search for files, but some folks believe that all the information traveling with a file poses a security risk. To purge a file of that excess information, follow these steps:

1. Summon the file's Properties dialog box.
2. Click the Details tab.
3. Click the link labeled Remove Properties and Personal Information at the bottom of the dialog box.
4. Click OK.

Watch Your Step!

Only certain types of files can have tags added to them. If you don't see the Tags field displayed for a file, tags can't be added to that file's description.

Certain files are hidden for a reason, usually because Microsoft doesn't want you spelunking in hidden folders or messing with hidden files. Even so, sometimes it's necessary to delve into hidden folders to make certain modifications in Windows.

When Things Go Wrong

The most common thing that goes wrong with files is that people lose them. Windows has a powerful Search command to compensate for this shortcoming — *see* Search.

Gold Rush Nuggets

Using the NTFS, a file in Windows Vista can be as big as 16 terabytes. That's 1,099,511,627,776 bytes, or as many bytes as the U.S. government spends in 20 nanoseconds.

Digging Elsewhere

Files, Folders, Icons, Search, Select Files, Shortcuts

Firewall

In the early days, the Internet was a freewheeling, open way to exchange information. It was used mostly by scientists, many of whom had few (if any) evil intentions. But then along came humanity, and people just can't be trusted. What the muddy masses discovered was that the Internet was pretty wild and free; it was like a summer cottage with the windows open and the doors unlocked. So, although not everyone abused things, enough people started prowling around the Internet that it became necessary to bolt the doors, lock the windows, and plug all the holes. The software that does that is a *firewall*.

WHERE'S THE GOLD?

You might think that the Windows Firewall is a program. Perhaps it is, but don't go looking for it on the All Programs menu. To check Windows Firewall, you need to go to the Control Panel.

To check the status of the firewall in Windows, open the Windows Firewall icon in the Control Panel or, from the Control Panel Home, choose Security and then Windows Firewall.

You can also start the Windows Firewall from the Run dialog box: Type **firewallcontrolpanel** in the text box and press Enter.

Advanced users can display the Windows Firewall with Advanced Security console. Here's how:

1. In the Control Panel, open the Administrative Tools icon or, from the Control Panel Home, open System and Maintenance, and then choose Administrative Tools.

2. Open Windows Firewall with Advanced Security.

You can also open the Windows Firewall with Advanced Security window by typing the command **mmc.exe WF.msc** in the Run dialog box.

The Windows Firewall with Advanced Security window contains specific options for controlling which ports are open or closed, and what type of traffic is allowed into or out of the computer. Obviously, the settings were made here by people who *really* know what they're doing.

Firewall icon

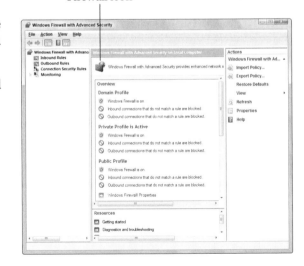

Windows Firewall isn't responsible for the UAC (User Account Control) warnings you see in Windows Vista. *See* User Account Control (UAC) for more information.

What to Do with It

A firewall is a simple thing. It monitors all network traffic coming into and going out of the computer. If the traffic has permission to enter or leave, it flows freely. When something unexpected happens, you're prompted to allow or deny that unexpected something, and that's how you protect your PC.

Disable the Windows Firewall

You don't need to enable the Windows Firewall if you have a hardware firewall protecting your computer. In fact, if you have a software firewall in addition to Windows Firewall, you can disable Windows Firewall.

To disable Windows Firewall, do this:

1. Open the Windows Firewall program.

2. In the upper right part of the Windows Firewall window, choose Turn Windows Firewall On or Off.

   The Windows Firewall Settings dialog box appears.

3. Choose Off (Not Recommended).

4. Click the OK button.

You can find hardware firewalls in most routers. If you have a broadband (high-speed) Internet connection, the cable, DSL, or satellite modem is most likely connected to a router, and then to your computer or a network. If that router has firewall protection, it's all you need; adding the Windows Firewall is redundant.

(Yes, I know that the Microsoft Help file claims you still need a local firewall to protect against worms. But, honestly, how often will you have an unknown computer connect to your network?)

Deal with a firewall warning

Don't be alarmed if you see a firewall warning appear. The warning means that the firewall is doing its job. Your job is to see whether the firewall is overreacting. You have three options:

Keep Blocking: This choice directs Windows to always prevent the program from getting into or out of the computer. It's a wise choice if you don't recognize the program being blocked or you aren't doing anything on the computer to cause Internet access.

Unblock: This is the "Good job, but you're wrong" button. Click to unblock legitimate programs that the firewall has mistakenly blocked from Internet access.

Ask Me Later: This option also blocks Internet access, but just once. If the same program tries to get on the Internet (or into your computer) again, you see the warning again.

The bottom line to knowing which option to choose is to be aware of what you're doing on the computer. Obviously, if you're just playing a game of Spider Solitaire while talking on the phone, and suddenly EVIL.EXE tries to access the Internet, you're wise to click the Keep Blocking button. Furthermore, you should investigate what the blocked program is up to and why it's installed on your computer.

Allow local network traffic through the firewall

One of the biggest problems with firewalls is that they impede traffic on your local network. Whenever you can't seem to access shared files or folders on another computer, blame the firewall.

To permit local network access in Windows Firewall, obey these steps:

1. Open Windows Firewall.

2. Choose Change Settings.

3. In the Windows Firewall Settings dialog box, click the Advanced tab.

4. Put a check mark by the Local Area Connection option.

5. Click OK.

Allow a specific program through the firewall

Although Windows may not trust some programs, you know better. To let a program out through the firewall when it's mistakenly blocked, follow these steps:

1. Open the Windows Firewall.

2. From the left side of the window, select Allow a Program through Windows Firewall.

3a. Look through the list of programs in the Windows Firewall Settings dialog box (on the Exceptions tab) and place a check mark by the one you want to allow through the firewall.

Or:

3b. Click the Add Program button and choose the program you want to add from the list, or use the Browse button to locate the program.

4. Click OK when you're done.

You can also remove programs from the list. Removing the program's check mark simply disables that program, blocking it once again. Selecting the program and clicking the Delete button not only disables the program but also removes the program from the list.

Watch Your Step!

Some users run more than one antivirus program, just to be safe. That's okay. But it's not okay to run more than one firewall program. If you do, you seriously slow down your Internet and network access. In other words, multiple firewalls hurt more than they help.

When Things Go Wrong

If you accidentally give permission to a specific program and then discover that you made a booboo, you can rescind that permission by doing this:

1. Open the Windows Firewall.

2. Choose Change Settings.

3. In the Windows Firewall Settings dialog box, click the Exceptions tab.

4. Select the program name in the scrolling list of exceptions.

5. Click the Delete button.

6. Click OK and (optional) close the Windows Firewall window.

Gold Rush Nuggets

The software firewall is based on the physical firewall, which is a way to protect buildings from burning down quickly. Physical firewalls are rated in minutes, as in how many minutes a raging fire would take to burn through the material. By installing firewalls, builders can improve the safety of their structures and ensure that most folks can get out before a fire starts to spread.

Windows Firewall isn't very good, at least not when compared with other available firewalls. If you're behind a hardware firewall in a router, you're okay. Otherwise, I can recommend the ZoneAlarm firewall from ZoneLabs (`www.zonelabs.com`).

Digging Elsewhere

Networking, Windows Defender

Folders

In the beginning was the disk. And it was good. And on the disk, you could store files. Lots of files. Dozens, hundreds, zillions of files. And things were scattered, so file lists took weeks to display. And, lo, the people were unhappy. Then came the folder, a deliverer from the vast waste of the disk chock-full o' files. By using the folder, files could be organized, like files into like folders. Even more so, folders could contain folders, called *subfolders,* allowing for even more organization. And the people looked upon this and yawned. Yea verily, preaching about disk organization with folders is an uphill battle.

| Folder icon | Folder containing files | Folder containing more folders | Folder contents preview |

WHERE'S THE GOLD?

Folders dwell on the PC's hard drive. In fact, the hard drive itself has one main folder, called the *root folder.* (It's also known by its archaic term, the *root directory.*) Folders can contain folders, called *subfolders,* so the answer to where you can find the gold is "all over your PC's disk drives and storage media."

Folders sport a folder icon, although you can customize the icon or choose another icon, if you want. Folders that are empty display an empty icon.

Folders that contain files use a folder icon that shows files.

Folders that contain more folders use a folder icon that shows more folders, and possibly files within those folders.

The contents of a folder are displayed in a window via the Windows Explorer program. *See* Windows Explorer. The contents are shown as icons; *see* Icons.

What to Do with It

Folders are created to store files. Specifically, folders help you organize files by keeping similar files together. It's the notion of file organization that baffles and confuses most computer users.

Make a new folder

To create a new folder, follow these steps:

1. Open the Windows Explorer window (if it's not open already).

 Press Win+E.

2. Browse to the folder in which you want the new folder created.

For example, to create a folder for family photos in the Pictures folder, browse to the Pictures folder.

3. Click the Organize button on the toolbar.

4. Choose New Folder from the Organize button's menu.

The new folder appears, ready for renaming.

5. Type a name for the folder.

See Rename for icon naming rules and regulations, although I recommend keeping the name short and descriptive.

6. Press the Enter key to lock in the folder's name.

7. Start using the folder.

Remove a folder

Folders are deleted just like any other icon. *See* Delete.

Rename a folder

Folders are renamed just like icons. *See* Rename.

Note that folders generally don't use extensions, although you can add extensions, if you want. Giving a folder an extension does nothing to the folder, nor does Windows treat the folder in any special or specific way if that folder has an extension.

Locate the root folder

The root folder is the main folder on each hard drive, disk drive, or storage media attached to your computer. All disks must have a root folder. To see any disk's root folder, obey these steps:

1. Open the Computer window.

2. Open any non-network disk drive.

Technically, I suppose that opening a network disk drive shows you that drive's root folder, but because of the nature of how disk storage is shared on the Internet, the folder you see may not be the drive's true root folder — not that it matters one whit this way or that.

Organize folders

The whole notion behind using folders is to keep your files organized. Sadly, there's no strict rule about folder organization. Most casual computer users don't care, and honestly, you have only a small price to pay for not organizing your stuff and being sloppy.

To organize folders, you use the same Cut, Copy, and Paste commands as you do for manipulating files. *See* Copy, Cut, and Paste Files for the details.

Place a picture in the folder icon

A folder icon reflects the contents of the folder, showing a little preview of the documents or folders graphically inside the folder icon. But you can place any image you want into a folder, such as the young booby chick shown in the figure earlier in this entry. Here's how:

1. Right-click the folder you want to modify.

2. Choose Properties from the pop-up menu that appears.

3. Click the Customize tab.

4. Click the Choose File button.

5. Use the Browse dialog box to locate and select an image file.

6. Click the Open button to choose the selected file.

7. Click OK.

To remove the image, follow the preceding steps but click the Restore Default button in Step 4, and then click OK.

Change a folder's icon

You can choose a new icon for any folder, replacing the standard folder icon with any of the icons that come with Windows or an icon you create yourself. Here's how:

1. Right-click the folder you want to modify and choose Properties from the pop-up menu that appears.

2. Click the Customize tab in the folder's Properties dialog box.

3. Click the Change Icon button.

4. Select a new icon from the Change Icon dialog box, or use the Browse button to locate another file chock-full of icons or an icon file you created yourself.

See Icons for more information.

5. Click OK to choose the new icon.

6. Click OK to close the Properties dialog box.

To restore the folder icon, repeat these steps but, in Step 4, click the Restore Defaults button.

Customize a folder for certain file types

Windows has custom templates for folders that contain specific file types. The templates are

✂ Documents

✂ Pictures and Videos

✂ Music (Details)

✂ Music (Icons)

A fifth template, All Items, displays files in a general way. But when you have a folder containing files of a specific type, it's a good idea to apply the proper template. Here's how:

1. Right-click in the folder window you want to modify.

2. Choose Customize This Folder from the pop-up menu that appears.

3. Choose from the drop-down list an appropriate template for the file's contents.

4. When the folder's subfolders contain similar types of files, put a check mark by the option Also Apply This Template to All Subfolders.

5. Click OK.

Change a folder's location

You can relocate specific folders in your User Account folder, placing those folders elsewhere on the network or on another hard drive attached to your computer. So, although it appears as though nothing has changed with the folder, its location has been changed. The official term for such a folder change is Client Side Redirect Folder.

For example, maybe you stored all your digital images on a network hard drive so that all computers, and even the television set, can access them. To have your account's Picture folder reflect that network picture location, follow these steps:

1. Right-click the icon for the folder you want to relocate.

2. Choose Properties from the shortcut menu that appears.

3. In the Properties dialog box, click the Location tab.

   If there isn't a Location tab, you can't relocate the folder.

4. Click the Move button.

5. Use the Select a Destination dialog box to locate and select the folder's location.

   Browse to a network or external drive to which the folder's files will be moved or where they may already exist.

6. Click the Select Folder button to choose the folder.

7. Click OK.

8. Click the Yes button to move any existing files and subfolders over to the folder you selected in Step 6.

To undo the change, repeat these steps, but in Step 4, choose Restore Default, and then click OK.

Watch Your Step!

Deleting a folder not only deletes the folder icon — it also deletes all files in the folder, plus any subfolders and their files. Be careful!

Choosing a new icon for the folder overrides the folder image that's already there.

When Things Go Wrong

Sometimes, to see the new folder icon, you must close the Windows Explorer window and then reopen it.

If you screw up terribly, consider first the Undo command; Ctrl+Z is the keyboard shortcut. *Also see* Previous Versions.

Gold Rush Nuggets

Folders were once called *directories*. Subfolders were *subdirectories*. This nomenclature still exists among old-timers. Even Microsoft hasn't fully purged the term *directory* from its vocabulary, specifically with regard to the *root directory*.

Digging Elsewhere

Compressed Folders, Encryption, File Compression, Files, Icons, Windows Explorer

Fonts

When computers made the move from ugly text-based mode to graphics mode, suddenly the weird typesetter term *font* went high-tech. The problem is that *font* is the wrong term. Whereas computer users refer to a *font,* typesetters prefer the term *typeface,* which I feel is more descriptive. Yet, in Windows (and in various applications), the term *fonts* refers to the appearance of the text on your computer.

WHERE'S THE GOLD?

Fonts all dwell in a special Fonts folder, which you can access from the Control Panel.

Opening the Control Panel's Fonts icon displays the fonts available on your computer, which all appear as icons, just like other files in Windows. The font icons differ, depending on the type of font.

Windows Vista uses OpenType fonts, which look good at any size and render well on both the screen and printer. The previous font type was TrueType, and you may still see some of those font files floating about.

The most ancient font type is the *raster* font, which is text set at specific sizes. At those sizes, the raster fonts look okay, but between and beyond those sizes, the raster fonts grow ugly.

What to Do with It

Fonts are there for you to use; both text and graphics programs let you pick from the assortment of fonts installed on your PC. Fonts are also used in Windows to display text, menus, and other fun things. It's a fun-filled forest of fonts!

Peruse available fonts in Windows

To review the fonts available in Windows, open the Control Panel's Fonts icon. From the Control Panel Home, choose Appearance and Personalization, and then click Fonts.

Fonts show up as icons. After all, each font is stored as a file on disk. (Files hold all sorts of information; *see* Files.) The files are named after the font typeface: Arial, Times New Roman, and Courier New, for example. Different font files may be used for the bold, italics, and bold italics fonts.

To preview what a font looks like, summon the Preview pane in the Windows Explorer window: From the Organize button's menu, choose Layout⇨Preview Pane.

 You can adjust the Preview pane's width by dragging left or right when pointing the mouse at the vertical line between the file list and the Preview pane.

Fonts icon

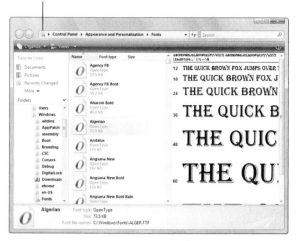

A better way to preview a font is to just double-click and open the Fonts icon. A special Fonts window appears, from which you can print the font by using the Print button.

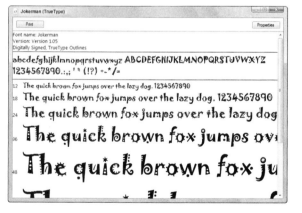

Add new fonts

Fonts come in font collections, which you can download from the Internet or obtain on a CD or other media. From whatever source, the idea is to install the fonts on your computer, making them part of your font repertoire. Here's how I do it:

1. Open the Fonts window.

2. Right-click in the window and choose Install New Font from the pop-up menu that appears.

3. Use the (primitive) Add Fonts dialog box to locate the media or folder in which the font files lurk.

4. Select the font or fonts to install.

5. Click the Install button.

6. Click the Close button when you're done and (optional) close the Fonts window.

You can also just drag fonts into the Fonts window from another window. That's the sneaky way, but it works.

Fonts are made available as soon as they're installed, although you have to close and reopen any open applications to access and use the newly installed fonts.

When downloading fonts from the Internet, you need to unzip or decompress the fonts before you can add them. Also, the Add Fonts dialog box is primitive; you can usually find your account folder by opening drive C:, the Users folder, and then the folder with your account name.

Remove fonts

To rid yourself of a font, simply delete its icon from the Fonts window. *See* Delete.

 Eureka As an alternative to deleting fonts, I recommend creating a special Dead Fonts folder, in which you can store fonts you may no longer need but don't want to erase. Follow these steps:

1. Create a Dead Fonts folder in your main account folder, the User Profile folder, if you haven't done so already.

   I created my Dead Fonts folder in my Junk folder. *See* User Profile Folder for more info on the Junk folder.

2. Open the Dead Fonts folder.

3. Open the Fonts folder.

4. Arrange the Fonts and Dead Fonts folders so that you can see both folder windows.

5. Drag a deadbeat font into the Dead Fonts folder.

   Dragging the icons *copies* the fonts; it doesn't move them. (Don't even try moving them — you can't.)

6. Delete the original font file in the Fonts folder; answer Yes at the confirmation prompt.

7. Repeat Steps 5 and 6 for all the fonts you want to store elsewhere.

Change fonts used by Windows

Windows uses fonts in menus, dialog boxes, and elsewhere to display information and text. You can change those fonts to anything you like, customizing Windows at your will and whim.

To change all fonts that Windows uses, consider using a new Windows theme. *See* Themes.

To change a font in a specific location, follow these steps:

1. Right-click the desktop and choose Personalize from the pop-up menu that appears.

2. In the Personalization window, choose Windows Color and Appearance.

3. Choose the link labeled Open Classic Appearance Properties for More Color Options.

   The Appearance Settings dialog box shows up.

4. Click the Advanced button.

   The Advanced Appearance dialog box lets you change the colors and fonts used by various elements in Windows.

5. Select a text item from the Item list.

   Text items include Active Title Bar, Icon, Inactive Title Bar, Menu, Message Box, Palette Title, Selected Items, and ToolTip.

6. Pick a new font, size, color, and optional bold or italics attributes for the text.

7. Repeat Steps 5 and 6 for each item you want to change.

8. Click the OK button when you're done, and (optional) click OK and close other dialog boxes and open windows.

The changes you make affect only your account on the computer.

Also see Themes for information on saving your changes as a theme.

Watch Your Step!

Deleting a font from the Fonts folder is a *permanent* thing. You're warned, but consider using a Dead Fonts folder, as described in the "Remove fonts" section, earlier in this chapter, rather than delete fonts outright.

Fonts consume computer resources. Believe it or not, a great deal of Windows effort is spent displaying and arranging fonts in windows. The more fonts your computer has installed, the greater the tax on your computer's efficiency. I recommend not going overboard with too many fonts. (Windows comes with a little under 400 fonts — I would say anything over double that number is excessive.)

When Things Go Wrong

Newly installed fonts don't show up in any programs unless you quit and restart that program after installing the new font.

Not every program you use may recognize every font installed on your computer. Also, some programs may come with their own set of specialty fonts, which you can't access or use from other programs.

Gold Rush Nuggets

Back in the old, text-based days, fonts were the domain of the printer, not the computer. If the printer could produce text in fancy fonts, you were in business. Otherwise, computers used boring, ugly text on the screen and boring, ugly text when printing.

Fonts dwell in the Fonts folder, found in the Windows folder, usually on drive C:. The Fonts icon in the Control Panel is merely a shortcut to the \Windows\Fonts folder.

Digging Elsewhere

Control Panel, Themes

FTP

One of the longest-lived Internet acronyms, far older than WWW, is FTP. Pronounced letters-only, FTP stands for File Transfer Protocol. What it refers to is the way files are sent and received between various computers on the Internet.

Most FTP is handled by a Web page. To download a program, you click a link and Internet Explorer handles the rest, safely transferring the files from the Internet into your computer. To send a program, you upload. For example, you may upload a set of photographs to share on a Web page. Both uploading and downloading are examples of what can be done on a Web page, but what also can be done by using FTP, which serves as a specific file transfer program.

WHERE'S THE GOLD?

FTP exists in many places in Windows. First, FTP can be a mode of operation for Internet Explorer (IE). You can use IE to browse to an FTP server in which you can access files and browse folders on the Internet.

Second, you can open an FTP window in Windows Explorer, which gives you the advantage of working graphically with remote files as icons, plus the ability to drag and drop files between an FTP window and a standard Windows Explorer window.

Third, and most nerdy, involves using FTP at the command prompt. The FTP command runs a text-based version of FTP, similar to the original FTP program on Unix computers. (I recommend that version of FTP for experts only.)

Finally, plenty of third-party FTP programs attempt to deal with the file transfer issues in various, often simple, ways. These programs offer more features and controls than the FTP implementations offered by Windows. Two examples are FileZilla (`http://filezilla.sourceforge.net`) and CuteFTP (`www.cuteftp.com`).

FTP works on the Internet by using the FTP protocol. The URL is `ftp`. (The URL for the Web is `http`.) Using a Web browser, you follow the URL with the address of an *FTP server,* a computer or software on the Internet that dishes up files. For example, `ftp://ftp.gnu.org` is the address of the FTP server at the Free Software Foundation.

You can get files from an FTP server. Those files are downloaded to your computer. The FTP command to get files is, obviously enough, `get`.

You can also send files to an FTP server. Those files are uploaded from your computer. The FTP command to send files to another computer is `put`.

What to Do with It

FTP is how you get files between your computer and the Internet. You can, for example, upload files to your personal Web space and create a Web page. Or, you can access an FTP server to download files too large for e-mail or files that you can't find on a Web page.

Connect to an FTP server

After obtaining the FTP server's name, you can access the server and its files by typing the FTP server name into the Address bar of a Web browser. For example, to visit the GNU software FTP server, type this address into the Internet Explorer Address bar:

```
ftp://ftp.gnu.org
```

Eventually, IE connects to the GNU server and displays a directory listing.

 Clue Most files available for public use are stored in a *public*, or *pub*, folder.

To browse to a folder, click its link. Note that the links may be labeled Directory rather than Folder.

To browse to a parent folder, choose the link toward the top of the page, Up to Higher-Level Directory.

You can also edit the Address bar to navigate the site, though.

Connect to a password-protected FTP server

Many FTP servers require passwords in order to get access, such as the server that hosts any Web space you might have. (Contact your ISP about your Web space and its FTP address.) When a password is required, you're prompted by a dialog box.

In the dialog box, type your username and password (you should know the drill from logging in to Windows), but note that the username and password you type are specific to the FTP site; they may not necessarily be the same username and password you use to log in to Windows or to pick up e-mail. Click the Log On button to connect to the FTP server.

You can use the Log On Anonymously check box to attempt an anonymous login, which many FTP servers accept for those without user accounts on their systems. Note that the anonymous access is very limited and often completely forbidden.

Disconnect from an FTP server

To cancel the FTP operation, simply close the Web browser window or browse to another location on the Internet.

Grab (download) a file from an FTP server

After connecting to an FTP server and accessing the files and directories on that site, you can start grabbing files.

To view a file, click its link. Note, however, that only certain types of files can be displayed in a Web browser window. These files include plain text, HTML or Web page documents, PDF files, certain media files (video and sound), and some graphics files.

To download a file, do this:

1. Right-click the file's link.

2. From the pop-up shortcut menu that appears, choose the Save Target As command.

3. Use the Save As dialog box to find a proper location (folder) for the file on your PC's disk system.

4. Click the Save button.

5. Click the Close button to dismiss the Download Complete dialog box.

   Or, you can choose the Open Folder command to view the folder in which the downloaded file was saved. Or, you can click either the Open or Run button to display the file or run it, respectively.

6. Close the IE window to disconnect from the FTP server.

Put (upload) a file to an FTP server

To send, or *upload,* a file to an FTP server, you need to do more than just use Internet Explorer. You must open the FTP server in a Windows Explorer window. That way, you ensure that you have full put and get file access. To make that happen, obey these steps:

1. Open a new Windows Explorer window; press Win+E.

2. Press the F4 key to select the Address bar.

3. Type the FTP address into the Address bar.

4. (Optional) Log in.

   Refer to the section "Connect to a password-protected FTP server," earlier in this chapter, for the specifics.

After logging in, you can browse the FTP server just as you browse any folder window. The bonus with this method, of course, is that you can drag-copy, or paste, a file or group of files from another Windows Explorer window into the FTP window. By doing so, you copy (upload or put) files to the FTP server.

You can also open a Windows Explorer FTP window from Internet Explorer: From the toolbar's Page button menu, choose the command Open FTP Site in Windows Explorer.

Don't forget to close the Windows Explorer FTP window when you're done.

Add an FTP server to the Computer window

I recommend keeping track of FTP servers that you connect to frequently by placing them in the Computer window. *See* Map a Network Drive for the details.

Use FTP at the command prompt

The Command Prompt window sports an FTP command, which is handy to use only when you're familiar with the traditional, Unix-based FTP command. Here are some pointers:

The command to start FTP is, logically, `ftp`. When you type `ftp`, you see the FTP program's prompt:

```
ftp>
```

Type **help** or **?** to see a list of commands. Type **help** followed by a specific command to see a terse, useless explanation of the command.

Here are some handy FTP commands to know:

ascii: The `ascii` command sets the file transfer mode to text.

binary: The `binary` command sets the file transfer mode to binary. Use this comment to ensure that nontext files are downloaded properly.

bye: End the FTP program and return to the command prompt.

cd: To change directories on the server, you use the `cd` command.

close: Disconnect from an FTP server.

dir: The `dir` command is also used to list files on the remote server.

get: Receive a file. Follow the `get` command with the name of a file on the FTP server; for example:

```
get unknown.mp3
```

ls: The `ls` command is used to list the files on the remote server.

open: Connect to an FTP site; the `open` command is followed by an FTP address (not a URL). So, to connect to GNU, you type

```
open ftp.gnu.org
```

This line is followed by logging in with a username and password. (Type **anonymous** for the username, and then type your e-mail address as the password, or obey the directions displayed on the screen.)

put: Send a file. The `put` command is followed by the name of the file to send; for example:

```
put archive.zip
```

pwd: The `pwd` command displays the current directory; it stands for *p*rint *w*orking *d*irectory.

Watch Your Step!

Although you can use Internet Explorer to visit an FTP site, the URL is `ftp`, not `http`. Plus, the FTP site most likely has an `ftp` prefix, not `www`.

Then again, some FTP servers recognize www and allow an FTP connection that way. When the connection doesn't work, check your typing.

FTP servers have timeouts. On some servers, the timeout can be quite long, but on others, the timeout may be as quick as 60 seconds. If you don't do anything (send, receive, or browse) during that period, the FTP server might disconnect you. If so, just log on again — and keep busy! (The timeout isn't in effect while you're sending or receiving files.)

You can't copy information from one FTP site to another. You must first copy the files to your own PC, and then you must copy them from your PC to the second FTP site (for example, to your own Web page).

When Things Go Wrong

If you don't see a login box for an FTP site in Windows Explorer, press Alt+F and choose the Login As command from the menu.

File transfers can be disrupted because of either a dropped connection or a dial-up modem timeout. If you're fast, you can reconnect to the Internet, and the transfer should pick up where it left off. If the transfer doesn't pick up, you have to start all over.

FTP may have trouble with your firewall. Normally, this shouldn't be an issue for Windows or for most hardware firewalls. If it is a problem, check the firewall to ensure that outgoing FTP requests are allowed.

Gold Rush Nuggets

FTP isn't a secure way to transfer files between two computers. First, your username and password are transmitted *unencrypted*, or in the open. Second, any data from any files you send are visible to so-called packet-sniffer programs. On a private network, this shouldn't be a problem, but be cautious when you're using FTP on a public network, such as a WiFi hotspot, cybercafé, airport, or other open location.

Digging Elsewhere

Address Bar, Compressed Folders, Internet Explorer

Game Controllers

Once upon a time, these things were called *joysticks*. But now the modern computer uses more than simple joysticks. Nope, those babies are called game *controllers*. There's more than just one joystick, more than one knob, and definitely more than one button on the thing. Now, it may also be called a game *pad*, but in Windows the key word is *controller*.

Game controllers need little, if any, explanation. I seriously doubt that any hard-core gamer needs to refer to this book before eagerly ripping the game controller out of its impenetrable plastic coffin, plugging the cable into the USB port, starting up the game, configuring the new controller — even if that's necessary — and beginning the onslaught. So, this stuff is for Mom and Dad or anyone older who chances to need a game controller.

Simply put, adding the thing is cinchy. Plug it in. All game controllers today are USB. They plug in, the computer recognizes them. You're done. Oh, a CD may come with the thing, but you probably don't have to install it first. Or, maybe you do. Read the directions.

There's a Game Controllers icon in the Control Panel: From the Control Panel Home, choose Hardware and Sound and then Game Controllers. Either way, a teeny Game Controllers window opens, listing any game controllers attached to your PC. Although you can adjust the game controller in this place, odds are pretty good that the game controller you purchased has its own, better configuration program; use that one instead.

Games

ames? But the PC is the serious computer, right? Well, not really. Although the PC has a reputation for numbers and serious business software, it remains perhaps the best platform for playing computer games. The sheer volume of available game software alone is reason to buy a PC over a Macintosh or gaming console. Even Windows itself comes with a slate of games, plus a special folder to make accessing the games easy.

WHERE'S THE GOLD?

Although computer games may be installed all over your PC's hard drive, for some reason Windows is able to find them and gather them all up in a virtual Games folder window. You can open that window by choosing Games from the Start button menu.

Games icon   Saved Games folder

If the Games command doesn't show up on the Start button menu, follow these steps:

1. Right-click the Start button.

2. Choose Properties from the shortcut menu.

3. Click the Customize button on the Start menu tab.

4. Scroll down to find Games in the list, and choose the option Display As Link.

5. Click OK to close the Customize Start Menu dialog box.

6. Click OK to close the Taskbar and Start Menu Properties dialog box.

I refer to the Games window as a *virtual* window. There's no real Games window; game information is collected and compiled by Windows itself.

In addition to the Games window, there's a Saved Games folder in the User Profile folder. The Saved Games folder is used for keeping game confirmation information, as well as high scores and other game-related info.

What to Do with It

More than just playing games happens in the Games window. Well, not much more.

Play a game

Playing a game is easy: Double-click to open its icon and start the game. This easy access is what makes the Games folder much better than having to sift through the All Programs menu to look for a game.

Read game information

When you select an icon in the Games window, additional information about the game appears in the Preview panel, on the right side of the window. Most importantly, the game's ESRB rating appears, which clues parents in to how appropriate each computer game is for their kids.

Download game information

To ensure that Windows Vista downloads information about the games in the Games folder, follow these steps:

1. Open the Games window.

2. Click the Options button on the toolbar.

3. Ensure that a check mark appears by the option Download Information about Installed Games.

4. Click the Update Game button (if it's available).

5. Click OK.

Build the Play menu

The Games window sports a Play button. Clicking the Play button simply plays whichever game icon is highlighted in the window. But the Play button also sports a menu, one that you can populate with various games, especially those that may not show up in the Games window, such as games on the Internet.

Here's how to populate the Play menu:

1. Open the Games window.

2. Click the triangle by the Play button to display its menu.

3. Choose Customize from the menu.

4. Click to select an unused Play command.

5. Click the Add button.

6. Type in (or paste) a Web page address, such as one where you can play an online game, or you can use the Browse button to locate a game on the hard drive.

 Clue   Games are installed in the C:\Program Files folder, usually under the game's name or by the game developer's name, such as LucasArts.

7. Type a name for the game's menu item.

8. Click the Finish button.

Set parental controls for games

Windows Vista sports a slew of parental control efforts, options designed to make parental types feel more comfortable about their wee ones using the PC. One such feature plays into the rating system assigned to computer games. It's designed to prevent kids of a certain age from playing those grown-up, violent video games. Here's how:

1. Open the Games window.

2. Click the Parental Controls button on the toolbar.

3. Choose the kid's account from the list of accounts displayed.

   Yes, Junior must have his or her own account on the PC for the parental controls to work. It should be a Standard account. See User Accounts.

4. In the User Controls window, under Parental Controls, choose the option On, Enforce Current Settings.

   The On option activates parental controls for the account.

5. In the Window Settings area, choose the Games link.

   The Game Controls window is where you can choose which games or which type of games the account has access to.

6. Choose Yes to allow Junior to play games.

7. Click Set Game Ratings.

8. Use the Game Restrictions window to set which type of ratings the account can have access to, plus whether to block unrated games. Click OK when you're done.

9. Choose Block or Allow Specific Games, and then block or allow the listed games or use the rating settings to control the account's access. Click OK when you're done.

10. Click OK and close the various open windows.

See also Parental Controls.

Watch Your Step!

Games tend to consume quite a bit of your time. Sadly, the office IT guys are aware of this problem, and at most large companies, the games that come with Windows are stripped from the office computers. That's one good reason to fly the Windows flag at half mast.

The Play menu can contain only five items.

If asked about which game rating system to use, I choose ERSB, which seems to be the most popular. It's the system that's most like the movie rating system.

When Things Go Wrong

Ensure that the Games window is configured to download information about games; otherwise, the Preview pane may not display game information.

Some older games may not be recognized by Windows and placed into the Games folder. Chances are that those games may not even work under Windows Vista in the first place.

Blocking games in Windows Vista may not necessarily block games that can be played over the Internet. So, when you see Junior playing Texas Hold 'Em Poker on Yahoo Games, don't blame Windows Vista.

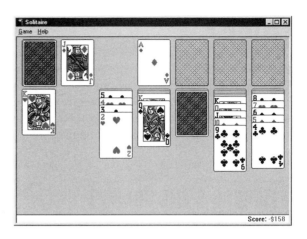

Gold Rush Nuggets

The original Solitaire game was included in older versions of Windows as both a game and a learning tool for people unfamiliar with using a computer mouse.

You might find even more games available on the Windows Update site. *See* Updates.

Digging Elsewhere

All Programs Menu, Parental Controls, Start Button and Menu

Guest

The lowliest of the low, the bottom rung on the user account ladder, is the Guest. In fact, it's so low that it's disabled on each Windows Vista computer. You must manually enable it to use it, and even then, having the account open and available is considered a security risk: The Guest account allows anyone to access your computer. Anyone! Even people in your own family, which is perhaps the scariest type of user imaginable!

The Guest account lies peaceful and undisturbed on every Windows Vista PC. It shows up in the list of all user accounts but typically appears disabled.

To visit with the Guest account, obey these steps:

1. Click your account picture at the top of the Start button's menu.

2. Choose the link Manage Another Account.

The Guest account appears in the list, but is disabled or "off."

When the Guest account is activated, it shows up with the list of other accounts when you log in to Windows or whenever the computer is locked or when switching users.

What to Do with It

The Guest account is intended for use by people who don't regularly use your computer, such as visiting relatives or someone who comes over to your house for a party and is really drunk and just dying to show you "this one thing" on the Internet and you dare not let them risk using your account (or any real account). *That* is why the Guest account exists.

Activate the Guest account

To activate the Guest account, click to select the account in the Manage Accounts window:

1. Click the Start button to display the Start menu.

2. Click your account picture at the top of the Start button menu.

3. Choose Manage Another Account.

4. Click the Guest account.

5. Click the Turn On button.

Disable the Guest account

I recommend keeping the Guest account disabled:

1. Click your account picture at the top of the Start button menu.
2. Click the link Manage Another Account.
3. Choose the Guest account.
4. Click the Turn Off the Guest Account link.

Log in as a guest

To use the computer as a guest, simply choose the Guest account when presented with the login screen. You don't have to enter a password, but keep in mind the warnings offered in the "Watch Your Step!" section. *See* Login and Log Off.

Watch Your Step!

Disabling the Guest account helps shore up computer security. In fact, if you don't plan on having any guests, do not activate the Guest account.

You cannot delete the Guest account. (You can disable it, however, as described in this entry.)

You cannot add a password to the Guest account. Because of that:

- ✕ Anything you save in the Guest account is available to anyone on the computer who logs in as a guest. So, when you save a document as a guest, it's available to anyone else who logs in as a guest; you have no protection.

- ✕ You can make changes to personalize the Guest account, and those changes are remembered by Windows, just as with a Standard or Administrator account. Note that any other user on the computer can log in as a guest and change things around again.

- ✕ Programs that require administrator-level access prompt the guest user to enter an administrator password to continue.

- ✕ As a guest user, you may not be allowed to access computers on the network unless those computers have their Guest accounts enabled.

When Things Go Wrong

The best way to avoid trouble is not to activate the Guest account in the first place.

Log in as an administrator to turn the Guest account on or off.

Gold Rush Nuggets

The Guest account in Windows Vista is different from accounts named Guest in other versions of Windows. Lots of Web pages that are out there have recommendations for enabling, disabling, password-protecting, and otherwise manipulating the Guest account that do not apply to Windows Vista. Be careful!

Digging Elsewhere

Administrator, Standard User, User Accounts

Help

"The truly miraculous thing," the advertising once said, "is that the computer itself can help you when you get into trouble." That was back in the 1970s. It wasn't true, of course. The computer *could* help you, but it didn't. As help moved from the old, dusty manuals to help available within the program, it still didn't get any better. Here it is in the 2000s, and I believe that finally the quality of the "help" offered by a computer might just be close to what people would agree is helpful. Maybe.

WHERE'S THE GOLD?

The help available in Windows Vista is perhaps the best-written of any version of Windows. It's not perfect, but it's not the scant, terse help of years gone by.

Help is found in most applications as a menu, typically the last menu on the right. The Help menu contains commands to access the Help system, a window displaying helpful information by topic and with the ability to search, plus other helpful menu items, including an About This Program command.

When you cannot see the menu, press the F10 key to display it.

In Office 2007, the Help system is activated by clicking the round, blue button with the question mark in it, located near the upper right corner of the window.

Help is also available via the F1 key on the keyboard. Stabbing at the F1 key pops up a general Help window or table of contents. Sometimes, the help you see when you press F1 is related to what you happen to be doing at the time.

Help button

Browse Help button

What to Do with It

Help is about *getting help!*

Search Help

The most popular thing to do with Help is search. You want to set margins on a printed page, for example. Here is how you can use Help to help you:

1. Press F1 to summon the Help thing.

2. In the Search Help box, type what you're looking for.

    For example, type **margins**.

3. Press Enter to start the search.

4. Peruse the results for something that matches what you entered in the Search Help box.

5. When nothing matches, type something more specific, such as **page margins**.

6. Repeat Steps 3 through 5 until one of the results looks valuable.

7. Click the result to read more information.

8. Close the Help window when you're done.

 Oftentimes, the first result is worth a stab, even when it doesn't seem like it makes much sense. Consider choosing that first result when the other results don't seem to make sense.

Use the online reference

The Help system can work like a book, complete with a table of contents and an index. To browse Help for any specific item, click the Browse Help button at the top of the Help window.

In browsing mode, you're presented with a series of general topics, which you can peruse like chapters in a book. Simply click a link to display more information; then read and, hopefully, gain some insight.

Run a troubleshooter

Deep down within the Help system, you find special gems called troubleshooters. A *troubleshooter* is an interactive Help session where you answer certain questions and, hopefully, end up solving a problem.

Sadly, the troubleshooters aren't all located in one place. To find them, you need to search.

Type **troubleshooter** into the Search Help text box.

 The main Troubleshooting section in Help is called Troubleshooting in Windows.

Choose a troubleshooter to run, and then answer the questions to find a way out of your dilemma.

Get help for older Windows programs

Using older Windows software in Windows Vista often results in disappointment when you try to get help. Rather than find help, you see a message scolding you for owning such antique software — or something like that.

The reason behind this is that Microsoft revamped its Help system, rendering the older version obsolete. To remedy the situation, and get help for older programs, you must download a new version of the `WinHlp32.exe` program from the Microsoft Web site. Here's the link:

```
http://support.microsoft.com/kb/
917607/
```

Watch Your Step!

The biggest problem with using any program's online Help system is not knowing what things are called. What you call "the box on the right" might have a specific name in Windows, and without knowing that exact term, it's hard to get help.

When Things Go Wrong

Help isn't available for everything. When the answer can't be found in the Help system, consider searching the Internet for help. But, beware! Not every site on the Internet offers quality help, nor should you blindly follow the advice of some random person you meet in a chat room.

Of course, books such as this one can be helpful in solving your computer puzzles!

Gold Rush Nuggets

A common saying about computer help is "Help isn't."

F1 wasn't always *the* Help key. In WordPerfect for DOS, one of the first PC programs to make extensive use of the function keys, the Help key was F3. Microsoft designed its programs to use the function keys for various duties, and no explanation was given for F1 as Help, although I assume that F1 was chosen because it's easy to find.

Digging Elsewhere

Keyboard Shortcuts, Search, Start Button and Menu

Hibernation

Inspired by various bears, Hibernation is a power management feature, much like Sleep or Suspend mode. When you hibernate your computer, everything in memory is saved to disk — all open files, running programs, the whole enchilada — and then the computer turns itself off. When you turn the computer on again, everything saved from memory to disk is loaded back into memory, which not only makes the computer start up faster but also means that you get back to work more quickly. Truly, if your computer has Hibernation as an option, it's much faster to hibernate the PC than it is to do a complete shutdown and restart.

Unfortunately, Hibernation is not available on all computers.

WHERE'S THE GOLD?

Of all the things Windows Vista can do that were also done in previous versions of Windows, the Hibernate command is the most difficult to find. There just isn't a Hibernate command, button, or option *anywhere*. Despite that, it's still possible to hibernate your PC.

The key to hibernating the computer is to change the function of one or more of the PC's power buttons. There are up to four of them:

- ✕ The main power button on the console

- ✕ The sleep, or "moon," button on the console (if present)

- ✕ A laptop computer's lid

- ✕ The Start menu's power button

To set any of these power buttons to put the PC into Hibernate mode, *see* Power Button.

What to Do with It

I use Hibernate for my computers rather than turn them off, especially my laptop, where I can just close the lid and slip the system into hibernation.

After assigning the Hibernate command to a power button (*see* Power Button), press the power button or click the Start menu's power button with the mouse.

 Clue When the Start menu's power button is set to Hibernate, the button is colored orange. When you point the mouse at the button, a pop-up bubble says, "Saves your session and turns off the computer. When you turn on the computer, Windows restores your session."

Watch Your Step!

Hibernation is not available on all PCs. When you cannot find the Hibernation option, your PC most likely doesn't support it. Confirm this with your computer dealer or manufacturer.

When Things Go Wrong

Yes, the Hibernate command is missing from the Start button's shutdown menu. But you can set the Start menu's power button so that clicking the button activates Hibernation. *See* Power Button.

Gold Rush Nuggets

Hibernation is different from the new Windows Vista sleep mode. Sleep mode doesn't completely power down the computer, whereas Hibernation turns the computer completely off. For laptops, hibernation saves battery power over sleep mode. *See* Sleep Mode.

Digging Elsewhere

Power Button, Shutdown Windows, Sleep Mode

Hidden Files and Folders

Shhh! One of the many attributes applied to files and folders in Windows is the *hidden* attribute. Designed as a security measure, hidden files and folders don't normally appear in a folder window, nor do they show up during a casual search for information. This keeps the file's or folder's contents secure — but it's only superficial security. It's possible to "display" hidden files. In fact, hiding files is something done by the operating system to keep casual computer users from snooping around and messing things up.

WHERE'S THE GOLD?

Hidden files and folders can lurk anywhere. Primarily, they exist in special system locations. For example, your User Profile folder has a special hidden folder named AppData, which contains support information for applications you run. By hiding the folder, Windows ensures that you don't go snooping around and messing things up. But, again, it's casual security because you can override the hidden file setting.

Hiding files happens specifically in the file or folder's Properties dialog box. On the General tab, in the Attributes area (at the bottom), is a check box labeled Hidden (just below Read Only).

The hidden file or folder itself doesn't show up in a Windows Explorer window — unless you direct Windows Explorer to display hidden files. When you do, the file or folder icon appears dimmed — kind of ghostly, in fact.

What to Do with It

Hiding files isn't necessary as a form of security, mostly because it's so easy to view hidden files.

Hidden folder   Visible folder

Hidden file   Visible file

See *Encryption* for better file security. Otherwise, hiding files is simply something you mess with when you're bored.

Hide a file or folder

To hide a file or folder, heed these directions:

1. Right-click the file or folder icon and choose Properties from the pop-up menu.

2. In the Properties dialog box, on the General tab, add a check mark by the Hidden item in the Attributes area.

3. Click OK.

The file is gone! Well, unless you've geared Windows Explorer to display hidden files; see the next section.

Display hidden files

To direct Windows Explorer to display hidden files, obey these directions:

1. Open the Control Panel's Folder Options icon.

   From the Control Panel Home, click Appearance and Personalization, and then click Folder Options.

2. In the Folder Options dialog box, click the View tab.

3. In the scrolling list, beneath Hidden Files and Folders, choose Show Hidden Files and Folders.

4. Click OK, and then close the Control Panel window, if you desire to do so.

To hide the files again, choose Do Not Show Hidden Files and Folders in Step 3.

Unhide a file or folder

To unhide a file or folder, first direct Windows Explorer to show hidden files, as described in the preceding section. Then repeat the steps from the section "Hide a file or folder," but in Step 2 remove the check mark.

(You might also want to configure Windows Explorer to once again hide previously hidden files.)

Watch Your Step!

Hidden files are generally excluded from being found by the Search command — unless you direct the Search command to look in hidden or system folders. *See* Search.

When Things Go Wrong

It's easy to forget about something that isn't there. Hiding files may work now, but when the file doesn't show up eventually, you may forget that it's there and someday waste time by re-creating it. Or, worse, you may remove all files in the folder and then remove the folder, all while being completely unaware that the hidden file still exists.

Gold Rush Nuggets

Another file attribute that hides files from view is the *system* attribute, which earmarks special files required by Windows to operate. System files are hidden from view and cannot be displayed in a Windows Explorer window; you must use the command prompt's DIR /A:S command to view the files.

Digging Elsewhere

Files, Read Only, Windows Explorer

History

S hocking but true: The Internet Explorer (IE) Web browser keeps track of every Web page you've been to. Every site. Every page. Linger anywhere on the Web, and IE makes a note of it. It's the *History* feature, and although it has wondrous appeal as an espionage tool, the real reason for IE keeping track of where you've been is to make it easier for you to return there again someday. Ah, to reminisce on the Web. . . .

WHERE'S THE GOLD?

Internet Explorer keeps your browsing history in a side panel in the IE window. To display the panel, click the star button on the left end of the toolbar, and then click the History button. The keyboard shortcut is Alt+C, Ctrl+H.

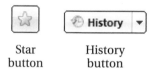

Star | History
button | button

The History list is a database of Web sites you've been to in the past 20 days or so. Sites are organized by time, with the most recent sites collected at the bottom of the list in the Today category, and then proceeding back in time as you get toward the top of the list.

Clicking a date or day heading displays a list of Web sites visited on that day, organized alphabetically. Clicking a Web site displays whichever pages were visited at that site.

See Address Bar for information on using the Back and Forward buttons, as well as the recently visited list. *See also* Favorites, the section "Close the Favorites area," for information on manipulating the History window in IE.

What to Do with It

Hark back to those days of yore, when you were younger and perhaps a bit more foolish but definitely forgetful. Revisit places you've known. Retrace your steps. And, above all, read your history because I hear that when you don't, you're doomed to repeat it.

Know your History

Where have you been? Just check the History list to find out! Click the star button on the left end of the toolbar, and then (if necessary) click the History button.

To view where you've been on a specific day, click to select that day. Then choose the folder representing each Web site you visited. (The Web sites are listed alphabetically, for some reason.) Finally, pages on each Web site are listed.

View History by Web site

The History button above the History list is a menu that can be used to sift and sort the data that's displayed. For example, to view the History list by Web site, click the button and choose By Site from the menu. All Web sites you've visited in the past 20 (or so) days are displayed alphabetically.

View the most popular places you visit

The History list is a database. As such, the information can be sifted and sorted. For example, to view the places you visit most often, follow these steps:

1. Display the History list.

2. From the History button menu, choose By Most Visited.

The list of Web sites you've visited in the past 20 (or so) days is displayed, with the most often frequented Web site listed first.

Track where you went

Reviewing the Web page history is done alphabetically, which I find odd. Yet you can review where you've been today in chronological order. From the History button's menu, choose the command By Order Visited Today.

Search through History

The History list is made even more effective because you can search through those pages you've been to. For example, you may not remember which day you were at a Web page, or you may not remember the site or even the page name, but you do remember something about *rutabaga*. Here's what you do:

1. Summon the History list.

2. From the History button menu, choose Search History.

3. In the Search For text box, type the text you want to search for.

4. Click the Search Now button.

A list of Web pages you've been to that contain the matching search text appear.

5. Choose a Web page to revisit that page.

Hopefully, you find what you're looking for.

Don't forget that you can also use a search engine to look for Web pages, although they may not be the same Web pages you've visited in the past.

When did you visit that Web page?

The History list tells you how long ago you visited a Web page, but it doesn't give you a date right away, nor does it tell you the time you visited a Web page — unless you do this:

1. Right-click a Web page link in the History list.

2. Choose Properties from the pop-up menu.

3. In the Properties dialog box, note the Last Visited date-and-time stamp.

4. Click OK to dismiss the dialog box.

Note that the Web site link's Properties dialog box indicates how many times you've visited a specific Web page.

Remove an item from History

Perhaps one of the most common questions I get asked via e-mail is how to remove an unwanted or embarrassing site from the History list. It's easy: Right-click the link and choose Delete from the pop-up menu. Click Yes to confirm, and the link is gone.

You can also click a Web site folder (which lists the individual page links): Choose Delete from the pop-up menu to remove the folder and all its links.

Delete the History

To remove all the History — including that potentially embarrassing list of recently typed Web pages — do this in Internet Explorer:

1. From the Tools toolbar button menu, choose Internet Options.

2. On the General tab, click the Delete button.

The Delete Browsing History dialog box appears.

3. Click the Delete History button.

4. Click the Yes button to confirm.

5. Close any remaining open dialog boxes.

You can also summon the Delete Browsing History dialog box by choosing the Delete Browsing History command from the toolbar's Tools button menu.

Set the History options

The History list is set to remember the past 20 days of Internet browsing and bustle. You can adjust this value up or down in IE:

1. From the Tools toolbar button menu, choose Internet Options.

2. On the General tab, click the Settings button in the Browser history area.

3. Enter the number of days to track history in the bottom part of the Temporary Internet Files and History Settings dialog box.

4. Click OK, and then click OK to close the Internet Options dialog box.

Disable History

To disable the History feature, run through the steps in the preceding section and set the number of days in Step 3 to 0.

Watch Your Step!

Choosing a Web site from the History list returns you to that Web site, but it does not show you a historical copy of the Web site. For example, if you visited a news site three weeks ago, choosing that news site from the History list shows you the site as it looks today; you don't see the same copy you saw three weeks ago. The History list doesn't work that way.

When Things Go Wrong

When setting the browsing history to zero days, you may notice that IE still keeps track of where you've been for the current day. I'm not sure whether this is a bug or a feature, but it's just the way the browser behaves.

Gold Rush Nuggets

If you really want to go back in time, you can use the Internet Wayback Machine. It gets its name from the old Jay Roach cartoon *Sherman and Peabody*, who used their Wayback Machine to time-travel. The Internet Wayback Machine is used to view what Web sites looked like years ago. For example, you can view Microsoft's Web page from 1996 or see what Amazon.com looked like in 1998:

```
http://www.archive.org/web/web.php
```

Digging Elsewhere

Address Bar, Favorites, Internet Explorer, Links Bar

Icons

Before computers went graphical, *icon* primarily referred to a painting of a holy person, something that you would normally find hanging in a church. The term could also refer to an individual who stands out as a symbol or who represents something. On your computer, an icon is a tiny picture used to graphically represent files or folders. The icon's image relates to the icon's purpose, so certain file types that have their own icons and files created by a program share an icon similar to the program's icon.

WHERE'S THE GOLD?

Windows has icons like an 8-year-old has the chicken pox. Icons are on the desktop, they're in windows, they're on menus. Icons are all over.

Generally speaking, icons are square or rectangular and vary in size from tiny to superlarge. The icon can have a fixed image, although Windows alters icons at larger sizes to display the file contents.

Special icons have *flags*, or symbols, associated with them. For example, a Shortcut icon features a curved arrow, shared files show the little sharing buddies, files awaiting download have a downward-pointing arrow superimposed, unavailable resources feature a red X, and so on. These flags cannot be removed, yet they are not a part of the original icon.

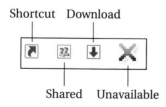

Shortcut   Download

Shared   Unavailable

What to Do with It

Icons represent files and folders mostly, so a lot of the things you can do with them — renaming, copying, deleting — are covered elsewhere; *see* Files and Folders. The activities listed in this entry are specific to the icons themselves.

Open an icon

To open an icon so that you can start a program or display a folder with more information, double-click the icon with the mouse.

You can open any selected icon, or group of selected icons, by pressing the Enter key. From the toolbar, you can click the Open button to open an icon or program, or click the Explore button to open a folder.

Right-clicking an icon displays a pop-up menu, from which you can choose either the Open or Play command.

Open an icon with a specific program

Each icon is associated with a specific program in Windows. Of course, some icons *are* programs, but those icons that represent data files typically open into the program that created them. To override that decision, follow these steps:

1. Right-click the icon.

2. From the pop-up menu choose Open With.

   Note that other commands may be available on the pop-up menu in addition to Open With — commands that open or play the file in a specific program.

   The Open With command does not appear for every type of data file.

3. Choose a program to open the file, from either the Open With submenu or the Open With dialog box.

   To see the Open With dialog box, choose the Choose Default Program item from the Open With submenu.

4. Click OK to close the Open With dialog box (if necessary).

Change which program opens an icon

Eureka

Data files are associated with certain programs. So, files of a certain type carry the same icon. The icon that's used is determined by Windows or, more often, by the program that opens the file. Changing which program opens a file is called *associating* the icon to a program. Here's how you can change which programs open which icons:

1. Open the Control Panel.

2. Open the Default Programs icon.

From the Control Panel home, choose Programs and then, beneath Default Programs, choose Make a File Type Open in a Specific Program.

The Set Associations window opens, listing a buncha filename extensions for every possible file found on your computer. (The filename *extension*, or the last part of a filename after the final period, is how Windows knows to which programs a given file belongs.)

3. Scroll through the list to look for the extension you want to change.

Clue

When you don't know the extension, use the information in the Description column to help you.

4. Click to select the extension, such as BMP for Windows bitmap files.

5. Click the Change program button.

   The Open With dialog box appears.

6. Choose the program to open the given file type from the list, or you can use the Browse button to locate a specific program — although I recommend caution when using that option.

7. Click OK.

8. Click the Close button when you're done.

The change takes place immediately; you do not need to restart Windows.

Change the icon's size

An icon's size is set by the Views menu in a window or by right-clicking the desktop and choosing Views.

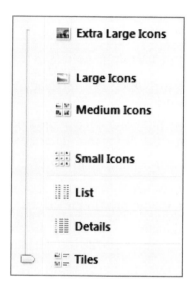

Four icon sizes are used by the various settings on the Views menu:

Extra Large: These icons occupy 270-by-270 pixels. At this size, Windows often previews the contents of certain file types.

Large: Large icons occupy a 96-by-96-pixel grid.

Medium: Medium icons occupy the traditional 48-by-48-pixel grid, which is also used for the Tiles option.

Small: Small icons are the teensiest, using a 14-by-16-pixel grid. These icons appear in the Small Icons, List, and Details views.

Arrange and group icons

Windows arranges icons by name or sorts them by group, but you can override that decision by right-clicking in any window (or on the desktop) and choosing how to arrange the icons with the Sort By submenu.

In Details view (choose Views⇨Details), you can click a column heading to sort the icons. For example, click the Date column to sort the icons chronologically. Click the column heading again to sort in reverse order.

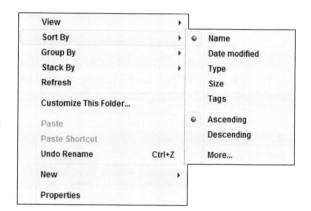

Icons can be ordered in groups, to keep files with similar attributes together. For example, right-clicking in a folder window and choosing Group By⇨Type arranges icons by file type.

Clue Choose Group By⇨None from the pop-up menu to remove the grouping.

Icons can also be *stacked,* or placed into subsets based on name, date, type, or other attributes. Right-click in a folder and choose a method from the Group By submenu.

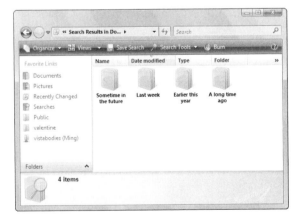

Assign a new icon image

It's impossible to assign a new icon to a program, well, as a mere mortal user. Programmers and software developers have the tools to create new icons and assign them to programs and data files. The only time you can change an icon is for a shortcut. Here's how:

1. Right-click the Shortcut icon.

2. Choose Properties from the pop-up menu.

3. Click the Shortcut tab in the icon's Properties dialog box (if necessary).

4. Click the Change Icon button.

   The Change Icon window appears, listing some common Windows icons.

5. Optionally, use the Browse button to locate more icon files on the hard drive.

6. Choose the icon you want.

7. Click OK to close the Change Icon dialog box.

8. Click OK to close the Properties dialog box.

You can also change the look of certain system icons on the desktop. *See* Desktop Icons. You can also change the icon for any folder. *See* Folders.

Eureka Most program files contain icons as well as DLL files. Also, specific ICO, or icon files, come chock-full of icons. Here are a few popular files for icons, found in the \Windows\Sytem32 folder:

```
Imageres.dll
Moricons.dll
Pifmgr.dll
Shell32.dll
```

Third-party programs exist that let you create icons. If you get such a program, make sure that it fully supports Windows Vista. Unlike previous versions of Windows, Windows Vista has special icon requirements.

Watch Your Step!

Associating an icon to the *wrong* program can have devastating consequences. Only when you're certain that a program not listed in the Open With dialog box is capable of *always* opening a given type of file should you proceed.

Icons are automatically arranged in a window. To override this feature, right-click in a window and choose View⇨Auto Arrange. Adding the check mark activates Auto Arrange, keeping the icons in order. Removing the check mark means that the icons aren't automatically arranged by Windows.

Icons can be placed anywhere in a window, and Windows remembers that location. To force Windows to align icons to a grid, right-click in the window and choose View⇨Align to Grid. (Placing a check mark by Align to Grid activates that feature.)

When Things Go Wrong

When icons change, it typically means that you installed a new program and the program has taken over the association of a certain file type. For example, if JPG graphics files are associated with the Windows Photo Gallery and after installing Adobe Photoshop the icon changes, you can assume that Photoshop has taken over association of the files. To reassociate the icon to the original file, follow the steps in the section "Change which program opens an icon," earlier in this chapter.

If you accidentally associate an icon with the wrong program, simply reassociate it to a proper program. Heed the steps in "Change which program opens an icon," and choose one of the Recommended Programs to open the file.

Grouping, or stacking, icons invokes the Windows Search command. To return to the original folder you were viewing, use the window's Back button.

Gold Rush Nuggets

The first commercially available graphical computer was the Apple Lisa. Its original icons were composed of special text characters and not graphical elements.

Icons on the original Macintosh computer occupied 128 bytes of storage space and were grayscale (black and white). Windows Vista icons are 1,536 times larger, or 196,608 bytes (and in full, glorious color).

Digging Elsewhere

Desktop Icons, Files, Select Files, Shortcuts, Windows

Internet Explorer

The Internet is merely a collection of computers that store, send, and receive information. To access that information, you need tools. The best tool is the World Wide Web and its companion Web browser software. Traditionally, Windows has included as its own Web browser Internet Explorer, which I shall abbreviate as IE (because it's late and I'm tired of typing). You use IE to browse the Web, get information, shop, entertain yourself, and do O so many things that it's pointless to list them all.

WHERE'S THE GOLD?

Internet Explorer is all over the place in Windows. You may find it atop the Start button menu, on the Quick Launch bar, or perhaps as an icon on the desktop. You can start it from the Run dialog box by typing **iexplore**. Or, IE may start all by itself when you type a Web page address in the Address bar. IE is everywhere!

What to Do with It

I hope that the computer revolution has carried you far enough into the 21st century that you can figure out the basic operation of a Web browser. Honestly, they're simple enough to figure out that extra instruction isn't necessary. Because of that, the following sections concentrate on some of the more useful yet not-so-obvious things that the program does.

Save an image from the Web page

It's not theft, of course, when you *borrow* an image from a Web page for your personal use. A pretty landscape or sunset, a winning goal, a quaint European village, or Miss August — they can all easily be saved to disk.

The key is to right-click the image. The commands in the middle of the pop-up menu all have to with graphics:

Show Picture: Used to display a missing picture — if the image is available.

Save Picture As: Summons a Save As dialog box, allowing you to save the image to disk.

E-Mail Picture: Links the image to your e-mail program, allowing you to send the image as an attachment to your online buddies.

Print Picture: Prints the picture on your PC's designated printer.

Go to My Pictures: Opens the Pictures folder (once called My Pictures).

Set As Background: Slaps the picture on the desktop's background as wallpaper.

Remember that most images on the Web are copyrighted and that you cannot reproduce them or use them in a way that makes money or in any manner that ticks off the copyright holder. When an image is in the public domain, you see a notice saying so. Note that most U.S. government images, such as the space imagery found on NASA's Web site (nasa.gov), are public and can be used freely.

Download a file

One useful thing you can do with IE is to download a program from the Internet. It may be a new device driver or a free program or some other software. The Web is full of such things.

When you download a file, you're transferring information from the Internet into your computer. This is the biggest security breach you'll ever accomplish with your computer, so you must truly know what you're doing.

Downloading works generally like this:

1. Click the Download button or link.

2. You may be taken to another page, one that lists even more download options or a page that says "Wait while your download starts."

3. Click the Close button when you see the download warning, and (optional) put a check mark by the option Don't Show This Message Again.

4. Click the bar atop the Web page window to see downloading options.

   The bar appears just above the Web page itself, below the tabs and toolbar.

5. Choose Download File from the bar's menu.

   The File Download Security Warning dialog box appears.

6. Click the Save button.

   Save the file to disk. That way, you have the original download, which you can reinstall if a problem occurs.

7. Use the Save As dialog box to save the file: Click the Save button.

   Generally speaking, the Save As dialog box should save the file in your account's Downloads folder. You can change the name to something more descriptive, especially when the file seems to have an odd or incoherent name.

   The file is transmitted to your computer, which is the technical meaning of the word *download*.

8. After the download is complete, click the Run button to install it.

9. Another security warning may appear, this one regarding an "unknown publisher." As long as the file is from a trusted source, you can click the Run button.

10. If faced with a User Account Control dialog box, click the Allow button.

Security on top of security! Oh, my!

11. At this point, the program's installer takes over; obey its directions until you're done.

The installer may ask you to approve its license agreement, choose which language to use, decide whether you want to place icons on the desktop, register the software, and answer other questions. Ensure that the installer places the new software in the `C:\Program Files` folder, or wherever you put your program files in Windows.

When the download is contained in a Compressed Folder or Zip file, you need to extract the contents of the Compressed Folder to continue. In Step 8 in this section, click the Open Folder button. *See* Compressed Folders for what to do next.

Check for phishing scams

A *phishing* scam occurs when one Web page pretends to be another, and does so for an evil purpose. For example, a page may look like your online banking page, even though it's not. The page is designed to fool you into surrendering vital banking information, which the Bad Guys then use to steal your money or identity or both!

Lots of people get fished in (or is that reeled in?) in by these scams. Because the Web page does the fishing and it's a fake Web page, they call it *phishing*.

IE comes with an anti-phishing scan. If you didn't activate the scan when you first ran Windows, here's how to confirm that it's on:

1. Start Internet Explorer.

2. From the Tools menu on the toolbar, choose Internet Options.

3. In the Internet Options dialog box, click the Advanced tab.

4. Scroll through the list to find the Phishing Filter heading.

5. Choose the item Turn On Automatic Website Checking.

6. Click OK.

When IE visits a Web site, it confirms that all the links go to where they claim they're going and that the Web page isn't a known phishing scam site. If so, you're notified.

To manually scan a Web page for phishing scams, click the Tools button on the toolbar, and from the menu, choose Phishing Filter➪Check This Website.

Watch Your Step!

Do not download anything you didn't ask for. The Bad Guys like to bring up pop-up windows that say "You must download this thing!" Don't. Often, the thing you download is a virus or worm or other nasty program.

Beware when downloading *codec* files to view movies. If you cannot see the movie on the Internet, you just cannot see it. You do not need a codec — even though that's the proper term. The "codec" ends up as a virus, not a codec.

Do not download EXE files that claim to contain text. For example, when you become totally pathetic and want to download a list of cheats for your favorite game, download a PDF or DOC file. Those are *document* formats. The EXE file is a *program,* which may contain cheats but most likely contains a virus.

Beware of Web sites that tell you to disable the phishing filter! That's the telltale sign of a Web page that wants to get something from you — not offer you information, entertainment, or advice.

When Things Go Wrong

When you download and install a nasty program, Windows offers many tools to help you out. First, try Windows Defender. Scan for nasty programs, and then use Software Explorer to stop and remove the program. *See* Windows Defender.

Second, try System Restore to bring your computer back to the way it was yesterday. *See* System Restore.

Gold Rush Nuggets

The Web exploded on the scene in 1993, yet Internet Explorer, released in 1995, was late coming to the party. Yet by 2000, IE owned 80 percent of the Web browser market, and by 2002 nearly 95 percent of all Web users were using IE as their Web browsers.

At one time, Microsoft offered a version of IE for Linux.

Digging Elsewhere

Address Bar, Cookies, Favorites, History, Refresh, RSS

Keyboard

Bored? Key bored? The PC's keyboard is based on the patented and highly successful IBM Selectric keyboard, itself a descendant of mechanical typewriter keyboards from the 19th century. Rumor has it that those devices were designed to *slow down* your typing so that the mechanism wouldn't get jammed. Even today, we put up with the awkward QWERTY typing system, and computer keyboards have staggered buttons on them, just like the ancient typewriter. Despite all that, the keyboard remains the primary way you communicate with your computer. The mouse is good for graphics, but the typing, text, and even shortcuts belong to the keyboard. It'll stay that way, too, until they can figure out how to get Mr. Computer to truly understand human speech. (I wouldn't hold my breath for that one.)

WHERE'S THE GOLD?

The keyboard can be found often lurking beneath your palms as you sit slack-jawed, astonished at how infuriating your PC can be.

The keyboard is divided into various regions to help you get lost more quickly: the standard typewriter keys, shift keys, function keys, cursor keys, and the numeric keypad, which also doubles as a set of cursor keys.

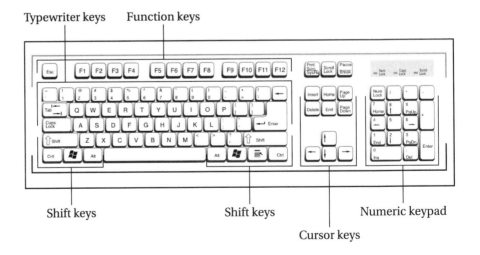

Typewriter keys   Function keys

Shift keys   Shift keys   Numeric keypad

Cursor keys

From the Control Panel, the Keyboard icon is used to open the Keyboard Properties dialog box, which can set the delay and repeat rates for the keyboard but do little else. (From the Control Panel Home, choose Hardware and Sound, and then click the Keyboard heading to see the Keyboard Properties dialog box.)

Windows also sports the *On-Screen Keyboard,* which is used to assist those who may have difficulty using a mechanical keyboard. To start the On-Screen Keyboard, pop up the Start button menu and choose All Programs⇨Accessories⇨ Ease of Access⇨On-Screen Keyboard.

The standard PC keyboard is quickly becoming a thing of the past. Newer keyboards have specialized buttons on them — buttons for navigating the Internet, adjusting the PC's speaker volume, or launching specific programs. They're not considered standard. You control the extra buttons by running a special program or accessing a special Control Panel icon.

What to Do with It

Obviously, the main thing to do with your keyboard is type on it. Type text. Type commands.

Or, slap the keyboard vigorously when the computer refuses to obey you!

Set the repeat and delay rates

The Keyboard Properties dialog box contains two keyboard settings: one for the repeat delay and the other for the repeat rate.:

Repeat delay: The pause that the computer takes before it begins rapid-fire repeating of a key.

Repeat rate: The frequency at which characters appear when you press and hold a key. I call it the "machine gun" feature; as with pulling and holding a machine gun's trigger, the longer you press a key on the keyboard, the more a certain character repeats.

Clue After choosing a repeat delay and rate, use the text box in the Keyboard Properties dialog box to check the settings. First, click the Apply button. Then press and hold a key. Check the delay and repeat. Adjust the settings as necessary. Click the OK button when things are peachy.

Use the On-Screen Keyboard

The On-Screen Keyboard allows you to "type" or access special keyboard functions by using the mouse. After summoning the keyboard, point the mouse and click a key to "press" that key and send its value to the computer for processing.

The gray shift keys must be clicked first to "shift" the next character you click.

Use the Keyboard menu to change the On-Screen Keyboard's appearance and behavior.

Choose whether to click the mouse or just hover it to select a key.

Simply close the On-Screen Keyboard's window when you're done using it.

Watch Your Step!

Set that delay rate too slow and the repeat rate too fast and you have one heck of a *slippery* keyboard!

When Things Go Wrong

The On-Screen Keyboard's appearance is set by using the Keyboard menu. The standard settings are Enhanced Keyboard, Regular Layout, and 101 keys. Use the Settings⇨Always on Top command to keep the keyboard above other windows on the screen.

Wireless keyboards need batteries, or perhaps need recharging every so often. Rather than break a stubborn wireless keyboard over your knee, consider checking its batteries or its charge.

Gold Rush Nuggets

The future of the PC keyboard is a bright one, literally. In a few years, computer keyboards will sport tiny LCD screens on their key caps. The screens will display information about each key, or list special functions as you use a program. There will even be keyboard "screen" savers and games, thanks to those 104 tiny little LCD screens on the key caps.

Digging Elsewhere

Control Panel, Keyboard Shortcuts, Mouse

Keyboard Shortcuts

Man does not compute by mouse alone. Yea, verily, occasionally the keyboard doth come in handy, especially when using many of the same commands over and over. Even more so in text-based applications, using the keyboard affords the swift-fingered soul quicker access to commands. Granted, you need to memorize the commands, but that's a small price to pay when you use something often.

Keyboard shortcuts can be found all over. The first clue is on a menu next to the command that the shortcut represents, such as Ctrl+Z next to the Undo command on the Edit menu.

Most keyboard shortcuts are, sadly, documented only in the online Help system. If you search for keyboard shortcuts, you see a list or two.

There are also *accelerator keys*, which can be used to activate the various menu commands. For example, to access File⇨Print, you can press Alt, F, P or Alt+F, P. *See* Menus for those details.

Finally, you can "roll your own" keyboard shortcuts, by assigning them to any shortcut icon in Windows.

What to Do with It

The notion behind keyboard shortcuts is to quickly access various commands without having to lift your laden hands from the keyboard and fumble for that slippery mouse. You can use certain keyboard shortcuts to do various things in Windows, and you can assign your own keyboard shortcuts to quickly run your favorite programs.

Also see Text Editing for information on text-editing shortcut keys used throughout Windows.

Ctrl (control) key shortcuts

Ctrl+A	Select all
Ctrl+B	Bold text
Ctrl+C	Copy
Ctrl+D	Font dialog box / Deselect
Ctrl+F	Find command
Ctrl+I	Italic text
Ctrl+N	New document
Ctrl+O	Open
Ctrl+P	Print
Ctrl+S	Save or Save As
Ctrl+V	Paste
Ctrl+W	Close window
Ctrl+X	Cut
Ctrl+Y	Redo
Ctrl+Z	Undo

(continued)

Ctrl (control) key shortcuts *(cont.)*

Ctrl+Alt+	Display a menu of system options Delete
Ctrl+F4	Close the document window
Ctrl+Esc	Display the Start button's menu
Ctrl+Shift+Esc	Display the Task Manager window
Ctrl+Tab	Display the next tab in dialog box (use Ctrl+Shift+Tab to move backward)

Alt key shortcuts

Alt+*letter*	Choose the command or option associated with the underlined *letter*
Alt+C	Display the table of contents in the Windows Help Viewer
Alt+Enter	Display the Properties dialog box
Alt+spacebar	Display the Control menu (*see* Windows)
Alt+Tab	Switch to the next window or switch between windows (*see* Multitasking)
Alt+Ctrl+Tab	Switch windows
Alt+Esc	Switch to the next program that's running
Alt+⇧	Go up one folder level in Windows Explorer

Shift key shortcuts

Shift	When inserting a CD, prevent the CD from automatically playing
Shift+F10	Display the pop-up shortcut menu for the selected item

Windows key shortcuts

Win	Display the Start button menu
Win+D	Show the desktop (minimize all open windows)
Win+E	Open the Windows Explorer window
Win+F	Display the Search Results window
Win+Ctrl+F	Display the Find Computers command window
Win+G	Cycle through Sidebar gadgets
Win+L	Lock the computer (return to the logon screen)
Win+M	Minimize all open windows (press Win+Shift+M to restore windows)
Win+R	Open the Run dialog box
Win+T	Cycle through the Taskbar buttons
Win+U	Display the Ease of Access window
Win+X	Display the Mobility Center (on laptops)

Win+Pause	Display the System Properties dialog box
Win+Tab	Visually cycle through open windows
Win+Ctrl+Tab	Flip through windows by using the keyboard
Win+spacebar	Bring forward the Sidebar

Win in these examples (and throughout this book) refers to the Windows logo key on the PC keyboard.

Function keys

F1	Help
F2	Rename file (or files)
F3	Search
F4	Display the Address bar
F5	Refresh the window (*see* Refresh)
F6	Switch between different parts of a window
F10	Activate or reveal the menu bar

Other keys

Delete	Delete item
Shift+Delete	Permanently delete file
Esc	Cancel
Tab	Move through elements in a dialog box or Web page (press Shift+Tab to move backward)

| Enter | OK |
| Spacebar | Turn check marks or radio buttons on or off |

Assign your own keyboard shortcut

Windows lets you create your own keyboard shortcuts, but only when you use a shortcut icon to run programs. But because Windows places all your programs on the All Programs menu, and each of those programs is a shortcut, it makes assigning keyboard shortcuts cinchy. Here's how:

1. Locate a shortcut icon, one that runs a program or performs a function to which you want to assign a shortcut key.

2. Right-click the shortcut icon, and choose Properties from the pop-up menu.

3. Ensure that the Shortcut tab is up front in the Properties dialog box.

4. Click in the Shortcut text box.

   It might say "None" in the box.

5. Press the keyboard shortcut to run that program.

   The keys you press appear in the Shortcut box.

 Clue I recommend that you use Ctrl+Alt+*letter* key combinations, specifically avoiding any key combination currently assigned to anything in Windows. Review the earlier sections in this entry for the list.

6. Click OK.

You can now use those keys to quickly launch the program that the shortcut icon references. *See* Shortcuts.

To remove the shortcut keys, repeat these steps, but press the Backspace key in Step 5 to remove the shortcut.

Watch Your Step!

You need to press a keyboard command only once. It's human nature to try the command again when things don't appear to be working. Yet I know many people who repeatedly press Ctrl+P to print, only to end up having several copies of the document (one for each Ctrl+P key press) printed.

Microsoft uses a special symbol to represent the Windows key.

Windows key

You need administrator privileges to apply shortcut keys to a program.

When Things Go Wrong

Some commands may not be available, so don't believe that your keyboard is busted when a command doesn't work. Instead, try accessing the menu-based version of the command. If the menu shows the command dimmed, you know that the command is unavailable. *See* Menus.

Gold Rush Nuggets

The Windows and Menu keys are the newest addition to the traditional PC keyboard. They brought the keyboard standard up from the 101-key keyboard to the 104-key keyboard. (Two Windows keys and one Menu key were added.)

The official name of the Windows key is the *Windows logo key.*

The Menu key might also be called the *Application key.* Whatever.

Back in the old days (about 20 years ago), programs were commonly sold with *keyboard templates,* pieces of cardboard that nestled atop the keyboards and listed common keyboard commands. WordPerfect for DOS, which has perhaps the most complex assortment of keyboard commands, had a poster-sized chart that you could hang on the wall, listing all the various key commands.

Digging Elsewhere

Keyboard, Mouse, Shortcuts, Text Editing

Links Bar

O ne overlooked part of Internet Explorer (IE), or any Web browser, is the Links bar. It's a toolbar, but one that you can customize and stock full of your favorite links — even menus. By using the Links bar, you can make navigating to your favorite Web sites a heck of a lot easier.

WHERE'S THE GOLD?

The Links bar normally doesn't show up; you have to conjure it into being. After it appears, it dwells above the main part of the Web browser window, either above or below the other toolbars. (Toolbars can be manipulated and moved; *see* Toolbars.) In IE, the Links bar seems to be fixed above the standard toolbar and tabs.

Links Toolbar

Toolbar handle

Links in the Favorites Links folder   Folders in the Favorites Links folder

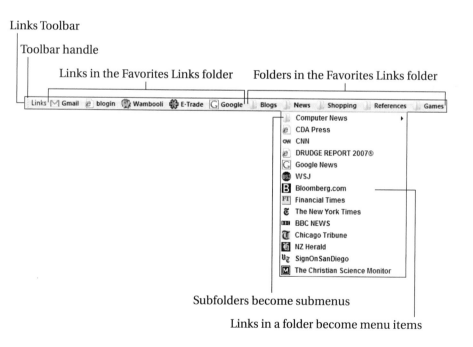

Subfolders become submenus

Links in a folder become menu items

Using the toolbar is a snap: Simply click a button to visit the corresponding Web page. You can also choose a menu to see a list of Web pages, or even submenus, from which you can choose some interesting place to go or Web site to visit.

What to Do with It

The Links bar is perhaps the handiest tool you can use to visit some of your favorite places on the Internet.

Display the Links bar

The easiest way to display the Links bar in Internet Explorer is to right-click the toolbar (or to the left of the toolbar). From the pop-up menu that appears, choose Links.

From the Tools toolbar button menu, you can alternatively choose Toolbars⇨Links.

See Toolbars for information on arranging the Links and other IE toolbars.

Add a link to the Links bar

The *Links bar* is simply a folder in the Favorites area in which you store, or bookmark, your favorite Web sites. (*See* Favorites.) Adding a link to the Links folder in Favorites is how you add a link button to the Links bar.

You can also grab a Web page's icon and drag it to the Links bar as a graphical, drag-and-drop method of adding a link: Grab the Web page's address by the icon on the far left side of the

Address bar, and then drag the icon to the Links bar. Release the mouse button to place the link on the toolbar.

To add a link to a menu on the Links bar, choose the folder name from beneath the Links folder.

Create a Links bar menu

Menus on the Links toolbar are nothing more than subfolders inside the Favorites Links folder. Those links inside the subfolder appear as menu items, and the subfolder itself appears as the menu.

Sub-subfolders appear as submenus. To add a subfolder, click the New Folder button when organizing the Links bar menu. *See* Favorites.

Edit the Links bar

The Links bar is edited along with other Favorites, as discussed in the Favorites entry. The only difference is that the edits you make to the Links folder appear on the Links bar.

You can graphically change the Links bar by using the mouse. You can drag links around on the Links bar, or you can right-click a link and, from the menu that appears, choose Rename to give it a new name or choose Delete to remove it.

Watch Your Step!

I prefer an *organized* Links bar. Because you can create folders and menus, consider putting some of your links into menus to help prevent the links from marching off the right side of the screen.

When Things Go Wrong

The Use Large Icons command affects only the standard IE toolbar; it doesn't change the size of the icons on the Links bar. (You can find this command by right-clicking a toolbar.)

Gold Rush Nuggets

The Links bar is often called the Bookmarks bar in Web browsers other than Internet Explorer. That's because those Web browsers logically refer to saved Web pages as bookmarks, not as Favorites.

Digging Elsewhere

Favorites, Internet Explorer, Toolbars

Live Search (Internet Explorer)

L ive Search is a feature on the new Internet Explorer (version 7) that allows you to search by typing text into a Live Search text box in the Internet Explorer window. Now, Internet Explorer doesn't do the search itself. Instead, it passes that text off to a major search engine, which does the search. The results are then displayed in the window, ready to illuminate your day.

Live Search dwells to the right of the Address bar in the Internet Explorer window. It looks like a regular Windows Search text box (*see* Search), but it's not. It's geared toward searching the Internet.

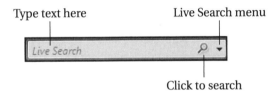

Type text here   Live Search menu

Click to search

The keyboard shortcut to access the Live Search text box is Ctrl+E.

Pressing Alt+Enter to search opens the results in a new tab.

What to Do with It

Searching the Internet isn't the problem. The problem is knowing what to type when you search! Sadly, Live Search doesn't solve that problem, but it does save you the extra step of visiting a search engine to search.

Search for something

Searching on the Internet with Internet Explorer (IE) version 7 works like this:

1. Click the mouse in the Live Search text box or press Ctrl+E.

2. Type the text you want to search for.

   For example, type **Calvin Coolidge Quotations.**

3. Press Enter to peruse the results.

Search text on a Web page

You search for text on a Web page, rather than across the Internet, by using the Find command, not Live Search. Press Ctrl+F to summon the Find dialog box, type the text you're searching for, and click the Next button.

Set the search engines to use

Perhaps the most important thing you can do with Live Search is set up your favorite Web search engine. No, believe it or not, you don't have to use the Windows Live or MSN search engine, even though Microsoft really, really wishes that you would. Here's how:

1. Click the downward-pointing triangle on the right side of the Live Search window.

2. Choose Find More Providers from the Live Search menu.

   A Microsoft Web page appears, listing common search engines, and it allows you to add your own.

3a. Choose a search engine from the Web page by clicking on its link.

   Or

3b. Use the Create Your Own form to enter your own search engine.

   Follow the directions on-screen to capture the search engine's URL. Press Ctrl+N to open a new Internet Explorer window; Ctrl+T opens a new tab.

4. If you want to make the new search engine the main, or *default*, search engine, put a check mark by the Make This My Default Search Provider option.

5. Click the Add Provider button.

6. (Optional) Repeat Steps 3 through 5 to add more search engines.

7. Close the window or tab when you're done.

 Clue When you set up multiple search engines, you can choose which one to use from the Live Search menu. The results are displayed immediately in the window after you choose another search engine.

To manage the search engine list, choose the Change Search Defaults command from the Live Search menu. In the Change Search Defaults dialog box, you can remove unwanted search engines from the list or choose a new search engine as the default.

Watch Your Step!

The text in the Live Search box changes to reflect any new search engine you choose. But it's still the same box and works the same way.

When Things Go Wrong

The key to searching is to properly phrase the question. Use only keywords; avoid using small words or writing the request using a complete sentence, which has no effect. (Most search engines ignore words like *the, an,* and *is*.) When words must be found together, enclose them in double quotes. Vary the word order when the first search doesn't meet your expectations.

Gold Rush Nuggets

Live Search gets its *Live* part from the Windows Live service, which is Microsoft's attempt to dethrone Google as the number one search engine. Windows Live Search was once known as MSN Search.

Digging Elsewhere

Search

Login and Log Off

In the realm of computers, a log isn't something a Canadian lumberjack rolls on. No, a *log* is an official record, like a ship's log or a written account of a journey. When you *log in* to a computer, you're registering your account name with the computer so that Windows knows who you are and can load your personal configurations and set things up just the way you like. (Furthermore, you use a password to ensure that you are who you say you are; *see* Passwords.) When you're done with the computer, you *log off.*

Logging in and logging off are part of using a computer. It's true that in the old days these tasks were options. Not so anymore.

WHERE'S THE GOLD?

Windows Vista sports a login screen, which is essentially where the prisoners identify themselves to the warden. Ahem!

The login screen shows your account's picture. When your account has a password (which I highly recommend), a box appears into which you can type that password.

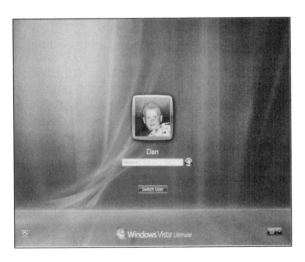

When more than one account is available on the computer, a screen listing all accounts appears first, from which you choose an individual account. Then the individual login screen appears.

Logging off is accomplished from the Start button menu. In the lower left corner, you can find the Shutdown Windows menu, and one of the options is Log Off.

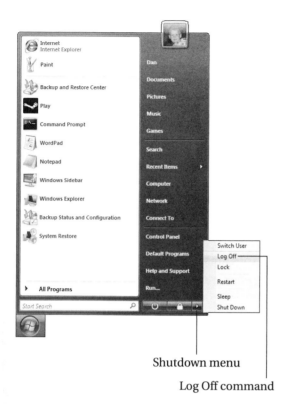

Shutdown menu

Log Off command

What to Do with It

The login screen is the first thing you "do" in Windows. So, realistically, it's not anything you do in Windows itself, but merely a door to pass through.

Create a login

To log in, you need a User Account on the computer. *See* User Accounts for information on creating an account, which then shows up in the Login window.

Log in

To log in, first choose your account from the list that's displayed (if there is one). Then type your password in the box and press Enter to get access to Windows.

If your account lacks a password, simply click the account picture to get in.

Log off

Logging off is the opposite of logging in. Essentially, it's like quitting Windows without turning off the computer. You end your Windows session, files are saved, programs are closed, and you end up back at the initial login screen.

To log off, follow these steps:

1. Open the Start button menu.

2. Choose the Log Off command from the Shutdown menu.

Logging off displays the initial login screen. From there:

✗ You can log in again.

✗ Someone else can log in.

✗ You can shut down the computer by using the Shutdown button.

The Ctrl+Alt+Delete menu also sports a Log Off button. *See* Ctrl+Alt+Delete.

Switch users

If your computer has more than one user account, you can switch between people using the computer without having to quit Windows or make anyone log off. This process is known as *fast user switching*. Here's how it works:

1. Open the Start button menu.
2. Choose the Switch User command from the Shutdown menu.
3. Choose another account.

Obviously, switching users works best when you have more than one user account on your PC.

You can find a Switch User button on the Ctrl+Alt+Delete menu. *See* Ctrl+Alt+Delete.

A Switch User button also appears on the screen when the computer is locked. See the following section.

Lock the computer

One way to keep the computer secure when you need to step away for a tad is to lock Windows. The easy way to do that is to press the Win+L key combination. The traditional way is to choose the Lock command from the Start button menu's Shutdown menu.

Locking the computer returns you to your account's Login window. To access the computer again, type your password. Or, you can click the Switch User button to log in under another account.

You can also lock the computer from the Ctrl+Alt+Delete menu: *see* Ctrl+Alt+Delete.

 Eureka Locking the computer is much more effective than waiting for a password-protected screen saver to kick in.

Check the log records

You can view which accounts log in or log off by using the Windows Event Viewer. (Yes, it uses the term *logon* rather than *login;* the two terms are interchangeable.) In the Event Viewer, open the Event Viewer (Local), Windows Logs, Security folder. In the list of events, the Task Category column shows either Logon or Logoff to indicate when various accounts have logged in or logged off. *See* Administrative Tools for more information.

Watch Your Step!

Logging off doesn't shut down Windows. *See* Shutdown Windows.

You can't disable the logon screen. If your previous version of Windows let you get in without logging in, recognize that was the way computers used to work. Computing in the present (and future) is about security. Security means everyone on the computer has an account, a username, and a password.

Switching users doesn't log you off; your account is still considered to be logged in, your programs idle, and any unsaved documents remain unsaved.

When Things Go Wrong

See Passwords for information on how to deal with missing or forgotten passwords.

Gold Rush Nuggets

To *log off* is to *log out* (logout), and sometimes it's written as one word, *logoff.* In fact, even *login* is often known as *logon* (log on). Oh, those crazy computer kids!

Digging Elsewhere

Administrative Tools, Ctrl+Alt+Delete, Passwords, Shutdown Windows, User Accounts

Magnifier

One of the Ease of Access tools available with Windows is the Magnifier, which you use to make things on the screen appear larger, easier to see. Although designed for the visually impaired, the Magnifier can be used by anyone. For example, I often use it to zoom in on graphics to see how they're constructed on a pixel-by-pixel basis.

You can start the Magnifier program from the Start button's menu. Choose All Programs➪Accessories➪Ease of Access➪Magnifier. You can also open the Ease of Access Center from the Control Panel, but that approach also activates the Narrator tool — and I don't like the computer reading to me.

On the screen, the Magnifier presents a preview window hugging the top of the desktop. (The preview window can float or dock to any edge of the desktop.) The preview window normally follows the mouse, showing the area on the screen where the mouse is pointing.

The Magnifier is controlled by a pop-up window. To activate the window, click the Magnifier button on the Taskbar. Click the Hide button to minimize the control window.

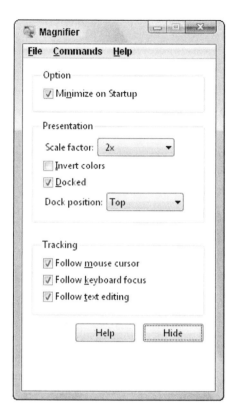

What to Do with It

The Magnifier can help you view or preview information on the screen that may be too tiny to view with the naked eye.

Change the zoom

The Magnifier's zoom is normally set to 2X, or twice as big as normal. You can choose higher zoom values from the Scale Factor menu button in the Magnifier control window.

Move the preview window

To change the preview window's location, use the Dock Position drop-down menu in the Magnifier control window. You can choose from four possible docked positions, one on each edge of the desktop.

You can also undock the preview window by removing the check mark by the Docked option. Use the mouse to drag around or resize the preview window.

Close the Magnifier

Put away the Magnifier when you're done with it: In the Magnifier control window, choose File⇨Exit. The keyboard shortcut is Alt+X.

Watch Your Step!

When the Magnifier's preview window is undocked, you can bring any window in front of it with the click of a mouse. In fact, when the Magnifier's preview window is undocked, it works like any other window in Windows. *See* Windows.

When Things Go Wrong

The Magnifier has a command to invert colors, which may cause some items to become more visible but can also really frustrate you. To undo the color inversion, choose Command⇨Invert Colors from the Magnifier control window or uncheck the Invert Colors check box.

Gold Rush Nuggets

Most programs have a Zoom tool you can use to make the contents of the window appear larger, easier to read. In Internet Explorer, you can find the Zoom tool in the lower right corner of the window; it's a pop-up menu labeled with the current zoom percentage.

Digging Elsewhere

Keyboard, Narrator

Map a Network Drive

Rather than continuously browse through the Network folder — opening computers, entering passwords, and digging deep — consider mapping a network drive. When you *map* a network drive, you're creating a local link to that remote network resource. So, rather than have to wade through the network or type a long network pathname, you simply access, for example, drive V: on your computer, which is the local link to that network drive.

WHERE'S THE GOLD?

There are two places where you can find the command to map a network drive. The first is in the Computer window, on the toolbar. The button is labeled Map Network Drive, but it's way off to the right; if the Computer window is too wide, the button appears only when you click the Show More chevron.

You find the second location for the Map Network Drive command when you open the Network window and browse directly to the shared folder you want to map. By right-clicking the folder, you can choose the Map Network Drive command from the pop-up menu that appears.

Either way, you choose the Map Network Drive command, and the Map Network Drive window shows up. (When you right-click a network drive, though, the Folder field is automatically filled in for you.)

What to Do with It

Mapping network drives is a great way to keep network resources close, almost local to your own computer.

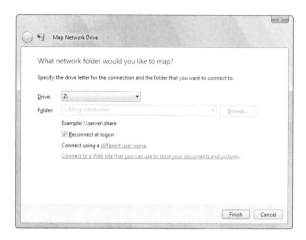

Map a network drive

To access a network drive, or a shared folder, as a disk drive on your own computer, follow these steps:

1. Open the Network window.

2. Browse to the computer and then the shared disk folder you desire.

3. Right-click the folder and choose Map Network Drive from the pop-up menu.

4. Choose a letter for the drive.

5. To have the drive map every time you use the PC, put a check mark by the Reconnect at Logon option.

6. Click the Finish button.

7. (Optional) Close the mapped drive window, which opens automatically after you map it.

Mapped network drives appear in the Computer window with network "plumbing" beneath them.

Mapped network drive icon

Plain folder icon for a mapped Internet drive

The drop-down Folder list contains network locations that you previously mapped. To remap an old location, simply pluck its network pathname from the list.

Map an Internet storage location

You can also map a network location on the Internet to the Computer window. A network location — such as a public folder on your Web space, an FTP site, or a picture uploading service — can easily be mapped to a disk drive letter in the Computer window. Here's how:

1. Open the Computer window.

2. Click the Map Network Drive button on the toolbar.

You may need to widen the window or click the Show More chevron, on the right end of the toolbar, to see the Map Network Drive command.

3. Near the bottom of the Map Network Drive window, choose the Connect to a Web Site link.

4. Click the Next button in the Add Network Location Wizard window.

5. Select the Choose a Custom Network Location option.

Well, unless you have some stuff on the MSN Communities, in which case, you're on your own.

6. Click the Next button.

7. Type the full Internet address (URL) for the resource you want to access.

Sometimes, typing FTP rather than HTTP works better for Web page URLs.

8. Click the Next button.

9. Choose an anonymous login or enter your username.

10. Click the Next button.

11. Enter a name for the resource.

The name appears in the Computer window, beneath the resource's icon.

12. Click the Finish button to test the connection.

13. Type your password in the FTP Logon dialog box; press Enter to log in.

The site appears in an FTP window, which means that everything works hunky and dory.

14. Close the FTP window.

A mapped Internet drive (FTP or HTTP file location) appears, using a plain folder icon in the Computer window.

Remove a mapped network drive

You don't really remove or eject a mapped network drive — you disconnect it. The simplest way to do that is

1. Open the Computer window.

2. Right-click a mapped network drive.

3. Choose the Disconnect command.

Watch Your Step!

When the network drive is unavailable, the drive's icon appears with a red X superimposed on it. The X means that the network resource is either offline or no longer available. (*See* Sync Center.)

Disconnecting a drive is permanent; even if you chose to reconnect a mapped drive at login, disconnecting the drive doesn't cause it to be reconnected when the computer starts.

Just typing an HTTP or FTP address doesn't grant you immediate access to an Internet resource. Generally, you must have an account on the resource and a specific address to which you can upload or download files.

When Things Go Wrong

Sometimes, the mapped drive may appear to be disconnected when it's not. Wait a second, and then press F5, the Refresh command key for the Computer window. *See* Refresh.

Gold Rush Nuggets

You can map a folder on your own computer as a network disk drive. As long as the folder is shared, you can use the Browse button to locate it "on the network" and map it to a drive letter. I don't know whether this mapping has any specific advantages.

Digging Elsewhere

Computer, Networking, Sync Center

Menus

Decisions, decisions. What's on the menu? Is it *prix fixe?* Maybe one from Column A and two from Column B? What about the à la carte menu? Forget the restaurant! On a computer, a menu is used to provide you with a list of handy commands. It's the simplest way to present commands and options, as opposed to using specific key combinations or having the user type text to get things going.

Menus are often found lurking just below the title bar in a window. The location is referred to as the *menu bar,* which may work just like any other toolbar (in that it can be rearranged) or be affixed to the top of the window.

Menus can also pop up, usually when you right-click an object, a window, or, honestly, just about anything. Unlike a menu bar, a pop-up window presents a single menu, although you often find submenus. This type of menu can be called a pop-up menu, context menu, or shortcut menu.

The most unique menu in Windows is the Start menu, which is really a form of pop-up menu attached to the Start button. *See* Start Button and Menu.

Toolbar buttons in Windows Vista often display menus, such as the Page button in Internet Explorer. The buttons that have menus sport a downward-pointing triangle.

Divider
Dimmed command (unavailable)
Menu bar   Alt-key shortcut
Command categories   Keyboard shortcut

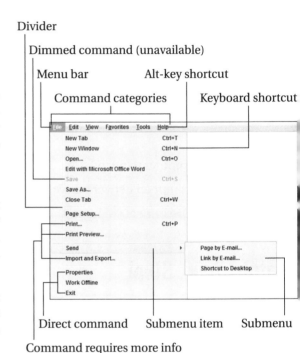

Direct command   Submenu item   Submenu
Command requires more info

keyboard shortcuts, as well as other gizmos in and about the window. But the menu provides basic access to a program's commands, functions, and options.

What to Do with It

You use menus to interact with various programs. The alternatives are toolbar buttons and

Choose commands

Menus are designed for interacting with the mouse. Click a menu heading, or category, to display commands related to the heading. Choose a command by clicking it, or display a submenu by clicking its command.

Some commands activate immediately. A command followed by an ellipse indicates that further action is required, a dialog box appears, or something else happens.

Activate or show the menu

Some Windows Vista programs may hide the traditional menu bar. Usually, the most common commands are available by using toolbar buttons or toolbar menus. But you can display a legacy menu: Press the F10 key. If that doesn't work, press the Alt key.

Pop-up menus are activated by right-clicking them. You can right-click just about anything in Windows to see a pop-up or shortcut menu.

Pressing the unusual Menu key on the keyboard activates the pop-up menu for a selected item on the screen.

Menu key

Choose commands with the keyboard

Many advanced users prefer accessing menus by using the keyboard rather than the mouse. If you

know the various accelerator keys, this method can be a fast way to use any program.

Using keys to access menus involves knowing which keys activate which menus. The basic key is Alt. Pressing the Alt key causes Windows to display underlines on its menus, indicating which keys activate which commands. For example, to access the Save command on the File menu, you press Alt, F, S. You can also press Alt+F and then S.

You can also use the arrow keys to access menu commands: Press F10 to activate the menu, and then use the keyboard's arrow keys to plow through the menus and select commands. Press the Enter key to activate a command.

See Keyboard Shortcuts for a list of common key combinations that quickly access specific commands.

Watch Your Step!

Some menu bars also work like toolbars in that they can be removed from the window. *See* Toolbars for information on how to re-dock a toolbar that becomes a floating palette.

Press the keyboard's Esc key to cancel or close a menu.

When Things Go Wrong

When you press F10 or the Alt key fails to show the menu, consider that the program may not have a menu. Press the F1 key for help and type **menu** or **menu bar**. If no help is available on either topic, assume that the program simply lacks a menu.

Not every menu command is available all the time. For example, the Paste command (on the Edit menu) is available only when something is available to paste into the program. (Unavailable commands appear dimmed on the menu.)

Gold Rush Nuggets

Menus on a computer are nothing new. Even the old text-interface programs used menus, although the menus were no more fancy than simple lists of choices.

Microsoft Office 2007 features programs that use a ribbon interface, shunning the traditional program menus. Supposedly, the next release of Windows will feature a similar interface.

Most programs share a common set of menus:

File: General file commands, such as Save, Open, Print, and Exit

Edit: Editing commands, such as Cut, Copy, Paste, and Undo

View: Commands to control the window's contents, display toolbars, and zoom in and out, for example

Window: Commands dealing with multiple windows and switching between windows, for example

Help: Helpful commands, plus information about the program and Web access

Digging Elsewhere

Keyboard, Mouse, Start Button and Menu, Windows

Modem

Modem is that rare computer word that often finds itself a punchline to some feeble high-tech joke. This ugly word is a contraction of *mo*dulator and *dem*odulator. A modem is a translator; it deals with communications, primarily computers that communicate by flinging data back and forth.

The modern computer modem is a high-speed, broadband number. A satellite modem. A cable modem. A DSL modem. One relic left over from the early days of computing is the dial-up modem. That dinosaur can still allow your PC to communicate with other computers and the Internet by using standard telephone lines. This entry covers that type of modem.

WHERE'S THE GOLD?

Dial-up modems can be internal or external, either dwelling inside the computer (on the motherboard or as an expansion card) or externally, as a boxy gizmo that adds way too many cables to your PC's cable mess. Logically, these two modem types are called *internal* modems and *external* modems.

Internally, the first place to find modems is in the Control Panel: Open the Phone and Modem Options icon, or, from the Control Panel Home, choose Hardware and Sound and then select Phone and Modem Options. Either way, you see the Phone and Modem Options dialog box. (The first time you try to open this dialog box, the Location Information dialog box appears instead; you can find more information about that dialog box in the section "Add an external modem," later in this entry.)

To use the modem, you need to create a connection. That chore is handled from the Network and Sharing Center, which you can open from the Control Panel's Network and Sharing Center icon; or, from the Control Panel home, choose View Network Status and Tasks from beneath the Network and Internet heading.

Phone and Modem Options icon   Network and Sharing Center icon

You can also use a modem to send or receive a fax. *See* Fax.

What to Do with It

Although you may never use your PC's dial-up modem, it's still there, and it still works. Consider it a throwback, but when the broadband connection is down, it's nice to have a backup.

Add an external modem

Internal modems are automatically configured with the rest of your computer; you shouldn't need to do any extra setup. This isn't true for external modems, which remain the final piece of PC hardware that must be manually configured after being connected.

Plug the external modem into one of your PC's COM, or serial, ports. Traditionally, COM1 is used for an external modem, although it makes no difference today. Unlike USB ports, serial ports don't recognize any devices connected to them. So, to tell Windows about your modem, you must follow these steps:

1. Open the Control Panel's Modem icon.

2. Fill in the Location Information dialog box, if necessary.

   Windows needs to know how to dial the phone from where your computer is located. Fill in the dialog box with the required information, and then click OK to proceed. (If you have a laptop PC, fill in information for your home or office where the laptop will be located most often.) You need to do this step only once.

3. In the Phone and Modems dialog box, click the Modem tab.

4. Click the Add button.

   The Add Hardware Wizard begins.

5. Click the Next button to have Windows probe for your modem.

If the modem is found, heed any remaining directions. You're done.

6. Click the Next button to manually set up your modem.

7. Choose your modem type from the list or, if you have an installation disk, click the Have Disk button.

8. Click the Next button.

9. Specify the modem ports.

   For example, choose COM1.

10. Click the Finish button.

    You're done.

Check the modem's status

To confirm that your PC's modem is working, heed these directions:

1. In the Phone and Modem Options dialog box, click the Modem tab.

2. Select your PC's modem.

3. Click the Properties button.

4. In the modem's Properties dialog box, click the Diagnostics tab.

5. Click the Query Modem button.

   When the modem is on, up, and running, some text information appears in the dialog box, which is the modem communicating its status with the computer. The appearance of that text generally means that things are okay.

6. Close the various open dialog boxes.

Configure dialing rules

Using a modem is like using a telephone, but the modem makes the call. So, the modem must hear a dial tone, and it must also obey the dialing and area code rules for wherever you're calling from. (Also note that long-distance and hotel-access charges apply to modem calls, just like any phone call.)

The good news is that you have a computer and it can be programmed to obey given dialing rules. Furthermore, the computer remembers different locations you visit. So, for example, when you and your laptop return to the same hotel, you can summon the dialing and area code rules you used earlier at that same location.

To set up dialing rules, follow these steps:

1. Open the Phone and Modem Options dialog box.

2. Click the Dialing Rules tab, if necessary.

3. Create a new location, if necessary.

   You should have a location for anywhere you plan to use the modem. If you have a desktop PC, you probably have just one location. Otherwise, create a new location by following these steps:

   a. Click the New button.

   b. Type the location name, such as **San Diego Hilton**.

   c. Enter the country and area code.

   d. Skip to Step 6.

4. Select a location.

5. Click the Edit button.

   The Edit Location dialog box appears.

6. Fill in the dialing rules as you know them.

   For example, enter any number you need in order to access an outside line, such as 8 or 9. Leave any box empty if you don't need to enter special numbers to dial the phone.

7. If you have call waiting (which would disconnect the modem), put a check mark by the To Disable Call Waiting, Dial option. Then choose the code you dial to disable call waiting.

8. Click the Area Code Rules tab and fill in the blanks.

   Area code rules are necessary when you must always dial a particular area code, never dial the code, or dial the code for only specific prefixes. Note that most phone systems in the U.S. allow you to dial an area code for local calls and for long distance.

9. Click OK when you're done setting area code rules.

10. (Optional) Click the Calling Card tab if you use a calling card to make phone calls.

11. Click the OK button when you're all done with the Edit Location dialog box, to dismiss that dialog box and pray to your favorite deity that it never returns.

12. Close the Phone and Modem Options dialog box.

Disable call waiting

Refer to the preceding section — up to Step 7, at least.

Set up the modem to contact your ISP

Connecting a dial-up modem to the Internet is a networking activity. The Internet is a network, and your PC's modem is the link between your computer and that network. Here's how you do things, if you have information from your ISP (Internet service provider) to help fill in the details:

1. Bring forth the Network and Sharing Center window.

2. On the left side of the window, click the Set Up a Connection or Network link.

   An ambiguous network wizard shows up.

3. Choose the third option, Set Up a Dial-Up Connection.

4. Click the Next button.

5. Enter your ISP's phone number, the number you dial to connect to the Internet.

6. Enter your Internet name and password.

   Remember that these items may be different from the name and password you use to connect to Windows.

7. Place a check mark by the Remember This Password option.

8. Type a name for the connection, such as your ISP's name.

9. (Optional) Put a check mark by the Allow Other People to Use This Connection option.

   Basically, this option lets other users on your computer share this Internet connection without having to set things up for themselves. Normally, that's okay.

At this point, you're done setting up the modem to contact the ISP. But the next, obvious step is to click the Connect button and connect to the Internet. You can do that now or back out and connect to the Internet at any time, as described in the following section.

Connect to the Internet

To connect to the Internet with your dial-up modem, you can either run an Internet program, such as Internet Explorer or Windows Mail, or do this:

1. Open the Start button's menu.

2. Choose Connect To.

   If you can't find this item, *see* Start Button and Menu.

3. Select the dial-up connection you want to make.

4. Click the Connect button.

Sit back and wait while Windows dials the modem and makes the connection.

Find the little modem buddies

After you connect, a new icon appears in the Notification Area. I refer to the icon as the *modem buddies,* but it's basically a network connection icon, indicating that you're online and using the Internet.

Check the modem speed

To confirm the modem's speed, double-click the modem buddies icon in the Notification Area. A pop-up window appears, listing information about your connection, including the speed and the length of time you've been online.

Disconnect the modem

To disconnect from the Internet, essentially hanging up the modem, right-click the little modem buddies icon in the Notification Area. From the pop-up menu that appears, choose the Disconnect command. That's it!

Watch Your Step!

An external modem must be turned on before it can communicate with the outside world.

The phone line used by the modem must not be in use by another device. For example, if someone tries to make a phone call or send a fax while the modem is online, the disruption can break the connection.

You don't disconnect from the Internet by simply closing your Web browser program or quitting your e-mail program. No, for a dial-up connection, you must manually disconnect, as described in the preceding section.

When you don't manually disconnect, the modem may hang up after a given timeout. Either your ISP disconnects you or a timeout value set within Windows does. To set the Windows timeout value, follow these steps:

1. Choose Connect To from the Start button's menu.

2. Right-click the Dial-Up Connection icon.

3. Choose Properties from the pop-up menu that appears.

4. In the Properties dialog box, choose the Options tab.

5. Set the timeout value by the Idle Time Before Hanging Up option.

6. Click OK and close any open dialog boxes or windows.

When Things Go Wrong

Despite a modem's advertised speed, your online speed is most likely slower. Modems don't top out at their best speeds unless ideal conditions exist, and that just doesn't happen with plain old phone lines. Even when you compare sessions, the modem doesn't always connect at the same speed.

Gold Rush Nuggets

Sadly, Windows Vista doesn't seem to come with a standard dial-up modem communications program. All previous versions of Windows came with the HyperTerminal program, a limited version of the Hilgraeve Software HyperACCESS program.

Digging Elsewhere

Add Hardware, Fax

Mouse

Communicating with the first computers involved directly rewriting the room-size behemoths. Eventually, a panel of switches was used to effortlessly program the beasts. As computers became interactive, teletypes were used for communications. Then came the advent of the computer monitor. The last hardware gizmo to fall into the computer's peripheral vision was the mouse. As computers moved from text to graphics, having a mouse became necessary to help manipulate those graphical doodads on the screen. As an input device, the mouse is second only to the keyboard as the way you tell the computer what you want to do. And, amazingly, sometimes the computer listens to you.

WHERE'S THE GOLD?

The mouse is often found lurking next to the computer keyboard, typically on the right but also on the left — and often under the sofa cushions for those wireless mice.

You manage your mouse by using the Control Panel's Mouse icon; from the Control Panel Home, choose the Mouse link, found under the Hardware and Sound heading.

The Mouse Properties dialog box is where you can tune, control, and mess with your computer's nonfurry rodent.

What to Do with It

Depending on how you use your computer, you may spend most of your time typing on the keyboard and spend relatively little time using the mouse. Games tend to require the use of the mouse more often, and graphics applications require full use of the mouse. Obviously, controlling and tuning the computer mouse can help make your PC day go a lot better.

Mouse icon

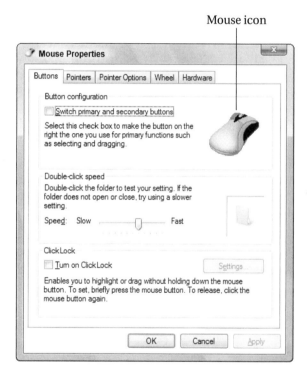

Basic mouse control

Several mouse activities are common in Windows, ways to manipulate the mouse to carry out certain operations on the screen:

Point: Move the mouse to a specific location on the screen, a graphical gizmo, or an object. Rolling the mouse on the desktop moves the mouse pointer on the screen.

Click: Press and release the mouse's main button, which is usually the left button. Point and click often happen one after the other.

Double-click: Give two swift clicks in a row.

Right-click: Press and release the mouse's non-main button, which is usually the right button.

Drag: Press and hold the mouse's main button, and then move the mouse to another location and release the button. This process has the effect of grabbing an object, moving it, and releasing it.

Right-drag: Use the right mouse button (the non-main button), rather than the left (or main), to drag.

Wheel-click: Click the mouse's center button, the wheel button. (The wheel button isn't available on all mice.)

Wheel-scroll: Roll the wheel button backward or forward, which scrolls up or down the document being viewed.

Wheel-pan: Press and hold the wheel, and then move the mouse around to pan a document in the same direction as the mouse. (This process can also be called a *wheel drag*.)

Wheel-tilt: Tilt the wheel button from side to side to pan a document horizontally. (This feature is found on only certain mice.)

Clue The best way to get used to using a computer mouse is to play a computer game, such as Solitaire or Minesweeper, both of which come with Windows. *See* Games.

Set mouse speed

Mouse speed is how fast the mouse pointer moves on the display as you move the mouse on the desktop. The mouse pointer can move lickety-split, or it can be slow and plodding. Set the speed by following these steps:

1. Summon the Mouse Properties dialog box.

2. Click the Pointer Options tab.

3. Use the slider to set the speed.

4. Click Apply to test the mouse speed.

5. Repeat Step 3, if necessary for adjustment.

6. Click OK.

The Enhance Pointer Precision check box helps adjust the mouse's accuracy when the pointer is moving slowly.

Make the mouse more visible

Options located at the bottom of the Pointer Options tab in the Mouse Properties dialog box can help you locate a wayward mouse on the screen. They include

Point trails: The mouse pointer grows a series of ghostly echoes that follow the pointer as you move it around the screen.

Point radar: Press and release the Ctrl button to make a series of concentric rings highlight the mouse button's location.

Don't forget that you can also select a larger mouse pointer. See the section "Change the mouse pointer," later in this entry.

Adjust double-click speed

When you have trouble getting the computer to recognize your double-click, try these steps to fix the problem:

1. Summon the Mouse Properties dialog box.

2. Click the Buttons tab.

3. Adjust the slider in the Double-Click Speed area.

4. Use the folder image in the dialog box to test your double-clicking prowess.

5. Repeat Steps 3 and 4 as necessary.

6. Click OK.

Use the left-handed mouse

Not all hope is lost if you're a southpaw. You can direct Windows to swap the mouse buttons, making the right button primary and the left button secondary, which is especially helpful if you're using the mouse with your left hand. Here's how to make the switch:

1. Conjure the Mouse Properties dialog box.

2. Click the Buttons tab.

3. Place a check mark by the Switch Primary and Secondary Buttons option.

4. Click OK.

One problem with this solution is that all Windows documentation, manuals, and online Help files assume that the *left* button is the main one. The nomenclature *right-click* would also be reversed for your mouse. I hope you can remember that!

Change the mouse pointer

One of the most distracting and amusing — I mean, engrossing and totally useful — things you can do in the Mouse Properties dialog box is to set a new mouse pointer. Here's how:

1. In the Mouse Properties dialog box, click the Pointers tab.

2. In the scrolling list, select a pointer to customize.

   Windows uses different types of pointers for different situations. You can change them all.

3. Click the Browse button.

   An Open dialog box appears, listing a slew of alternative mouse pointers.

 Clue The CUR files are standard mouse pointers. ANI files represent animated mouse pointers.

4. Choose an alternative pointer.

   Use the preview window in the bottom of the Browse dialog box to see what the pointer looks like and gauge its size.

5. Click Open to select the new pointer.

6. Repeat Steps 2 through 5 to modify other pointers.

7. Click OK.

Apply a mouse pointer scheme

Windows comes with preset mouse pointer *schemes,* collections of similar pointers all with a design in mind. To choose a scheme, obey these instructions:

1. Open the Pointers tab in the Mouse Properties dialog box.

2. Choose a scheme from the Scheme drop-down list.

3. Preview the selected pointers.

4. Click OK to select the scheme you want.

Likewise, when you choose your own slate of modified mouse pointers, you can save your selections as your own scheme: Click the Save As button on the Pointers tab and give your scheme a name.

Watch Your Step!

The Mouse Properties dialog box isn't standard on all computers. The contents — specifically, the tabs — depend on which type of mouse is attached to your computer and how many buttons or options the mouse has. For example, the Wheel tab appears only if you have a mouse with a wheel button.

When Things Go Wrong

You can use the keyboard to do many things a mouse can do. For example, you can press Alt+spacebar to activate a window's control menu, from which you can manipulate the window by using the keyboard rather than the mouse. *See* Keyboard Shortcuts.

If the mouse seems to jump to various items, especially in a dialog box, you probably have the Snap To option set. To remove it, go to the Pointer Options tab in the Mouse Properties dialog box and remove the check mark in the Snap To area.

To reset the original Windows mouse pointer theme, choose Windows Aero (System Scheme) from the Schemes drop-down list.

Gold Rush Nuggets

One of the first PC programs to make use of the mouse was Microsoft Word. At the time, using a mouse on a PC was so unusual that the Word software was often bundled with a free Microsoft mouse.

The PC mouse has traditionally had two buttons. In the early days, pressing both buttons simultaneously was the mouse equivalent of the Cancel command.

Mouse pointers are kept in the \Windows\ Cursors folder.

Digging Elsewhere

Keyboard, Themes

Multitasking

Can you multitask? Most people can, but only with simple tasks. For example, some folks can walk and chew gum at the same time. Some people can doodle while they talk on the telephone. But most people can't carry on two conversations at once, let alone really, truly be able to do homework while watching television. That's merely a human limitation, though: Your computer is not only capable of doing many things at once — it's also happy to do so.

WHERE'S THE GOLD?

Multitasking isn't anything you find in Windows. No, it's a feature of the operating system. In Windows, you can have several programs running at the same time, all of them working at their various tasks. The key is simply to start up different programs.

Although many programs can run at once and you need to quit something only when you're really done with it, you can, of course, use only one program at a time. That program or window is said to be in the *foreground*. Any other programs are in the *background*.

Most programs rely on user input. So, when a program in the background needs user input, it merely sits patiently and waits until it's put into the foreground and receives input.

What to Do with It

The idea behind multitasking is to be productive. While you're downloading a file, you can be working on a document and have a graphics program open, for when you need to create an illustration.

Multitasking is about saving time, being productive, and getting the most from your computer.

Run several programs at once

You don't need to use an incantation or a special sacrifice to multitask in Windows: Simply start up one program after another. *See* Programs.

For example, on my computer, I typically have Microsoft Word, Internet Explorer, and my e-mail program running, plus perhaps iTunes or some other music program motivating me with Mozart. All programs run at the same time, but I can *use* only one program at a time.

Find the top program

In a multitasking operating system such as Windows, the lone program you're using is said to be *in the foreground*. Graphically, that's shown on the screen as the top, or front, window.

When you're confused about which window is on top, note how it's colored: Background windows appear dimmed or in subdued colors, and the top window is always more colorful.

You can also check the Taskbar on the top window. The top window has a button on the

Taskbar, and that button looks different from other buttons; it looks like it's been pressed.

No, the button is not *depressed*. Buttons don't have emotions, and, anyway, the background programs would have the depressed buttons.

When the Windows desktop is on top, all other windows are in the background. *See* Desktop.

Select a background program

To bring forward a program that's in the background, either click its window or choose its Taskbar button.

Minimize a program

Rather than quit a running program, if you just need to set it aside for a while, consider minimizing its window: Click the leftmost button in the window's upper right corner. *Also see* Windows.

Minimize   Preview of
button   open windows

 To minimize all open windows, press Win+M on the keyboard, or use the Win+D command to display the desktop.

Switch between programs

There's no point in multitasking unless you can switch between the various running programs.

You have multiple methods of managing multitasking mayhem:

Use the Taskbar. Click a program's or window's button on the Taskbar to switch to that window.

Press Alt+Esc. The Alt+Esc key combination moves you from one window to the next, in sequence, until you cycle through all open windows.

Press Alt+Tab. The Alt+Tab, or *cool* switch, allows you to cycle through all open windows. Press and hold the Alt key and then tap the Tab key. As you do, a pop-up window shows tiny previews of all open windows (and the desktop). Keep tapping the Tab key to select different windows. Release the Alt key to switch to the highlighted window.

Desktop

 When you press Alt+Ctrl+Tab, the pop-up window remains on the screen when you release the keys. Then use Tab (or Shift+Tab) to scroll through the preview windows; press Enter to select a window that you want to switch to.

Press Win+Tab. The Win+Tab key combination switches between windows in a fancy graphical way, flipping each window in a perspective view: *Flip 3D*. As with Alt+Tab, you press and hold the

Win key while tapping the Tab key to cycle through the windows (and desktop).

On keyboards without a Windows key, you can pull off the Win+Tab or Flip 3D trick by running the Window Switcher program, found on the Quick Launch bar.

Use the Task Manager. Finally, you can use Task Manager to switch between programs. Press Ctrl+Shift+Esc to summon the Task Manager window. *See* Task Manager.

Copy and move data between programs

Another benefit to running two or more programs at a time is that you can copy, cut, and paste to share information (both text and graphics) between programs. *See* Copy, Cut, and Paste Data for the details.

Watch Your Step!

Remember that you don't need to quit one program to use another; keep all programs open as long as you need to use them.

The Flip 3D effect is available only if your PC has the graphics horsepower to display the animation.

When Things Go Wrong

Hopefully, when one program dies, it doesn't take the whole computer with it. If you find that you can't switch to a program, check the Task Manager window to see whether the program's status is Not Responding. If so, use Task Manager to end the program. *See* Task Manager.

Gold Rush Nuggets

DOS's inability to run more than one program at a time led to its decline and the supremacy of Windows. But back in its day, DOS had many multitasking utilities that performed far better than early versions of Windows. In fact, Microsoft's own DOS Shell program was better at handling multiple programs than Windows was at the same time. What? You've never heard of DOS Shell? Well, there's a reason for that!

Digging Elsewhere

Copy, Cut, and Paste Data; Programs; Task Manager

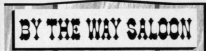
Narrator

One Ease of Use feature in Windows is Narrator, a tool that can read aloud text that appears on the screen. I prefer to call it the Annoy-rator because it never really seems to read what I want; the interface is a wee bit vague. But, at least it remains a tool that's available for folks who may need a little assistance with text on the screen.

Start the Narrator from the Start button's menu. Choose All Programs⇨Accessories⇨Ease of Use⇨ Narrator. The Narrator control window appears, and the nice lady with the computer voice reads the window to you. That's about as helpful as things get.

Switching to a window makes the Narrator attempt to read the window's contents. For simple windows, this works well: The Narrator reads the window's title and then the contents. That's exactly how things should work. But complex windows, such as on a news site on the Internet, don't fare as well. Rather than read the window, Narrator simply announces how many items are present. It doesn't even say "Ta-da!" after doing so — it just stops reading.

Now, I could stop there, but I won't because I have some blank space left on this page to continue writing. Basically, Narrator falls shorts in that it lacks an interface with your windows. For example, you should be able to click the Control menu or right-click in a window and find a command that lets Narrator read the text. Perhaps you could select text and right-click it so that Narrator can read that selection. But these types of commands are lacking, which makes the whole point of Narrator seem rather futile.

When you recognize the severe limitations of Narrator, you can close its window by clicking the Exit button.

Network Window

The Network window displays icons representing computers and network resources available on a local-area network. It's the main window through which you can explore the local network and access network gizmos, and it's the gateway to other networking goodies located deeper in the bosom of Windows.

WHERE'S THE GOLD?

You can summon the Network window from many places. If the Network icon appears on the desktop, opening that icon displays the window. (*See* Desktop Icons.)

You can also choose the Network command from the Start button's menu.

Finally, any Windows Explorer window grants you access to the Network window from the Address bar: Click the leftmost triangle on the Address bar and choose Network from the menu that appears.

The Network window shows other computers on a peer-to-peer network, networking devices, printers, disk drives, and other resources.

Network icon

window. Opening the icon displays a list of resources available on that computer, including shared folders, files, printers, and modems.

What to Do with It

The Network window is merely a gateway through which you can access network resources or other places in Windows where the true networking control happens.

Browse the network

To see what resources are available on the network, open a computer icon in the Network

Visit Networking HQ

The Network window serves as a quick door into the Network and Sharing Center, which is where the real networking activity takes place in Windows Vista. To get there, click the Network and Sharing Center toolbar button. *See* Networking.

Watch Your Step!

A computer on the network doesn't show up in the Network window when that computer is turned off or hibernating.

Connecting to some computers on the network requires that you have permission. A Login dialog box may appear, prompting you for a user ID and password. Only users who are known to that computer can access the resources. *See* Share Stuff on the Network.

Even if you're given open access to a computer, you may not have full access. That means that you can only view or copy files from the other computer; you can't delete, modify, or create new files.

When Things Go Wrong

Whether a networking gizmo shows up in the Network window depends on how the network is configured. Some network printers, for example, may not appear in the Network window unless the printer has been configured to be part of the local workgroup. *See* Networking for specific networking issues.

Gold Rush Nuggets

In previous versions of Windows, the Network window was referred to as the Network Neighborhood and was later called My Network Places.

Digging Elsewhere

Computer, Control Panel, Networking, Share Stuff on the Network

Networking

After years of torturous labor and research, computer scientists have gotten the *working* into networking. No longer do you need an IT guy to come to your home or small office and help set things up. Hardware-wise, you plug in a cable that you can't plug in incorrectly. Software-wise, Windows comes with all the tools and toys you need to connect the various PCs in your home and office and then add a printer, a router, and a high-speed modem. There. That should be all I need to write about networking, but it's not. The computer scientists need a few *more* years.

WHERE'S THE GOLD?

Networking has both hardware and software parts. On the hardware side, your PC most likely has a network interface card, or NIC, installed. The physical evidence is an RJ-45 jack (or hole) on your computer, into which you plug a network cable.

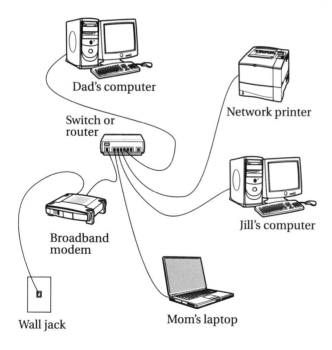

Dad's computer

Switch or router

Network printer

Jill's computer

Broadband modem

Wall jack

Mom's laptop

The other end of the network cable typically goes to a hub, switch, or router, which connects other computers and their cables. Toss in a few printers and maybe a modem, and you have a computer network.

On the software side, networking is one of those Control Panel things. The Network and Sharing Center icon in the Control Panel opens the Network and Sharing Center window, from which all things networking flow. From the Control Panel home, choose Network and Internet and then Network and Sharing Center.

Network
and Sharing
icon

System
icon

The Network and Sharing Center window is home plate for all networking activities and things interesting. From that lone window, you can do just about anything regarding networking in Windows.

While your computer is connected to the network, you might see a tiny icon in the Notification Area, which I call the networking buddies. The icon blinks during high network activity. Pointing the mouse at the buddies displays a pop-up window listing the current network status; clicking, double-clicking, or right-clicking the buddies displays a pop-up menu. *See* Notification Area for information on turning the buddies on or off.

On the Start button menu, you might find a Connect To item (on the right), which is used to connect to various networks — specifically, wireless networks. *See* Start Button and Menu for more information on displaying this item and also a link to the Network window.

Speaking of which, a Network window provides a peek into various networking devices near or connected to your computer. *See* Network Window for more information on the Network window.

What to Do with It

Networking is about sharing resources, but that topic is covered in this book under the Share Stuff on the Network entry. For this chapter, networking is about getting things working.

Configure networking stuff

Windows comes with a wizard that guides you through network setup. If you've not yet configured your computer to be on a network, follow these steps:

1. Open the Network and Sharing Center window.

2. Choose the Connect to a Network link on the left side of the window.

3. Choose an existing network from the window (if any networks appear in the window).

4. Click the Connect button.

Confirm that the network is working

When the network is up and running, you can open the Network window and see your own computer listed. If other computers and network devices are listed, you can be *very* sure that everything is working just fine. *See* Network Window.

Set the workgroup name

For a peer-to-peer network, which is the basic type of network you find at home or in a small office, all computers should share the same workgroup name. Here's how to check and set the workgroup name:

1. Open the Control Panel's System icon.

   From the Control Panel Home, choose System and Maintenance, and then choose System.

2. In the System window, locate the Computer Name, Domain, and Workgroup Settings area.

3. Click the Change Settings link.

   The System Properties dialog box appears.

4. Click the Computer Name tab.

5. Click the Change button.

   The Computer Name/Domain Changes dialog box appears.

6. Ensure that Workgroup is chosen.

7. Type a workgroup name.

   Don't use any spaces; type ALL CAPS.

8. Click OK, and then close any other open dialog boxes or windows.

9. Restart Windows if you're prompted to do so.

It doesn't matter what you name the workgroup; it's just easier to use the network when *all* computers share the same workgroup name.

 For security reasons, I recommend against using the workgroup name WORKGROUP or MSHOME, which tend to be the standard names. The bad guys rely on people not changing these names, which makes it easier for them to get into your computer.

Check the network status

A View Status link appears in the Network and Sharing Center window. You can find the link on the left, in the area devoted to your network(s).

Click that link to see a dialog box summarizing the network's condition.

You can also see a pop-up display of the network's status by pointing the mouse at the little networking buddies icon in the Notification Area.

Connect to a wireless network

I'll be honest: The best way to connect to a wireless network is to use any specific software that came with your computer to support the wireless adapter. That's the easy way. The Windows way, which works almost as well, is to do this:

1. Open the Start button's menu.
2. Choose the Connect To command.
3. In the Connect To window, choose a wireless network from the list.
4. Click the Connect button.
5. If you're prompted for a copious password, type one.
6. Select Public if you're out in public — at a wireless café or public library or anywhere else that the network is shared by unknown humans. Choose Private only for your own, wireless router at home or the office.
7. Save the network connection information, which should come in handy later.
8. Click Close, and you're connected.

Check the Notification Area to confirm that you're connected. When the signal is lost, you're notified. You're also notified when more wireless networks become available.

Disconnect from the wireless network

You don't have to disconnect from a wireless network. When laptopping, for example, I simply turn off the laptop or shut the lid. That's enough to disconnect, and the computer is only mildly annoyed at the missing connection the next time I start the thing.

If you're desperate to disconnect, right-click the Wireless Networking icon in the Notification Area. Choose the Disconnect command from the pop-up menu that appears.

Disable your wireless connection

When I use my laptop computer on an airplane, I'm careful to ensure that I turn off the wireless networking adapter. Supposedly, the wireless transmission can interfere with the airplane's operation — which is something I'd rather not do. So, instead, I do this to disable the wireless networking gizmo:

1. Open the Networking and Sharing Center window.
2. On the left side of the window, choose Manage Network Connections.
3. Right-click the icon representing your wireless networking adapter.
4. Choose Disable from the pop-up menu that appears.

The wireless network adapter no longer transmits or receives information when it's disabled.

To reenable the adapter, repeat the preceding steps, but in Step 4, choose the Enable command.

Customize the network

Clicking the Customize link in the Network area of the Network and Sharing Center window displays a window in which you can change various network settings.

For example, you can name your network something other than Network. (Note, though, that Windows uses this name to refer to the network connection; it's *not* the workgroup or domain name.)

You can specify whether your network is public or private: Use the Private setting when the network is in your home or office and is isolated from outside access. Use the Public setting when your network is open to the public.

You can even change the Network icon, although I don't recommend it: People expect the Network icon to look the same on all versions of Windows.

Check the network map

Windows Vista can display a map of your network, listing all computers and how they're connected to the network. Well, listing *most* of the computers; Windows Vista is best at recognizing other Windows Vista computers.

To see the map, open the Networking and Sharing Center window. Click the link that says View Full Map. Windows thinks for a bit and then displays the Map window, outlining how and where various devices are connected to the network and the Internet.

Note that some computers and devices may not show up on the map. In the illustration nearby,

the computer MING is a Windows 98 computer. NETDRIVEALPHA is a network hard drive.

 To get your Windows XP computers to show up on the network map, you need to install something called the LLTD Responder. On your Windows XP computer, visit this link:

`http://go.microsoft.com/fwlink/?LinkId=70582`

Get your PC's MAC address

Some forms of wireless networking security require that you discover your PC's wireless adapter's MAC address. This has nothing to do with hamburgers. MAC stands for Media Access Control. Say "mack."

To discover your PC's MAC address, follow these steps:

1. Open the Network and Sharing Center window.

2. Click the View Status link.

3. Click the Details button.

4. In the list presented in the Network Connection Details window, look for the Physical Address item.

A MAC address is composed of six pairs of numbers or letters, such as

```
01-23-45-67-89-AB
```

5. Click the Close button and (optional) close other windows.

Repair the network

Windows has some self-diagnostics you can try when the network is acting particularly fussy. Here's what you can do:

1. Open the Network and Sharing Center window.

2. From the left side of the window, choose Detect and Repair.

3. Wait and watch.

Honestly, I've never seen the thing work, so I can only guess what happens next. But it's worth a try.

Watch Your Step!

Here's some general advice for using a wireless network in public: Avoid doing anything on the Internet that would seriously compromise your security. Don't do online banking. Don't use your credit card (or transmit your credit card number). Avoid logging in to sensitive Web sites where your password may be literally plucked out of the air. Although I don't think you should

be paranoid, and it's nice to get away with a laptop from time to time, you should still remain cautious in public.

Disabling a wireless network adapter means that it stays disabled until you manually reenable it.

When Things Go Wrong

When you can't find any network available in the Network and Sharing Center window, your computer might not be equipped with networking hardware or the hardware might not be functioning. Ask your computer dealer.

When you don't see other computers on the network, first ensure that the other computers (or devices, such as network printers) are on; computers must be turned on to use the network. Second, ensure that all computers on the network share the same workgroup name. This is vital for peer-to-peer networks, the kind used in small offices and at home.

Gold Rush Nuggets

The networking protocols used by the PC, as well as by the entire Internet, are referred to as *Ethernet*. Computer pioneer Robert Metcalf coined the term from the words *ether* and *net* (from network). Ether, or rather *aether,* was once thought to be the medium that carried light.

Digging Elsewhere

Network Window, Share Stuff on the Network

Notepad

The Notepad program almost didn't make it into Windows Vista. Although Notepad has been included in all Windows releases since the first version back in the 1980s, the argument was offered that modern computer users don't need a text editor. The argument lost. Notepad continues its tradition of providing basic text-editing abilities when needed in Windows.

You can find the Notepad program on the Start button's menu. Choose All Programs⇨Accessories⇨ Notepad. The program is used to edit plain-text files. Anything, from simple lists to computer configuration files or even Web pages, can be created or edited (although only in text mode) in Notepad. It's a powerful and useful tool.

Notepad is a text editor. That means it deals only with text — characters, symbols, and numbers — but not any formatting, fancy indents, character attributes, or colors, and definitely no graphics. Just plain text. And, you can find a lot of places in a computer where plain text is used and required.

The Notepad window is as boring as a program can get. You can open, edit, or create text files. Again, that's just text, although Notepad lets you pick a font to use from the Format⇨Font menu.

For viewing text files, you can use the Format⇨Word Wrap command to ensure that long lines of text don't extend off to the right for infinity. With Word Wrap on, text is as wide as the Notepad window.

Notepad features basic Find and Replace commands — Copy, Cut, and Paste, plus the F5 key, which can be used to insert a date/time stamp.

Most text files end in TXT, which is the standard three-letter file extension for text. Notepad can also open plain-text log files (often ending with LOG), Windows batch files ending in BAT, and Web pages saved to disk (HTM or HTML, for example). The Web pages appear as plain text, showing only the Web page formatting and text.

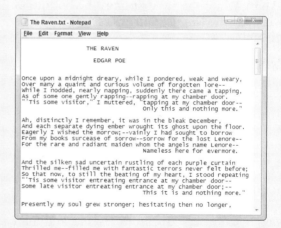

Notification Area

I suppose that the Notification Area started out innocently enough. Perhaps someone at Microsoft thought that the Taskbar looked lonely, so he decided to put the time display over there, off to the right. The whole notion is that occasionally (or more often than that), Windows or certain programs need to *notify* you of various conditions or events. So the little icons often grow cartoon balloons with explanations of events. Or, the icons may just sit still and do nothing until they're clicked, double-clicked, or right-clicked. Yes, it's rather random — sort of like the Notification Area itself!

WHERE'S THE GOLD?

The Notification Area dwells on the opposite end of the Taskbar, away from the Start button (*see* Taskbar). When the Taskbar lines the bottom of the display, the Notification Area sits squat on its right end.

The Notification Area thrives with tiny icons, each representing a program, task, or process running inside the computer. For example, most antivirus programs are accessed via a tiny icon in the Notification Area. Many graphics drives have tiny icons in the Notification Area, which you can use to adjust the PC's display.

You control the Notification Area by using the Control Panel's Taskbar and Start Menu Properties dialog box. You can open the Taskbar and Start Menu icon in the Control Panel to get to this dialog box, but you can take a shortcut:

1. Right-click the time on the chevron next to the Notification Area.

2. Choose Properties from the menu that appears.

Taskbar and
Start Menu icon

What to Do with It

You don't need to do anything with the Notification Area. You can sit and watch. You can wait for it to notify you. Or, you can madly click the various icons and hope that something productive comes of it.

Use an icon

Most of the icons in the Notification Area don't sit there to look pretty. At the least, you can point the mouse at an icon to see a pop-up bubble displaying the icon's status or the situation of whatever the icon is monitoring.

Clicking certain icons once displays a pop-up menu of options.

Right-clicking an icon may display a control menu from which you can select options to control the program that displays the icon.

Double-clicking an icon may also display a menu or window in which you can do more things regarding what the icon represents.

Display more or less of the Notification Area

The Notification Area originally hung open all the time, like a yawning garage door revealing all the junk you don't want to keep in your house. To close or open the Notification Area's garage door, use the Show More chevron, located on the Notification Area's western border.

When the chevron points to the left, icons are hidden. Click the chevron to show all the icons.

When the chevron points to the right, the entire contents of the Notification Area are shown. You don't need to click the right-pointing chevron; the Notification Area closes automatically after a few moments.

Show or hide Notification icons

You can display a Notification Area icon in three ways:

Hide when inactive: The icon isn't visible as long as whatever the icon controls isn't busy.

Hide: The icon is always hidden.

Show: The icon is always visible.

To control the visibility of each dang doodle icon that could possibly appear in the Notification Area, heed these steps:

1. Summon the Taskbar and Start Menu Properties dialog box, and then choose the Notification tab.

2. If necessary, place a check mark by the Hide Inactive Icons option.

3. Click the Customize button.

   The Customize Notification dialog box lists every potential teensy icon that might appear or has appeared in the Notification Area. The item to the right of the icon's name determines its current visibility. Clicking that item displays a menu from which you can set a new visibility status.

4. Choose whether to show, hide, or hide when inactive any given icon, especially one that bugs you.

5. Click OK, and then click OK to close the Taskbar and Start Menu Properties dialog box.

Click
to show
menu

Notification Area icons   Current status

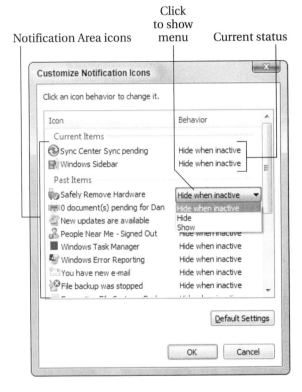

Display the time

To ensure that the time display shows up in the Notification Area, obey these steps:

1. Conjure up the Taskbar and Start Menu Properties dialog box, and then click the Notification tab.

2. Place a check mark by the Clock option.

3. Click OK.

To hide the Clock display in the Notification Area, repeat the preceding steps and remove the check mark in Step 2.

Display the volume control

To control whether the PC's software volume control appears in the Notification Area, heed these steps:

1. Beckon forth the Taskbar and Start Menu Properties dialog box, and then click the Notification tab.

2. Put a check mark by the Volume option.

3. Click OK.

Display the network guys

Windows displays a tiny twin computer icon in the Notification Area, which is used to confirm your connection to the local-area network or to the Internet. To determine whether the thing shows up, follow these steps:

1. Summon the Taskbar and Start Menu Properties dialog box, and then click the Notification tab.

2. Plant a check mark by the Network option.

3. Click OK.

Display the power meter

Battery-operated computers, which most folks call *laptops*, can have their power meters displayed in the Notification Area, which serves as a constant reminder that wireless-and-free computing comes with its limitations. To throw that power meter into the Notification Area mix, do this:

1. Bid come the Taskbar and Start Menu Properties dialog box, and then click the Notification tab.

2. Click to put a check mark by the Power option.

3. Click OK.

The Power option is available only on battery-powered PCs.

Watch Your Step!

Most users, and many manuals and tech support people, assume that the time and volume controls sit in the Notification Area.

In earlier versions of Windows, controlling what did and didn't appear in the Notification Area was done by using individual icons in the Control Panel. For example, controlling the clock's visibility was handled by the Date and Time icon. This is no longer the case with Windows Vista.

When Things Go Wrong

No, there's no way to make the Notification Area disappear. That Show More chevron is always there, unless:

The chevron doesn't appear when all the icons in the Notification Area are visible, meaning that no icons are hidden.

Gold Rush Nuggets

Once upon a time, the Notification Area was called the system tray.

Click the clock in the Notification Area to see a nifty monthly calendar.

Digging Elsewhere

Taskbar

Open

O pen, sesame! In Windows, the word *open* does, in fact, reveal all sorts of hidden treasure, but there's nothing magical about it (unless you believe that anytime the computer works properly, it can be considered *magic*). *Open* is what you do to an icon when you double-click it — you open that file to either run a program, open a document in a program, or get faced with that delightful "What the hey?" dialog box. Within your applications, the Open command summons the Open dialog box, from which you can pry open icons without having to leave the comfy luxury of the application. Open is quite a versatile thing.

WHERE'S THE GOLD?

The Open command is attached to each icon you see in Windows. The icon has assigned to it a specific action that takes place when the icon is double-clicked. For many icons — programs, documents, and folders — double-clicking the icon opens the icon, either running the program, loading the document into an application, or opening the folder to reveal its contents.

To see the Open command attached to any icon, right-click the icon. The top portion of the pop-up menu lists the primary commands associated with the icon.

Open exists primarily as a command in applications that deal with or create documents. The Open command is found on the File menu, and it's shown in this book as File⇨Open. The keyboard shortcut is Ctrl+O.

The Open command summons the Open dialog box, which you can use like a mini–Windows Explorer window to hunt down various files on disk for use by the application.

What to Do with It

The Open command opens things. It gives your applications access to various documents saved to disk, and it allows you to open icons to see what mysteries they hold.

Open an icon

To open an icon, double-click the icon with the mouse. You can also press the Enter key, which activates the Open command for an icon you've selected (although that's not always a certainty).

To open a group of documents, for example, select the documents and then press the Enter key. *See* Select Files. You can also open a group of documents by selecting them and then pressing F10 and choosing File⇨Open from the menu that appears.

Summon the Open dialog box

The Open dialog box allows an application to fetch a previously saved document and open it in a window for viewing, modification, or printing, for example. The command to summon the Open dialog box is File⇨Open or the keyboard shortcut Ctrl+O. You might also have an Open toolbar button.

Clue The Open dialog box has another name in Windows: Browse. The Browse dialog box works just like the Open dialog box, although it's generally used for choosing a file to serve a function, as opposed to opening a file for editing.

Use the Open dialog box

The Open dialog box generally works like this:

1. Look through the list of files to find the one you want.

Navigation pane   Address bar   Display only files of this type

Show or hide folder tree   Folders   Matching files

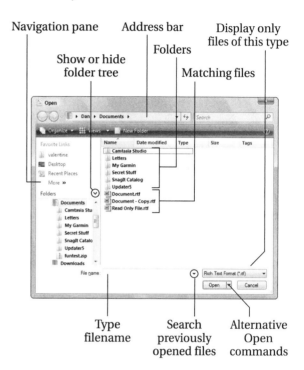

Type filename   Search previously opened files   Alternative Open commands

2. If you see the file, click it to select it and click the Open button, or just double-click the icon. Otherwise:

3. Choose another location from the Address bar, Favorite links, or Folder tree, or open a folder to continue looking for the file you want.

4. Repeat Steps 2 and 3 until you locate the file you want to open.

Also see Address Bar and Windows Explorer, given that the Open dialog box is basically a mini–Windows Explorer window.

Select files of a given type

To help you locate the files you need, the Open dialog box features a filter of sorts. The File Type button, located in the lower right part of the dialog box, can be used to narrow the types of files displayed.

For example, to see only JPG files in a graphics program displayed for the Open dialog box, choose JPG as the file type.

To see all files, use the All Files option or the old DOS wildcards: `*.*` (`All files`). Be aware that just because a file is listed in the window is no guarantee that the application can properly open it.

Watch Your Step!

Avoid randomly opening icons. Some icons may run programs that do weird things to your computer.

Some icons may have commands other than Open associated with double-clicking, such as the Play command associated with a music file.

Most Windows applications use the same Open dialog box, perhaps with subtle variations. Be on the lookout for certain applications that sport their own, unique Open dialog boxes. They may not look the same, but their basic operation and purpose haven't changed.

When Things Go Wrong

If you can't find the file you're looking for, use the Search text box. *See* Search.

Corrupted files, or files that have had their extensions mistakenly changed, may not open. When they do open, they may display improperly or crash the program.

Gold Rush Nuggets

The original term for opening a file was *load.* That's because you transferred the file's data from disk storage and loaded it into memory storage. In fact, in the first version of Microsoft Word (in 1983), the command to open a file was T for Transfer and then L for Load.

Digging Elsewhere

Files, Save, Search, Windows Explorer

Paint

Paint is the name of a graphical program that comes with Windows. It was one of the first "free" programs included with the original version of Windows as a bonus — a $59 value, or some such. Back in its day, it was a heck of a graphics program. But now it's more of a novelty or toy than a serious painting or drawing application.

You can find the Paint program on the Start button menu: Choose All Programs⇨Accessories⇨Paint. You can use the Paint program to edit any graphics image on your PC: Select a graphics file's icon and, from the toolbar's Preview button menu, choose the Paint command.

The Paint window shows a menu bar, a tool palette, and a color palette. In the middle is a resizable canvas on which the painting takes place. You can stretch and shrink the canvas by grabbing one of the tiny blue squares on its bottom or right side.

You create stuff in Paint by using the drawing tools in the upper part of the toolbox. Options for the tool appear below the toolbox, and they specify line thickness, whether a shape is drawn with a border or interior, and other settings.

Colors are chosen for both foreground and background painting. You set the foreground color by clicking the mouse; the background color, by right-clicking the mouse. Likewise, drawing with the left mouse button held down draws in the foreground color; drawing with the right mouse button draws in the background color.

The Image menu has a few tricks, including resizing, stretching, skewing, and rotating the image or a selected block.

You can type text only if the Text tool is selected *and* the image isn't zoomed. Choose View⇨Text Toolbar to change the font and text size. Note that after you switch to another tool, the text you type cannot be edited.

By using the File⇨Save As command, you can save images in a variety of formats. The standard format is BMP, Windows Bitmap. Paint can also save or open JPG, GIF, TIF, and PNG images.

Parental Controls

The computer is a learning tool, certainly. It opens up a world of possibilities. No kid should be without a computer. But as a parent, you recognize the dangers the computer harbors: On the Internet alone, you have to contend with porn, foul programs, and predators. Video games can be violent and disturbing. And, what's to keep Junior from playing on the computer for hours on end? Hey! Get outside! Play in the mud, like I did when I was your age! But I digress. Windows Vista is the first Windows release that sensibly deals with the issue of kids and computers. It's done by something called Parental Controls.

WHERE'S THE GOLD?

Parental Controls seems like an odd name, given that kids' behavior is being controlled, not the behavior of the parents. Some would claim there's a link. But I digress. . . .

You find the Parental Controls by opening the Parental Controls icon in the Control Panel. From the Control Panel home, choose the link Set Up Parental Controls for Any User (found beneath User Accounts and Family Safety).

Parental Controls icon

Opening the Parental Controls icon displays the Parental Controls window, from which you choose an account to control and then specify which controls you feel will work best.

 Eureka To make Parental Controls work, you have to configure Windows Vista with an Administrator account for you (the parent) and a Standard account for each kid. Ensure that everyone uses passwords.

What to Do with It

Nothing substitutes for an involved parent. Yet it's unreasonable to assume that you can be there monitoring what Junior does on the PC all day long — even when you're in the same room. Therefore, Parental Controls can be implemented in varying degrees, depending on how young your children are or how much you trust them.

Turn on Parental Controls

Parental Controls are turned off for all accounts in Windows by default. You have to activate the controls before you can use them. Here's how:

1. Summon the Parental Controls window.

2. Select the account that you want to control.

 Clue Only Standard accounts can have the Parental Controls set.

3. In the upper left part of the window, beneath the Parental Controls title, choose On, Enforce Current Settings.

4. Review the settings or make new settings in the User Controls window.

Various sections that follow describe these settings.

5. Click OK when you're done.

The User Controls window is a home plate for the four areas in which you can limit an account:

✗ The Web

✗ Time limits

✗ Games

✗ Applications

You can find a summary of the various settings on the right side of the window. Peruse the

Activity Log for details. (See "Check to see what Junior has been up to," later in this entry.)

Disable Parental Controls

To remove the Parental Controls, you can disable each item individually or simply turn off all Parental Controls: Repeat the steps from the preceding section, but in Step 3, choose the Off option.

Determine when Junior can use the PC

One of the most useful things you can do is to limit when a kid can use the computer. Sadly, enforcing the time with your voice doesn't seem to work. Suddenly, that one-hour limit becomes 90 minutes because "I have to find a save point, Mom! If I don't find a save point, I'll lose my place!" or "I'm in the middle of a boss battle!" or "I have to say goodbye to my friend and he's AFK (Away From the Keyboard)!" Yes, this handy tool puts an end to that. Here's what you do:

1. Bring up the Parental Controls User Controls window for the account you want to modify.

2. Choose Time Limits.

3. Use the mouse to plot out which hours for which days of the week your offspring is allowed access to the computer.

The darkened squares indicate an hour when the computer is off limits.

Undarkened squares indicate times when Junior can use the PC.

4. Click OK, and then close other windows.

The account that you limit can't be used during blocked hours; the user can't log in, and if he's using the computer, the computer logs him out at the given time. Yes, the computer can be heartless and cruel.

Create a list of okay/not okay Web sites

One way to limit where your kids go on the Internet is to create a list of okay Web sites — for example, the Microsoft site, Wikipedia, Yahoo Mail, and other places on the Internet that you feel would have a positive effect on your kids. To create the list, follow these steps:

1. Summon the Parental Controls window.

2. Choose the account that you want to limit.

3. In the User Controls window, choose Windows Vista Web Filter.

4. In the Web Restrictions window, choose Block Some Websites or Content.

   This option must be set for you to apply other restrictions.

5. Choose the Edit the Allow and Block List link.

6. Type the name of a Web site, good or evil, into the Website Address text box.

7. Choose Allow for a safe, good Web site, or choose Block to prevent access to a given Web site.

8. Repeat Steps 6 and 7 for various Web sites.

9. To further restrict access, put a check mark by the Only Allow Websites Which Are on the Allow List option.

10. Click OK, click OK again to close the Web Restrictions window, and close all other windows.

When Junior attempts to access an unknown Web page, a warning appears: "Windows Parental Controls has blocked access to this Web page."

Block Web sites by content

Rather than sit and endlessly type blocked and allowed Web sites, you can direct Windows to do most of the decision making for you. Just follow these steps:

1. Choose an account to modify in the Parental Controls window.

2. Choose Windows Vista Web Filter.

3. If necessary, remove the check mark by the option Only Allow Websites Which Are on the Allow List.

4. Choose either High, Medium, or Custom for the Web Restriction Level.

   If you choose Custom, you can select which individual topics will be restricted.

5. Click OK, and close other windows.

Disable file downloads

Downloads bother me the most about my kids on the Internet. They read some fake ad or visit some "fun" Web site that entices them to download something. Not knowing any better, they download, and then the whole computer is infected with some foul program or virus. To stop that, do this:

1. From the Parental Controls window, select an account that you want to restrict.

2. Choose Windows Vista Web Filter.

3. At the bottom of the Web Restrictions window, put a check mark by the Block File Downloads option.

4. Click OK, and close other windows.

Allow or forbid certain games

Without getting into all the (gory) details, it's easy to restrict which games Junior can play. Do this:

1. Open the Parental Controls window and choose the account that you want to modify.

2. Choose Games.

3. In the Game Controls window, click Yes to allow your kidlet to play games.

   Choosing No disables all game playing on the computer.

4. Choose Set Game Ratings.

5. If required, choose a game rating type.

   I prefer the ESRB ratings.

6. Choose the option Block Games with No Rating if you really don't trust your kid.

7. Select the highest game level you want to allow, such as Teen or Mature.

8. Click OK.

9. Back in the Game Controls window, choose Block or Allow Specific Games.

10. In the Game Overrides window, choose which games to specifically block.

11. Click OK when you're done.

12. Click OK to close the window, and then close all other windows, when you're finished.

 Some games are Internet-based. Mostly, those types of games are harmless fun, but some can be violent or objectionable. The best way to prevent those types of games from being played is to block the specific game sites. See "Create a list of okay/not okay Web sites," earlier in this entry.

Limit which programs can be used

Just as you can crank down on which games can or can't be played, you can determine which programs installed on your PC are okay for Junior to use and which ones you'd rather not have him mess with. Here's how:

1. Open the proper account in the Parental Controls window.

2. Choose Allow and Block Specific Programs.

3. Choose the second option, [User] Can Only Use the Programs I Allow.

4. Place a check mark by each program you want Junior to have access to.

 Click the Check All button, and then you can simply remove check marks from those programs you'd rather have Junior not mess with.

5. Click OK.

Check to see what Junior has been up to

To help keep an eye on Junior, direct Windows to turn on Activity Reports for when he uses the computer: In the Parental Controls window, under his account settings, choose the On option, under Activity Recording.

To review the Activity Log, choose the link on the right, View Activity Reports. A window appears, listing Web sites visited, time the computer was used, e-mail, blocked programs, and so on.

 By clicking Generate Report, in the upper left of the Activity Viewer window, you can save the information to disk, where you can open it in any text editor or word processor and print it, or just keep it on disk for future reference.

Watch Your Step!

The Parental Controls can be applied only to an account that is logged out. If you have trouble applying the controls, check the list of users on the computer and have any other users log out, and then make the necessary changes.

When Things Go Wrong

Bottom line: Communications. I recommend against slapping down the controls and then having your kid be surprised by them. Instead, explain your concerns. And, have him give you an update on what he may feel is too restrictive.

Gold Rush Nuggets

The Clever Naming Department has come up with the term *censorware* for software that controls what you do on your computer.

Digging Elsewhere

Games, Passwords, User Accounts

Password Reset Disk

Your computer recognizes that you're human. Out of sheer pity, it provides a way for you to recover your password when you, as a silly human, forget that password. By using the password reset disk, you can gain access to your PC by setting up a new password when you forget the old one. Obviously, this handy tool is worth looking into.

WHERE'S THE GOLD?

Setting up a password reset disk is done in the User Accounts window, where you set or reset your password in the first place. I recommend creating the password reset disk each and every time you change your account's password.

Incidentally, the password reset disk isn't necessarily a *disk* at all. Only if you use a floppy disk — which I don't recommend — is it really a disk. Otherwise, a removable USB media drive, such as a Flash drive or thumb drive, is ideal for use as a password reset "disk."

What to Do with It

Creating the password reset disk is the most important step. Hopefully, you'll never need it.

Create a password reset disk

Anytime you create or change your password in Windows, immediately make yourself a password reset disk by following these steps:

1. Attach a USB drive to your computer, such as a thumb drive or other removable media drive.

Although Microsoft suggests that you can use a floppy disk, I find them too unreliable for this purpose. Also, you cannot use a USB hard drive or CD/DVD drive. I prefer the key chain type of thumb drive.

2. Close the AutoPlay dialog box, if it appears.

3. Open the Control Panel User Accounts icon (if necessary).

4. Click the Create a Password Reset Disk link on the left side of the window.

   The Forgotten Password Wizard starts up.

5. Click the Next button.

6. Choose the media you inserted in Step 1.

7. Click the Next button.

8. Type your current password.

9. Click Yes if prompted to overwrite the existing password backup information.

   This prompt may appear twice.

10. Click the Next button and then the Finish button, and you're done.

11. Properly remove the USB drive and keep it in a safe place.

    See Safely Remove.

Use the password reset disk

To save your butt and get into Windows when you forgot your password, and providing that you were smart enough to create a password reset disk, gingerly follow these steps:

1. Attach the USB drive, the password reset disk, to your computer system.

   Or, if you didn't heed my admonishment, stick the floppy disk containing the password rescue file into the floppy drive.

2. Try typing the password again.

   You have to incorrectly enter a password in order to see the prompt for the password reset disk.

3. Click OK.

4. First, use the password hint to try to remind yourself of the original password.

5. Second, click the Reset Password link.

6. Click the Next button in the Password Reset Wizard.

7. Choose the media serving as your password reset disk.

8. Enter your new password (twice) plus a password hint.

   See Passwords for tips and hints.

9. Click the Next button and then the Finish button.

   But you're not done!

10. Log in to Windows using the new password.

After using the password reset disk, make a new one! Run through the steps in the preceding section.

Use the password reset disk for other things

The password reset disk needs only a small amount of space for the teensy, tiny file Windows uses to restore your password. So, feel free to use the disk for other things as well. Just be careful when cleaning the disk that you don't accidentally remove the password file (See the "Gold Rush Nuggets" section.)

If you want to be sneaky, use a media card from your digital camera as the password reset disk. As long as you don't lose the disk, and you can easily attach it to the PC; who would suspect?

Watch Your Step!

Yes, obviously, anyone else who gets hold of your password reset disk can reset your password and get access to your computer. My suggestion is to keep the disk or media in a safe, secure place.

Each user on the computer should have his own password reset disk or media. When you use the same disk to save a second password, any password previously saved on that disk is erased.

Floppy disks. Who needs 'em? They are very, *very,* unreliable, especially over the long haul. Find yourself a nice USB thumb drive, such as one you can attach to your key ring. Use it as the password recovery disk.

The password reset disk helps you when you forget your Windows login password. It does not know about any other passwords you may have, such as an e-mail account or ISP account or accounts on various Web pages.

When Things Go Wrong

When you forget your password, look at the two prompts below the password input box. The first prompt offers a hint about your password. You can use the hint first; hopefully, to remember your password. Try that before using the disk.

If the disk or media doesn't work, use another as your password reset disk.

When your password reset disk seems corrupted or the file cannot be found, well, then, have another user on the same computer, a user with an administrator-level account, log in and restore your missing password. *See* Administrator.

Gold Rush Nuggets

The password reset disk contains a single, small file named USERKEY.PSW, which is used to unlock the password. Don't get nerdy on me here: The file is encrypted.

Digging Elsewhere

Administrator, Passwords

Passwords

You need two pieces of identification to get into the Windows prison, er, computer system. The first is your login name or your account name. That name says who you are, but to verify that information, you must also supply a password. This is common stuff for computers; anyone who has been using e-mail or has been out online shopping is familiar with the account name/password scheme of things. The bottom line is *security*. The password protects your account and your stuff from prying, meddling eyes and from those who wish ill will upon you. Passwords are Good Things.

WHERE'S THE GOLD?

Windows hides the actual password assigned to your account somewhere deep inside the computer. The password itself is encrypted. There's no point in my being specific about the location; the bad guys can figure it out for themselves.

As far as you're concerned, the password is used whenever you log in to Windows. That can be when Windows first starts, when switching users, or when recovering from sleep mode or hibernation.

Passwords are created, reset, and removed by using the User Accounts icon in the Control Panel. To get there from the Control Panel Home, choose User Accounts and Family Settings, and then choose User Accounts.

User Accounts
icon

What to Do with It

Passwords are for using. In fact, the more you use your password, the more likely you are to remember it. You can dabble with your password in a number of ways in Windows.

Enter your password

Passwords are typed when you first start Windows, switch users, log in, or revive the computer after a screen saver has done its duty. This is simple: Type the password into the box.

The text you type does not appear on the screen. Again, that's for security. So, you must be careful as you type!

Press the Enter key to send your password off for verification.

If you make a mistake the first time, check to see whether the Caps Lock key is on (passwords are case sensitive), and try again. Also note the password hint that appears.

Change your password

Security experts recommend that you change your accounts password at least once every 60 days. Honestly, I have enough trouble just getting people to use passwords in the first place, let alone change them. But when the urge hits you or you feel intense social pressure, follow these steps:

1. Click the Start button to display the Start menu.

2. Click your account picture in the upper right part of the Start menu.

   That's the shortcut to get to the User Accounts window.

3. Choose Change Your Password.

4. Type your current password.

5. Type the new password you want.

6. Type the new password again to confirm that you have it down.

   That's because you can't see the password displayed, so you must rely on your typing skills here.

7. Type a password hint.

   Hint: The password hint must not be the same as your password!

8. Click the Change Password button.

Remove your password

I see no reason to remove a password, especially on an Administrator account. But the ability is there nevertheless, so if you feel compelled, you can sneak through these steps:

1. Display the Start button's menu.

   Click the Start button or press the keyboard's Windows key.

2. Click your account picture in the upper right part of the Start menu.

3. Click the Remove Your Password link.

4. Enter your current password.

5. Click the Remove Password button.

Your account is now without a password. It's unprotected. It's naked. I beseech you to continue with the next section.

Add a password

Do be a *doo-bee* and use password protection for your account in Windows Vista. Here's how to add a password if your account lacks one:

1. From the Start button menu, click your account picture in the upper right corner.

2. Choose the link Create a Password for Your Account.

3. Type the new password.

   Refer to the later section "Watch Your Step!" for information on creating a *strong* password.

4. Retype the password to confirm that you can type it "in the dark."

5. Type a password hint, some text to remind you about your password.

6. Click the Create Password button.

Configure Windows to force you to reset your password

Eureka

You can direct Windows to remind you to change your password every so often. Again, having to change a password is a beneficial part of computer security. To direct Windows to force you to reset your password every so often, you must do two things.

First, you must allow your account's password to expire by following these steps:

1. Summon the Run command.

   Press the Win+R key combination.

2. Type **compmgmt.msc** into the box and press the Enter key.

   The Computer Management console appears.

3. On the left side of the window, choose Local Users and Groups.

4. In the center part of the window, double-click to open the Users folder.

5. Right-click your user account name and choose the Properties command from the pop-up menu.

6. In your account's Properties dialog box, on the General tab, click to remove the

check mark by the Password Never Expires option.

7. Click OK, and close the Computer Management window.

Second, after setting the password to expire, you should check the expiration time limit for passwords on your PC:

1. Open the Administrative Tools icon in the Control Panel.

2. Open the Local Security Policy icon.

3. From the left side of the window, choose Account Policies.

4. In the center of the window, double-click to open the Password Policy folder.

5. Double-click to open the Password Policy Age option.

6. Set the number of days to retain passwords.

7. Click OK, and close the various windows.

After the given number of days has passed (refer to Step 6), you're prompted to enter a new password when you log in to Windows.

Watch Your Step!

Passwords are case sensitive. The passwords *blorf*, *Blorf*, and *BLORF* are all different according to Windows.

Security experts advise using a *strong* password. Here's the skinny:

- ✗ The password should be at *minimum* 8 characters long.

- ✗ The password cannot be any word or name you can find in a dictionary.

- ✗ Avoid using your account name as a password.

- ✗ Do not use your name, street name, company name, pet's name, or any other names or information you could be directly associated with.

- ✗ The best password contains a mixture of upper- and lowercase letters *plus* a number *plus* a symbol character. Symbol characters can be any punctuation mark or symbol found on a computer keyboard.

Sometimes, a good password is simply a combination of two unrelated words. For example:

Lichen+Swe3t

Kleen!Germ$

Bride%Ugly

Another tactic is to use the first letters of something you can easily remember. For most men, that's not their anniversaries:

AnvIZON3/19

I recommend keeping a written copy of your password, just in case you forget. The best way to do this is by keeping it "hidden in plain sight." For example, write your password on two or three consecutive days on a calendar. Write down your password as an entry in your address book or in a recipe file. The idea is to keep the password handy but not in an obvious way.

Password hints are most helpful when you have a repertoire of several passwords that you use in various places. For example, I have passwords I use that begin with the letters *S, V, H,* and *M.* Therefore, my password hint is often the first letter of whichever password I've chosen.

The worst element in the computer security chain of command is *you,* the human. In most cases where computer security is broken, people voluntarily tell others what their password is. Don't tell anyone your password! When you feel that a password has been compromised, change it!

When Things Go Wrong

If you forget your password, an administrator on your computer can change it for you. *See* Administrator.

I highly recommend creating a password reset disk to assist you if you ever forget your password. *See* Password Reset Disk.

Gold Rush Nuggets

The Windows password is not the same thing as your e-mail password. Although you may use the same password, and Windows may automatically enter your password for you when you're checking e-mail, be aware that they aren't the same. Many passwords are involved with using a computer. Just because you type one once doesn't mean that you're done for the day.

Windows 95, 98, and Me provided password prompts when Windows first started, but they could be bypassed by a simple press of the Esc key. So much for security!

Digging Elsewhere

Administrator, Login and Log Off, Password Reset Disk, Screen Saver, User Accounts

Pathnames

A *pathname* is a full address for a file, specifying its exact location in your computer system. A pathname is similar to a Web page address in that it defines an exact location. For advanced users, typing a pathname is sometimes quicker than navigating through graphical hard drives and folders.

Pathnames are buried with every file on your computer. Each file has a longer pathname, which gives the file's exact location: the disk drive, the parent folders, and, finally, the file's full name (first part plus extension).

A traditional pathname starts with the disk drive letter and a colon, followed by the names of folders separated by backslashes, and, finally, the filename.

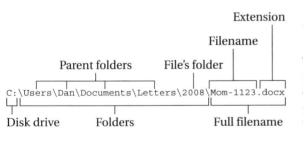

The pathname shown in this figure references the file MOM-1123.DOCX, which is found in the 2008 folder, located inside the Letters folder, which is further located in the Documents folder, in Dan's account folder inside the Users folder on drive C.

A *network* pathname, which gives the location of a file or folder on a network as opposed to only on your PC, begins with two backslashes and the name of the shared network resource (a shared hard drive elsewhere on the network). Beyond the resource name, the rest of the path works the same as a local pathname.

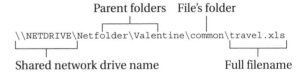

What to Do with It

You can do two things with a pathname: Use the name to locate a file (to "follow the path," as it were), and type a pathname to access a specific file, which is really a nerdy thing to do, echoing back to the text-based days of computing.

Read a pathname

Pathnames, like street addresses, are read from left to right. You begin with the disk drive or network device and then open the folders, eventually finding the file or folder you need. For example:

```
C:\Program Files\Microsoft Office\
   Templates\1033\
```

To get to the mysterious folder 1033, follow the path and these steps:

1. Open the My Computer window.

2. Open drive C:.

3. Open the Program Files folder.

4. Open the Microsoft Office folder.

5. Open the Templates folder.

6. Open the 1033 folder.

Read a network pathname

Network pathnames indicate a location on a network, beginning with the name of a shared network resource or the name of a shared network computer. For example:

```
\\XOG\Travel\2008\Chicago\June\
```

To venture off to the June folder on the network, take these steps:

1. Open the Network window.

2. Open the XOG computer or network resource.

3. Open the Travel folder.

4. Open the 2008 folder.

5. Open the Chicago folder.

6. Open the June folder.

Type or edit a pathname

Pathnames appear in the Address bar of the Windows Explorer window. To edit or type a pathname, press the F4 key or click the folder icon on the left end of the Taskbar with the mouse.

You can use all the standard Windows text-editing commands — including using the mouse to select text — when editing or typing a pathname.

As you type the pathname, Windows does a search for folders matching what you type. Often, it's easier to select the path you need from the drop-down list of matching folders.

Watch Your Step!

Pathnames use backslashes in Windows. On the Internet, and in other computer operating systems, forward slashes are used. In fact, you can use forward slashes some of the time in Windows, but it's best to stick with the backslashes to avoid errors.

Whenever a pathname contains a space, enclose the entire pathname in double quotes. For example, this pathname might be okay:

```
C:\Program Files\Sims\
```

But this pathname is better:

```
"C:\Program Files\Sims\"
```

Pathnames can be in either upper- or lowercase.

When Things Go Wrong

Check your typing!

When you're following a path and it suddenly leads nowhere, the indicated folder most likely isn't on your disk drive. In that case, use the Search command to try to locate the wayward folder. *See* Search.

In some cases, a folder in a pathname may be a system or hidden folder, which doesn't show up in the Windows Explorer window. *See* Hidden Files and Folders.

Gold Rush Nuggets

Pathname is often abbreviated as just *path*. The difference is that a pathname ends with a filename. A path indicates a folder.

The drive letter is often optional, although it must be concluded in a *full* pathname.

A pathname can be 260 characters long — max. This is also the maximum length for a filename, although officially the length being limited is that of a pathname, which includes the filename, folders, and various backslashes and junk.

Digging Elsewhere

Address Bar, Run, Search

Pop-Ups

When I was a kid, *pop-ups* referred to those cool books where the pages literally popped up, creating three-dimensional scenes and often having moving pieces. What a thrill for a kid! But in the cold, stark reality of the Internet, a pop-up isn't a delightful thing. Specifically, *pop-ups* refers to advertisements, ones that pop up in new windows right in front of the window you really want to see. Although the pop-up window is an effective advertising technique, it's also an annoyance to many Internet users. Fortunately, the Internet Explorer (IE) program offers you a clear and clean way to block the annoying pop-up windows.

WHERE'S THE GOLD?

Pop-ups lurk on the Internet. In fact, you can't tell which Web page will throw one your way. Basically, the pop-up window appears over the page you're viewing, generally in a smaller size, and the window lacks any toolbar or controls. It's just an ad! It bugs people, especially when more than one pop-up window pukes forth from the same Web page.

Pop-ups are controlled in IE through the Pop-Up Blocker Settings dialog box.

To see this dialog box, obey these steps:

1. Open Internet Explorer.

2. From the Tools button menu on the toolbar, choose Internet Options.

3. In the Internet Options dialog box, click the Privacy tab.

4. Click the Settings button to view the Pop-Up Blocker Settings dialog box.

You can also get to the settings from the Tools button on the IE toolbar: Choose Tools⇨Pop-Up Blocker⇨Pop-Up Blocker Settings.

Working the pop-up blocker happens as you use IE; you can decide whether to block specific sites, unblock sites, or dispense with the various bleeps and warnings.

What to Do with It

Normally, the pop-up blocker is turned on in IE. You can, however, disable it (if you're bold). You can also tune and adjust it to meet your Web-surfing needs.

Activate the pop-up blocker

To ensure that the pop-up blocker is on, click the Tools button on the IE toolbar and choose Pop-Up Blocker⇨Turn On Pop-Up Blocker.

To disable the pop-up blocker, choose Pop-Up Blocker⇨Turn Off Pop-Up Blocker.

Stick a pop-up in a tab

Maybe you want to see pop-ups, but not necessarily as pop-ups. Internet Explorer can shove what otherwise would be a pop-up window into a tab by using its tabbed browsing feature. Here's how to work things:

1. From the IE toolbar, click the Tools button.

2. Choose the Internet Options command.

3. Click the General tab (if necessary) in the Internet Options dialog box.

4. Click the Settings button in the Tabs area.

5. In the Tabbed Browsing Settings dialog box, ensure that there's a check mark by the Enable Tabbed Browsing option.

6. Choose Always Open Pop-Ups in a New Tab.

7. Click OK, and then click OK to close the Internet Options dialog box.

Deal with the pop-up warning

Rather than annoy you with a pop-up advertising window, Internet Explorer annoys you with a pop-up window telling you that a pop-up window was just thwarted. (Well, to me, it's a wash.)

Put a check mark in the Don't Show This Message Again box. Then click the Close button. Note the information bar along the top of the Web page window that says, "Pop-up blocked. To see this pop-up or additional options, click here . . . " This information bar comes into play when dealing with other aspects of pop-ups.

See the pop-up "just this once"

To view the pop-up suppressed in Internet Explorer, click the information bar near the top of the window and choose the item Temporarily Allow Pop-Ups.

If the pop-up turns out to be something useful, such as a secondary news or information window, you might consider allowing pop-ups for that site. Do so by clicking the information bar and choosing the command Always Allow Pop-Ups from This Site. Click Yes in the confirmation dialog box, and you're set.

Add a site to the exceptions list

To allow pop-ups for a site, click the information bar and choose the command Always Allow Pop-Ups from This Site. Or, you can make the settings manually in the Pop-Up Blocker Settings window: In the Address of Website to Allow box, type the address of the site from which you want to allow pop-ups. Click the Add button.

 Eureka Copy the address from the IE Address bar, and then paste the address into the Address of Website to Allow box.

Disable the warning, or the beep

The pop-up warning information bar can be disabled: Click the bar, and then choose Settings⇨ Show Information Bar for Pop-Ups. By removing the check mark by the option Show Information Bar for Pop-Ups, you disable the information bar.

To fix the beeping problem, remove the check mark by the Play a Sound When the Pop-Up Is Blocked option.

To reenable the warnings, visit the Pop-Up Blocker Settings window and remove the check mark by the item Show Information Bar When a Pop-Up Is Blocked. Click the Close button.

Change the beep

Rather than disable the beep, consider changing the sound that's made when a pop-up window is blocked. To do so, summon the Sound dialog box, and then click the Sounds tab (as described in the Sounds entry). Scroll through the list to find the Windows Explorer heading, and look for the Blocked Pop-Up Window option. Choose a new sound, per the directions in the Sounds entry.

Watch Your Step!

When you block pop-ups too tightly, you may not see features on some Web sites, such as menus or windows with video content. Consider adding those sites to your exception list to see the menus or windows.

When Things Go Wrong

Some pop-ups persist, even though you block them. Generally, this is a sign of spyware infection. *See* Windows Defender to find out how to check for spyware on your PC.

Pop-ups can also appear in special windows — usually, Flash animations. You can try setting your pop-up blocker to its highest setting: Open the Pop-Up Blocker Settings window and, from the drop-down Filter Level list, choose High: Block All Pop-Ups (press Ctrl+Alt to override).

Gold Rush Nuggets

Another type of pop-up window is the *pop-under* window. This type of window appears beneath the window you're viewing, so you don't see the annoying advertisement until you close the Web browser window. Yes, the pop-up blocker stops them as well!

The most offensive type of pop-up is the *mouse trap*. Basically, when you close the pop-up window, another pop-up window opens to replace it. Or, sometimes two pop-up windows may replace one pop-up window.

Digging Elsewhere

Cookies, Internet Explorer, Windows

Power Button

Long gone are the days when a computer had a simple on-off switch. Nope, like many other electronic gizmos, the PC has a power button. The *power button* is used to turn the computer on, but once the computer is on, the power button's function can be anything — which includes turning the computer off, putting it to sleep, hibernating, or doing nothing.

WHERE'S THE GOLD?

The PC's physical power button is found on the front of your computer console. Punching it turns the computer on. When the computer is on, the power button's function is handled by Windows, so punching it again can do any number of things, from turning the computer off to putting it to sleep to making popcorn (or so my kids tell me).

1. Open the Power Options icon in the Control Panel.

| Power Options icon | Start menu power button | Shield indicates updates will be installed during next shutdown or restart |

2. From the links on the left side of the Power Options window, select Choose What the Power Buttons Do.

The Power Options System Settings window is where you can control not only your PC's power button but also the "moon," or sleep, button.

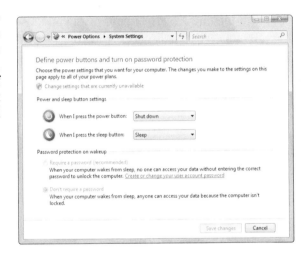

In addition to the PC's physical power button, a virtual power button is located on the Start button's menu. Its function can be set just like the physical power button. To see the current setting, point the mouse at the Start menu power button.

For Shutdown, the button is colored red. The pop-up balloon says, "Closes all open programs, shuts down Windows, and then turns off your computer."

For sleep mode, the button is colored gold. The pop-up balloon says, "Saves your session and puts the computer into a low-power state so that you can quickly resume working." *See* Sleep Mode.

For Hibernate, the button is colored gold. The pop-up balloon says, "Saves your session and turns off the computer. When you turn on the computer, Windows restores your session." *See* Hibernation.

There's also a *hidden* power button on the Ctrl+Alt+Delete menu. *See* Ctrl+Alt+Delete.

What to Do with It

The power button itself is punched with your finger. The power button on the Start menu is jabbed with the mouse. But the big issue in both cases is *What happens next?*

Change the power and sleep buttons' function

Configuring the function of the PC console's power button is done as follows:

1. Open the Power Options System Settings window.

2. To set the function of the power button, choose an item from the drop-down menu.

3. To set the function of the sleep button (if your PC has one), choose an item from the drop-down menu.

4. Click the Save Changes button.

Each button can have up to four options available:

Do nothing: Pressing the console button does nothing — nothing, I tell you!

Sleep: The button activates Windows Vista sleep mode.

Hibernate: The button activates Hibernate mode.

Shut down: The button turns off the computer.

Set the function on the Start menu's power button

Lurking in the lower left part of the Start menu is a power button. As with the real-life power button, its function can change.

Here's how:

1. Open the Power Options icon in the Control Panel; or, from the Control Panel Home, choose System and Maintenance, and then choose Power Options.

   The Power Options window appears.

2. Choose any link that says Change Plan Settings.

3. In the Edit Plan Settings window, choose Change Advanced Power Settings.

4. Scroll through the list of plan options to find the item Power Buttons and Lid.

5. Open the + (plus sign) by Power Buttons and Lid.

6. Open the + (plus sign) by Start Menu Power Button.

7. Click the button (yes, it's a button) by the word Setting.

8. Choose Sleep, Hibernate, or Shutdown from the drop-down menu.

9. Click OK to close the Power Options dialog box, optionally closing the Edit Plan Settings window as well.

Watch Your Step!

Laptop computers have another power "button": When you shut the laptop's lid, you can tell the computer to shut down, hibernate, sleep, or do nothing. To set the lid's function, repeat the steps from the section "Set the function on the Start menu's power button," but in Step 7 choose Lid Close Action.

When Things Go Wrong

A tiny shield icon in front of the Start menu's power button indicates that system updates will be installed the next time you shut down or restart Windows. *See* Updates.

Even if you utterly disable the function of the console's power button, you can still turn off your PC from the Start button's Shutdown menu. *See* Shutdown Windows.

Gold Rush Nuggets

Some PCs also have a secret, real-live on-off switch on the back of the console.

Digging Elsewhere

Hibernation, Sleep Mode, Shutdown Windows, Start Button and Menu

Previous Versions

A bold new feature in Windows Vista is the ability to recall older versions of files that you would otherwise not have access to. The feature is called *Previous Versions*, and it allows you to recover an older rendition, or *shadow copy*, of a file. This can save your butt when you accidentally overwrite a file, save over a file, copy over a file, or just want a previous version of a file you're updating. With Previous Versions, you can quickly recall that older shadow copy of a file, or even a backup you've made, essentially restoring something that would be otherwise difficult or impossible to recover.

WHERE'S THE GOLD?

All files in Windows Vista sport the Previous Versions feature. It's found lurking in the file's Properties dialog box. Here's how to summon the thing:

1. Right-click the file or folder's icon.
2. Click the Previous Versions tab.

 The shortcut here is to right-click the file or folder icon and then choose Restore Previous Versions from the pop-up menu.

For Previous Versions to work, System Protection must be activated. The restore points that System Protection creates make the shadow copies shown in the Previous Versions list available.

Here's how to confirm that System Protection is doing its part to make Previous Versions function:

1. Press Win+Break to bring up the System window.

2. From the left side of the window, choose System Protection.

3. Ensure that a check mark appears by the disk drive (or drives) listed in the Automatic Restore Points area.

4. Click OK, and close any other open windows.

See also System Restore.

The Previous Versions tool also monitors any backups you make, allowing you to recover an older version of a file that you've backed up. *See* Backup.

What to Do with It

The best thing to do with Previous Versions is to recover files that most likely wouldn't be recovered in previous versions of Windows. It's cinchy.

Peruse a previous version of a file

Before you restore a shadow file I recommend taking a peek to ensure that it's what you want. Obey me:

1. Display the file's Previous Versions list.

2. Select the shadow copy or backup to view.

3. Click the Open button.

   The shadow or backup copy opens in the program that created it, allowing you to view its contents.

4. Use the File⇨Save As command to recover the file, or just close the program window.

Restore a previous version of a file

To restore a shadow copy or file backup, do this:

1. Summon the file's Previous Versions list.

2. Select the copy you want to recover.

3. Click the Restore button.

4. Click the Restore button again to confirm, or use the Restore Files Wizard to recover the file from backup media.

It's also possible to restore a file by first trying to restore the folder containing the file. Simply locate the older edition of the folder, and then click the Open button to open that shadow copy. From there, you can drag or copy the file you want from the folder shadow copy.

Create a duplicate of a previous version

Restoring a shadow copy or backup replaces the file currently on disk, and it does so in a manner that cannot be undone. Often, a better choice than clicking the Restore button is to use the Copy button to create a duplicate of the older file version. Here's how:

1. Conjure up the Previous Versions list.

2. Select an older rendition of the file to recover.

3. Click the Copy button.

4. Select a destination folder or media in the Copy Items window.

   You can also, optionally, create a new folder.

5. Close the file's Properties dialog box.

Watch Your Step!

Working on a single file, updating it several times a day, creates only one shadow copy. This is because shadow copies are created by the System Restore program when it creates new restore points. So, if you want to create several restore points a day, Windows makes multiple shadow copies of a file. But note that configuring System Restore that way consumes a revolting amount of disk space. *See* System Restore.

 When you restore a previous version to the same folder as the current version, the current version is irrevocably erased; it cannot be recovered.

Using the Disk Cleanup tool to remove restore points also deletes shadow copies of files. *See* Disk Cleanup.

You cannot restore shadow copies of Windows files or folders. Just use System Restore to recover your computer when you're having operating system woes. *See* System Restore.

Having older editions of files available may constitute a security risk. To eliminate the shadow copies, use System Restore or Disk Cleanup to delete old restore points. Or, if you find the Previous Versions feature utterly offensive (security-wise), simply disable System Restore. *See* System Restore.

When Things Go Wrong

The Restore button isn't available when Windows cannot restore the selected file (for whatever reason). In that case, try to open or copy the file instead.

 The Previous Versions feature does not work when System Restore is disabled or when the restore points have been removed.

Gold Rush Nuggets

Another term for restoring a previous version of a file is to *downgrade*.

Digging Elsewhere

Backup, Files, Recycle Bin, System Restore

Printers

Next to the monitor, the printer is the main way to get information out of a computer. Yes, the printer is an *output device*. It's not as flashy as a monitor. For example, it's dreadfully slow to play games on the computer printer. But the printer does provide that all-important *hard copy*, or printed material that you can show others, verifying that you do more with your computer than play games or type cryptic messages to your friends on the Internet.

The printer is both a hardware and software thing in your computer world.

As a hardware thing, the printer sits on or near your computer desk, often elsewhere on the network, and its job is to spew out sheets of printed material. But for Windows, Printers refers to a special window.

To display the Printers window, open the Printers icon in the Control Panel; from the Control Panel Home, click the Printer link beneath the Hardware and Sound heading.

Printers icon

Your main printer has a check mark.

You can open the Printers folder from the Start button's menu, if there's a Printers command on the right side. If not, you can configure the Start button menu to add the command. *See* Start Button and Menu.

The Printers window lists various printing devices available to your computer. This includes local printers (or printers connected directly to your PC), network printers, virtual printers, and fax machines.

What to Do with It

The Printers window is not where you go to print stuff; it's where you go to control the printer. The only time printing control comes into play is when a printer screws up, and then you can do some troubleshooting in the Printers window, but that's about it.

Add a new printer

Attaching a printer to your computer in the 21st century is really cinchy. As long as it's a USB printer, just plug it in. Windows Vista should recognize it instantly and install software for the printer, and then you're done.

When Windows is too stubborn to recognize a printer you've just attached to your computer, first check the printer's documentation to see whether there's a CD or DVD to use and directions to follow. Otherwise, follow these general steps:

1. In the Printers window, click the Add a Printer toolbar button.

2. Choose Add a Local Printer.

3. Choose the printer port.

 Clue If you're using the PC's printer port, it's named LPT1 in the drop-down list.

4. Click the Next button.

5. Choose the printer's manufacturer.

6. Choose the printer's make and model.

7. If the printer came with a CD or DVD, click the Have Disk button and follow the directions there.

8. Click the Next button.

9. Type a name for the printer.

   Don't worry about the name now; you can always rename the printer icon just as you can rename any icon in Windows. *See* Rename.

10. Click the Next button.

11. To test the printer, click the Print a Test Page button.

    Ensure that the printer is turned on.

12. Click Finish.

The test page spews forth from the printer in a matter of moments.

Add a network printer

Network printers are a little more involved to add. Unlike in previous versions of Windows, a network printer doesn't automatically attach itself in Windows Vista unless it has a *signed driver,* or proof that the printer driver isn't a virus or other nasty program.

To add a network printer or a wireless printer, obey these vague steps:

1. Click the Add a Printer toolbar button in the Printers window.

2. Choose Add a Network Wireless or Bluetooth Printer.

3. If your network printer shows up in the list, click to select it. Skip down to Step 9.

4. Click the button that says The Computer I Want Isn't Listed.

5. Type the computer's network pathname if you know it (*see* Pathnames), or just skip to Step 6 when you don't know it. If the computer is found, skip down to Step 9.

6. Choose the option to type in a TCP/IP address or host name, if you have that information from the network server or gizmo that puts the printer on the network.

7. Click the Next button.

8. Enter the device type, host name or IP address, or port name according to the directions that came with the printer's networking interface.

9. Click the Next button.

10. (Optional) Click the Print a Test Page button.

   Ensure that the network printer is turned on and available before you try this.

11. Click Finish.

Test a printer

Although you can test print a printer when it's first installed, it's often necessary to test the printer later, to ensure that it's still connected and that no problem occurs between Windows and the printer. To test the printer, heed these directions:

1. Open the Printers window.

2. Right-click the printer's icon.

3. From the pop-up menu, choose the Properties command.

4. On the General tab in the printer's Properties dialog box, click the Print Test Page button.

5. Click OK.

Wait for the test page to print.

Set the main printer

Out of the hoard of potential printers you can make available to your PC, one is the main printer, the *default*. That's the printer that Windows chooses for you when you don't specifically choose a printer.

To set the main printer, do this:

1. Open the Printers window.

2. Select your main printer from the list.

3. Click the Set As Default toolbar button.

The main printer sports a green button with a white check mark on its icon.

 You can always choose another printer from any Print dialog box.

Remove a printer

Whether or not you've physically removed the printer, you can rid the Printers window of any printer icon by selecting the icon and pressing the Delete key on your keyboard. *See* Delete.

Open a printer's window or queue

Opening a printer icon in the Printers window displays that printer's queue, or a list of any documents waiting to be printed.

Files waiting to be printed appear in a *queue*. You can use the mouse to rearrange the order of any document that isn't currently printing. (Only the top one is printing.)

You can also click to select a document and then press the Delete key to cancel that document from printing. *See* Printing for more information.

To pause printing, choose Printer⇨Pause Printing. Resume printing by choosing Printer⇨Pause Printing again (to remove the check mark).

When the window is empty, no documents are waiting in the queue. This happens often for short documents or when the printer itself has lots of internal memory.

Watch Your Step!

A printer must be on for it to work and be detected by Windows. Furthermore, some printers must be *online* or *selected* before they can accept information from the computer.

Pausing and resuming printing may result in lost pages from your document.

When Things Go Wrong

Documents may not cancel or pause printing immediately. That's because each printer has internal memory and it takes a while for the document stored in that memory to *spool* out into the printer.

Gold Rush Nuggets

Back in the bad old days, computer users had to not only install their own printer hardware but also *write* the printer software. As an old-timer, I've written driver software for three different printers. It was fun, but not part of a happy, easy computer experience.

The printer that came with the NeXT computer (circa 1989) had a vocal interface with the computer. For example, when the printer was out of paper, a charming Englishwoman's voice said, "The printer is out of paper!"

Digging Elsewhere

Control Panel, Printing

Printing

The final result of your efforts, after that last edit, that last swipe of the mouse, that last save, i printing. It's the act of getting your information out of the computer and onto paper, where it ca exist in the real world and delight or horrify other people, depending on the document's purpose

WHERE'S THE GOLD?

Printing is found in all applications as well as in programs that offer up information for the printing task. The command dwells in the same place, on the File menu: File⇨Print.

In Internet Explorer, the Print command is found on the toolbar on the Print button menu.

The keyboard shortcut for the Print command is Ctrl+P.

Many programs feature a Print toolbar button, but, unlike the Print command or Ctrl+P, it immediately prints the document on the computer's main printer. The Print command and Ctrl+P summon the Print dialog box, where printing can be refined.

The Print dialog box is where you can customize the print job, choosing a specific printer, perhaps setting printer options, or choosing how many copies or which pages to print.

The Print dialog box sports standard features but may look different from program to program.

See Printers for information on the Printers window, as well as how to cancel a printing job.

What to Do with It

You use the Print command, and the Print dialog box, to print. It's all about printing!

Print your document

To print your document, or whatever you're creating in Windows, do this:

1. Ensure that the printer is on, stocked with paper and ink, and ready to print.

2. Choose File⇨Print, or press Ctrl+P.

3. Click the Print button in the Print dialog box.

When the program sports a Print toolbar button, simply click that button to print your document on the main printer.

Print a single page

To print a single page from your document you'll need to open the Print dialog box. Input the number of the page to print in the Pages text box. Click the Print button.

 If the program has a Print Preview command, use it to help determine which page it is you want printed.

A simpler way to print a single page is to move the cursor to the page you want to print, then open the Print dialog box and choose Current Page from the Page Range area. Click the Print button.

Print a range of pages

To print a range of pages in a document, specify the page-number range in the Pages text box. Use a hyphen to separate the beginning and ending pages: 3–8 for example, to print pages 3 through 8.

To print an odd lot of pages, use commas to separate the individual pages or ranges: 4,15,27 prints pages 4, 15, and 27; 2, 5-8, 10 prints pages 2, 5, 6, 7, 8, and 10.

Print a document twice (or thrice)

To produce multiple copies of a document, use the Number of Copies spinner. Either manually type the number of copies you want, or manipulate the spinner gizmo with the mouse to set the number of copies.

 The Collate option determines whether the document copies come out as complete sets of different documents or whether all the first pages print and then all the second pages, in which case you need to manually collate to assemble the documents later.

Choose another printer

You can print to any printer attached to your computer, even a printer on the network or a wireless printer. Just choose that printer from the Print dialog box's list o' printers.

Set page margins

Setting the margins on your document's page is generally done in a Page Setup dialog box, which you can conjure up by choosing File⇔Page Setup. The Print command is just for printing.

Print the screen

Windows lets you print what you see on the display. It's called a *screen dump* or "printing the screen." Believe it or not, the Print Screen (or PrtSc) button on your keyboard handles most of the task. Here's how:

1. Set up the display as you want.

2. Press the Print Screen key.

3. Open the Paint program, or any program into which you can paste graphics.

   See Copy, Cut, and Paste Data.

4. Press Ctrl+V to paste in the screen image.

From this point, you can manipulate the image, print it, save it to disk — whatever. The key to capturing the screen is the Print Screen key.

 Eureka Windows Vista also comes with a program called Snipping Tool. It's a better screen capture program and is more flexible than using the Print Screen key. From the Start button menu, choose All Programs⇔Accessories⇔Snipping Tool.

Print a window

The Print Screen key can be used to capture just a single window or dialog box: In the preceding section, press Alt+Print Screen in Step 2.

Watch Your Step!

Avoid the temptation to try to print something a second time when the first time doesn't work. Generally, that merely leads to printing two (or more) copies of the document, which isn't what you want. Sometimes, the best thing to do is just sit and wait.

When you don't choose a specific printer, Windows figures that you mean to use the main printer, which is chosen in the Printers window. *See* Printers.

Avoid using the Print Screen key to copy text. Print Screen is a graphics command. When you want to copy text from one window to another, select the text and press Ctrl+C on the keyboard. *See* Copy, Cut, and Paste Data.

When Things Go Wrong

Check to ensure that the printer is on, ready to print, stocked with paper, and supplied with ink. Ensure that the printer's cable is fully attached.

Open the Printers window and open the icon for the printer you're using. Check the queue to ensure that your document is there. Oftentimes, the queue lists the reasons why a document isn't printing.

See Printers for information on stopping a print job.

A discolored printout means that one of the printer's color ink cartridges is low. Change the cartridge.

Gold Rush Nuggets

It's been over 20 years since computers began using graphical operating systems. All that time, users have requested a Print command for a folder window, and we just cannot get Microsoft (or Apple!) to comply. How tough is it?

Digging Elsewhere

Fax, Open, Printers, Save

Problem Reports and Solutions

A treasure I've discovered in Windows Vista is a great diagnosis and error reporting tool, one that has the potential to deal with Windows woes and actually fix them, if a solution becomes available. The treasure probably has some official name, but I refer to it by its window title, Problem Reports and Solutions.

WHERE'S THE GOLD?

The Problem Reports and Solutions window can be summoned from the Control Panel: Open the Problem Reports and Solutions icon, or from the Control Panel Home, choose System and Maintenance and then Problem Reports and Solutions.

The Problem Reports and Solutions window offers you a list of current problems, suggestions, and solutions. Things to meet. Places to do. People to go.

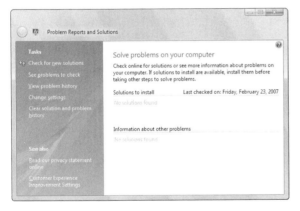

What to Do with It

The Problem Reports and Solutions window is a great place to start your Windows troubleshooting duties. Visit it whenever something weird happens. Well, weird as in "out-of-the-ordinary weird." Windows can get pretty weird.

Report problems and check for solutions

To see what's wrong and whether anything can be done, open the Problem Reports and Solutions window, and then choose the link on the left that reads Check for New Solutions.

Some problems may require information to be sent to Microsoft. If so, click the Send information button.

Review the solutions that are found (if any), and follow the directions on the screen.

See the problems that plague your PC

To review the full, massive list of problems, choose the link View Problem History on the left side of the Problem Reports and Solutions window. The list that's displayed tells you which programs have caused trouble, the problems they caused, when they were caused, and whether a report was sent to Microsoft.

To clear the list, click the link Clear Solution and Problem History.

Set problem reports to happen automatically

Windows should report problems and get solutions without your having to bother with the Problem Reports and Solutions window. To confirm that, or to change settings, click the Change Settings link, on the left side of the window.

Ensure that solutions are automatically checked. You can, optionally, click the Advanced Settings link to control specific aspects of the reports, such as forbidding some programs from triggering a new report.

Watch Your Step!

Obviously, this tool works best when you have an Internet connection.

When Things Go Wrong

By the very nature of the Problem Reports and Solutions window, things *have* gone wrong! The way to deal with it is to check with the Microsoft mothership to see whether a solution is handy. If so, Windows attempts to fix itself. If not, at least Microsoft is aware of the problem.

Some older Windows programs cause problems in Windows Vista. *See* Programs for information on running older programs in a special compatibility mode.

Gold Rush Nuggets

When you feel nerdy, summon the Run dialog box, type **wercon.exe**, and press Enter, and soon you'll see the Problem Reports and Solutions window. I'm guessing that WERCON stands for Windows Error Reporting Console.

Digging Elsewhere

Help, Safe Mode, System Restore

Programs

A *program* is merely a file, one that contains instructions that tell the computer to do something. The file is also configured so that the computer knows to *run,* or *launch,* the file, obeying the code it holds, as opposed to trying to open the file in some other program. In the world of computers, the general term *program* refers to any such file, also called an *executable file.* Sophisticated programs are dubbed *applications*, usually because they do something specific or in a specialized way. A collection of applications is often referred to as a *suite.* Maintenance programs are *utilities* or *tools.* Whatever the term, the thing is a program.

Where's the Gold?

Programs can dwell anywhere in the computer's long-term storage system. After all, programs are merely files and, as such, they can exist anywhere a file exists. In Windows, however, programs have a specific location.

In Windows, programs are primarily found on the first hard drive (drive C), in the Windows folder tree for system programs and in the Program Files folder for all other applications.

Programs are manipulated from the Programs and Features icon in the Control Panel. *See* Uninstall Programs.

What to Do with It

Programs are what your computer is all about. You didn't plunk down that hard-earned money just to sit and stare in awe of Windows itself. No! Using your computer is about using programs!

Install a new program

Program installation in Windows is cinchy. For commercial programs that come on a CD or DVD, insert the disc into the drive, and AutoPlay should immediately start and run the installation program. (*See* AutoPlay.) If not, open the Computer window, right-click the drive icon, and choose the Install or Run Program command.

Software downloaded from the Internet is installed by either running the program directly or removing the program from a compressed folder and then running the Install or Setup program. *See* Compressed Folders.

Uninstall a program

Programs must be properly removed, not merely deleted from the hard drive as you would delete an icon or folder. *See* Uninstall Programs for the details.

Start a program

Most programs are started from the All Programs menu, found on the Start button menu. *See* All Programs Menu.

Programs can also be started by creating a short-cut icon on the desktop. *See* Shortcuts.

Another place to start a program is the Quick Launch bar. *See* Quick Launch Bar.

Quit a program

When you're done using a program, you close its window to quit. (*See* Windows.) You can also choose the File⇨Exit command, if it's available.

Cajole an older program to work

Some ancient Windows programs may not work in Windows Vista. Before giving up on such programs, there are a few tricks worthy of attempting, to rouse an antique piece of software to life. Here's what to do:

1. Right-click the prehistoric program's icon to summon its Properties dialog box.

   You must click the original icon, not a shortcut. To locate the original icon from a shortcut icon, *see* Shortcuts, the section "Find the original file."

2. Click the Compatibility tab.

3. Click to place a check mark by the item Run This Program in Compatibility Mode For.

4. Choose the earlier version of Windows under which the program was designed to run.

5. (Optional) Choose a display option from the Settings area.

Most of those options can be ignored for recent programs; only very old programs may require such settings. My advice is to run the program first. If the color scheme looks goofy, try one of the display options to repair it.

6. Click the OK button.

7. Attempt to run the program.

Determine which programs are running

The simple way to see which programs are running is to peruse the Taskbar, which shows each running program as a button. (*See* Taskbar.)

You can also use the Task Manager to see a tidier list of running programs; unlike the Taskbar, the Task Manager lists each running program only once. *See* Task Manager.

Of course, many programs are running in the computer at once. The Taskbar and Task Manager list only those programs run by you, the computer operator. Windows itself runs a multitude of programs, tasks, services, and such.

Switch between programs

Windows lets you use several programs at once; you don't have to quit one program to start another. This ability is referred to as *multitasking*. *See* Multitasking.

Set automatic startup programs

Windows runs various programs when the computer first starts, most of which are internal programs, special services, or support programs for software or hardware on the PC. You can also set your own programs to run automatically at Startup. Here's how:

1. Find the program you want to start automatically whenever you log in to Windows.

   Search the All Programs menu for the program, or use a shortcut icon on the desktop.

 Eureka You can also choose a file or folder to automatically open when Windows starts: Find the file or folder icon by using the Windows Explorer program.

2. Right-click the program (or icon) and choose Copy from the pop-up menu.

3. Right-click the Start button and choose Open from the pop-up menu.

4. Open the Programs folder icon.

5. Open the Startup folder icon.

6. From the toolbar's Organize button's menu, choose the Paste command.

   You want to paste a copy of a program shortcut icon. But when you're pasting a file or folder, choose the Paste Shortcut command instead.

7. Close the Startup window.

Windows automatically runs or opens any icon found on the All Program's Startup menu.

To prevent a program from automatically starting, simply delete its icon from the Startup menu.

Specify which programs run when more than one program can do the job

Some things you do on your computer may trigger a war, an all-out battle over which program gets to do the job. Activities such as composing e-mail, checking a calendar, visiting the Web, playing music, or viewing images might fall under the control of two or more programs. To determine which program wins control, follow these steps:

1. Open the Control Panel's Default Programs icon.

   From the Control Panel Home, choose Programs and then Default Programs.

2. Click the Set Your Default Programs link.

   A list of programs appears.

3. Select a program from the list.

4. To make that program the *default*, or the program that Windows uses first, click the Set This Program As Default link.

   For example, when you need to send e-mail, you can choose one of the listed e-mail programs as the default. The same holds true for media programs, Internet programs, and others.

5. With the same program still highlighted, select Choose Defaults for This Program.

   The window changes to list a hoard of filename extensions associated with the selected program.

6. To ensure that the selected program always opens the listed file type, put a check mark by the filename extension.

   For example, if you want AIF audio files to open in QuickTime rather than in Windows Media Player, put a check mark by AIF, AIFF Format Sound.

7. Repeat Step 6 for all file types you want to associate with the program.

8. Click the Save button.

9. Click OK when you're done with the Set Default Programs window, and (optional) close the Control Panel window.

Use Windows Defender Software Explorer

The Windows Defender program also lists all programs running in the computer, as well as startup programs. Windows Defender is designed to protect your computer from attack by bad programs, so the list of startup and running programs is presented to help you better control what's going on inside Mr. PC.

To view the Windows Defender Software Explorer, follow these steps:

1. Open the Control Panel's Windows Defender icon.

   From the Control Panel Home, choose the link, beneath Programs, labeled Change Startup Programs; skip to Step 5.

2. Click Tools.

3. Choose Software Explorer.

4. Choose Startup Programs from the Category Button list.

5. Select a program from the list to view information about that program.

   To stop the program, click the Disable button; to remove the program from the Startup program list, click Remove.

6. Choose Currently Running Programs from the Category button list.

   Naughty programs can be halted by selecting them and clicking the End Process button.

7. Close the Windows Defender window as well as the Control Panel window.

Watch Your Step!

Avoid the temptation to randomly roam the computer's hard drive looking for files to run. Honestly, if you don't know what an icon represents, you really shouldn't be opening it or trying to access its guts.

Quitting a program without saving a file one last time results in a warning dialog box displayed. Your options are Save, to open a Save As dialog box or use the Save command to save the file and then quit; Don't Save, which quits the program without saving the document; and Cancel, which returns you to the program (does not quit).

 Eureka Some older Windows programs don't run under Windows Vista. These include games, older DOS programs, and disk utilities.

Avoid stopping any program or process unless you have a good reason to. *See* Task Manager.

When Things Go Wrong

Some older programs will not install on Windows Vista no matter how hard you try.

Some programs in the Windows folder, as well as support programs found in the Program Files folders, are meant to be run at the command prompt. As such, double-clicking their icons to run them in Windows appears to have no effect, but indeed the program may have run. Again, my advice is not to mess around with running unknown programs.

Don't be surprised when you don't find all the automatic startup programs in the All Program's Startup folder. Remember that there's a second Startup folder, one that is shared by all users. To edit it, right-click the Start button and choose Open All Users, and then proceed with the steps described earlier in this chapter.

Gold Rush Nuggets

Program files in Windows sport the EXE filename extension, where EXE stands for *executable*. The program's icon, however, varies with the program.

Some executables may end in DLL, although these are mostly operating system support files and not programs you would run directly. DLL stands for Dynamic Link Library, if that helps.

Older Windows programs used the COM and PIF extensions. The BAT extension identifies command-line batch files. VBS is used for Visual Basic scripts.

Digging Elsewhere

All Programs Menu, Shortcuts, Uninstall Programs, Windows

Public Folder

The Public folder is the place on your computer where you put files you want to share with other folks, either people with another account on your computer or humans on the computer network. The Public folder is geared to work easily and work best with such sharing.

WHERE'S THE GOLD?

The Public folder is part of the Public account in Windows Vista, which is an account just like your personal account. Essentially, the Public folder is the User Account folder for the Public account.

Public Folder
icon

The Public folder can be found in the folder tree in the Windows Explorer window, and also in expanded Save As and Open dialog boxes. (*See* Open and Save.)

From the Address bar, the Public folder is found as a menu item on the rightmost triangle's menu. *See* Address Bar.

Displaying the desktop in the Windows Explorer window shows the Public folder (although the Public folder may not appear on the actual desktop).

Physically, the Public folder is located in the main Users folder, usually on hard drive C. To get there from your User Account folder window, press Alt+↑, and then open the Public Folder icon.

Within the Public folder, you find a series of sub-folders, each with the Public prefix:

- ✗ Public Documents
- ✗ Public Downloads
- ✗ Public Music
- ✗ Public Pictures
- ✗ Public Videos

These are preset folders, just like the ones in your account. The theme, as with your personal folders, is *organization*.

What to Do with It

The Public folder is where you place files and folders you want shared with anyone. It's definitely not for your private stuff.

Work with files in the Public folder

Files can be placed in the Public folder by using the Copy or Cut commands and then pasting the file into the Public folder. *See* Copy, Cut, and Paste Files.

You can also create your own custom folders in the Public folder, folders that everyone can share, such as common project folders or subfolders within the Public folders already there.

Share the Public folder

The Public folder is automatically available for reading, writing, and modifying to all users on the same computer. *See* Share Stuff on the Network for information on making the Public folder available to all computers on the network.

Restrict Public folder access

It's possible to limit who on your computer has access to the Public folder. *See* Access Control for the details.

Watch Your Step!

I recommend against saving any files directly to the Public folder. Instead, place only *copies* there. That's because other users on your computer, and perhaps on the network, have full access to the Public folder and can delete or modify those files without your permission.

When Things Go Wrong

When you cannot access the Public folder, it most likely means that your account is *not* protected by a password. Only password-protected accounts can access the Public folder. *See* Passwords for details.

Gold Rush Nuggets

The Public folder replaces the old Shared Documents folder in Windows XP.

Digging Elsewhere

Share Stuff on the Network, Windows Explorer

Quick Launch Bar

I'd like a turkey-and-provolone sandwich and a bag of chips, and do you have Coke or Pepsi? What? Wrong bar? Oh! I see. Quick *Launch* bar. And I was hungry! Oh, well.

In Windows, the Quick Launch bar is one of the Taskbar's optional toolbars. The bar's purpose is to store a handful of icons that let you quickly start, or *launch,* some popular programs, utilities, or Windows features.

WHERE'S THE GOLD?

The Quick Launch bar dwells on the Taskbar, traditionally just to the right of the Start button, although it can be positioned anywhere on the Taskbar. (*See* Toolbars.)

As with most things in Windows, the Quick Launch bar is merely a representation of something else going on somewhere else. In this case, the Quick Launch bar merely contains shortcuts to various programs or Windows features.

The Quick Launch bar's shortcuts are located in the hidden Quick Launch folder, buried in your User Profile folder tree. To see the location, right-click the Quick Launch bar and choose Open Folder from the pop-up menu that appears. Of course, it's easier to mess with the Quick Launch bar directly than to waste time in its secret folder.

What to Do with It

The Quick Launch bar exists to help you quickly start some of your favorite programs or to access Windows features such as the Run dialog box, the Switch Between Windows command, or the desktop.

Display or hide the Quick Launch bar

To ensure that the Quick Launch bar is visible, follow these steps:

1. Right-click the Taskbar.

2. Choose Toolbars⇨Quick Launch.

To hide the Quick Launch bar, repeat these steps, which removes the check mark next to the Quick Launch option on the Toolbars submenu.

Add an icon to the Quick Launch bar

Icons are added to the Quick Launch bar in a number of ways. First, before adding an icon, note that the Quick Launch bar uses shortcut icons. Don't place full programs or file icons directly on the Quick Launch bar.

The easiest way to place an icon on the Quick Launch bar is to drag and drop it: Drag the icon to the Quick Launch bar with the mouse.

To place an icon from the All Programs menu on the Quick Launch bar, right-click the icon and choose Add to Quick Launch from the pop-up menu that appears. (*See* All Programs Menu.)

Remove an icon from the Quick Launch bar

To rid the Quick Launch bar of an icon, simply drag that icon off the Quick Launch bar and onto the desktop. Of course, that process merely shifts the icon's location. To remove the icon, right-click it and choose the Delete command from the pop-up menu that appears.

Change the icon size

Quick Launch bar icons can appear tiny or large. I prefer large icons, which are easier to see, but when the Quick Launch bar becomes burdened with icons, smaller icons are better.

To set the icon size for the Quick Launch bar, right-click the Quick Launch bar. Choose View⇨Large Icons to see big icons or View⇨Small Icons for smaller icons.

Watch Your Step!

Avoid putting too many icons on the Quick Launch bar. As an alternative, consider merely creating shortcuts on the desktop rather than on the Quick Launch bar.

When Things Go Wrong

When the Quick Launch bar sports more icons than it is wide, a button appears at its right end. Clicking the button displays the rest of the Quick Launch bar's icons. Consider resizing the Quick Launch bar to fix this problem; *see* Toolbars.

Clue Right-clicking the Quick Launch bar is an art. To confirm that you got it right, the pop-up menu should feature the View command on top.

Gold Rush Nuggets

The Quick Launch bar is a feature of Internet Explorer (IE), not of Windows. It was introduced with IE version 4. Note that you can still use the Quick Launch bar, even if IE isn't your main Web browser.

Digging Elsewhere

Programs, Taskbar, Toolbars

Read Only

Read only books; use newspapers to line your bird cage. But that's not exactly what *read only* implies when it comes to computers.

The term *read only* applies to computer storage, either computer memory (RAM) or disk storage. The normal mode of operation for storage is read/write, meaning that information (data) can be read from the storage device and written to the storage device. When information is flagged as read only, it means that it can only be read; the storage device cannot be written to, and the information cannot be erased or modified. It can only be read; hence, read only.

WHERE'S THE GOLD?

There are three types of read only. The first regards read-only memory, or ROM, which is used on the PC's motherboard for storing long-term, unchanging information (although many PCs now use flash memory rather than ROM). You cannot change ROM.

You can mess around with two types of read only. The first type applies to media, such as a CD-ROM or a write-protected disk. This status isn't really buried anywhere, but it's apparent when you examine the media in the Computer window.

Read-only media always shows zero bytes free. For example, a CD or DVD shown in Tile view displays zero bytes free below the disc icon.

Otherwise, the Details pane must be visible when the media is highlighted to view the space-free value.

Read only exists more commonly as a file attribute, a weak form of protection to apply to a file or folder to prevent its accidental modification. The attribute can be found at the bottom of the file's Properties dialog box, on the General tab.

Read-only protection is weak because it's easy to disable read-only status for a file, and that read-only protection does not prevent the file from being accidentally deleted.

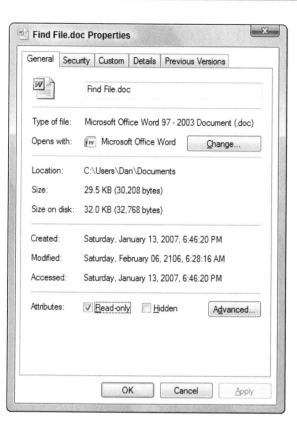

read-only status removed when they're pasted to a hard drive or other, non-read-only media. But you can still mess with read-only files and certain older disks.

Add or remove read-only file permissions

Setting or resetting the read-only attribute on a file is cinchy:

1. Right-click the file's icon.

2. Choose Properties from the pop-up menu.

3. On the General tab, click to remove or add the check mark by Read-Only.

4. Click OK.

A check mark by Read-Only indicates that the read-only attribute (and protection) is on. No check mark means that the file can be freely modified.

Write-protect a disk

One feature of older, removable disks was that they could be write-protected, essentially enabling the entire disk to be read only. This prevented the disk from being accidentally reformatted (erased) and the files on the disk from being modified.

What to Do with It

Fortunately, the issue of read only doesn't pop up that often in Windows Vista, not as often as in earlier versions of Windows. For example, files copied from a CD or DVD now have their former

Floppy disks were write-protected by sliding a tiny tile on the disk's corner. When the tile exposed a hole through the disk's case, the disk was write-protected. A similar sliding-tile technique was also used on removable magneto-optical disks.

Watch Your Step!

Read-only files and folders can be copied, moved, renamed, or deleted. When you're copying, moving, or renaming, the read-only attribute is retained.

No warning is given when you open a read-only file and attempt to edit it. The only time you know that something is up is when you use the Save command; Windows refuses to save over the original, read-only protected file. A warning dialog box alerts you to this problem.

You cannot modify a file's read-only status while that file is stored on a CD or DVD. Copy the file to the hard drive or some other media, and then you can work on the file.

When Things Go Wrong

Remember that read-only protection does not prevent a file from being renamed, moved, or deleted. If you cannot find your read-only file, use the Windows Search command to locate it. *See* Search.

Gold Rush Nuggets

Read-only status offers more protection at the command prompt. A read-only file cannot be deleted or overwritten when using the command prompt.

Digging Elsewhere

Discs (CDs and DVDs), Encryption, File Compression, Hidden Files and Folders

Recycle Bin

Windows isn't harsh when it comes to deleting files and folders. Rather than rub out a file, sending it to the bottom of the proverbial bit sea, Windows puts the deleted file on ice. More specifically, the deceased file goes into a digital limbo known as the Recycle Bin. There it lingers, waiting for potential revivification or eventual death, depending on how fervent you are about deleting files and on how full the hard drive is becoming.

The Recycle Bin is often found as an icon on the desktop, although that's not a guarantee. (*See* Desktop Icons.)

When the Recycle Bin icon cannot be found on the desktop, use any Windows Explorer window to find it. The Recycle Bin can be located in the folder tree part of the Navigation pane (in the lower left part of the window), or, from the Address bar, you can click the leftmost triangle and choose Recycle Bin from the drop-down menu.

Opening the Recycle Bin displays your dearly departed folders and files just as though they were alive and well and living in any folder on your computer system.

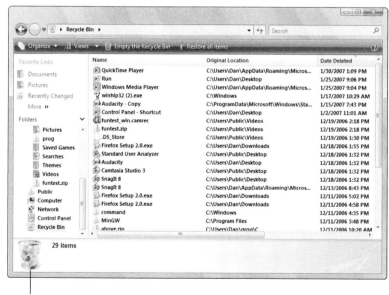

Recycle Bin icon

Clue I prefer to view the Recycle Bin's contents in Details view; choose Details from the toolbar's Views button menu. One advantage here is that you can quickly sort the files by clicking a column heading, such as clicking the Date Deleted heading to sort the deleted files by the date that they passed away.

What to Do with It

The Recycle Bin is so handy that you'll wish you had a similar device for real life. Imagine a gizmo that can reconstruct things you tossed out, making them good as new again. That would be something!

Restore a file or folder (undelete)

To restore a file you previously deleted, heed these steps:

1. Open the Recycle Bin.

2. Select the file or folder.

3. Click the Restore This Item button on the toolbar.

Clue The restored item is placed back into its original folder location. See "Preview where files will be restored," later in this entry.

Restore a file to another folder

Normally Windows places a restored file from the Recycle Bin back in the exact location (disk drive and folder) from which that file was removed. But you can override that decision by following these steps:

1. Open the Recycle Bin.

2. Right-click the file (or folder) to restore.

3. Choose Cut from the pop-up menu.

4. Open the folder window, the location where you want to restore the file.

5. From the toolbar's Organize button's menu, choose Paste.

You can also substitute Ctrl+X for the Cut command in Step 4, and Ctrl+V for the Paste command in Step 5.

Preview where files will be restored

There are two ways to see where a file will be restored when it leaves the Recycle Bin.

The first location is the Recycle Bin window's Details pane. The folder location for any selected file shows up in the Details pane. That works in any view.

In Details view, you can use the Original Location column. If that column isn't visible, follow these steps:

1. Ensure that Details view is used to display the Recycle Bin's contents.

If Details view isn't already selected, choose Details from the toolbar's Views button.

2. Right-click any column heading in the list of deleted files.

3. Choose Original Location from the pop-up menu.

You can change the Details view column order by dragging a column heading left or right.

To make a column wider, double-click the mouse on the line that separates each column.

Restore everything

To restore the entire Recycle Bin and put all the deleted files back to their original locations, click the Restore All Items button on the Recycle Bin's toolbar.

Empty the Recycle Bin

The toolbar button named Empty the Recycle Bin does just that: purges the Recycle Bin of all its files, eliminating the opportunity for you to recover anything.

Manual purges can be done as well. What I typically do is arrange the Recycle Bin's files by date and then remove the oldest files from the list. You can also sort the files by size and remove some of the larger ones, which helps keep the smaller files around longer.

Display the Recycle Bin's Properties dialog box

The Recycle Bin Properties dialog box provides access to all the gizmos and gadgets you need to control the Recycle Bin's operations and duties.

To display the Recycle Bin Properties dialog box, open the Recycle Bin window and choose Properties from the toolbar's Organize button's menu.

You can also view the Recycle Bin Properties dialog box by right-clicking the desktop's Recycle Bin icon and choosing Properties from the pop-up menu.

Set the Recycle Bin capacity

The Recycle Bin occupies but a small sliver of hard drive space, generally about 10 percent of the overall drive capacity. This value can be changed for all drives or individually set for each hard drive. Do this:

1. Display the Recycle Bin Properties dialog box.

2. Choose Custom Size.

3. Enter a new value for Maximum Size (MB).

4. Click OK.

When multiple drives are present, you can configure each drive's storage values independently.

Clue   I recommend a setting between 5 and 10 percent of the hard drive's overall capacity for the Recycle Bin's size. *See* Disk Space for more information on retrieving a hard drive's overall capacity value.

Watch Your Step!

The Recycle Bin cannot recover a previous version of a file you recently saved. To do that, you need to use the Previous Versions command. *See* Previous Versions.

Windows automatically purges files from the Recycle Bin as needed. Purging is done to older files first, but only when the Recycle Bin becomes full or exceeds the capacity you set for it. (See the

section "Set the Recycle Bin capacity.") In many cases, when there's enough room, files can stay in the Recycle Bin for a long time.

Files in the Recycle Bin cannot be opened or previewed. Restore the file and then open it.

The Recycle Bin is often purged when freeing up disk space. *See* Disk Cleanup.

Deleted e-mail messages *do not* go to the Recycle Bin. It's up to your e-mail program to manage deleted messages. Some programs sport a trash or Recycle Bin–like feature for recovering deleted messages.

When Things Go Wrong

The toolbar buttons in the Recycle Bin window change depending on what is selected. For example, you find the Restore All Items button only when nothing is selected in the window. When one icon is selected, the button is renamed Restore This Item. When several items are selected, the button is renamed Restore The Selected Items.

Older files have a slim chance of being recovered because of the way the Recycle Bin operates. When you cannot find the file to restore, it's done gone for good.

Some third-party disk utilities may be able to recover files that the Recycle Bin has long forgotten.

Uninstalled programs are not stored in the Recycle Bin. To reinstall the program, use the original CDs or downloaded archive. *See* Uninstall Programs.

Gold Rush Nuggets

The Recycle Bin first appeared in Windows 95. Before then, deleted files could not be recovered unless a special program (utility) was used.

Files are stored in the Recycle Bin in a compressed state and therefore occupy less disk space.

The Recycle Bin itself exists as a hidden system folder in the root directory of each hard drive.

Digging Elsewhere

Delete, Previous Versions, Uninstall Programs

Refresh

I suppose that some people avoid the Refresh command because they don't understand it. That's sad. The Refresh command is quite useful, especially when dealing with removable disks, as well as folders or Web pages where the content can change even as you're viewing it. By using the Refresh command, you're assured that what you're looking at is updated and fresh.

WHERE'S THE GOLD?

As a button, the Refresh command lingers on the right end of the Address bar, in either Windows Explorer or Internet Explorer. This makes sense because what's being refreshed is whatever item is referenced by the Address bar.

Refresh   "Busy" icon
button

On the keyboard are two choices for refreshing what you see: the Ctrl+R keyboard shortcut or the F5 key. Why F5? Who knows?

What to Do with It

There are a few instances where Refresh is entirely useful, nay, necessary:

Update a networked folder

When a folder is shared on a network, there's a possibility that others on the network may be modifying files. To get the most recent picture of the folder's contents, use the Refresh command.

View files on a removable disk

When you remove the disk, you should close the window displaying the disk's files. But you can be sneaky by keeping the window open and waiting for the disk to be replaced. After it's replaced, use the Refresh command to update the disk's contents in the window.

Update what's shown on a Web page

News and other up-to-date Web pages change their contents often. To view the most recent copy of a Web page, use the Refresh command. In a way, refreshing a Web page is like reloading it from scratch, but without having to retype the Web page's address.

You can also use the Refresh command when a Web page refuses to load or is unavailable. Often, merely refreshing is necessary to make the Web page visible.

When a Web page is refreshing itself, a "busy" icon appears next to the page address in the Address bar, or by the page name on a tab when the Internet Explorer tabbed browsing feature is enabled.

Update a device in the Sync Center

When you don't see an attached device in the Sync Center program, click the Refresh button to force an update.

Watch Your Step!

Refreshing the content of a removable disk when the disk isn't in the drive leads to obvious and predictable trouble. This is why I recommend properly removing disks and other media — as opposed to simply removing a disk manually from your computer system.

Windows Vista is smart enough to recognize when you manually remove a disk or other media; Windows Explorer closes that disk's window.

When Things Go Wrong

Refresh works, although the results may not be visible on the screen. When nothing changes, assume that nothing has changed, not that Refresh is broken.

When you're certain that Refresh isn't giving you the most current version of a Web page, empty the Web cache and try again. *See* Web Page Cache.

When Refresh refuses to update a network drive, disconnect from the network, and then reconnect to view the updated drive.

Gold Rush Nuggets

Different Web browsers use different Refresh command buttons, although generally speaking, the Ctrl+R keyboard shortcut seems to be common.

Some Web pages contain an automatic refresh, where the page is automatically refreshed on the screen after a given duration.

Web pages can also sport a *meta refresh*, which causes the browser to be redirected to another Web page.

Refresh may also refer to the rate at which the image is updated on a computer monitor. The refresh rate is measured in Htz, or cycles per second. The higher the refresh rate, the less a monitor flickers.

Digging Elsewhere

Address Bar, Windows

Registry Editor

Windows assaults your eyeballs with an assortment of dialog boxes, controls, windows, options, buttons, and gizmos that help you control and manage your computer. Pretty much everything you need to do can be done in some obvious, logical way (although that point is debatable). Internally, Windows stores all those settings, all that configuration information, in a single place. That place is the Registry. To view or to mess with the Registry, you use a tool called the Registry Editor.

WHERE'S THE GOLD?

The Registry has two parts. One is internal, stored in memory and updated as the computer runs. Another part is stored on disk, loaded into memory when Windows starts. Together, both parts form the Registry.

Start the Registry Editor by summoning the Run dialog box (Win+R) and typing **regedit**. Press Enter to see the Registry Editor window.

The Registry Editor presents information in one of those hierarchical tree-structure things: Click the white triangle by a folder to open a folder or branch; click the black triangle to close a branch. Information contained in a folder, if anything, appears on the right side of the window.

Each item in a folder is a *key*.

Keys that contain values (numbers) have a blue icon.

Keys that contain text have a red icon.

Keys are edited by double-clicking to open the key and then typing in new information. The stuff you type depends on the key being edited.

Key with text

Name	Type	Data
(Default)	REG_SZ	(value not set)
PublisherPolicyChangeTime	REG_QWORD	0x1c771bb28ca373a (12819616306051;
StoreArchitecture	REG_BINARY	00 00 00 00
StoreFormatVersion	REG_BINARY	30 00 2e 00 30 00 2e 00 30 00 2e 00 35

Key with values

The Registry is divided into five root keys, each of which contains *subkeys*. Here's how things are organized:

HKEY_CLASSES_ROOT: This key contains file association and data sharing information. It's a copy of information that exists elsewhere in the Registry.

HKEY_CURRENT_USER: This key contains information specific to the user currently logged in to Windows, including personal settings and other account information. It's a copy of the user's information held in the next key.

HKEY_LOCAL_MACHINE: This key contains information about the PC's hardware as well as information about Windows.

HKEY_USERS: This key contains personal information and settings for all users who have accounts on the computer.

HKEY_CURRENT_CONFIG: The information in this key is copied from the HKEY_LOCAL_MACHINE key regarding the PC's configuration when it started.

What to Do with It

The only time you should venture into the Registry Editor is when directed to do so by someone else, such as when following directions on a Web site, from technical support, or in a book.

Explore the Registry

Oftentimes, you're told where to go in the Registry. You're given a pathname, similar to the pathname for a file. The pathname is your road map for locating specific information.

For example, any programs Windows starts up when the computer starts are listed in this key:

```
HKEY_LOCAL_MACHINE\SOFTWARE\
MICROSOFT\WINDOWS\CURRENTVERSION\RUN
```

To display that key, open each folder as you read from left to right, using the backslash character (\) as a separator:

```
HKEY_LOCAL_MACHINE
Software
Microsoft
Windows
CurrentVersion
Run
```

When you finally open, or select, the last folder, Run, you see a list of any programs that Windows runs when it first starts the computer.

 You can adjust the width of the left part of the Registry window by pointing the mouse at the dividing bar between the left and right parts of the window. Drag the mouse to the right to make the left part wider.

Search the Registry

When you don't know where something is, the easiest way to find it is to use the *power of the computer* to help you locate the missing info tidbit. The Registry Editor has such as tool. Here's how to use it:

1. Open the Registry Editor.

2. Click to ensure that the top value, Computer, is chosen from the left side of the window.

   You want your search to start there.

3. Press Ctrl+F to summon the Find dialog box.

4. Type the text to look for.

For example, type your name (or just your last name).

5. When you know in which part of the Registry database the information is found, put a check mark by that item in the Look At area. Otherwise, keep all items checked.

6. Click the Find Next button.

The Registry is a massive database, so it takes a while for the search to work. (It's also not indexed, as is the Search command when you look for files.)

When the result is displayed, you can do what you will with the information: edit it, delete it, whatever. But make sure you know what you're doing before you just randomly change things.

 Eureka   To search again for the same tidbit o' text, press the F3 key.

Change a key

To change a key value, double-click the tiny key icon, either the red "ab" for text information or the blue 0101 thing for a value. Type the new value into the dialog box that appears. Click the OK button to save your changes.

Add a key

When you're instructed to add a key, do this:

1. Find the proper folder for the key on the left side of the window.

2. Click to ensure that the folder is selected.

3. Choose Edit⇨New, and then from the New submenu, choose the type of key you were directed to create.

4. Type a name for the key, and then press Enter.

5. Double-click to open the key.

6. Type the key's value.

7. Click OK to set the value and finish creating the key.

Delete a key

To remove a key, simply select it and press the Delete key on the keyboard. Answer Yes in the confirmation dialog box.

Back up and restore the Registry

Some technical instructions may recommend that you back up the Registry before you start messing around. I concur. Do this:

1. Open the Registry Editor.

2. On the left side of the window, choose the top item, Computer.

The directions work to back up whichever part of the Registry you choose. To back up the whole Registry, you must choose Computer.

3. Chose File⇨Export.

4. Use the Export Registry File dialog box to find a location for the Registry data file.

The dialog box works just like the Save As dialog box.

5. Give the Registry backup a filename.

6. Click the Save button.

The Registry is a *huge* database. The whole thing weighs 106MB on my hard drive. Be careful where you back the sucker up.

To restore a Registry backup, do this:

1. Open the Registry Editor.

2. Choose File⇨Import.

3. Use the Import Registry File dialog box to find your Registry backup.

4. Click the Open button to restore the Registry.

The Registry backup is read in from disk and restored.

Watch Your Step!

Changes to the Registry affect the entire computer system. Honestly, if you can make the change without going into the Registry, use that other way first.

You cannot restore the Registry when portions of it are being used. Be sure to close all open programs and try again. If that doesn't work, attempt to restore the Registry in Safe mode. If that doesn't work, use System Restore.

When Things Go Wrong

System Restore should fix any Registry boo-boos you happen to make. *See* System Restore.

Gold Rush Nuggets

So many people, would-be computer geeks, desire the Registry Editor to be more than what it is. They fantasize that the Registry Editor is full of hidden secrets (including that Run Faster option) and settings that will make them all-powerful users. The truth is not so inspiring: The Registry Editor is a dull place. Pray that you don't have to go there often.

Before the Registry existed, Windows was controlled by editing text files. These text files ended in INI, such as `WIN.INI` or `SYSTEM.INI`, and therefore they were often called "innie" files. The problem with INI files was that they quickly grew complex and cumbersome. Because there were no solid rules regarding INI file contents, things quickly became disorganized. Yet, because INI files might still be used by some programs, there exist INI files in the Windows folder on your computer's hard drive.

Digging Elsewhere

Device Manager, System Information, System Restore

Remote Desktop Connection

Have you ever wanted to use your main computer from a remote location? Say, to access your office computer while you're out on the road with a laptop? Me neither, but despite the incredibly loud silence on the issue, Microsoft has built into Windows something called the Remote Desktop Connection. You use it to access one Windows Vista computer from another, and it allows you to use that remote computer just as though you were sitting there at the console, even though you may be zillions of miles away.

The Remote Desktop Connection causes me to raise an eyebrow, primarily for security systems. Allowing your computer to be accessed remotely over the Internet is like leaving for a vacation with all your home's windows and doors wide open and a sign out front saying Free Stuff. But, theoretically, the Remote Desktop Connection has some security precautions built in. At least, I hope so, because I've tried the thing out and — to my knowledge — no one used my home computer except me and my laptop from a coffee shop two miles down the road.

The Remote Desktop Connection is started from the Start button menu. Choose All Programs⇨ Accessories⇨Remote Desktop Connection. No, you don't have to do anything else; Windows comes with all the security items to allow Remote Desktop Connection to open full throttle, although it does take administrator access to get things going.

To make the connection, you need the IP address or domain name (Internet pathname) to the computer you want to access. You must have an account on that computer, complete with a password, for the thing to work.

Most important, you're probably wondering how to disable the thing. That's cinchy: Open the Control Panel's System window. From the links on the left side of the window, choose Remote Settings. You should see the System Properties dialog box with the Remote tab forward. Remove the check mark by the option Allow Remote Assistance Connections to This Computer. (Even though it's not part of Remote Desktop, it's a good thing to disable.) Then choose Don't Allow Connections to the Computer. Click OK. There. You're safe.

By the way, I use a remote access program for my laptop when I really need to use the desktop remotely. The name of the program I use is RealVNC, and I discuss using that program in my book *Laptops For Dummies,* Second Edition (Wiley Publishing, Inc.).

Rename

Files are named at birth, just like humans. Rather than have two excited parents and an oogling baby, files are named by a semi-befuddled computer operator and a Save As dialog box. The reason the Rename command exists is that, just like those excited parents, not every computer operator is blessed with a rational mind when faced with the opportunity to name something.

You can use the Rename command to apply a new name to just about any icon in Windows, including icons for disk drives, printers, network thingies, and other stuff.

The Rename command itself is handy from the keyboard: the F2 key. I use (and remember) that key command because I use the keyboard to type the new name anyway. So, it makes sense. But you can also find the Rename command on the Windows Explorer toolbar, on the Organize button's menu. You can also right-click an icon and choose Rename from the pop-up menu.

What to Do with It

I suppose the icons I rename the most are those pictures that come from my digital camera. The camera dubs the images with some weird date-time code name. After copying the image to the hard drive, I use the Rename command to give the image a more descriptive name, especially those images I plan on e-mailing or using elsewhere — say, in the Christmas letter.

Rename a file or folder

To rename a file or folder, follow these steps:

1. Click to select the file or folder.

2. Press the F2 key.

3. Type the new name.

   If the filename extension is showing, do not change it!

4. Press the Enter key to lock in the new name.

 Eureka

After you press the F2 key, the filename becomes selected. You can use Windows text-editing commands to edit the name at that point or simply retype a new name.

Rename a group of files

Windows lets you rename a group of files, but the files are not renamed individually. Instead, each file is given the same name plus a numbered suffix. Here's how it works:

1. Select the group of files to rename.

   See Select Files.

2. Press the F2 key.

The first file in the list is selected for renaming.

3. Type a name for the group, like a first name or common name.

4. Press Enter to lock in the name.

Each selected file is given the name you typed (Step 3), but also a numeric suffix in parentheses. For example, if the first file is renamed Text File, the next three files selected are named:

Text File(2)

Text File(3)

Rename a disk drive

Disk drives can be given names, although officially it's not a name — it's a *label*, and it has absolutely no effect on anything other than your eyeballs. Here's how to rename a disk drive:

1. Open the Computer window.

2. Click to select a hard drive, removable drive, or network drive.

3. Press F2 to rename the drive.

Windows "bonks" at you when the drive cannot be renamed.

4. Type the drive's new name.

5. Press the Enter key to lock in the name.

Rename a printer

One of the more esoteric things you can rename is a printer. I can see the reason: The name Color Laser Jean's Office might make more sense than HP4550N. Here's how to rename a printer:

1. Open the Printers window.

From the Control Panel, open the Printers icon; from the Control Panel Home, choose Printer beneath the Hardware and Sound heading.

2. Right-click the printer you want to rename.

3. Choose the Rename command from the pop-up menu.

4. Type a new name for the printer.

5. Press the Enter key to lock in the name.

Watch Your Step!

Do not rename any file or folder that you didn't create yourself. Never rename any file or folder outside of your User Profile Folder, and avoid renaming those folders Windows pre-created for you in the User Profile folder (Documents or Pictures, for example).

Windows coughs and sputters when you attempt to rename a file using one of the following characters:

" * / : ? \ | < >

A filename can be no longer than 260 characters, but that 260-character limit is applied to the full pathname in addition to the filename. (*See* Pathnames.) My advice is to keep filenames short and descriptive.

You cannot rename a file when another file of the same name exists in the same folder. (The files can be of different types, but two files of the same type cannot have the same name.)

When Windows is configured to show filename extensions (*see* Files), the Rename command can be used to change the extension, although this is not a good thing. Try not to change the filename extension.

When Things Go Wrong

Chances are that the rename operation failed because you used a forbidden letter in the new filename or that the name is already used by a file on disk. If so, try again with another name.

Pressing Ctrl+Z, the Undo command's keyboard shortcut, undoes renaming boo-boos.

Gold Rush Nuggets

Windows was once a minion of the DOS operating system. Under DOS, a file could have only eight characters in its name, followed by a period and up to three characters for the filename extension.

Digging Elsewhere

Files, Icons, Save, Select Files

RSS

A lot of Web pages are updated on a regular basis. To assist you in finding new information on Web sites that you visit regularly, the RSS feed was developed. *RSS,* which stands for Really Simple Syndication, is a way to alert you to new information on a Web page so that you don't have to surf from page to page to see what has changed. Instead, you can get all your updates and read new information as it comes in.

RSS is a Web browser feature. Although you can find separate RSS reader programs available, the ability to read and organize RSS feeds is included with Internet Explorer (IE), starting with version 7, the version originally shipped with Windows Vista.

To find an RSS feed, look for the XML icon on a Web site. RSS feeds can be found on any Web site, typically one that has updated or changing content. The most common Web sites are *blogs,* or We*b logs,* which are public diaries or forums you can visit for news or gossip or to pound your online enemies into the digital dirt.

When you find the actual RSS feed itself, locate the Subscribe to This Feed button or click the Subscribe to This Feed button on the toolbar. A dialog box appears, similar to the one that appears when you add a site to your Favorites list (*see* Favorites). Type a name for the RSS feed, site, or blog; optionally, organize it in the Feeds list (again, similar to Favorites); then click the Subscribe button.

To review feeds you've subscribed to, click the star button on the toolbar, and then click the Feeds button; or, you can press Alt+C and then Ctrl+J. The feeds area lists RSS feeds you've subscribed to; again, similar to Favorites. In fact, you can organize and work with the Feeds list just like Favorites. (*See* Favorites, and this time, I mean it!)

To use the list of feeds, select a subscription. The last information or post appears in a special format in the main part of the IE window. You can use the toolbox on the right to search, sift, and sort through the information that's displayed, but note that you're seeing only the updated information from the Web site, not the real Web site itself.

XML icon	RSS icon	Add to Favorites button	Favorites button

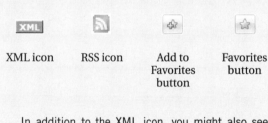

In addition to the XML icon, you might also see either the text RSS Feed or Subscribe to Comments icon. RSS feeds might also be flagged by the RSS icon. However it's set up, the icon, graphic, or text is your clue that changing information exists on the site and that selecting the icon, graphic, or text is how you can subscribe to the RSS feed and get that updated information.

Run

I find it amusing that the command used to start programs on a computer is often called *run*. Sure, there are alternatives: Start. Launch. Load. Open. Initiate. Transfer. But run holds special meaning because it also can imply a panicked departure. Sit down at the computer. Be brave. Now . . . *run!*

The Run command in Windows harkens back to the days when computer users started programs by typing the program name at a command prompt. In fact, that's exactly what the Run command does: It presents a dialog box that lets you type in the name of a program, any program inside the computer, and run that program directly. Power users love the Run command. Mere mortal users may encounter it from time to time, mostly because it's a quick shortcut, often more convenient than digging through a graphical interface to find a program. Plus, with the Run command, you can specify *options* or *parameters* for certain programs, which is something that graphical interfaces don't allow.

WHERE'S THE GOLD?

The Run command exists in its own dialog box, which coincidentally tends to appear in the lower left part of the screen, where the Start menu dwells. But summoning that dialog box might require a bit of magic.

The easiest way to conjure the Run dialog box is to press the Win+R combination on the keyboard.

The Run command might be available on the Start menu itself, but only when Windows is configured to present it that way. (See "Add the Run command to the Start menu.")

There's also a Run command on the All Programs menu, found on the Accessories submenu. Because of that, the command can also be copied to the desktop as a shortcut, placed on the Quick Launch bar, or messed with as you can mess with any program shortcut icon.

What to Do with It

Truly, the Run dialog box allows you to run any program on your computer, including secret superuser programs that require special options. Actually, using the Run command isn't the issue; it's knowing what to type that's important.

Run a program

To run a program, you must know the program's name — what to type. The Run dialog box sports a Browse button to peruse for a file, but what's the point when you can use the Windows Explorer program to do that anyway?

To run a command, press Win+R to bring up the Run dialog box. Type a command into the box, and then press the Enter key or click the OK button.

Open a Web page

You can also use the Run dialog box to open any Web page: Simply type a Web page address into the box and press Enter, and then your Web browser opens and loads that Web page.

Retrieve a previously typed command

The Run dialog box sports a command history, allowing you to easily recall previously typed commands. Simply use the down arrow to select a command; press Enter, and the command runs.

Place a Run icon on the desktop

To make the Run command handy, create a shortcut on the desktop:

1. Click the Start button to display the Start menu.

2. Choose All Programs.

3. Choose Accessories.

4. Right-click the Run command on the menu.

5. Choose Send To⇨Desktop (Create Shortcut) from the pop-up menu.

6. Click the mouse on the desktop to hide the Start menu.

Put a Run icon on the Quick Launch bar

The Run command can also dwell on the Quick Launch bar, which is a handy location when you find yourself using the Run command often:

1. Complete the steps in the preceding section.

2. Drag the Run command's shortcut icon to the Quick Launch bar.

3. (Optional) Delete the copy of the Run command on the desktop.

Unlike with other commands on the Start menu, you cannot use the Add to Quick Launch command on the Run icon. *See* Quick Launch Bar.

Add the Run command to the Start menu

The Run command already exists on the All Programs menu, but once upon a time it existed as a command on the Start menu. You can relive those days by following these steps:

1. Right-click the Start button and choose Properties from the menu.

2. Click the Customize button on the Start Menu tab.

3. In the scrolling list of links, folders, and frolic, find and select the Run Command item.

4. Click to put a check mark by the Run command.

5. Click OK, and close the Taskbar and Start Menu Properties dialog box.

Clear the Run command history

1. Right-click the Start button and choose Properties from the shortcut menu.

The Taskbar and Start Menu Properties dialog box appears.

2. Ensure that the Start Menu tab is up front.

3. In the Privacy area, remove the check mark by the item Store and Display a List of Recently Opened Programs.

4. Click OK.

Watch Your Step!

The Run command is literal. It doesn't assume that you meant to type **mspaint** when you typed **mspiant**.

By its nature, some of the commands you type into the Run dialog box are of an advanced nature. It's important to type the commands properly. Changes in some command options may adversely affect your computer.

When Things Go Wrong

Check your typing and try again. You can edit text in the Run command's input box just as you can edit text anywhere in Windows.

Some commands may not produce any results on the screen. This doesn't mean that the command didn't work, but simply that it has no viewable output.

Gold Rush Nuggets

You can use the Search input box, found on the Start menu, as an alternative for some commands that the Run command uses. Simply type the program name into the Search box, and then choose the proper command from the list provided. This trick doesn't, however, let you type command line options, as can be done with the real Run dialog box.

Here's the Run dialog box for Windows 3.1, 1992:

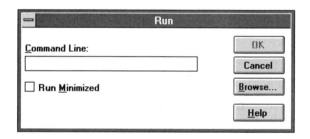

Digging Elsewhere

All Programs Menu, Pathnames, Standard User, Start Button and Menu

Safe Mode

Windows has a special mode of operation called *Safe mode*. In Safe mode, Windows starts up but does not load, or loads a limited set of, support programs or device drivers. Basically, when you start the computer in Safe mode, you're just seeing Windows in action — no other software. That way, you can determine whether any problems occur with Windows itself or with other software you may have installed on your computer.

WHERE'S THE GOLD?

Safe mode provides an alternative way to start Windows; rather than start normally, the computer runs in a limited mode of operation. This may happen automatically whenever a major problem occurs, or you can choose to start the computer in Safe mode as part of a general troubleshooting procedure.

Safe mode itself looks different from the regular way you're used to seeing Windows. First, your video driver isn't loaded, so Windows shows up in low resolution; things look bigger. Second, the desktop background is gone. Third, the windows and Taskbar look different, not in the standard, fancy *aero* interface. Finally, the words *Safe Mode* appear at the corners of the desktop, along with the Windows version number.

To manually control whether your computer starts normally or in Safe mode, use the System Configuration window. Start System Configuration by using this Search cheat:

1. Pop up the Start button menu.

2. In the Search box, type **system**.

3. Choose System Configuration from the top part of the results list on the Start menu.

You can also start the System Configuration window by typing **msconfig** in the Run dialog box. (*See* Run.)

The System Configuration window contains many options for starting Windows, including some tools that will help you diagnose problems that Safe mode doesn't cover.

If you're too late, you have to start over. You must press F8 (and you need to press it only once, not press and hold it) *before* the graphical Windows logo shows up.

4. Choose the proper startup option from the Advanced Boot Options menu.

Here are the choices worth selecting:

Safe Mode: Enter standard Safe mode for diagnostics and repair.

Safe Mode with Networking: Enable networking commands under Safe mode.

Safe Mode with Command Prompt: Start the Windows command prompt (for techies only).

Start Windows Normally: To hell with Safe mode; just start the computer.

5. Press Enter to start the computer in the proper Safe mode (or not).

6. Log in (if prompted) using a password-protected Administrator account.

7. Fix the problems.

This step involves diagnostics and tools covered elsewhere in this entry and in this book.

8. Restart Windows.

What to Do with It

Safe mode is for diagnostic purposes. Basically, when the problem still exists in Safe mode, you know that it's a problem with Windows. If the problem doesn't exist, the solution lies in fixing other software you've installed on the computer.

Start the PC in Safe mode

Safe mode starts automatically whenever a problem occurs in Windows. The on-the-fly method to enter Safe mode when the computer starts works like this:

1. Turn on or restart your computer.

2. If the computer boots into multiple operating systems, start by choosing Windows Vista.

3. Before the Windows logo appears, press the F8 key.

Configure the computer to start in Safe mode

To force the computer to start up in Safe mode, which is often easier than trying to stab the F8 key to death upon startup, do this:

1. Conjure up the System Configuration window.

2. Click the Boot tab.

3. Put a check mark by the Safe Boot option.

4. Click OK.

5. Click the Restart button to start Windows in Safe mode.

When the computer restarts, Windows comes up in Safe mode automatically. You can then fix problems, or refer to the next section, because Windows continues to start in Safe mode until you direct it not to.

Configure the computer to start normally

When Safe mode has started automatically, or when you press the F8 key to start Safe mode, the computer restarts automatically in Normal mode — as long as any problems were fixed, of course. But, when you manually configure the computer to start in Safe mode, you need to manually reset things to start normally. In Safe mode, you can do this:

1. Bring forth the System Configuration window.

2. On the General tab, choose Normal Startup.

3. Click OK.

4. Click the Restart button to start Windows normally.

Fix problems in Safe mode

When problems still exist in Safe mode, the problem lies with Windows, not with other software installed on your computer.

The first step you should take is to run System Restore. Select a restore point that was set before the bad thing happened. (Of course, you don't need to be in Safe mode to run System Restore.) *See* System Restore.

The second step you should take is to check the Device Manager for misbehaving devices. You should look in three problem spots, especially when the problem isn't present in Safe mode: display adapters, network adapters, and the power management software (found under System devices and named Microsoft ACPI-Compliant System). *See* Device Manager.

You can also use the Device Manager to update or roll back *device drivers*, which are the software programs that control the various hardware doodads in your computer. Even so, using System Restore often fixes these problems and is easier to use.

Fix startup problems outside Safe mode

Safe mode helps determine whether the problem is with Windows itself. When the problem isn't with Windows, you can check out other startup programs that load after Windows does. They're handily listed in the System Configuration window. Here's what to do:

1. Open the System Configuration window.

2. Click the Startup tab.

   You see listed a slew of startup programs, including some from Microsoft. One of these could be the problem child that's causing you startup woe.

3. Disable all startup items: Click the Disable All button.

4. Click the OK button.

5. Click the Restart button to restart Windows.

6. Confirm whether the problem still exists.

   If it does, the solution may lie elsewhere: Open the System Configuration window on the Startup tab and click the Enable All button; click OK and then restart. You're done.

7. Open the System Configuration window after restarting Windows.

8. In the Startup tab, reenable one of the options.

   Put a check mark by an option to reenable it.

9. Click OK.

10. Click the Restart button to restart Windows.

    If the problem crops up again, the last item you check-marked is the culprit; contact the developer for a fix. Otherwise:

11. Repeat steps 7 through 10 until you locate which startup program is causing you woe.

Yes, this is an involved way to troubleshoot startup problems, but it works. The only thing you don't really have control over is whether he developer knows about the issue and has provided a solution.

 Clue Use Google to look up the developer's name and help find its Web site on the Internet. The developer is listed in the System Configuration window, on the Startup tab, in the Manufacturer column.

Watch Your Step!

Safe mode is for diagnosing and fixing problems. You should not work in Safe mode or run programs other than diagnostic or repair utilities. Don't try to get your work done in Safe mode. And, when all your PC offers is Safe mode and you cannot start your computer otherwise, have a professional look at it.

When Things Go Wrong

Remember that Safe mode only helps you identify and fix *Windows* problems. For problems with other programs, refer to the developer's Web page for suggestions and cures as well as software updates.

Safe mode, and all the other various software cures for PC ills, don't address hardware failure issues. For example, when your PC's hard drive is about to fail, there's no software solution to fix it. (You should back up your data and replace the drive, and then restore your data on the new drive.)

Gold Rush Nuggets

The name Safe mode, of course, implies that running Windows in its normal configuration should be called Unsafe mode.

Digging Elsewhere

Device Manager, Help, Problem Reports and Solutions, System Restore

Safely Remove

The Safely Remove command is used to detach a removable drive from your computer system. So, when you're done using that USB media card reader or IEEE DVD drive, you can detach it from the PC without having Windows go all verklempt on you.

WHERE'S THE GOLD?

There are two places to find the Safely Remove command. The first is by right-clicking a removable storage device in the Computer window; the Safely Remove command can be found on the shortcut menu.

The other place to find the Safely Remove command is lurking in the Notification Area. Clicking the icon displays a pop-up menu of removable devices. Right-clicking the icon displays a one-item menu that you can use to access the Safely Remove Hardware dialog box.

What to Do with It

You need to use the Safely Remove command to detach a removable storage device from your PC. This is not the same as ejecting media (*see* Discs [CDs and DVDs]). For example, you eject a DVD from a DVD drive, but you must *safely remove* the DVD drive when you want to detach it.

Work in the Computer window

To safely remove a media card reader or external USB disk drive, follow these steps:

1. Open the Computer window.

2. Right-click the device to remove it.

   When you're using Category view, you can find all the devices in the Devices with Removable Storage area.

3. Choose Safely Remove from the shortcut menu.

The device's icon may disappear, or you may see a pop-up balloon from the Notification Area, telling you that the device can be safely removed.

Use the Notification Area

The quick way to detach a removable drive is to use the Safely Remove icon in the Notification Area:

1. Right-click the Safely Remove icon.

Safely Remove
icon

   You may need to click the Show More button on the Taskbar to see all the icons in the Notification Area.

2. Choose the device to remove from the pop-up list.

3. Click OK when notified that the device can be removed safely.

Display the Safely Remove Hardware dialog box

The Safely Remove Hardware dialog box is summoned by double-clicking the Safely Remove Hardware icon in the Notification Area.

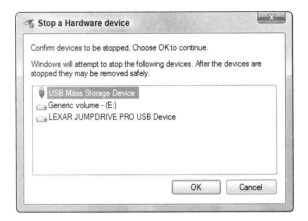

To remove a device, choose the device from the list and then click the Stop button.

Watch Your Step!

You cannot remove a drive that is *busy* (it has open files or is somehow being accessed by the computer).

Yes, it is easy simply to rip out the drive. The risk you take is lost or damaged files on the media.

The Safely Remove Hardware dialog box is not necessary when you need to remove hardware that's internal to your PC, such as when replacing a video card or removing a modem. Windows recognizes such changes automatically, although you may be required to reauthenticate Windows when your PC starts after a hardware update.

When Things Go Wrong

Try using the Eject command first to remove the media. That action confirms that the device isn't busy. If you can eject media, you should freely be able to remove the drive.

Sometimes, it pays to close programs and windows and then even wait a spell before trying to safely remove hardware.

If all else fails, restarting the computer generally makes attached hardware unbusy.

Gold Rush Nuggets

The command to manually run the Safely Remove Hardware dialog box is

```
RunDll32.exe
    Shell32.dll,Control_RunDLL
    hotplug.dll
```

This command can be typed into the Run dialog box, or it can be used when creating a desktop shortcut icon to the Safely Remove Hardware dialog box.

Digging Elsewhere

Discs (CDs and DVDs), Notification Area

Save

You can save money, save time, save the whales, save your soul. In Windows, the important thing to save is the stuff you create on your computer. The process is quite technical, involving taking raw, binary data from the computer's memory and saving it as a *file* on disk. Windows handles all the dirty work, and you merely need to tell it where to save the file and what to name the stuff. That duty is handled in one, compact location, the Save As dialog box, summoned by either the Save or Save As command.

WHERE'S THE GOLD?

The Save command is found in nearly every program that creates something or offers a way for you to collect something and save it as a file on your computer's storage system. There are two commands for saving:

Save As: The first command is Save As, which initially creates the file, assigning it a name and possibly a file type, and then setting a location — a specific disk drive, storage media, and folder — for the file.

Save: The second command is Save, which merely takes any information you previously saved to disk and updates the file, resaving the new information.

Both commands are found on the File menu: File⇨Save As and File⇨Save. The keyboard shortcut is Ctrl+S, which activates the Save As command when information hasn't yet been saved, and activates the Save command afterward.

A toolbar may also have a Save icon, which also represents the Save As and Save commands.

The Save As command itself summons the Save As dialog box, which is full of gizmos and doodads to assist you with the file-saving operation.

Filename

Choose another location

Current folder (in which file will be saved)

Choose another folder

Previously saved files

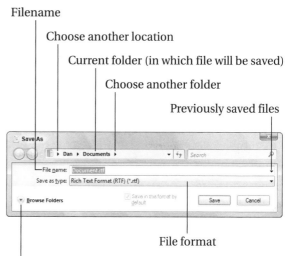

File format

Display full-on Windows Explorer-like dialog box

What to Do with It

Save is possibly the best command you could ever use. So use it! Save your stuff! Often!

Save information to disk

The first time you use the Save command, or use the Save As command directly, you see the Save As dialog box. Here's how you work that dialog box:

1. Optionally, choose a location for the file: Use the Address bar to select a specific disk drive or folder for your stuff. (*See* Address Bar.)

2. Optionally, select a file format by using the Save As Type drop-down list.

3. Type a name for the file.

   The Windows file-naming rules apply: *See* Rename for the details.

4. Click the Save button, or press the Enter key.

Typing the filename extension isn't necessary; Windows adds it automatically for you. In fact, if you're in the habit of typing, say, .DOC for your documents, you may find them looking like this on disk:

```
filename.doc.doc
```

 Clue　A saved file's filename appears on the document's title bar.

Save (update) information on disk

After saving a document to disk the first time, which essentially dubs the file with a name and specifies a location, any later Save commands merely update the file on disk with the new information you created. Just press Ctrl+S to save, or choose File⇨Save, or use the Save button on a toolbar.

Automatic file save

Some applications feature an *autosave* feature, which automatically saves your data to disk, even when you haven't initially saved your file. Refer to the application's Help system for information on autosave.

Save a file as a specific file type

Most Save As dialog boxes sport a drop-down list from which you can choose a file type. I call it the Save As Type drop-down list.

Normally, you don't need to mess with the file type when saving a file. Only when you know that you need a certain file type should you choose that other format. For example, when saving graphical images for the Web or as e-mail attachments, you should use the PNG or JPEG file format, not TIFF or Photoshop.

Some applications sport a File⇨Export command, which is also used to save information in a nonnative file format.

Save a file under a new name

You can conjure up the Save As dialog box any time you like after saving a file. You might, for example, save another copy of the file in another folder (although I recommend using Shortcuts for that; *see* Shortcuts). Another reason may be to save the file in another format (or type) or with another name.

To save a file with a new name, choose File⇨Save As. Then type the new name into the Save As dialog box. Click Save, and the file has a new name. The original file still exists, so be aware of that when updating the file.

And, of course, if you need two copies of a file, you can always duplicate a file. *See* Copy, Cut, and Paste Files.

Create a new folder for the file

As part of your disk organization, you may deem that your new file creation deserves its own folder. Yes, you can create a folder from within the Save As dialog box: Click the Browse Folders button. Then, when the Save As dialog box takes on its Windows Explorer persona, you can click the New Folder button on the toolbar. *See* Folders for more information on making new folders.

Watch Your Step!

Save your files right away! Don't wait! Save your stuff as soon as you've done a few things, written some text, drawn a picture, or whatever. Save!

Update your files as you work by using the File⇨Save command (Ctrl+S). Use it often!

You must obey the Windows file-naming rules when you save a file to disk. *See* Rename.

Do not save a file to disk by using the name of a file that already exists. When you do, you overwrite the original file. (Windows warns you before this happens.)

Do not save files directly to a floppy disk or CD-R/DVD-R. Instead, save the file to the hard drive *first*. Then copy the file to another location. *See* Copy, Cut, and Paste Files.

You cannot undo a Save command.

When you don't save files and then quit a program, Windows warns you. Click the Save button to summon a Save As dialog box, or click the Cancel button to return to the program.

 Saving files touches on disk organization in a big way. As long as you save your files in a logical location, you'll remember where to find them next time. Of course, this advice generally falls on dead ears, which is why Windows Vista comes with such a powerful Search command. *See* Search.

When Things Go Wrong

Saving a file over an existing file *erases* the original file. The only way to recover it is to use Windows Vista Previous Versions. *See* Previous Versions.

When you doubt that a file was saved, press Win+E to summon a Windows Explorer window. Browse to the folder where you believe that your file was saved, and confirm that it's there. If so, and if the file's size isn't zero (use Details view), you're okay!

Gold Rush Nuggets

The icon used for the Save toolbar button is generally a floppy disk icon — even though most computers sold today no longer sport floppy drives.

Digging Elsewhere

Address Bar, Files, Open, Rename

Screen Saver

In the beginning, computer monitors were cheap and suffered from an image persistence problem. When you ran one program day after day, such as the old WordPerfect or 1-2-3 spreadsheet, an image of that program would *burn* into the monitor's phosphor. The end effect was that the computer looked like it was running WordPerfect (or whatever) even when the computer was turned off! To fix this problem, and fight the peril of phosphor burn-in, screen saver software was introduced. Over the years, the screen savers became more complex, involving fancy graphics, text, images, and so on. Thanks to better technology, the issue of phosphor burn-in soon became a thing of the past, yet the screen saver remained.

WHERE'S THE GOLD?

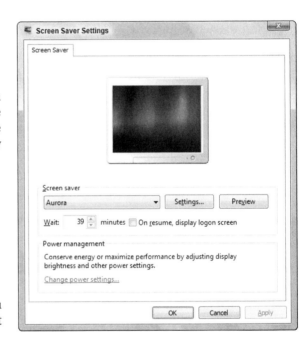

Screen savers are controlled from the Screen Saver Settings dialog box, summoned from the massive Personalization window. To conjure forth the Screen Saver Settings dialog box, follow these steps:

1. Right-click a blank part of the desktop.

2. Choose Personalize from the pop-up menu.

3. In the Personalization window, choose Screen Saver.

The Screen Saver Settings window appears, from which you can choose a screen saver, how it works, when it shows up, and other stuff.

What to Do with It

The screen saver is more than a visual toy — eye candy. It can be used to help secure your computer while you're away. But you have to apply a password!

Choose a screen saver

Windows comes with a slew of screen savers, all of which are listed in the Screen Saver drop-down list in the Screen Saver Settings dialog box.

Choosing a screen saver from the list displays what it looks like in the tiny preview window.

Clicking the Preview button displays the screen saver's preview full-screen. Move the mouse or press the Ctrl key to hide the screen saver.

The Settings button displays a special dialog box where some screen savers can be customized; text can be input, speed changed, and other options set or reset. Not every screen saver uses the Settings button.

Use your own picture as a screen saver

Choose the Photos screen saver from the drop-down list, then click the Settings button to use images stored on your computer as a screen saver. Options displayed when you click the Settings button help customize which pictures are displayed and how they appear.

I recommend creating a special folder within the Pictures folder. Name it Screen Saver, and place into that folder only those images you'd like to see on your screen saver. (Use shortcuts to your images to avoid using too much disk space; *see* Shortcuts.)

You can also use pictures from the Windows Photo Gallery, should you decide to use that program for managing images.

Set the kick-in time

The screen saver takes over the screen (it's actually a window, though a special type of window)

whenever you haven't typed anything or moved the mouse for a while. That while is set using the Wait box in the Screen Saver Settings dialog box.

Values to wait can range from 1 minute (not recommended) to 9999 minutes, which is just under 7 days (not recommended either).

Set the screen saver timeout to something *less than* the time specified to sleep the monitor. *See* Sleep Mode.

Apply a password

As a security precaution, put a check mark by the option "On resume, display logon screen." Providing that your account is password protected (which I recommend), that ensures that no one can saunter by and access your computer while the screen saver is running.

Wake up the system

To end the screen saver and return to Windows, jiggle the mouse or press any key on the keyboard. For "any key" I recommend the Ctrl key. Either one.

Disable the screen saver

Choosing (None) in the Screen Saver Settings dialog box disables the screen saver.

It's possible to temporarily disable the screen saver, such as when you're watching a video or doing something where the screen saver may kick in at an undesired time. This feature is available in Windows Media Player:

1. From the Now Playing tab's menu, choose More Options.

2. In the Options dialog box, locate the Player tab.

3. Remove the check mark by the item Allow Screen Saver During Playback.

Watch Your Step!

The computer's energy-saving abilities turn off the computer monitor, which also turns off the screen saver. When you set the monitor to "sleep" before the screen saver kicks in, you'll never see the screen saver! *See* Sleep Mode.

Avoid obtaining "screen savers" from the Internet. Many of them are advertisements or, worse, nasty programs that you cannot get rid of. Windows Vista may warn you, but you may be tempted to ignore the warning. Don't. Unless you're certain of the source — a notable software developer or hardware vendor you trust — avoid any third-party screen savers.

Obviously, using your own images in a screen saver involves thoughtful consideration of those images that appear.

Screen savers are affected when you select a desktop theme. *See* Themes.

When Things Go Wrong

Check to ensure that sleep mode isn't kicking in before your screen saver activates; *see* Sleep Mode.

Yes, Windows can die while the screen saver is still up and entertaining you. When you cannot seem to wrest control over a PC with a screen saver running, press the power button and wait. If that doesn't work, press and hold the power button until the computer turns itself off (usually about 5 seconds). Then restart Windows.

Gold Rush Nuggets

Early PC screen savers simply blanked the screen. The first PC screen saver was written by programmer John Socha in 1983. John was the author of the popular Norton Commander, and he coined the term *screen saver*.

The After Dark screen saver program was one of the most popular for early versions of Windows. Its images included the famous Flying Toaster graphics, plus screen savers customized with popular television and comic book characters.

Digging Elsewhere

Display, Passwords, Sleep Mode, Themes

Search

Despite all the effort and urging that go into the concept of file organization and properly naming files, people are just sloppy or lazy or both. Files accumulate like clutter in a garage. Eventually, nothing makes sense and nothing can be found. Fortunately, Windows Vista features a powerful information-location command named Search. Using Search, you can locate long-gone files or even text in e-mail messages. It's simple and powerful. Yet it's also an admission of guilt in that such a powerful tool wouldn't be so valuable if folks would just organize files and name them properly in the first place.

WHERE'S THE GOLD?

The Search command is ubiquitous, most commonly as a text box that contains the word *Search* in faint lettering on one side and a tiny blue magnifying glass on the other side.

The Search input boxes can be found in two common locations:

✕ The upper right corner of any Windows Explorer window

✕ The lower left corner of the Start button's menu

You can also choose the Search command, when it's available, from the Start button's menu. *See* Start Button and Menu.

When a search is performed, the Search Results window appears and displays the files that were found.

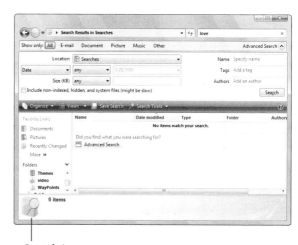
Search icon

Clicking the Advanced Search button displays a panel where you can enter more details about the search.

A set of predefined searches, saved as Search Results windows, can be found in your User Account folder, inside the Searches folder.

Be careful to note when Windows Explorer is showing a Search Results window. (It can even happen when you group icons in a window.) The Search Results window is *not* a folder window, but rather a display of files matching a search. To restore the window to a normal folder window, click the X at the right end of the Search text box, click the Back button by the Address bar, or simply close the window.

What to Do with It

Missing anything?

Choose the correct Search box

Choosing which Search box you use is important because the search is relative to what you're looking at. For example, to find any document on your computer, you do this:

1. Open the Computer window.

2. Type all or part of the document name into the Search box.

In addition to looking for documents with matching names, Search also looks inside documents and e-mail messages for matching text.

3. Press the Enter key.

The results are displayed in the Search Results in Computer window; the title tells you that the search results are those files found from the Computer window and all subfolders and files.

To search only in the User Account folder, follow these steps:

1. Open your User Account folder.

2. Type the information to search for in the Search box.

3. Press the Enter key.

The files that are found are displayed in the Search Results in [Your Account Name] Window.

Using the Search box on the Start menu searches your entire computer, like so:

1. Press the Windows key to summon the Start button's menu.

2. Type the information to search for in the Start menu's Search box.

3. Press the Enter key.

The results appear in the Search Results in Indexed Locations window. See "Set indexed locations," later in this entry, for more information.

Search for a wayward file

Here's what to do when you need to find that file and you don't remember where you put it:

1. Pop up the Start button's menu.

2. In the Search box, type the name of the file as best as you can remember it.

3. Press the Enter key to start the search.

4. Locate your file in the Search Results window.

Remember that the Search Results window also shows file *contents,* so you may have to scroll through the list to find your exact file.

Refine your file search

When the search results show lots of files but not the file you wanted, you need to do some refinement, like this:

1. Click the Advanced Search link.

2. Choose where to look for your file from the Location drop-down list.

3. Type the filename into the Name box.

4. Click the Search button.

When the file still isn't found, you can rest assured that it's not on your PC, at least not with the name that was provided. Try searching again, but look for the file's contents. Refer to the next section.

Search for text somewhere on your PC

Windows Search not only searches for files by name, but also automatically looks inside files for contents. It even looks inside e-mail messages. To find text just about anywhere on your PC, do this:

1. Type the text to search for into the Start menu's Search box.

2. Press Enter.

   Theoretically, all the files you see contain the word or words you searched for.

3. To narrow the choices, choose a specific file type from the toolbar.

   For example, to narrow the search to e-mail messages, click the E-mail button.

4. Select a file to preview its contents.

5. Repeat Step 4 until you find the file you want.

Search through files recently created

The Searches folder contains some preset searches you can use to search for specific things, such as files you recently created. Here's how that works:

1. Open your User Account folder.

2. Open the Searches folder.

3. Open the Recent Documents Search icon.

4. Peruse the list for the file you're after.

The files are listed in Details view, sorted by date; the most recent files appear at the top of the list.

Search for files of a given size

I use the search-by-size type of search to locate potentially huge files on my computer — files that make me question why I have them because they occupy so much space. It's a good exercise, but it involves an advanced search. Here's one way to pull it off:

1. Choose Search from the Start button menu.

   If the Search command isn't available, display the desktop and press the F3 key.

2. Click the downward-pointing chevron by the Advanced Search option to display the advanced searching options.

3. From the Size (KB) drop-down menu, choose the Is Greater Than option.

4. Type **5000** in the text box.

You're searching for files greater than 5 million bytes (5MB, more or less).

5. Click the Search button.

Save a search

When creating a custom search or a complex search or any type of search you do repeatedly, consider saving the search. To do so, simply click the Save Search button on the Search Results window's toolbar.

Use the Save As dialog box to give your search a descriptive name, and then click the Save button. As long as you don't mess with anything else in the Save As dialog box, the search is saved in the Searches folder, where you can use it over and over again.

Set indexed locations

The Search command is so lickety-split fast because Windows takes time out of its day to index just about every file on your computer's hard drive. It then uses that index to help speed up the search, by searching the index instead of plodding through every file on disk.

The indexed locations (which you may have seen when searching from the Start menu's Search box) are set by using the Control Panel's Indexing Options icon. From the Control Panel Home, choose System and Maintenance and then Indexing Options.

To change where Windows indexes files, click the Modify button. Click the Show All Locations button to reveal everywhere that Windows looks for its search indexes. Remove check marks by those items you want to exclude from the search, or add check marks by items to include.

Adding too many items slows down the searches as well as the process of creating the index.

You can click the Advanced button for even more options, including options to filter out certain file types (which might save time).

Watch Your Step!

 Start with the proper Search text box. When you choose the wrong Search text box, you automatically narrow the locations in which Windows searches. When in doubt, use the Search text box on the Start button's menu.

Encrypted files are *not* indexed. You can direct Windows to override this setting: In the Indexing Options dialog box, click the Advanced button. Then put a check mark by index-encrypted files. Note that this kind of searching removes the secure aspect of the encrypted files! (*See* Encryption.)

Quite a few wags out there have recommended using the Search text box on the Start menu as a replacement for the Run command. This method works, but it's just easier to place the Run command on the Start menu and not waste so much of the computer's time on a search. (*See* Start Button and Menu.)

When Things Go Wrong

Try searching again, using different text to search for. Eventually, you might have to accept that the file you're looking for might just be gone. (This is when I could remind you again of the value of backing up your PC, but I won't; *see* Backup.)

Gold Rush Nuggets

Whether it's called Find or Search, the underlying function is the same: to locate things. But over Microsoft's history, it has changed the command name from Search to Find and back to Search again.

Digging Elsewhere

Files, Folders, Live Search (Internet Explorer), Run, Windows Explorer

Security Center

Windows Vista is all about security. Several programs that come with Windows are specifically designed to protect your PC, your programs, and your precious files from the various nasty things that threaten and loom on the high-tech horizon. To keep all those things organized, use the Windows Security Center, a sanctuary of sanity in a sea of high-tech sin.

WHERE'S THE GOLD?

The Security Center is found in the Control Panel: Open the Security Center icon, or from the Control Panel Home, choose Security and then Security Center. Either way you get there, the Windows Security Center is displayed.

The Security Center window provides a central location to access four other types of programs in Windows.

By itself, the Security Center is really nothing more than a door into those four other programs:

Firewall: A firewall protects your computer from being invaded by programs that abuse weaknesses in the Internet. *See* Firewall.

Automatic Updating: By keeping Windows up-to-date, you ensure that any security releases, updates, patches, and fixes are installed when they're needed. *See* Updates.

Security Center icon

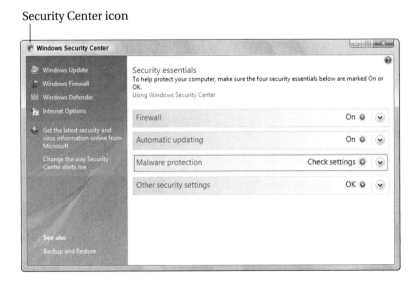

Malware Protection: Both anti-spyware and antivirus programs are recommended to help protect your computer against attacks by nasty programs. Windows provides some spyware protection with its Windows Defender program (*see* Windows Defender). Antivirus protection must be provided by a third-party utility (*see* Antivirus).

Other Security Settings: Two options in this part of the Security Center window deal with Internet security as well as with the User Account Control security warnings. *See* User Account Control (UAC).

What to Do with It

You can use the Security Center window as a way to access individual security places in Windows. Honestly, it's an extra step. When you get to know Windows Vista well, you probably won't bother with the Security Center window.

Visit another security place in Windows

The Security Center window is information-only. Although you can display or hide each of the four areas, nothing in each area affects your security settings. To change the settings, choose one of the links on the left side of the window:

✕ To set automatic updates, choose Windows Update.

✕ To work with the Firewall, choose Windows Firewall.

✕ To check malware protection, choose Windows Defender.

✕ To work with other security settings, choose Internet Options.

Change how the Security Center alerts you

The only specific thing you can do in the Windows Security Center is disable the warnings it displays. Follow these steps:

1. Open the Windows Security Center.

2. Choose the link on the left side of the window, Change the Way Security Center Alerts Me.

3. Choose the option Don't Notify Me and Don't Display the Icon (Not Recommended).

4. Close the Security Center window and bid it *adieu*.

If you feel more comfortable having the Notification Area icon appear, or when you can truly tolerate the warnings, repeat these steps and change the option in Step 3.

Watch Your Step!

Security is good, especially on a Windows computer. But don't let the various layers and multiple forms of security lull you into reckless behavior. The most common way people compromise their PC's security is by being lazy or forgetful. Remember: The Bad Guys use clever social engineering to trick you into doing things you otherwise would not do. Always be on guard, no matter how much security you have installed on your PC.

When Things Go Wrong

Windows Security Center may not recognize other firewalls or antivirus software you have installed. Even so, it continues to bother you when these items are not set. The solution? Disable the security warnings from the Notification Area, which is covered elsewhere in this entry.

Gold Rush Nuggets

The Windows Security Center made its first appearance in Windows XP with the release of Service Pack 2, back in August 2004.

Digging Elsewhere

Antivirus, Firewall, Updates, Windows Defender

Select Files

To work with a group of files (or icons) at one time, you must corral them all into a group, marked as a herd, gathered up and set down. If you don't live on a ranch, the proper term is *selecting*. In fact, even individual files must be selected before you can manipulate them. But when you're crafty, you can select a swath of files, wide, complete, or choosey. After you select them, you're free to manipulate the files in a number of ways.

WHERE'S THE GOLD?

The skills required to select files lie in the palm of your hand, specifically when the palm of your hand cradles the computer mouse.

Selection commands are also available on menus in Windows Explorer. The Select All command can be found on the toolbar's Organize button's menu. Pressing the F10 key to reveal the hidden menu bar gives you access to the Select All and Invert Selection commands on the Edit menu.

What to Do with It

Selected icons become a group of files, a group on which you can perform various file manipulation tasks. Your first step is to mark the files you want as a group.

Select a single icon

To select a single file in a window, click that file with the mouse.

You can also select an icon from the keyboard by pressing the first letter of the icon's name. If you type quickly, you can type the first few letters of an icon's name to select that icon. Or, use the arrow keys to select neighboring icons.

Select all icons in a window

The Select All command is used to select all icons in a window: All files and folders. Everything. The keyboard shortcut is easy to remember: Ctrl+A. From the Organize button's menu, you can choose the Select All command.

Select all but a single icon

To select all but one icon in a window, follow these steps:

1. Select the oddball icon, the one you do not want selected.

   Yes, you read that correctly.

2. Press F10 to activate the Windows Explorer menu.

3. Choose Edit⟳Invert Selection.

If you have trouble with the Invert Selection command, you can do this instead:

1. Press Ctrl+A to select all icons in the window.

2. Press and hold the Ctrl key (either one).

3. Click the icon or icons you do not want selected.

The Ctrl+click action deselects the icons.

4. Release the Ctrl key.

Select an odd lot of files

You have a number of ways to select an odd lot of files or icons. The easiest is to use the Ctrl-click method.

Normally, when you click the mouse to select an icon, only that icon is selected. But, when you press and hold the Ctrl key on the keyboard, clicking the mouse continues to select icons. I call it a Ctrl+click ("control click").

To select any old odd bunch of icons, do this:

1. Click the mouse to select the first icon.

2. Press and hold the Ctrl key.

3. Click other icons, keeping that Ctrl key down.

As long as the Ctrl key is down, each icon you click is selected.

4. Release the Ctrl key.

Rope up files with the mouse

The graphical way to select files is to play cowboy and select them with the mouse: Drag the mouse down and to the right. As you drag, the

mouse pointer creates a square with a dashed line. All icons within the square are selected.

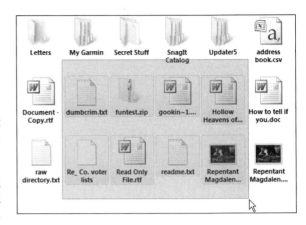

You can add to the files you rope with the mouse: Press the Shift key as you drag the mouse. The files you drag over are added to the selection.

Select a swath of files

Eureka
Oftentimes you select files of a certain ilk: files created yesterday, all JPG files in a folder, or files named from M to Z, for example. The best way to do that is as follows:

1. Choose Small Icons, List, or Details from the Views toolbar button menu.

2. Right-click in the window.

3. Choose Sort By and then the proper item from the Sort Buy submenu.

For example, to select all graphics files in a window, choose Sort By⇨Type.

4. Click to select the first item in the list.

5. Shift+click to select the last item in the list.

   Press and hold the Shift key as you click the mouse.

   All items between the first click and the Shift+click are selected.

Clue As long as you properly sort the icons in the list (Step 3), the Click/Shift+click trick works. You can even press Ctrl+click and then Ctrl+Shift+click to select a second swath of files in the list.

Deselect

To deselect individual icons, use the Ctrl+click trick on each selected icon; Ctrl+clicking a selected icon deselects that icon.

To not select any files, you can press Ctrl+A and then choose Edit⇨Invert Selection from the F10 menu, but it's just easier to click in the window at a spot between icons, which deselects everything.

Watch Your Step!

You can select files from only one folder at a time.

File commands (Cut, Copy, Rename, Delete) affect all selected files.

When using the mouse to drag over icons, ensure that you start above the icon, not exactly on the icon (which drags the icon around). I generally start to the upper left of an icon and then drag down and to the right.

When Things Go Wrong

Windows can be configured to require a single click to open icons rather than the standard double-click. When that change is made, it means that you must drag the mouse over icons to select them; you cannot select icons by clicking them. (*See* Windows Explorer under the heading "When things go wrong," for more information.)

Use the Refresh command (F5) in a window if you seem to have trouble selecting icons.

Changing the view (from the toolbar's Views menu) often reveals icons that may be hidden or not visible and, therefore, difficult to select.

Gold Rush Nuggets

Back in the bad old days, computer files were selected as a group by using filename wildcards. Even today, that text-based method is often faster and more efficient than selecting files in a graphical operating system. The problem is remembering which commands to type and properly using the wildcards.

Digging Elsewhere

Cut, Copy, and Paste Files; *Delete*; *Files*; *Icons*; *Rename*; *Text Editing*

Share Stuff on the Network

Sharing takes courage. It's about overcoming your selfish desires and accepting that you can give something to someone else regardless of the consequences. Or, perhaps there's the occasional veiled threat regarding returning the shared item in its pristine condition. On the computer, of course, sharing is about *resources*. Specifically, it's about sharing stuff on a network: stuff like your printer, disk drives, and the occasional modem or two. Although it may take courage to share your stuff on the network, it can be done safely and with relatively no consequences.

WHERE'S THE GOLD?

Sharing is an option attached to the devices that can be shared, primarily folders and printers. The Sharing command is easily accessed from the pop-up shortcut menu found by right-clicking a folder or printer icon.

Before you can share anything, you must tell Windows that it's okay for it to be friendly with its network neighbors. That action happens in the Control Panel's Network and Sharing Center; from the Control Panel Home, click the Set Up File Sharing link, found under the Network and Internet heading.

Network and Sharing Center icon

A shared icon

Shared icons sport a tiny "sharing buddy" flag in the lower left corner. *See* Icons.

What to Do with It

Having two or more computers that are not networked just doesn't make sense. By networking the computers, you allow them to share files, share a single printer, and share an Internet connection. It all begins with teaching your PC to share.

Configure your PC to share

Windows does not come out of the box all ready to share its stuff. That's because you need to be careful about sharing anything with anyone. When you're comfortable, you can set up Windows for sharing by following these steps:

1. Bring forth the Network and Sharing Center.

2. Activate Network Discovery; set it to On.

3. Activate File Sharing; set it to On.

4. To limit access to your computer, activate Password-Protected Sharing.

Setting this option means that only users with accounts on your computer can access the computer's resources. In my small, secure office, I leave this option turned off.

5. Activate Media Sharing to share any music, pictures, or videos from your PC.

I leave this option off because, honestly, I have nothing to share!

Share the Public folder

The only folder you really want to share on your PC is the Public folder. That's where you should copy files that need to be accessed on the network, or retrieve files copied to your PC from others on the network.

To share the Public folder, do this:

1. Visit the Network and Sharing Center.

2. Click the chevron to display more information for public folder sharing.

3. Choose Turn On Sharing so that anyone with network access can open files, which is the read-only option. Or, you can choose Turn On Sharing so that anyone with network access can open, change, and create files, which is the full-access option.

4. Click the Apply button, and then (optionally) close the Network and Sharing Center window.

To unshare the Public folder, repeat these steps but in Step 3 choose Turn Off Sharing (people logged on to this computer can still access this folder).

Share a folder you own

In addition to sharing the Public folder on the network, you can share individual folders you own with other users on the same computer. This is not network sharing! In fact, it's an utterly pointless thing to do unless you have more than one user on the same computer. But, if you're so inclined, here are the steps to take:

1. Open the folder you want to share.

2. Press Alt+↑ to move *up* one folder, to the folder's parent folder.

3. Right-click the folder's icon and choose Share from the pop-up menu.

The File Sharing window appears.

If you don't see the File Sharing window, and instead see the folder's Properties dialog box, you're opening a folder that you do not own. Do not share that folder; close the dialog box by clicking Cancel.

4. If you see a button that says Change Sharing Permissions, click it; otherwise, skip to Step 5.

Administrators automatically share their folders with each other, so when you have more than one administrator on your PC, you'll discover that all your folders are shared.

5. Choose whom to share the folder with from the drop-down list.

The list contains the names of other users on your computer; sharing is first a PC-with-itself thing. To share with everyone on a network, choose the Everyone item.

6. Click the Add button to add the selected user to the list.

7. Click the Share button.

Standard users need an administrator's password to complete this operation.

8. Click the Done button.

And, the folder's icon is blessed with the magical Sharing Buddies flag.

To stop sharing the folder, follow Steps 1 through 3; in Step 4 click the Stop Sharing button, and then click Done.

Share any folder on the network

An administrator can flag which folders to share on the network in addition to sharing the Public folder. I do not recommend this strategy. But, if you're still reading, you probably don't care. So, here:

1. Right-click the folder icon representing the folder you want to share.

2. Choose Properties from the pop-up menu.

3. Click the Sharing tab.

4. Click the Advanced Sharing button.

5. Put a check mark by the top item, Share This Folder.

6. Type a share name, just in case the folder's given name is generic or would be confusing on the network.

For example, Stuff and Templates are great folder names, but they might not explain things well on a network. Better names are Joyce's Stuff or Jim's Travel Templates.

7. Click the Permissions button.

8. Ensure that Everyone appears in the list of group or user names. If not:

a. Click the Add button.

b. Type **Everyone** into the bottom text box.

c. Click the Check Names button.

d. Click OK.

9. To allow full access to the folder, click the Full Control check box in the Allow column; otherwise, the Read button in the Allow column should be checked, which provides read-only access.

10. Click OK to close the Permissions dialog box.

11. Click OK to close the Advanced Sharing dialog box and share the folder.

12. Click the Close button to dismiss the Properties dialog box.

And, the folder is sanctified with its teensy sharing flag.

Share a printer

Sharing printers attached to your computer is simple (thankfully). Here's all you need do:

1. Open the Network and Sharing Center.
2. Click the Show More chevron by Printer sharing.
3. Choose Turn On Printer Sharing.
4. Click the Apply button.
5. Close the Network and Sharing Center window.

That's it. Every printer attached to your PC, including virtual printers (such as print capture utilities) are shared, and their icons sport the little sharing buddies flag.

Unshare a printer

When you have printers you don't want to share, you can manually unshare them by doing this:

1. Open the Printers window.
2. Right-click the icon representing a shared printer.

   It's not a printer you're using on the network, but rather a printer attached to your PC — one that has an icon with the sharing buddies on it.

3. Choose Sharing from the pop-up menu.

4. On the Sharing tab of the printer's Properties dialog box, click the Change Sharing Options button.
5. Remove the check mark by Share This Printer.
6. Click OK.

The printer's icon should lose the little sharing buddies flag, which is your confirmation that the printer is no longer being shared on the network.

Review which folders (and printers) you are sharing

To help you get a grip on the folder-sharing situation, you can have Windows display a list of the folders you're sharing, not only on your PC with other users but also on the network. The secret is found in the Network and Sharing Center window.

In the bottom of the window, choose the link Show Me All the Files and Folders I Am Sharing. The Search Results window displays any folders on your computer that you're sharing with other users. These are *not* necessarily folders shared on the network.

To see which folders are available from your computer to others on the network, click the link Show Me All the Shared Network Folders on This Computer. The window that's displayed shows not only shared folders but also any available shared printers.

Watch Your Step!

See Networking for information on configuring Windows to use a network. You must be part of a network or workgroup for this file-sharing non-sense to work.

A firewall can interfere with sharing folders and printers on a network. You must configure the firewall to allow local traffic between your PCs.

You cannot access a shared folder or printer when the host computer is asleep or turned off.

When Things Go Wrong

The biggest problem with accessing other computers occurs when those computers have password-protected files and folders. In some cases, it's simply a matter of knowing the password to access the folder. But, with Windows Vista, you must also have an account on the computer, which makes things a tad more difficult. That's why I recommend not activating password-protected sharing.

Only the Public folder is shared on the network. Individual folders you share do not appear on the network, but are available only to other users on the same computer.

Gold Rush Nuggets

Before computer networking became common, the way information was shared between personal computers was by *sneakernet*. Sneakernet was not a program. It was not hardware. It consisted of human beings walking between computers. Humans often wear sneakers as shoes; hence, sneakernet.

Digging Elsewhere

Networking, Printers, Public Folder

Shortcuts

A shortcut is a copy of a file but without the bulk. It's a way to litter the hard drive with a file here, a folder there, and programs everywhere, but without losing a lot of disk space by making multiple and redundant copies of the same file over and over. Windows uses shortcuts on the desktop, on the Start menu, and elsewhere. You can also create your own.

Shortcut icons lurk not in the misty bit stew of your computer's nether regions. No, they wear something akin to the scarlet letter, a little arrow badge in their lower left corner, which indicates that the icon is a shortcut, not the real McCoy.

Shortcut
icon

Microsoft recommends that you put only shortcuts on the desktop (in addition to the standard desktop icons; *see* Desktop Icons).

All programs on the Start menu are shortcut icons referencing the original program installed elsewhere on the hard drive. Programs referenced on the Quick Launch bar are shortcuts. In both cases (on the Start button's menu and on the Quick Launch bar), the icon lacks the tiny arrow in the lower left corner, yet the icons are still shortcuts.

Shortcut icons can also reference locations on the Internet. Web page shortcuts, for example, can be stored on your computer for quick access to Web pages. In fact, when you create a Favorite (or "drop a bookmark") on the Web, you're creating a shortcut to a Web page and storing it in a place where the Web browser can easily access the shortcut again.

What to Do with It

You can do anything with a shortcut icon that you can do with any other icon in Windows. The idea behind the shortcut is to provide you with a handy reference to a file, folder, disk drive, or program without duplicating the entire original file.

Create a shortcut

Shortcuts are created just like a file copy operation. The difference is in the way the file is pasted; rather than use the Paste command, you must choose the Paste Shortcut command, from either the traditional File menu, the Organize toolbar button's menu, or the right-click shortcut menu in the location where you're creating the shortcut. Step by step, it goes like this:

1. Click to select the file you want to shortcut.

   It can be a file or folder.

2. Press Ctrl+C to copy the file.

3. Open the *destination,* the location where you want to place the shortcut icon.

4. Right-click in the destination to summon a pop-up menu.

5. Choose Paste Shortcut from the menu.

See also Copy, Cut, and Paste Files for more information on moving and copying files.

Place a shortcut on the desktop

 Eureka It's easy to create a desktop shortcut, to either a favorite program, favorite data file, or even a folder for a current project: Just right-click the item, and from the pop-up menu, choose Send To⇨Desktop (create shortcut).

Create a shortcut to a disk drive

My PC's Z drive is its backup disk. To keep that disk drive handy, I create a shortcut to the drive on the desktop. Here's how:

1. Open the Computer window.

2. Right-click the drive you want to shortcut.

3. Choose Create Shortcut.

4. Close the Computer window.

The shortcut appears on the desktop.

You can also create a shortcut to any disk drive by copying the drive's icon and then choosing Paste Shortcut, as described earlier in this section.

Find the original file

Each shortcut references an original file elsewhere on the disk storage system. To find that original file, right-click the shortcut icon and choose Open File Location from the shortcut menu. A Windows Explorer window opens, revealing the original file icon, which is selected.

Create a Web page shortcut

Web page shortcuts are created when you press Ctrl+D and visit a Web site. Depending on the Web browser, you're given the option to place that bookmark into a Favorite folder or a specific location. That's one way.

You can also choose to right-click a Web page and choose Create Shortcut from the pop-up menu. That places on the desktop a shortcut icon referencing the Web page; open the icon and you revisit the same Web page.

Finally, you can drag the Web page address from the Address Bar to the desktop or into a folder to create a Web page shortcut. Point the mouse at the icon on the far left side of the address, and then drag the sucker out of the Web browser window.

Delete a shortcut

Feel free to delete any shortcut on the computer; deleting a shortcut doesn't delete the original file.

When deleting a shortcut on the desktop, you may be prompted by a confirmation dialog box that repeats information about how it's "okay" to delete a shortcut, which isn't the real file. Disabling the Delete Confirmation warning for the Recycle Bin fixes that annoyance: *See* Delete.

Copy, move, or rename a shortcut

Shortcuts work like any other file or icon in Windows. You can copy, move, or rename a shortcut. *See* Copy, Cut, and Paste Files; and Rename.

 Sometimes Windows sticks the text "shortcut" onto a shortcut's filename. I think that's wholly unnecessary; the little arrow on the shortcut icon is clue enough that the icon is a shortcut. It's perfectly okay to rename such an icon.

Change the shortcut's icon

One thing you can do with a shortcut that you cannot do with any other file icon is to give it a new image. *See* Icons for the details.

Watch Your Step!

No, you cannot remove the wee little arrow from a shortcut icon.

Don't create a shortcut to a shortcut. When you already have one shortcut icon and need to make a second, simply copy the first shortcut icon.

Do not e-mail shortcuts. Although opening the shortcut on your PC displays the original file or folder or runs the named program, e-mailing the shortcut does absolutely nothing for the person who receives it.

When Things Go Wrong

When the Paste Shortcut command isn't available, either you cannot create a shortcut in the given location, or you did not properly select and copy the original file in the first place.

When the Open File Location command isn't available, the shortcut references an internal Windows command, not a file on disk. This is true for shortcuts to the Run command, to Show Desktop (on the Quick Launch bar), and to other specific Windows commands.

Shortcuts every so often lose track of the file they originally reference. That's because there's no real connection between the original file and any of its shortcuts. Windows attempts to remedy the situation by trying to track down the absent original. When it cannot find the original, Windows may present a list of suggested similar files that it found, from which you can choose the original. Or, you can use the Browse button to locate the original.

When an original file, folder, or program is gone for good, you simply delete the shortcut.

Gold Rush Nuggets

Other operating systems refer to a shortcut as an *alias*.

In Windows, the shortcut file type has the LNK filename extension. LNK stands for *link*.

Digging Elsewhere

Copy, Cut, and Paste Files; Desktop; Files; Keyboard Shortcuts

Shutdown Windows

When you're finished using the computer, your final task to take is to officially shut down Windows. You save your data, optionally quit your programs, and then tell Windows that you're done. Windows does some tidying up and then turns off and shuts down its various programs, processes, and services. Your account is logged off, and then the computer bids you farewell and turns itself off. You sit there for a few seconds, to ensure that you haven't been fooled by the thing, and, yes, it really turns off.

WHERE'S THE GOLD?

Turning off Windows doesn't seem to be as important a thing as starting Windows. For me, I would expect some huge, glorious menu or fancy button. But, no. Turning off Windows has been relegated to the Start menu. Yes, it's ironic. And it's sad because the Shutdown menu is but a teensy submenu on the Start button menu.

The Shutdown Windows menu lists several options for suspending or ending your Windows session.

There are also various Shutdown buttons in Windows, such as the one found on the Ctrl+Alt+Delete menu. (*See* Ctrl+Alt+Delete.) Generally speaking, clicking the button shuts down Windows, although you may see a pop-up menu of options to choose from.

When a power button has a circle with a vertical line in its middle, the power button's function is to turn off the computer.

Shutdown menu

Shut down the computer

Restart Windows

Turns the computer off	Restarts, sleeps, or hibernates the computer

When a power button has a broken circle with a vertical line up top, the power button's function is to restart, sleep, or hibernate the computer.

What to Do with It

By shutting down Windows, you free yourself to do other activities that human beings have done for thousands of years. It's amazing how far we've come as a species.

Shut down Windows

You have many ways to properly shut down Windows. The most obvious is to choose the Shutdown command from the Shutdown menu: Pop up the Start button menu, click the Shutdown menu's triangle, and choose the Shutdown command.

There's a Shutdown button on the Ctrl+Alt+ Delete menu. *See* Ctrl+Alt+Delete.

There's a Shutdown button on the login screen. *See* Login and Log Off.

The console's power or sleep buttons can also be used to shut down Windows. *See* Power Button.

Restart Windows

When you restart Windows, you do everything necessary to shut down the computer but then start everything back up again. In the olden days, the term *warm boot* was used instead of restart, but the concept is the same: For some reason, Windows needs to clear its head and start things over. Here's how:

1. Pop up the Start button menu.

2. Click the Shutdown menu, in the lower right corner of the Start button menu.

3. Choose the Restart command.

As with a shutdown, you're prompted to save any unsaved files. Windows shuts down and then starts itself up again.

Restarts are often done automatically, especially after installing some types of software or when changing some aspect of Windows. You can postpone such a restart, but you don't gain the benefits of any changes until after the restart takes place.

Prevent Windows from automatically restarting

Sometimes, you may notice that Windows restarts over and over again, almost starting up but then failing and starting all over again. This is a feature of Windows (believe it or not) whereby Windows restarts itself whenever it encounters a problem. It's called *automatic restart.*

To disable automatic restart, press the F8 key before the Windows logo appears when you start Windows. Pressing F8 displays the Advanced Boot Options menu. From the menu, choose the item labeled Disable Automatic Restart on System Failure. Press Enter.

Although this trick may work, it doesn't fix the problem causing the restart. *See* Problem Reports and Solutions, Safe Mode, and System Restore for more information.

Schedule a restart or shutdown

You can use the Windows Task Scheduler to have your computer automatically turn itself off at a given time. *See* Task Scheduler for an example.

Watch Your Step!

Windows doesn't shut down when you have programs with unsaved files in them. You're given the opportunity to save the files. I highly recommend that you do so.

You're warned whenever other users are logged on to the computer and you attempt to shut down or restart Windows. Be careful! You have no way to tell that other users who are logged in have unsaved files; if you shut down anyway, others can lose their stuff. Have everyone log out before you shut down or restart.

When Things Go Wrong

Windows attempts to shut down your computer by using software — specifically, the power management software, which controls the function of the console's power button. When nothing seems to work, you can use the emergency shutdown technique: Press and hold the console's power button. After about five seconds, the PC turns itself off.

Gold Rush Nuggets

Believe it or not, in the old days you just turned off the computer when you where done. Some folks did things "properly," by quitting various programs and even going as far as to *park* the hard drive. But most folks just flipped the PC's on–off switch. Thunk! Computer off.

The original term for restarting a computer was *warm boot*. A *cold boot* is when the computer is first started; the machine is cold because it's not on. (Computers get warm while they run.) The term *boot* refers to the software that loads the operating system, pulling it up by its "bootstraps," so to speak.

Digging Elsewhere

Login and Log Off, Power Button, Safe Mode, Sleep Mode

Sidebar

A new toy, er, *tool* that's included with Windows Vista is the Sidebar. It's a special docking place along the right side of the desktop, where you can float various tiny programs, or *gadgets*. The programs display information, interact with the Internet, or provide diversion from the routine humdrum of using a computer.

WHERE'S THE GOLD?

The Sidebar usually appears on the right side of the desktop. It's kind of a fat toolbar, although it sports a distinctive edge only when you point the mouse its way. Adorning the Sidebar are teensy programs called gadgets. *Gadgets* display information or interact with you, and they can be moved, controlled, added, or dismissed.

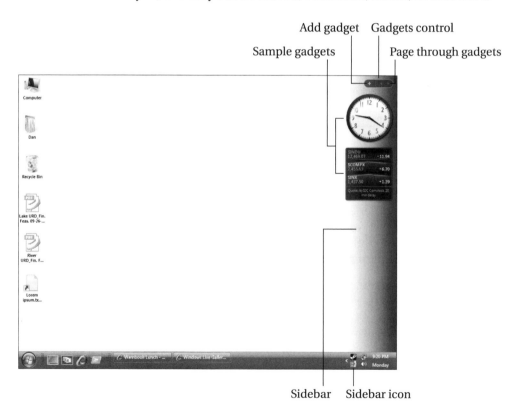

Add gadget   Gadgets control

Sample gadgets   Page through gadgets

Sidebar   Sidebar icon

The Sidebar itself is a program. It's found on the Start button menu's All Programs menu. Choose All Programs⇨Accessories⇨Windows Sidebar.

While Sidebar is running, it places a tiny icon in the Notification Area. Right-clicking the icon displays a pop-up menu with options fun and interesting. For example, choosing Properties from the pop-up menu displays the Sidebar's Properties dialog box.

Clicking the Add Gadget button (+) on the Sidebar displays a window full of gadgets, and often pages of them. These gadgets are installed on your computer, but not necessarily stored on the Sidebar.

Gadgets are obtained from the Internet, in a special part of the Microsoft Windows Live Web site called the Windows Live Gallery. The Gallery is a quick hop away from the window full of gadgets, which contains a shortcut link to the site.

Each gadget is manipulated in different ways, depending on the gadget. Some have menus, and some have buttons, but all gadgets have a little tab on the left that appears whenever the gadget is selected. You use the tab to close, modify, or move the gadget.

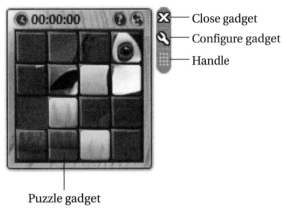

Close gadget
Configure gadget
Handle

Puzzle gadget

What to Do with It

The Sidebar comes in handy as a diversion or as a quick way to get at a handy tool, such as a calculator or online quick reference. It's completely optional, so you can use the Sidebar however you see fit.

Turn the Sidebar on

The Sidebar is turned on when Windows first loads, although it may have since been disabled. To reactivate it, use the Start button menu: Choose All Programs⇨Accessories⇨Windows Sidebar.

Make the Sidebar start when Windows starts

To control whether the Sidebar automatically starts when Windows starts, do this:

1. Right-click the Sidebar itself or the Sidebar icon in the Notification Area.

2. Choose Properties from the pop-up menu.

3. Place a check mark by the top item, Start Sidebar When Windows Starts.

4. Click OK.

See also Programs for information on making other programs start automatically with Windows.

Page through gadgets

The Sidebar can hold only so many gadgets at a time. To see any additional gadgets, click the right-pointing triangle in the Gadgets control, at the top of the Sidebar.

Eureka You can drag a gadget off the Sidebar and out onto the desktop, which allows you to see more gadgets. To drag a gadget, click to select that gadget and then use the gadget's handle to drag.

Gadgets on the desktop stay on the desktop; only those gadgets directly on the Sidebar flip from page to page as you use the Gadgets control.

Put the Sidebar on the left side of the desktop

You move the Sidebar to the "other" side of the screen by using the Sidebar Properties dialog box. Click the Right button to put the Sidebar on the right side of the desktop; click the Left button to put the Sidebar on the left.

Clue Summon the Properties dialog box by right-clicking the Sidebar or the Sidebar icon in the Notification Area.

Put the Sidebar on top of or behind other windows

The Sidebar can be always visible, floating on top of all other windows on the desktop. Or, you can configure the Sidebar to be more of a background or desktop feature. Either way, the magic button is in the Windows Sidebar Properties dialog box: Put a check mark by the option labeled Sidebar Is Always on Top of Other Windows.

Turn off the Sidebar

To hide the Sidebar, right-click the Sidebar and choose Close Sidebar from the pop-up menu.

To reactivate the Sidebar, right-click the Sidebar icon in the Notification Area and choose the Open command.

Quit the Sidebar

To close the Sidebar, ending the Windows Sidebar program, do this:

1. Right-click the Sidebar icon in the Notification Area.

2. Choose the Exit command from the pop-up menu.

3. Click the Exit Sidebar button in the confirmation dialog box.

Add a gadget

To add a new gadget to the Sidebar click the Add Gadget button, found atop the Sidebar (the + button). The Add Gadget button displays a Gallery window of gadgets, which you can page through.

To add a gadget from the Gallery, simply drag its icon to the Sidebar from the Gallery window.

 Close the Gallery window when you're done.

Display a list of running gadgets

To see which gadgets the Sidebar is now using, follow these steps:

1. Right-click the Sidebar or Sidebar icon in the Notification Area.

2. Choose Properties from the pop-up list.

3. In the Windows Sidebar Properties dialog box, click the button labeled View List of Running Gadgets.

4. Click the Close button when you're done with the View Gadgets window.

5. Close the Windows Sidebar Properties window.

Remove a gadget

To remove a gadget from the Sidebar, click to select the gadget, and then click the gadget's X (Close) button. You can also close gadgets from the View Gadgets window, which is discussed in the preceding section.

Find and install new gadgets

Microsoft stocks its Windows Live Web site with gobs of gadgets you can download and install for use in Windows. Here's how it's done:

1. Start the Sidebar if you haven't already.

2. Click the + button atop to the Sidebar to summon the Gadget Gallery window.

3. Click the link found in the window's lower right corner: Get More Gadgets Online.

   Yes, you're going on the Internet.

4. Browse through the Web site to find a gadget that interests you.

5. When you find your gadget, click the button Download to Sidebar.

6. Click the Install button to confirm the download.

7. In the File Download box, choose Save.

8. Click the Save button in the Save As dialog box.

I recommend saving all downloads in the Downloads folder.

9. After downloading the gadget, click the Open button in the Download Complete dialog box.

10. Click the Install button to add the downloaded gadget to the Sidebar.

11. Optionally, repeat Steps 4 through 10 to download more gadgets.

12. Close the Web browser window.

Uninstall a gadget

To remove a gadget from the Gallery window, essentially uninstalling it, open the Gallery window (see "Add a gadget," earlier in this entry), and follow these steps:

1. Right-click the gadget you want to uninstall.

2. Choose the Uninstall command from the pop-up menu.

3. Click the Uninstall button to confirm.

 Eureka The relative manner in which gadgets are easily removed is why I recommend downloading and saving gadgets to your account's Downloads folder. That way, you can open the folder and double-click a gadget to reinstall it.

Adjust a gadget

Most gadgets can be adjusted or manipulated. The way you adjust the gadget and the type of adjustments you make depend on the gadget. For each one, though, the *technique* is the same:

1. Click to select the gadget.

2. From the tiny tab that appears in the upper right corner, click the tool, or "wrench," button.

3. Make any adjustments.

4. Click the OK button to confirm.

For example, you can adjust the Clock gadget to display one of a number of interesting clock faces, set the time zone, or show the second hand.

Watch Your Step!

I recommend downloading gadgets only from the Windows Live Web site. Other gadgets may appear from time to time elsewhere on the Internet. Only when the gadget is available from a Web site or source you trust should you install it.

When Things Go Wrong

If the Sidebar suddenly disappears, click the Sidebar icon in the Notification Area. If that doesn't work, right-click the Sidebar icon and choose the Open command.

Gold Rush Nuggets

Sad to say, but the Windows Vista Sidebar is just a pale imitation of the better-looking and superior OS X Dashboard, found on Apple's Macintosh computer. Although both have similar gizmos, the Dashboard is designed to zoom on and off the desktop, which eliminates a lot of clutter.

Digging Elsewhere

Desktop, Notification Area

Sideshow

In the Windows Sideshow feature, a separate gizmo is used in conjunction with the computer to display information. It really has nothing to do with showing slides or even displaying graphics. No, it's more of a *side*show than a slideshow.

The first step to getting Windows Sideshow to work is to obtain a Sideshow-compatible device — an external PDA, a cellphone, a television, a remote control, or another gizmo slapped with a Windows Sideshow Compatible sticker or label.

You connect the gizmo to your computer, and Windows then uses the gizmo's screen as a second monitor to display information. Specifically, you can place Sidebar gadgets on the gizmo's screen. The gadgets continue to be displayed whether the PC is on, off, sleeping, or severely distracted.

To control the Sideshow, you must open the Sideshow icon in the Control Panel; or, from the Control Panel Home, choose Hardware and Sound and then Windows Sideshow.

In the Windows Sideshow window, you can choose which gadgets display what information on the various external screens you might have attached to your computer.

Again, the key to getting Sideshow to work is having a Windows Sideshow–compatible device that connects to the computer. Whether this makes your life easier is, of course, debatable, but it's *another* something that Windows can do.

By the way, remember that this feature is named *Side*show, not *Slide*show.

Sleep Mode

One of the PC's energy-saving features is the ability to put the computer to sleep, which is something new. In the old days, computers put people to sleep. But now you can put your computer to sleep, resting its weary hard drives, closing its heavy screen, and whispering its blazing microprocessor in a blissful state of low-power slumber. Rather than have to repeat all that, the function is simply referred to as *Sleep mode.*

Sleep mode has changed over the years. The name was originally *Stand-by* mode, and the hardware was originally designed for laptop computers. Sleep mode once merely turned off the display, powered down the hard drive(s), and switched the microprocessor into a slower, low-power state. Sleep mode does all that now, but it also saves all your unsaved data to the hard drive, similar to Hibernation (*see* Hibernation). Unlike in Hibernation mode, the computer isn't truly powered off when you enter Sleep mode.

WHERE'S THE GOLD?

There are two parts to Sleep mode in Windows. The first is where you can manually force the computer to sleep. The second part controls automatic sleeping and other power management settings.

Sleep mode is present on the Shutdown menu, identified by the padlock button on the Start button menu.

You can also "sleep your computer" by pressing the PC's power button, but only when that button has been configured to sleep the computer. *See* Power Button.

Automatic snoozing is controlled through the Power Options icon in the Control Panel; from the Control Panel Home, choose System and Maintenance (or Hardware and Sound) and then click Power Options. Opening the Power Options icon or item displays the Power Options window, your home place for power management in your PC.

Power Options icon	Virtual power button on the Start menu

The monitor fades, the hard drive warbles to a smooth stop, and the computer is asleep.

Sleep mode can also be entered by punching the PC console's power button. *See* Power Button for information on how to set that up.

Sleep mode can be entered by clicking the virtual power button on the Start button menu. See the next section.

What to Do with It

Sleep mode saves energy. It also provides a type of security in that, after waking up the computer, you need to log in again. The new mantra from Microsoft is that you should, in fact, sleep your computer rather than turn it off. (I'll leave that decision to you.)

Put the computer to sleep

You have a number of ways to sleep the computer, although the most consistent one is to choose the Sleep command from the Start button menu's list of shutdown options:

1. Click the Start button.

2. Click the triangle button next to the padlock icon (in the lower right corner of the Start button menu).

3. Choose Sleep.

Assign Sleep mode to the Start menu's power button

The Start menu sports a virtual power button in the lower middle area. To set this button's function, heed these steps:

1. Open the Control Panel's Power Options window.

2. Click one of the Change Plan Settings links.

3. Choose Change Advanced Power Settings.

   The Power Options dialog box appears.

4. In the scrolling list, click the + (plus sign) by the Power Buttons and Lid item.

5. Click the + (plus sign) by the Start Menu Power Button item.

6. Click the word following *Setting* and choose the Sleep command from the popup menu.

7. Click OK, and optionally close any other windows you opened.

Wake up the computer

The computer can be roused from Sleep mode in several ways:

✘ Press a key, such as the Ctrl key, on the keyboard.

✘ Jiggle the mouse a wee bit.

✘ Press the PC console's power button.

In a few seconds, Windows comes back to life and presents the logon screen. *See* Login and Log Off.

Set Sleep mode timeouts

Sleep mode happens automatically after a given period of inactivity. So after a period of your not tapping a key or moving or clicking the mouse, the computer naturally falls to sleep, just like Granddad on the sofa after Thanksgiving dinner. To set the timeouts for Sleep mode, obey these steps:

1. Open the Control Panel's Power Options window.

2. From the links listed on the left side of the window, choose Change When the Computer Sleeps.

3. Set a timeout period to turn off the display.

4. Set a timeout period to put the computer to sleep.

5. Click Save Changes, and optionally close the Power Options window.

The display timeout merely disables the computer's signal to the monitor, which causes modern PC monitors to enter their low-power modes.

The computer timeout determines when the entire system (hard drives, microprocessor, *and* monitor) enters low-power mode.

Disable the wake-up password

When the PC recovers from Sleep mode, it displays the logon screen and requires you to enter a password to continue. That's just good security! When you're the only person using the PC, and you feel that things are secure enough anyway, you can disable the wake-up password. Here's how:

1. Open the Control Panel's Power Options window.

2. From the list of tasks on the left side of the window, choose Require a Password on Wakeup.

3. If the Don't Require a Password option is available, skip to Step 5.

4. Choose the link Change Settings That Are Currently Unavailable.

5. Select the item Don't Require a Password.

6. Click Save Changes.

7. Close the Power Options window.

Prevent the mouse from waking up the computer

Some mice may be oversensitive and can wake up the computer if you tap on the desktop or look at the computer in the wrong way. To prevent that, follow these steps:

1. Open the Control Panel's Device Manager icon.

From the Control Panel Home, choose Hardware and Sound, and then choose Device Manager.

2. In the Device Manager window, click the + (plus sign) by Mice and Other Pointing Devices.

3. Double-click to open your PC's mouse, as listed beneath the text *Mice and Other Pointing Devices*.

4. In the mouse's Properties dialog box, click the Power Management tab.

5. Remove the check mark by the item Allow This Device to Wake the Computer.

6. Click OK and, optionally, close the Device Manager and Control Panel windows.

Disable Sleep mode

If you want to be environmentally evil, or perhaps you have no desire to see a computer sleep, you can utterly disable Sleep mode for your PC. Simply repeat the steps from the preceding section and choose Never for both display and computer timeouts.

Watch Your Step!

If you want to enjoy your PC's screen saver, ensure that the display timeout is *greater than* the screen saver timeout. For example, after 20 minutes your screen saver kicks in, but after an hour the monitor sleeps (and goes dark). *See* Screen Saver.

Laptop computers have different power management options and settings. For example, on a laptop, you can determine what happens powerwise when you close the laptop's lid while the laptop is on. For more information, refer to my book *Laptops For Dummies,* 2nd Edition (Wiley Publishing, Inc.).

When Things Go Wrong

Sleep mode isn't available on all PCs. For example, power management options may be disabled from the PC's BIOS or System Setup program. Or, Sleep mode may be disabled by your organization's computer manager.

It's normal for some PCs to have their power or hard drive lights flash or fade in and out while the computers are in Sleep mode.

Not every PC can recover from Sleep mode by pressing its power button.

If your PC crashed while sleeping, you have to start it up normally to recover. Press and hold the console's power button until the computer turns itself off. Then start the PC normally.

Gold Rush Nuggets

The U.S. Environmental Protection Agency (EPA) introduced the volunteer labeling program Energy Star in 1992 as a way to identify energy-efficient gizmos. Many electronic devices, including DVD players, MP3 players, and television sets, now have computer-like Sleep modes.

Digging Elsewhere

Hibernation, Power Button, Shutdown Windows

Sounds

The difference between music and noise really depends on how old you are and whether you've ever been exposed to John Cage. All seriousness aside, whether it's music, noise, a beep, or something resembling a digital grunt, the thing is called *sound* as far as the computer is concerned. From silence to symphony, sound covers a lot of ground — and quickly!

WHERE'S THE GOLD?

Although you cannot hold sound in your fist, you can control it, especially when the sound is oozing from your computer's speakers. There are hardware controls, which you find on your PC's speakers, on the headphones (if you use those), or on an external sound system. Those things you control by using your fingers or, if you're really lazy, a remote control.

In Windows, sound exists and is controlled in a variety of places depending on whether you're dealing with creating sound or controlling the volume.

Sound volume is controlled primarily by using the Sound icon in the Notification area. (*See* Notification Area.)

Sound is set by using the Sound icon in the Control Panel; from the Control Panel Home, choose Hardware and Sounds, and then choose Sound. The Sound dialog box is where sound hardware is configured, and also where sounds can be assigned to events.

Sounds themselves are saved as files on disk. (The sound is simply digital information encoded into a file, just as a JPG or PNG is a digital representation of an image.) To play the sound file, double-click. The sound file most likely will play in the Windows Media Center unless you have other audio software installed. (*See* Programs.)

You can also create your own sound files, if your computer has a microphone, or recording device, attached.

What to Do with It

Annoy the neighbors!

Display the Sound icon in the Notification Area

When dealing with sound on your PC, you must have the Sound icon displayed in the Taskbar's Notification Area. *See* Notification Area for the details; this entry assumes that the Sound icon is visible.

Sound icon in Notification Area

Sound icon in the Control Panel

Set the PC's overall volume

To make the PC's whisper quiet or loud enough to wake the dead, click the Sound icon in the Notification Area to display the pop-up volume control.

Use the slider on the volume control to make the PC louder (up) or softer (down). The volume control gizmo controls the overall volume of *all* sound in the PC. Although other programs, such as Windows Media Center, may have their own volume sliders, the volume control in the Notification Area is the *master.*

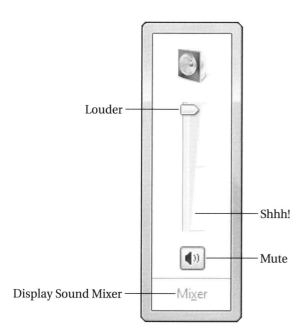

Louder

Shhh!

Mute

Display Sound Mixer

Mixer

Make it mute!

To mute the speakers, do this:

1. Click the Sound icon in the Notification Area.

2. Click the Mute button, just above the word *Mixer.*

To unmute the sound, repeat these steps.

Note that the Sound icon in the Notification Area changes to indicate that the speakers have been muted.

Set the volume for individual noise generators

The Windows sound mixer window is labeled Volume Mixer. Display it by clicking the Mixer link from the volume control.

The Volume Meter window displays multiple sound-generating voices in your computer, such as sounds from applications, from the MIDI generator, Line In, and other sources. You can set the individual volume for each gizmo or mute individual gizmos as you please.

For example, if you detest MIDI music annoying you from some childish Web page, you can mute all MIDI music by clicking the Mute button in the MIDI column of the Volume Meter window.

Play a sound file

Sound files play when you open them, just as graphics files are displayed when you open them. As with graphics files, however, you may want to pick which application plays the sound file: Click to select the sound file, and then use the toolbar's Open button's menu to choose which application plays the sound.

Of course, when Windows Media Player is the only sound-playing program you have, it's the only item on the list.

Record a sound file

Windows comes with the primitive sound recording program Sound Recorder. It's pitiful. But it comes with Windows. To record your own voice, do this:

1. Connect a microphone to the Mic-In jack (colored red or pink) on your PC.

2. From the Start button menu, choose All Programs⇨Accessories⇨Sound Recorder.

3. Click the Start Recording button.

4. Talk. Sing. Be entertaining. Just direct it into the microphone.

5. Click the Stop Recording button.

6. Save the file.

A better audio-recording program is Audacity. Be sure that you get the Windows Vista–compatible version from:

`http://audacity.sourceforge.net/`

 You can also record sound from other devices, such as a VCR, tape recorder, or ancient turntable. Simply connect the audio output from the device to the PC's Line In jack, and then use a program like Sound Recorder (or Audacity).

Assign sounds to events

One of the more entertaining things to do in Windows is assign sounds to certain events or activities. It's fun. And, it's not really a waste of time: It's considered serious computer configuration. Really. They pay people six digits in Silicon Valley to do such things.

1. Open the Sounds icon in the Control Panel.

2. Click the Sounds tab.

3. Choose an event from the scrolling list.

4. To hear the current sound, click the Test button.

5. Choose another sound from the Sounds drop-down list:

   The list displays related sound files, but it's not a complete list of all sound files on your computer.

6. Use the Browse button to locate a sound file not shown on the drop-down list.

   Windows uses WAV (wave) format sound files for its events.

7. Use the Text button to confirm the sound.

8. Repeat Steps 3 through 7 for each sound you want to modify.

9. Click OK, and close the Control Panel window.

Use a sound scheme

Windows lets you save your sound settings (events and their sounds) as a scheme on disk. You can also select from preset sound schemes, which changes all Windows sounds at once. Here's how:

1. Click the Sound tab in the Sound dialog box.

2. Choose a preset scheme from the drop-down list.

3. (Optional) Choose various sounds from the scrolling list of sounds and use the Test button to check things out.

4. Click OK.

Eureka You can choose the No Sounds scheme when you prefer blissful silence.

You can also create your own custom sound list. In fact, anytime the drop-down list says "whatever scheme" followed by "modified," it means that you've made some of your own changes. To save them to disk for later recall, click the Save As button and use the Save As dialog box to save your scheme to disk.

Disable the Windows theme song

To turn off the music that Windows plays when it starts, follow these steps:

1. Open the Control Panel's Sounds icon.

2. In the Sound dialog box, click the Sounds tab.

3. Remove the check mark by the Play Windows Startup sound item.

4. Click OK, and close the Control Panel window.

Watch Your Step!

Some Windows events to which you can assign sounds may appear vague: Asterisk, Exclamation, and Question, for example. That's because they're different types of warnings.

Save your own, custom sound files as the WAV file type when you plan to use them for Windows sounds. (Other popular file types include MP3, WMA, and AIFF.) WAV is the standard file format for saving audio with the Sound Recorder application, but not with the Audacity program.

When Things Go Wrong

Dag Nabbit You may also have a volume control on your PC's speakers (or headphones). That hardware control has the final say-so over how loud, soft, or non-existent sound that's coming from your PC can be.

Ensure that Windows knows about your PC's sound system. When it doesn't, Windows makes assumptions, one of which is that your PC has no microphone input or other obvious sound controls. The best way to inform Windows is to use the driver CD that came with your PC — the CD (or DVD) that contains the computer's sound system files.

Gold Rush Nuggets

Windows keeps its sound files in the Windows\ Media folder.

There was some debate at Microsoft over whether to have a startup sound and whether users could disable it. Many people object to the sound, and I'm sure that you've been places where you heard it and thought, "There's some dork starting Windows." But in the end, sanity won the day, and you can, indeed, disable the sound that Windows plays when it first starts.

Digging Elsewhere

Control Panel, Notification Area, Themes

Speech Recognition

Ah! The holy grail of computing continues to be speech recognition. Blame Mr. Spock. Back on *Star Trek,* he never typed into a computer. No, Mr. Spoke *spoke* to the computer. He addressed it as "Computer" (although in practice, the crew of the Enterprise would most likely give the computer a name, even a boring one like `enterprise.uss.ufp`). Ever since then, computer enthusiasts and amateurs have longed for the same thing. O to be able to sit at a PC and mutter, "Get my stock quotes, check today's headlines, get my mail, and see whether Belinda is on her Webcam." But, is it just a dream?

Surprisingly, Windows comes with basic speech recognition abilities. Although Mr. Spock would be disappointed, folks who prefer speaking to the PC over typing (or who cannot type) will find it a decent if not acceptable alternative.

The problem with speech recognition software in general is that it must be trained. You need to spend time in front of the computer reading and reciting so that the software can recognize your voice. A minimum of three hours is necessary to get the computer trained. And, the more time you spend dictating and the computer spends learning, the better it understands you. Eventually, speech recognition works flawlessly, or so it says in the brochure.

To get started with speech recognition, open the Control Panel's Speech Recognition Options icon, or, from the Control Panel Home, choose Ease of Access and then Speech Recognition Options. Next choose the link Start Speech Recognition and follow the steps.

Remember that speech recognition works only after training; don't expect to sit down at the computer in the morning and be dictating like some fictional starship science officer by the afternoon.

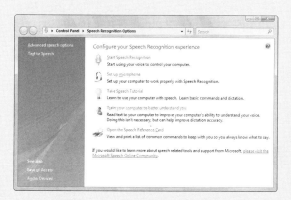

Standard User

Three types of users are on a Windows Vista computer: First is the glorious *administrator,* who has full control and power over the computer and can access all the bells, whistles, and graphical goodness that the PC has to offer. Amen. Second is the mere, humble *standard user,* who can use the computer at will but is limited in his abilities to alter the computer in such a way as to affect other users. The third is the pitiful *Guest* account user, which is really the bus station lavatory of computer accounts: No one wants it, but it's there if you need it. Quickly. For most folks using a PC, these differences mean nothing. The *default* or only account on a PC is Administrator. Microsoft recommends that you create a second, Standard User account for daily computer use.

WHERE'S THE GOLD?

User information is ensconced in the User Accounts window, which you can access by opening the User Accounts icon in the Control Panel. The window explains which type of account you have, and it also provides access to change other accounts from one account type to another.

What to Do with It

Honestly, you're supposed to do everything as a standard user, unless you're working with something that affects all users on the computer. In that case, Microsoft desires that you log in to the Administrator account.

Create a Standard User account

When you have an Administrator account and desire to comply with Microsoft's wishes, you should set up a separate Standard User account to use for your daily computer activities. Here's how to do that:

1. Log in under an administrator-level account.

   When you're the only person using the computer, that's *you!*

2. Open the Control Panel.

3. Open the User Accounts icon.

   In the Control Panel Home, choose User Accounts and Family Safety, and then choose User Accounts.

4. Choose Manage Another Account.

5. Click the Create a New Account link.

6. Type the name for the account.

7. Ensure that Standard User is selected.

8. Click the Create Account button.

The account is created and appears in a window listing other accounts on the computer. I recommend logging in as that user and applying a good password to the account. *See* Login and Log Off and Passwords.

Run an application with administrator privilege

When you're not the administrator, you can temporarily run a program with administrator privilege. To do so, right-click the program's icon and choose Run As Administrator from the shortcut menu. This action is necessary for only specific programs that affect all users, such as antivirus programs or other utilities.

The keyboard shortcut for running an application with administrator privilege is to press Ctrl+Shift as you open an application.

You can permanently assign administrator privilege to an application by following these steps:

1. Right-click the program's icon.

2. Choose Properties from the shortcut menu.

3. In the program's Properties dialog box, click the Compatibility tab.

4. Place a check mark by the option Run As Administrator.

When running an application with administrator-level privilege as a standard user, you're prompted to enter the password for an administrator-level account. Simply choose the account (if there's more than one), type the password, and click the OK button to continue.

Watch Your Step!

As a standard user, you cannot install or remove any software or hardware from the computer. (Well, you can physically remove the hardware, but you cannot tell Windows about the changes unless you log in as an administrator.)

Standard users cannot make any changes to the computer that affect all users. For example, you cannot edit the portion of the All Programs menu that contains settings for all users. You're also banned from deleting or changing certain system files that administrators can access.

When Things Go Wrong

Each account on the computer is unique and separate. So, when you set up a new Standard User account, it's the typical dull account that everyone gets in Windows; you have to add any custom settings, sounds, graphics, and other things to the account. Or, to share stuff with your Administrator account, use the Public folder. *See* Public Folder.

Gold Rush Nuggets

The reason behind using the Standard User account rather than an Administrator account is security. As a standard user, you automatically have a lower level of access to the types of things that nasty programs — spyware, viruses, Trojans, worms — need in order to do their dirty work. By running the PC as an administrator, you remove one layer of protection.

Digging Elsewhere

Administrator, Guest, User Accounts

Start Button and Menu

The key that unlocks Windows is the Start button. It's the spot to go to when you want to start up anything in Windows: Run a program, open a folder, configure windows, or just mess around. It all starts with the Start button, which displays the Start button menu.

The Start button dwells on the far end of the Taskbar; when the Taskbar rests at the bottom of the display, the Start button is found on its left end, nestled in the lower left corner of the display.

By clicking the Start button, you display the Start menu. The Start menu can also be displayed by pressing the Windows (Win) key on the PC keyboard or by pressing the Ctrl+Esc key combination.

You control the Start menu mostly by using the Taskbar and Start Menu Properties dialog box. You can summon that dialog box by opening the Control Panel's Taskbar and Start Menu icon; or, the best way to see the dialog box (the shortcut) is to right-click the Start button and choose Properties from the pop-up menu. Ensure that the Start Menu tab is chosen inside the dialog box.

What to Do with It

Naturally, you use the Start button and its menu to start things. This concept is so well known that Microsoft decided not to apply the name Start to the Start button in Windows Vista.

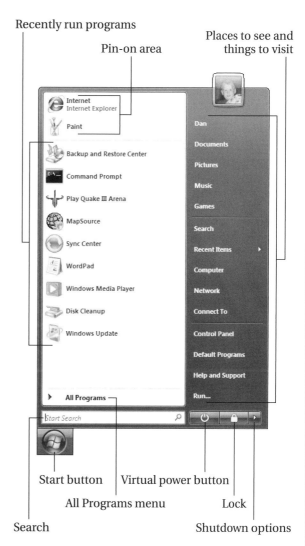

Recently run programs

Pin-on area

Places to see and things to visit

Start button

Virtual power button

All Programs menu

Lock

Search

Shutdown options

Run a program

The Start button menu is one of many places you can go in Windows to start programs. Programs can be chosen from the pin-on area, the list of recently run programs, or from the All Programs part of the menu. *See* All Programs Menu.

Search for stuff

The Start button menu is also home to one of the many Search boxes in Windows. You can use Search to locate files and information all over your PC. *See* Search.

Go to somewhere in Windows

The right side of the Start button menu lists various and sundry places you can visit in Windows, popular folders, the Control Panel, the Run and Search commands, plus other items. Some of these items are commands, and others are menus.

To specify what shows up on the right side of the Start menu and whether it's a link or a menu, refer to the section "Add and remove items from the right side," later in this entry.

Shutdown Windows

The lower right part of the Start button menu deals with options for ending your Windows day, including sleep, lock, and a submenu full of logoff and shutdown options. *See* Shutdown Windows.

Place a program in the pin-on area

The *pin-on* area is the upper left portion of the Start button menu. In older versions of Windows, this area was simply the top of the Start button menu, whereupon certain popular programs would roost. Obviously, accessing programs on such a perch is easy and consistent, so it's a desirable position.

To post one of your most-favorite programs to the pin-on area, do this:

1. Right-click the program's icon.

   The icon can be a shortcut icon on the desktop, an icon in the Quick Launch bar, a menu item on the All Programs menu, or even an icon listed in the Start menu's list of recently run programs.

2. From the pop-up shortcut menu, choose the command Pin to Start Menu.

Place Internet programs in the pin-on area

There's no need to pin your Internet programs — specifically, the Web browser and e-mail program — to the Start menu. That's because those programs have their own priority method for being pinned. Here it is:

1. Right-click the Start button and choose Properties from the pop-up menu.

2. Click the Customize button.

3. To pin your Web browser to the Start menu, place a check mark by Internet Link (near the bottom of the dialog box).

4. Optionally, choose a Web browser from the button menu.

5. To pin your e-mail program to the Start menu, place a check mark by E-Mail Link.

6. Optionally, choose an e-mail program from the button menu.

7. Click OK, and close any other open dialog boxes or windows.

In the old days, Microsoft automatically pinned Internet Explorer and Outlook Express (or Outlook) to the top of the Start menu. Thanks to advancing technology and multiple lawsuits, you now have that option yourself.

Clear the recently run programs list

Windows keeps track of each program you run, placing it on the Start menu in the list of recently run programs. The list is updated as you open and run programs, making it easy for you to access the programs you run most often. For some, however, the list is a security risk, and it should be eliminated or cleared. Here's how:

1. Right-click the Start button and choose Properties from the pop-up menu.

2. Remove the check mark by the option labeled Store and Display a List of Recently Opened Programs.

3. Click OK.

This list of recently run programs is now cleared — and disabled. To reenable it, repeat these steps but add the check mark in Step 2.

Set the size of the recently run programs list

To set the size of the recently run programs list, follow these steps:

1. Right-click the Start button and choose Properties from the pop-up menu.

2. Click the Customize button.

3. Set a new value by the option Number of Recent Programs to Display.

Windows presets this value to 9.

4. Click OK, and then click OK to close the other dialog box.

The more items you have in the recently run programs list, the taller the Start menu can get.

Purge the list of recently opened files

Windows keeps track of the programs you run, keeping them on the Start menu's Recent Items submenu. That menu offers you a quick way to access those programs you run most often, but it might also provide a security risk in that it shows other users which programs you've been working on.

To empty the list of recently opened files, do this:

1. Right-click the Start button and choose Properties from the pop-up menu.

2. Remove the check mark by the option labeled Store and Display a List of Recently Opened Files.

3. Click OK.

Add and remove items from the right side

You can control which items appear on the right side of the Start button menu. You can determine whether some of the items are links, which open other windows, or menus, which display submenus listing more options, icons in the named folder, or what-have-you. It's all controlled by following these steps:

1. Right-click the Start button.

2. Choose Properties from the pop-up menu.

3. Click the Customize button.

4. Use the scrolling list to add or remove items from the right side of the Start button's menu:

   a. Place a check mark by an item to display that item.

   b. Choose Display As Link for an item to display that item as a command.

   c. Choose Display As a Menu to display the item's contents as a submenu.

   d. Choose Don't Display the Item to remove the item from the menu.

5. Click OK when you're done customizing, and then click OK to close the other dialog box.

To restore things to the way they were when Windows first came out of the box, click the Use Default Settings button (after Step 3).

Use the antique Start menu look

Some people enjoy the way that Windows 98 or Windows NT displayed the Start button menu. Back then, the menu was stark. Naked. Aesthetically pleasing. Boring.

To relive those days, follow these steps:

1. Right-click the Start button.

2. Choose Properties from the pop-up menu.

3. Choose Classic Start Menu.

4. Click OK.

Watch Your Step!

Most Windows Vista documentation assumes that you're not using the Classic Start menu.

When Things Go Wrong

The buttons from which you can choose alternative Web browsers or e-mail software (see the earlier section "Place Internet programs in the pin-on area") are disabled when your PC lacks alternatives to the Internet Explorer or Windows Mail programs, which come with Windows. If you have such programs and they still don't show up, just manually pin them to the Start button's menu as described in this entry.

Gold Rush Nuggets

The Start button was named Start in each version of Windows that had a Start button. Windows 95 even had a "bouncing arrow" that said *Start here* next to the Start button, as though the word *Start* weren't enough to clue you in to the button's function.

Digging Elsewhere

All Programs Menu, Run, Search, Taskbar

Sync Center

You can argue that Windows has thrown in everything, including the kitchen sink, but sink is spelled *sync* in this case and it stands for *synchronize*. Officially (or, according to the dictionary), *synchronize* means to cause things to occur or take place at the same rate or time. On a computer, synchronize is often the process of making information on one computer match up with information on another. You can do that manually, which is a chore, or you can use the Sync Center to have things done for you automagically.

The Sync Center is a program. To start it, from the Start button menu, choose All Programs⇨ Accessories⇨Sync Center. You can also view the Sync Center window from the Control Panel: Open the Sync Center icon, or from the Control Panel home, choose Network and Internet and then Sync Center.

The Sync Center window displays any folders being synced, plus any errors or conflicts that have occurred as part of a synchronization.

With files in sync, you can browse to network folders and access files even though the network may not be connected. For example, you can access files on a laptop even though the laptop isn't there. And when you do connect the laptop, the Sync Center synchronizes files between the two devices.

To set up a folder for synchronizing, first locate the folder on the network. Right-click the network folder and choose the command Always Available Offline. That sets up the synchronization between the two computers.

To force a folder to update, right-click it and choose the Sync command. Otherwise, the Sync Center does its own updating on a schedule that you can look up in the Task Scheduler (*see* Task Scheduler). Otherwise, you can check current synch-ups in the Synch window by opening the Sync Results icon.

Note that you cannot sync folders on computers running some versions of Windows Vista.

Sync Center icon

System Information

Windows provides you with a tool that answers the question "What the heck is going on in my computer?" The tool is the System Information window, and it displays information about your PC's hardware, software, and various programs. The System Information window is an information tool. You can use it to help troubleshoot or to answer tech support questions.

WHERE'S THE GOLD?

Unlike so many other tools, System Information can be easily found on the Start button menu. Choose All Programs⇨Accessories⇨System Tools⇨System Information.

From the Run dialog box, you can open the System Information window by typing **msinfo32** and pressing Enter.

The System Information window lists both hardware and software information about what's going on in your computer.

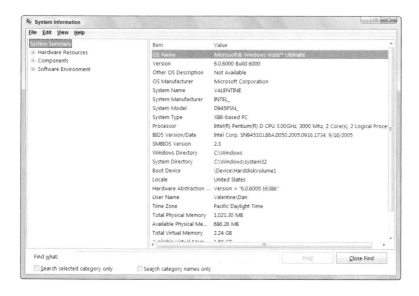

What to Do with It

The System Information window places hardware and software information in one location. That's handy.

Discover which CPU is in your PC

A common question people ask is which CPU, or microprocessor, dwells in their PC's bosom. Sometimes the CPU type is named on a sticker on the front of the console. But the System Information window should be used to get the real answer (or at least the best answer without opening up the case and looking directly at the microprocessor itself!).

In the System Information window, choose System Summary on the left. On the right, look in the Item column for Processor. The text to the right of Processor describes in detail which CPU is harbored in your computer.

Determine how much memory the computer has

After the microprocessor question, folks most want to know how much memory is installed in their computers. Again, this answer is found in the System Information window by selecting the System Summary category: On the right side of the window, look for the Total Physical Memory item.

On my computer, the value shown is 1,021.30MB, which is close enough to the one gigabyte of RAM that I paid for when I bought the computer. Other items worth noting:

Available Physical Memory: How much of the computer's memory is *not* being used. The lower this value, the more sluggish the computer's performance.

Total Virtual Memory: Represents virtual memory, a disk-based supplement to physical memory (or RAM). This value is set internally by Windows, although the more physical memory your computer has, the less it has to rely on virtual memory.

Available Virtual Memory: Reveals how much virtual memory is being used. If the value is less than the Total Virtual Memory value, I recommend buying more RAM for your computer. You should see a noticeable performance increase by doing so.

Memory information can also be found in the System window. (Open the Control Panel's System icon to see it.) Don't be confused when the memory information in the System window appears different from the System Information window's values; the System window *rounds* the value.

Check the Windows version

If you're confused about which Windows version you're using or you need to know the specific Windows release numbers, you can check in the System Information window. Click the System Summary item on the left; on the right, the top item, OS Name, tells you the official Windows version name. The second item, Version, gives you a specific release and build number.

The Windows version can also be found in the System window; open the Control Panel's System icon to see that information.

List any known hardware problems

In addition to using the Device Manager, you can use the System Information window to help locate potential hardware problems. In the System Information window, on the left, choose Components and then select the Problem Devices option. On the left, you see any known hardware problems.

(On my computer, a digital camera, or *Webcam*, appears in the list of problem devices. The camera is connected to my PC's USB port, but I don't have software for the camera to enable it.)

Review network connections

A common question that people ask me by e-mail is "Who is using my computer?" This question comes up because when you quit Windows, you might see the message "Others are using your computer. Shutdown anyway?"

Don't be alarmed! The "others" mentioned in the warning message are most likely connections on the network. (They may also be other users logged in to your PC.) To check the network connections in the System Information window, choose Software Environment, Network Connections on the left side of the window. The right side of the window then reveals who is connected to your computer and which network resources your computer is connected to. *See* Share Stuff on the Network for more information.

Watch Your Step!

Many, many things go on inside the computer. Not everyone knows everything that goes on, so please do not use any information gathered and displayed by the System Information window to determine whether you should modify anything in Windows. If you do, ensure that you set a restore point before going forward. *See* System Restore.

When Things Go Wrong

Sometimes, the System Information window may take a few moments to refresh. Just sit and wait. If you think that the program has "hung," check the Task Manager to see whether it's responding. *See* Task Manager.

Gold Rush Nuggets

γνωθI σεαυτον is Greek for "know thyself." The System Information program is the computer's attempt at knowing itself, although keep in mind that the computer is very bad at self-diagnosis.

Digging Elsewhere

Device Manager, Help

System Monitor

Your computer uses resources to make all the action happen. *Resources* include computer memory — which is perhaps the biggest resource — and also how much of the microprocessor is being used and the number of programs that are running; it also includes graphical and other types of resources. Having too many resources is just *wonderful*: Your computer runs well with few problems. Too few resources can make your computing experience sluggish. The solution is, generally, to add more memory or upgrade to a more powerful microprocessor.

System Monitor was the original name of a tool used in Windows to examine system resources. Sadly, System Monitor is no longer included with Windows Vista, although other tools are available. Even so, I still refer to them as the System Monitor.

WHERE'S THE GOLD?

Taking the System Monitor's place are two locations in Windows: one where you can quickly check resources and another where you can monitor resources over time.

Your first stop is the Performance tab in the Task Manager window: Press Ctrl+Shift+Esc to bring up the Task Manager window, and then click the Performance tab for a quick summary of system action.

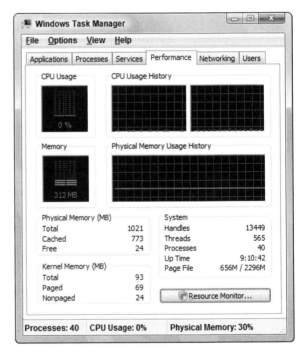

Your second stop is the Resource Monitor. To get to this location, click the Resource Monitor button on the Task Manager's Performance tab; close the Task Manager and behold the wonders of the Resource Monitor window.

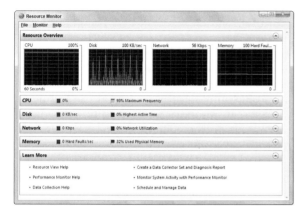

You can also launch the Resource Monitor from the Run dialog box: Type **perfmon** and press Enter.

What to Do with It

Sadly, the only thing you can do about resources, at least from within Windows, is to monitor them. Watching resource consumption can clue you in to what's happening inside the PC and, at minimum, tell you where else to look.

Review the Task Manager's Performance tab

The Task Manager's Performance tab lists two graphs and three areas to help describe current resource usage inside the computer.

CPU Usage: This meter and graph show how much effort the microprocessor is exerting.

Memory: The memory meter and graph display how much computer memory is being consumed. (Memory is renewable, so closing programs and windows frees up memory.)

Physical Memory (MB): This area lists overall memory statistics.

Kernel Memory (MB): Memory used by the Windows operating system is shown in this area (as opposed to memory used by programs or by you, the user).

System: This area shows various tidbits about the computer. Note the Up Time value; it tells you how long your computer has been turned on and running.

Check the Resource Monitor

The Resource Monitor window lists five large buttons. The first button most likely is "open," and it displays four moving graphs. Below the graphs are the other four large buttons, each covering a different system resource. To reveal more information about a resource, click its button.

Resource Overview: This area shows a set of four graphs that track overall resource activity in the computer.

CPU: The table displayed under the CPU heading lists running programs and processes, giving each an ID number (*PID,* for Process ID), a description, and various other info nuggets.

Disk: This area lists disk activity, including a huge list of open, running programs and files. You can track CPU usage from the Disk area by using the PID of each disk image.

Network: The Network area lists various programs that are communicating with other computers on the network or Internet. You may see some activity here as certain tasks take place in the background in Windows, such as checking your e-mail, updating windows, getting help, or performing other processes that access the Internet.

Memory: The Memory area shows all running processes and how much memory each one is consuming.

 Remember that you can sort the various tables in the Resource Monitor by clicking the table head. To see which resources are using the most memory, click the Memory button to display that information, and then click the Commit (KB) column heading.

How to tell when you have a memory leak

A *memory leak* is a lingering computer problem from which no one is immune. Normally, when a program quits, it releases the memory it was using back to the operating system, which can then allot that memory to some other program. But when a program *leaks* memory, it doesn't release the memory it used. In fact, the program tends to slowly consume more and more memory, which makes the computer act sluggish and eventually stop.

You cannot fix a memory leak, but you can spot one in the Resource Monitor. Simply track memory usage over time by using the Memory graph in the Resource Overview area at the top of the window. If memory use steadily grows, and you're not running any more programs, you may have a memory leak.

Finding which specific program is leaking is tough because you have to restart the computer and test each program individually. Even then, when you find the guilty program, only the software developer can fix the actual leak.

Watch Your Step!

Don't freak out at the things that go on in the computer. True, the Resource Monitor is by far the most informative tool for seeing what's going on in your computer. But just because you may see random tasks come and go or watch network access spike and then flat-line doesn't necessarily mean that some evil program has taken over your computer.

When Things Go Wrong

Remember that the Resource Monitor is merely a diagnostic tool; it doesn't fix anything. The fix for most resource problems is to buy more memory or a faster microprocessor.

Another good idea is to ensure that Windows and its files are always up-to-date. *See* Updates.

Gold Rush Nuggets

The System Monitor, er, Resource Monitor window is a great tool for demonstrating how multi-tasking works in Windows. By opening another window *in front of* the Resource Monitor (but not full screen), you can still see the charts in the Resource Monitor working in the background. That's one way to prove that the computer is doing more than one thing at a time.

Digging Elsewhere

Task Manager

System Properties

A popular dialog box to visit in previous versions of Windows was the System Properties dialog box. In that dialog box, you could discover which version of Windows you had or how much memory was installed on your computer. You could visit the Device Manager, configure system items, set the computer and network names, configure System Restore, and do a whole host of interesting things. The System Properties dialog box is truly a useful place, as are its Windows Vista counterparts.

WHERE'S THE GOLD?

The System Properties dialog box still exists, but it's been split into two beings. The first is the System window.

You summon the System window by opening the System icon in the Control Panel; or from the Control Panel Home, choose System and Maintenance and then System. Or, from the desktop, you can right-click the Computer icon and choose Properties to see the System window.

The System window displays a lot of the information once found on the General tab of the System Properties dialog box. But, it's not quite the same thing as the old System Properties dialog box. To get there, you must click the Advanced System Settings link, found on the left side of the System window.

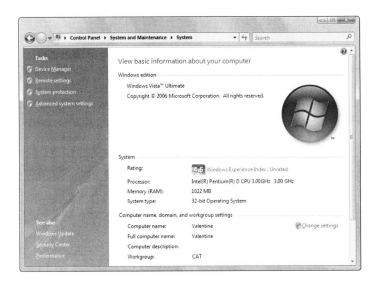

The System Properties dialog box looks more like what folks remember from the Windows XP days (and before).

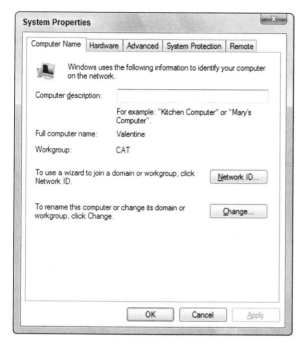

Note that you can quickly summon the System Properties dialog box directly from the Run dialog box. The command to type is **SystemPropertiesComputerName**. Or, to see the Hardware tab, type **SystemProperties Hardware**. To see the Advanced tab, type **SystemPropertiesAdvanced**. (You get the idea.)

What to Do with It

The System window and System Properties dialog box are informational tools as well as places where you can tune the Windows operating system. Most of these activities are covered specifically elsewhere in this book.

Determine which version of Windows you're using

To find out which version of Windows Vista you have, summon the System window and read the topmost item.

To specifically see which version of Windows you have, summon the Run dialog box and type **winver**. Click OK to see the About Windows window, which tells you more detailed information.

Determine how much memory is installed on your PC

The System window displays memory information in the second area, System. Also listed is the CPU clock speed, although that information may not be totally accurate.

See also Task Manager and System Monitor for more information on memory and its usage.

About that Experience rating

One of the most annoying items in the System window is the Windows Experience Index. It's a value from 1.0 through 5.9 that grades your computer's performance, kind of like rating floor routines at a gymnastics competition, but supposedly more objective (and without that biased judge from Romania).

Clicking the Windows Experience Index link in the System window displays the Performance Information and Tools window, where you can see individual ratings for various resources in your computer.

The idea behind this ratings system is so that you can boast about how much better your PC is than your co-workers'. Seriously, it supposedly has something to do with the Windows Vista *experience*, which means that it's easier to judge which software your computer can handle by using the experience rating value when you go shopping. Or so they say.

Watch Your Step!

There are things you can do in the System Properties dialog box that affect the entire computer. Don't go around messing with things unless you fully understand how they affect your PC.

When Things Go Wrong

You can improve your PC's performance instantly by adding more memory. Windows Vista supposedly needs a minimum of 512MB of RAM, but 2GB (or four times what's recommended) is a more realistic figure. A faster, larger hard drive helps. And, a nice, speedy microprocessor never hurt any computer.

When goofing up settings in the System Properties dialog box, your best recourse is System Restore. *See* System Restore. Of course, if you use the System Properties dialog box to disable System Restore, you're really out on a limb as far as troubleshooting goes.

Gold Rush Nuggets

The System Properties dialog box first appeared in Windows 95.

Digging Elsewhere

Device Manager, System Restore

System Restore

The System Restore feature is a wonderful solution to many of the common problems that plague Windows. In short, you can use System Restore to take your computer back in time, back to when it was working properly or before you made so many changes and screwed things up that there just wasn't anything else you could do. Truly, System Restore is a lifesaver.

WHERE'S THE GOLD?

As a utility, the System Restore command dwells on the All Programs menu along with most other available programs and applications.

To run System Restore, from the Start button menu, choose All Programs➪Accessories➪System Tools➪System Restore.

You can manually run System Restore by typing **rstrui** into the Run dialog box. *See* Run.

The most obscure place to find System Restore is in the System Properties dialog box. Summon it this way:

1. Open the Control Panel's System icon, or from the Control Panel Home choose System and Maintenance and then System.

2. From the links on the left side of the System window, choose System Protection.

In the System Properties dialog box, the System Protection tab contains items that control System Restore, such as which hard drives are affected. The Create button can be used to set a new restore point, or the System Restore button can be used to run System Restore.

What to Do with It

System Restore is about keeping your computer running well and keeping you, the computer operator, happy. That's accomplished by setting and using restore points as you work on, with, or against the computer.

Set a restore point

A restore point is a snapshot of your computer's condition, settings, and options at a certain point in time. The restore point is set so that, in case something nasty happens later, you can restore your computer to its operating condition when the restore point was set.

Normally, it's not necessary to create a restore point, because System Restore is configured to create restore points automatically. But, to manually set one, heed these steps:

1. Summon the System Properties dialog box, the System Protection tab.

2. Click the Create button.

3. Type a description for the restore point.

    For example, type **Just before I started messing with my computer**.

4. Click the Create button.

5. Click OK in the confirmation dialog box.

6. Close up other dialog boxes and windows.

Clue The best time to create a restore point is just before you start messing with the computer, installing new software, or adding new hardware. (Most software installation programs automatically set restore points.)

Set up automatic restore points

Windows is configured to create restore points every day at midnight as well as each time you turn on the computer. You don't need to mess with this schedule, although you can review it in the Task Scheduler: Open Task Scheduler Library, Microsoft, Windows, System Restore to see the schedule. *See* Task Scheduler.

Restore your system

When things run amok and trouble surrounds you like subpoenas and a congressman, you should turn to System Restore to bring your computer back to the way it was — hopefully, before the problems set in.

Note that restoring your system restarts Windows! Be sure that you save your stuff before you do this:

1. Start System Restore.

2. Choose Recommended Restore.

Or, if the problem predates the recommended restore point, select Choose a Different Restore Point, click Next, and pluck the restore point from the list that's presented.

3. Click Next.

4. Click the Finish button to restore Windows.

5. Click the Yes button to confirm and to restart Windows.

A confirmation dialog box appears after the computer has restarted and you log back in to Windows.

Disable System Restore

Some folks consider System Restore to be a security problem — specifically, the ability to recover previous versions of files because those previous versions may contain sensitive information. Another reason to disable System Restore is to free up all the hard drive space it consumes.

To disable System Restore, bring up the System Properties dialog box and select the System Protection tab. Remove the check mark by the disk drive(s) System Restore is monitoring. Click OK.

If you choose to disable System Restore, I highly recommend that you take on the regular task of backing up your computer. *See* Backup.

Watch Your Step!

The quicker you are to use System Restore to solve problems, the more successful you'll be. It's when you try to restore to a week (or longer) ago that you have trouble getting your system back.

Setting too many restore points consumes a heck of a lot of disk space.

When you disable System Restore, you also remove the ability of Windows to restore previous versions of files and folders. *See* Previous Versions.

When Things Go Wrong

Restore points vanish when you use the Disk Cleanup program. Beware! *See* Disk Cleanup.

When System Restore fails to solve the problem, the problem may not be with Windows but, rather, with an application you're running or the computer's hardware.

Gold Rush Nuggets

System Restore was formally introduced with Windows Me. Curiously, System Restore was available in Windows 98, but only from the command prompt.

Digging Elsewhere

Backup, Previous Versions

Tabbed Browsing

A new feature in Internet Explorer (IE), but one that has been in competing Web browsers for a few years now, is tabbed browsing. The tabbed feature allows for multiple Web pages to be viewed in a single program window. It can often be handier to use multiple tabs rather than try to manage multiple Web pages in multiple windows.

Tabs appear on top of the Web page window, alongside the IE toolbar buttons, between Favorites and Home. Each tab represents an open Web page, one that can be switched to or viewed within the same window.

Tabbed browsing is controlled from the Tabbed Browsing Settings dialog box.

The Tabbed Browsing Settings dialog box controls the specifics of how tabs work in IE. Note that making changes often requires you to quit IE and then restart.

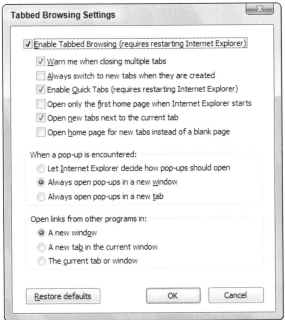

Close button

Tab List   Current tab   New tab

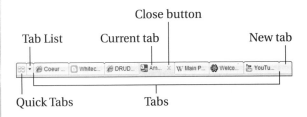

Quick Tabs   Tabs

Here's how to display that dialog box:

1. From the IE toolbar, choose Internet Options from the Tools button menu.

2. On the General tab in the Internet Options dialog box, click the Settings button in the Tabs area.

What to Do with It

I suppose you can use tabbed browsing however you want. I tend to open related links in tabs while I'm on one Web page so that I can continue reading related materials without closing the same window. Or something like that.

Activate tabbed browsing

When you don't see the tabs, or are sick of seeing the tabs, you can turn them on or off. To do so, summon the Tabbed Browsing Settings dialog box. Put a check mark by the top item, Enable Tabbed Browsing, and then click OK and close the Internet Options dialog box. Or, remove the check mark to disable the tabs.

Remember that you must close all open IE windows before you can display or close the tabs.

Use a new tab

To use a new tab, click the New Tab button to the right of any current tabs. The new tab shows either a blank screen or your home page.

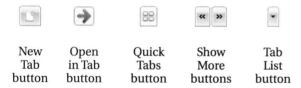

| New Tab button | Open in Tab button | Quick Tabs button | Show More buttons | Tab List button |

You can also summon a new tab by pressing Ctrl+T or by opening a link in a tab, as discussed in the next section.

Open a link in a tab

To open a link in a tab rather than in the current window, right-click the link and choose Open in New Tab from the pop-up menu.

Open a Favorite in a tab

To open an item from the Favorites list, move the mouse to the far right of the item until the Open in Tab button appears, and then click that button. *See* Favorites.

When you click the Open in Tab button next to a folder in Favorites, every link in the folder opens in its own tab.

Switch to a tab

The easiest way to switch between tabs is to click the tab you want with the mouse. From the keyboard, you can also press Ctrl+Tab to cycle through the various tabs. (See also the next two sections.)

Preview tabs

The Quick Tabs feature allows you to see all the tabs in mini-preview windows.

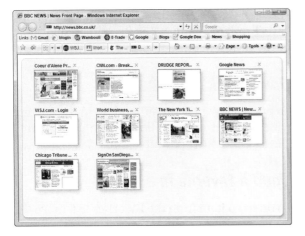

Tabs view, click the X button by any window preview.

The keyboard shortcut to close the current tabbed window is Ctrl+W or Alt+F4.

The mouse shortcut to close any tab is to click the tab by using the mouse's wheel button.

To close all tabs except for the current one, press Ctrl+Alt+F4.

Closing all tabs is the same as closing the IE window. When you do so, you see a warning. It can be disabled in the Tabbed Browsing Settings dialog box.

To use this feature, click the Quick Tabs button when more than one tab is open or press Ctrl+Q.

To switch to a window, simply click it with the mouse.

Find one tab among many

When more tabs are open than can fit on the screen, use the Show More chevrons to the right or left of the tabs to shuffle over to tabs unseen to the left or right.

You can see a quick list of all Web pages that are open in tabs by clicking the Tab List button. Choose a Web page to bring forward from the drop-down list that's displayed.

Close a tab

You can close any tab you're viewing by locating the X (Close) button on the tab. Or, from Quick

Watch Your Step!

One thing I have a difficult time with is finding which tabbed window is alerting me. For example, when a tabbed window reloads or blocks a pop-up window, I hear a tiny "dah-bleep" sound. There's no way to tell which window is having issues without clicking each successive tab and taking a peek.

Some Web page links automatically open in a new window. To have them open in a new tab instead, open the Tabbed Browsing Settings dialog box and choose the option A New Tab in the Current Window.

When Things Go Wrong

You cannot close the last tab window without closing the entire IE window as well.

If you would rather look at a new tab later, remove the check mark by the option Always Switch to New Tabs When They Are Created, found in the Tabbed Browsing Settings dialog box.

To have your home page, instead of a blank page, open on a tab, go to the Tabbed Browsing Settings dialog box and put a check mark by the option Open Home Page for New Tabs Instead of a Blank Page.

Gold Rush Nuggets

Tabbed browsing is merely a new interface on an old idea. The old idea was known as the MDI, or Multi Document Interface. You might still see some programs (such as QuickBooks) use it. Basically, the MDI was several tiny windows inside one main window. The windows were managed by using the Windows menu, yet each tiny window existed only within the main window. Microsoft Office used this type of interface until Office 2000.

Digging Elsewhere

Internet Explorer

Task Manager

I n the early days of Windows, the Task Manager was more important than it is now. That's because those early versions of Windows lacked a Taskbar. The Task Manager window was one of the tools you used to switch between programs, or just to see which programs were running. Today's Task Manager retains that feature but also has other, nerdier things in it. Some of them you may find useful, but most are for trivial purposes only.

WHERE'S THE GOLD?

For a dozen years, Windows users could summon the Task Manager by pressing Ctrl+Alt+Delete. When you do that now, a menu screen appears, from which you must choose the Task Manager button. Only then does the Task Manager window show up. That's possibly the most awkward way of summoning the Task Manager.

Task Manager
icon

From the keyboard, the Task Manager shortcut is now Ctrl+Shift+Esc.

The handy mouse shortcut to the Task Manager window is to right-click the Taskbar and choose Task Manager from the pop-up window.

Finally, the geekiest way to summon the Task Manager is to type **taskmgr** in the Run dialog box. *See* Run.

The Task Manager window contains multiple tabs, each of which monitors the various things going on in the computer.

Applications: A list of currently running programs or open windows, exactly mirroring the buttons on the Taskbar.

Processes: The programs running within the computer, including system tasks, support programs, and the whole ball-o-wax.

Services: A list of activities running in the background to help Windows do its thing. One process may be responsible for running several activities.

Performance: Details information about the computer's CPU, memory, and resource use. Lots of techy stuff.

Networking: Network activity monitor and information.

Users: List of users logged in to or connected to the PC.

What to Do with It

It seems like the Task Manager would best be something to keep away from. Hardly! There are plenty of times when a tool like the Task Manager comes in handy.

Keep the Task Manager on top

The Task Manager window can be treated uniquely, by keeping it on top of other windows. To turn this feature on or off, follow these steps:

1. Summon the Task Manager.
2. Choose Options⇨Always on Top.

A check mark by Always On Top means that the Task Manager window appears on top of all other windows all the time. Removing the check mark makes the Task Manager behave like other windows.

Switch tasks

You can use the Task Manager window to switch between running programs, although I admit that there are other, quicker ways to do so. *See* Multitasking.

Find a process

To see which process is associated with a running program, follow these steps:

1. Conjure forth the Task Manager.
2. Click the Applications tab.
3. Right-click an application.
4. From the pop-up menu, choose Go To Process.

The Processes tab is brought forward, and the process associated with the selected program is highlighted.

Going to a process is often required for troubleshooting purposes — specifically, to kill the process; after the process is identified, click the End Process button. This is often done to halt viruses or nasty programs that may infect your PC.

Monitor system performance

One of the most boring things you can do with the Task Manager window is click the Performance window and watch. Watch. Watch. Watch.

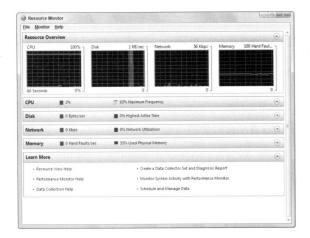

Far more interesting for monitoring system performance is the Resource Monitor. To open it, click the Resource Monitor button on the Performance tab in the Task Manager window. Or, you can type **perfmon.exe** in the Run dialog box.

Quit a program

You can use the Task Manager to quit any program. It isn't necessary (see the following section anyway) unless you're having trouble getting to the program's window. If so, follow these steps:

1. Display the Task Manager window.

2. Click the Applications tab.

3. Click to select the program.

4. Click the End Task button.

5. Close the Task Manager window.

The End Task button merely sends the *shutdown* notice to a program, just as though you had closed the program's window or chosen the File⇨Exit command. Nothing big.

Kill off a snoozing program

When a program seems to stubbornly refuse to respond, move, or quit, you can summon the Task Manager to kill it off:

1. Bring up the Task Manager window.

2. Click the Applications tab (if necessary).

3. Look for the program and confirm that its status message says "Not responding."

   If the program is listed as Running, I advise waiting for a while; the program may simply be slow and need time to catch up.

4. Click to select that process.

5. Click the End Task button.

Additional steps may be required, depending on how stubborn the program is.

Watch Your Step!

Do not randomly kill processes or end services. Only do so when directed to by an online help system, technical support, or some other authority.

When Things Go Wrong

Some programs just cannot be killed, even in the Task Manager. The next step you should take is to restart Windows. If that doesn't work, and only when that doesn't work, you must manually restart the PC: Press and hold the power button for at least 5 seconds, and the computer turns itself off.

You can hide the Task Manager's menu and tabs by double-clicking the mouse just inside the window border. Double-clicking again restores the Task Manager window to its previous look.

If the Task Manager is set to be hidden when minimized, you have to look for its icon in the Notification Area. It looks like a tiny green square. Double-click the green square icon to show the Task Manager again. To disable hiding the minimized Task Manager window, choose Options⇨ Hide When Minimized from its menu bar.

Gold Rush Nuggets

The Task Manager program is named `taskmgr.exe`.

In early versions of Windows, the Task Manager (nearby) was summoned by double-clicking the desktop.

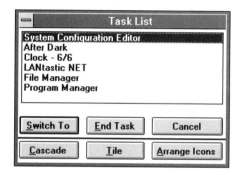

Digging Elsewhere

Ctrl+Alt+Delete, Taskbar

Task Scheduler

The Task Scheduler is a handy tool that has been available in Windows for a while. It's one of those automated features that you once read computers had (something about saving time and drudgery) but never really saw before. (Computers don't save time; they simply take out a loan on time from other devices around the home or office.) You can use the Task Scheduler to have the computer perform certain activities or automatically run programs at given times or under certain circumstances. The activities are generally utility or maintenance operations. I had a friend who configured his Task Scheduler to direct the computer to ring like a telephone while he was at lunch, much to the distress of his co-workers.

WHERE'S THE GOLD?

The Task Scheduler is an administrator-level thing; it's not for the casual user. Therefore, you find it buried in the Control Panel's Administrative Tools icon. Here's one way of finding it:

1. Open the Control Panel.

2a. Open the Administrative Tools icon, and then open the Task Scheduler in the Administrative Tools window.

Administrative   Red
Tools icon   Error
          icon

or

2b. From the Control Panel Home, choose System and Maintenance, and then on the next page choose Schedule Tasks, beneath the Administrative Tools heading.

The Task Scheduler window appears. It's a management *console*, not really a window (but why pick nits?).

Task information

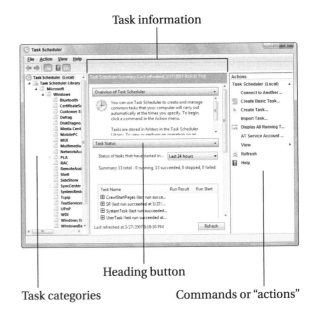

Task categories

Heading button

Commands or "actions"

The quickest way to summon the Task Scheduler console is to bring up the Run dialog box (Win+R) and type **mmc.exe taskschd.msc**. Press the Enter key to start the Task Scheduler.

What to Do with It

The first thing I think of is scheduling pranks because, honestly, in Windows Vista, most of the serious stuff is already scheduled for you.

Review scheduled tasks

Windows Vista automatically schedules many routine tasks. These tasks include regular disk maintenance, such as checking for errors or defragging, plus backup and system tasks, like setting restore points. To review these and other tasks that the computer does, follow these steps:

1. Summon the Task Manager window.

2. Beneath Task Scheduler (Local), open the Task Scheduler Library.

   Tasks are organized in a folder/tree structure.

3. Open the Microsoft folder and then the Windows folder.

   The folder you see contain tasks related to the folder name.

4. Select the Defrag folder.

   The Defrag folder contains tasks related to running the disk defragmentation program. (*See* Defrag.) In the central part of the window, you see a list of tasks related to Defrag.

Beneath the list is a tabbed interface where the task is scheduled.

5. Choose the Scheduled Defrag task from the top of the central part of the window.

   The Triggers column describes when the task runs or what causes the task to run. On my PC, Defrag runs at 1:00 a.m. every Wednesday.

6. If necessary, click the General tab, in the lower central part of the screen.

   The General tab's Security options show that Defrag is run by the SYSTEM user, which is Windows itself. You should also see that Defrag is run whether a user is logged in or not (although tasks cannot be run when the computer is turned off).

7. Click the Triggers tab.

   On the Triggers tab, you find the task's *schedule,* or a list of events that can trigger the task to start, such as the PC's being idle or when starting or shutting down Windows.

8. Click the Actions tab.

   Actions is where the action is, where the command dwells that runs the actual task. The command for Defrag is the *pathname* to Defrag (where %windir% is a placeholder for the Windows folder, or directory), and the command line version of Defrag is specified with -c and -i options. (The -c option directs Defrag to defragment all hard drives on the PC, and the -i option is undocumented but most likely means to run Defrag with no visual feedback, or *invisibly.*)

9. Click the Conditions tab.

A very useful option, the Conditions tab helps the task deal with unusual circumstances.

10. Click the Settings tab.

The Settings tab contains more options — seemingly, more conditions.

11. Click the History tab.

The History tab describes when the task was most recently run as well as whether it was successful.

12. Repeat Steps 4 through 11 for other tasks in folders to review how they work.

For example, the System Restore folder contains the task that controls how and when a restore point is set (*see* System Restore). The Windows Backup folder holds tasks that control how and when the computer's hard drives are automatically backed up. Note that some folders don't contain any tasks.

13. Close the Task Manager window when you finish your review.

Confirm that a task has run

Perhaps you're like me and you have that old "trust issue"; you're just not certain that a scheduled task has taken place. To confirm or dismiss your fears, do this:

1. Open the Task Manager window.

2. From the folder list, choose the top item, Task Scheduler (Local).

3. In the central part of the window, look for the Task Status heading button; optionally, click the button to display the status of tasks that have started.

4. Choose a time period from the menu button.

5. Locate your task in the list.

6. Click the + (plus sign) button to expand the task to review its status.

Refer to the Run Result column to determine whether the task was successful.

For more information, you can dig a little deeper. With the Task Manager window open, follow these steps:

1. Open the folder tree to find your task's folder.

2. Click to select your task's folder.

3. Click to select the task in the folder, the task you want to confirm.

4. Click the History tab in the lower central part of the window.

You should see six entries for each task:

Task engine received message to start task

Task started

Action started

Created task process

Task completed

Action completed

The task can fail at any of the first four entries: The task engine can fail to receive the message, the task can fail to start, the action can fail, and the task itself (the program run) can foul up.

When a problem occurs, you see the red Error icon in the General column, and the text for the Task Category reflects the error, such as `Task Start Failed`.

To see more information, click to select a failed task item, and then use the General tab, at the bottom of the window, to read more information — although I admit that the information isn't very helpful.

Create a folder for your own tasks

Although you can create tasks in any folder, you should create your own folder and use it to store your tasks, or go all organization-crazy and create subfolders for tasks — if you have a whole hoard of them.

Creating a task folder is supercinchy:

1. On the left side of the Task Manager window, click to select the Task Scheduler Library folder.

2. On the right side, under Actions, choose New Folder.

3. Type a new name for the folder, and press the Enter key or click OK.

The folder appears beneath the Task Scheduler Library folder, on the left side of the window.

Create a new task

Despite its seemingly overwhelming nature, tasks are easier to create in the Task Manager than in previous versions of Windows. Those vast controls and options let you create customized tasks. The only problem you have is thinking of which tasks to run; Windows already does most of the required tasks.

1. Create a folder for your tasks.

   Refer to the preceding section.

2. Click to select your task folder on the left side of the Task Manager window.

3. From the Actions pane, choose Create Task.

   The Create Task dialog box appears.

4. Type a name for the task.

   For example, type **Annoying Warning**.

5. Type a description.

   For example, type **Message that's displayed every 10 minutes**.

6. Click the Triggers tab.

   Triggers determine when the task runs.

7. Click the New button to set a trigger.

   The New Trigger dialog box shows up.

8. From the Begin a Task drop-down menu, choose the interval or trigger for the task.

9. Fill in the rest of the New Trigger dialog box according to the trigger you set.

For example, if you choose On a Schedule, use the rest of the dialog box to set the schedule, such as daily or weekly or every 10 minutes.

10. Click OK to set the trigger.

11. Optionally, repeat Steps 8 through 10 to set additional triggers.

12. Click the Actions tab.

Actions tell the task what to do.

13. Click the New button to display the New Action dialog box.

14. Choose an action from the Action menu button.

15. Fill in the rest of the information according to the action you chose.

16. Click OK to close the New Action dialog box.

17. Click the Conditions tab.

Conditions help you refine when and how the task takes place.

18. Set any conditions as necessary.

19. Click the Settings tab.

Settings are simply options not listed anywhere else — basically, stuff that helps you complete the task.

20. Make any necessary changes on the Settings tab.

21. Click the OK button.

The task is created and listed in the folder. You can optionally close the Task Scheduler window at this point, but my guess is that you'll want to test-run the task to ensure that it works. Refer to the following section.

Test-run a task

To test-run any task, follow these steps:

1. Open the Task Scheduler window.

2. Open the folder containing the task to test.

3. Click to select the task from the upper central part of the window.

4. Beneath Actions, choose the Run command.

5. Observe your task.

Note that the task may appear in a window *behind* the Task Scheduler; check the Taskbar for its window.

If all goes well, close the Task Scheduler window and be on your merry way. Otherwise, you can modify the task, as covered in the next section.

Edit a task

Some tasks require fine-tuning. To change a task, do this:

1. Beckon forth the Task Scheduler window.

2. Select the task's folder.

3. Choose the task to modify.

4. Choose Properties under Actions to display the task's Properties dialog box.

Or, you can just double-click the task to open its Properties dialog box.

5. Change the task by clicking appropriate tabs and making necessary changes.

Use the Edit buttons to change the Triggers or Actions.

6. Click OK to save the changes.

Consider test-running the task after making your changes; see the preceding section.

Disable or enable a task

Rather than delete a task, consider disabling it. By disabling a task, you prevent it from running on schedule or being triggered by some event, and you keep the task around. That way, if you desire, you can reenable the task at a later time.

To disable a task, click to select the task in the center window, and then choose Disable from the Actions list.

A disabled task appears in the upper center portion of the Task Scheduler window with the word *Disabled* in the Status column.

To enable a task, select a disabled task in the list, and then click the Enable button from the Actions list.

Delete a task

To remove a task, utterly deleting it, do this:

1. Open the Task Scheduler window.

2. On the left side of the window, select the folder containing the task.

3. Select the task to destroy from the list in the upper center part of the window.

4. I suggest that you consider exporting the task to save it for later — just in case:

   a. Choose Export from the Actions list.

   b. Use the Save As dialog box to find a location for your task.

   c. In the Save As dialog box, optionally give your task a name.

   d. Click the Save button.

5. Choose Delete in the Actions part of the window.

6. Click the Yes button to confirm deleting the task.

Tasks that you export can be imported by using the Import Task command in the Actions list.

Schedule when people can use the computer

You can determine when users can use the computer by employing the Parental Control's time limit function on a Standard account. *See* Parental Controls.

Schedule automatic shutdown

Windows Vista doesn't sport an automatic shutdown feature, but you can craft one yourself, thanks to the Task Scheduler. To do so, create a new task for the Task Scheduler per the directions earlier in this entry. Here are the details for each tab:

General: Set the name as **Shutdown**, and for the description, type **Turn the computer off** (or whatever you feel is appropriate for the type of shutdown you're doing).

Triggers: Set the schedule for when you want to shut down the computer. For example, daily at 11:00 p.m. or perhaps after 2 hours of idle time.

Actions: The name of the command is, surprisingly, *shutdown,* but it's a command-line program. So, for the action, choose Start a Program. For the program/script, type the following line:

```
%windit%\system32\shutdown.exe
```

Type that line *exactly* as you see it here: two percent signs, two backslashes, no spaces, no final period.

In the Add Arguments box, type one of the following commands:

/s	Turns off the computer
/r	Restarts the computer
/h	Puts the computer into hibernation mode

You must specify one of those options. For example, /s shuts down the computer.

Information on the Conditions and Settings tabs may be set as you please.

After creating the task, test-run it: Close all windows and programs, saving any open files. Then click the Run action with your shutdown task selected to see how it works. On my screen, a warning dialog box is displayed before the computer shuts down. *See also* Shutdown Windows.

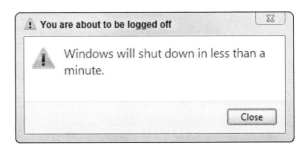

Watch Your Step!

Tasks cannot run when the computer is turned off.

Try not to create tasks inside the Windows folder or any of its subfolders. Create and use your own folder for tasks, as described in this entry.

Do not delete tasks created by Windows (within the Windows folder).

You cannot recover a task you deleted.

When Things Go Wrong

The Task Scheduler window is a *console*. It has three panes: left, right, and center. To control the visibility of those panes, use the View menu.

Many of the Actions listed in the Actions pane are also available on the Actions menu.

Sometimes tasks fail because the conditions that you set the task to run under never happen. Sometimes tasks fail because of something that happens in the program. The best way to prevent a task from failing is to *test-run* it, or schedule it to take place when you can watch what it does. Then, after observing and fixing the task, you can set it to run at the original time.

Gold Rush Nuggets

The Task Scheduler was known as the Task Manager in previous versions of Windows. Of course, the Task Scheduler is far more complex and precise.

Digging Elsewhere

Backup, Shutdown Windows, System Restore, Task Manager

Taskbar

Windows doesn't offer many gizmos on the desktop. All in all, it's rather plain. There's the desktop itself, which can be either plain as a picture or pockmarked like the moon with icons. Beyond that, you have only the noble Taskbar, a virtual anchor for just about everything else you do in Windows. It's home to the Start button. It's home to the Notification Area. It's home to the programs you run and play with while you do that thing called Windows.

Next to the desktop, the Taskbar is the easiest thing to find in the Windows interface. Its home location is the bottom of the desktop, although in reality it can dwell on any of the display's four edges.

The Taskbar sports three major parts: the Start button, the Taskbar itself, and the Notification Area. On the Taskbar itself, you can have other toolbars, such as the Quick Launch bar, and then buttons or stacks of buttons representing running programs and open windows.

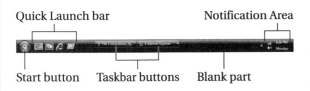

Quick Launch bar   Notification Area

Start button   Taskbar buttons   Blank part

Controlling the Taskbar happens in the Taskbar and Start Menu Properties dialog box. You can open the Control Panel's Taskbar and Start Menu

icon to display the dialog box, but the quickest way is as follows:

Taskbar and Start
Menu icon

1. Right-click a blank part of the Taskbar.

2. Choose Properties from the pop-up menu.

3. If necessary, click the Taskbar tab.

What to Do with It

The Taskbar is a useful tool. You use it to access the Start button, to switch programs, to view running programs, and to do a whole host of interesting and useful things.

Mess with a Taskbar button

Each open window or running program on the desktop has a corresponding button on the Taskbar. The button appears whether the window is restored, maximized, or minimized. *See* Windows.

Right-clicking a Taskbar button displays the window's control menu.

As more windows are opened, buttons on the Taskbar shrink to accommodate the windows.

Stack similar buttons

You can stack or group similar windows on the same Taskbar button. For example, if you have six Word documents open at a time, they can all use the same button rather than add to the Taskbar clutter. To stack similar buttons, follow these steps:

1. Summon the Taskbar and Start Menu Properties dialog box.

2. On the Taskbar tab, place a check mark by the Group Similar Taskbar Buttons item.

3. Click OK.

A group button displays the number of windows, the program name, and then a triangle indicating that the button is also a menu. To pluck one of the individual windows, click the button and choose the window from the pop-up list.

To close all windows in a group, right-click the group button and choose the Close Group command.

Display window previews on the Taskbar

As long as you have the proper version of Windows Vista *and* a capable graphics adapter in your PC, you can direct the Taskbar to display a tiny preview window as you point at each button. Here's how to engage that feature:

1. Conjure forth the Taskbar and Start Menu Properties dialog box.

2. Ensure that the Taskbar tab is forward.

3. Put a check mark by the Show Preview Windows (Thumbnails) item.

4. Click OK.

The image displayed is a *real-time* image, which means that if the window's contents are changing, you see the changes shown in the preview window.

Lock or unlock the Taskbar

The Taskbar is normally locked, which means that you cannot change its size, rearrange toolbars on the Taskbar, or move the Taskbar to another edge of the screen. Yes, locking the Taskbar is a good thing; I've done lots of PC troubleshooting with worried folks whose Taskbars have run astray. But, if you want to modify the Taskbar, you have to learn how to unlock it:

1. Right-click a blank part of the Taskbar.

2. Choose Lock the Taskbar.

Removing the check mark unlocks the Taskbar. Repeating the steps to put a check mark by the Lock the Taskbar option locks the Taskbar again.

Clue When the Taskbar is unlocked, it grows an upper ridge. Also, each toolbar on the Taskbar grows a dimpled "handle," which is used to manipulate the toolbar. *See* Toolbars.

Move the Taskbar

The Taskbar can dwell on any edge of the display: top, left, right, or bottom. To move the Taskbar, heed these steps:

1. Unlock the Taskbar (if necessary).

2. Point the mouse at a blank part of the Taskbar.

3. Drag the mouse to another edge of the screen.

4. Lock the Taskbar.

The Taskbar doesn't move until the mouse gets close to the edge of the screen, and then the Taskbar *snaps* to that edge.

Resize the Taskbar

The Taskbar can be as thick or thin as you need it. As Windows comes out of the box, the Taskbar is a bit thinner than I like it; I prefer my Taskbar about two window buttons tall. To adjust the Taskbar height, follow these steps:

1. Unlock the Taskbar.

2. Point the mouse at the Taskbar's inside edge, where the Taskbar and desktop meet.

3. Drag the mouse inward, toward the center of the screen to make it thicker, or outward toward the outside of the screen to make it thinner.

   As you drag the mouse, the Taskbar changes its thickness.

4. Release the mouse to set the Taskbar size.

5. Relock the Taskbar.

Eureka Rather than make the Taskbar superskinny, in which case it can be difficult to see, consider using the Taskbar's auto-hide option. See the next section.

Automatically hide the Taskbar

When you prefer screen real estate over seeing the Taskbar all the time, consider using the Taskbar's automatic hiding feature. Activate the feature thusly:

1. Summon the Taskbar and Start Menu Properties dialog box.

2. Place a check mark by the Auto-Hide the Taskbar item.

3. Click OK.

The Taskbar slithers down to the bottom lip of the display as you use the computer. To show the Taskbar, point the mouse at the bottom edge of the screen.

Keep the Taskbar on top

The Taskbar normally likes to be always on top, overlapping any windows displayed on the screen. To make the Taskbar appear more humble, you can direct Windows to treat it like any other window. Here's how:

1. Bring forth the Taskbar and Start Menu Properties dialog box.

2. Remove the check mark by Keep the Taskbar on Top of Other Windows.

3. Click OK.

The Taskbar now lurks behind windows, and windows can overlap the Taskbar.

To summon the Taskbar, you can press Win+D to show the desktop, from which you can access the Taskbar.

If you prefer to keep the Taskbar on top of all other windows, repeat the steps in this section but add the check mark in Step 2.

Add or remove a toolbar

The Taskbar is home to a host of toolbars, some of which you may find handy and some of which only serve to create the muddled appearance that so many PC users seem to enjoy. To add or remove a toolbar from the Taskbar, heed these steps:

1. Right-click a blank part of the Taskbar.

2. Choose the toolbar to add (or remove) from the pop-up menu's Toolbar submenu.

You have several toolbars to choose from:

Address: *See* Address Bar.

Windows Media Player: Displays a mini-control panel for the Windows Media Player when the player is on and playing something.

Links: Displays the same links as found on the Internet Explorer Links bar.

Tablet PC Input Panel: Displays a button that allows you to summon the input panel for your overpriced laptop.

Desktop: Displays icons and folders found on the desktop.

Quick Launch: *See* Quick Launch Bar.

Toolbars that are already visible have a check mark by their names. *See also* Toolbars for information on how to manipulate the toolbars on the Taskbar because they tend to get scrunched up and unmanageable.

Watch Your Step!

The number of windows you need in order to form a group button depends on the Taskbar's width. Generally speaking, having four or five windows open for the same program is about all it takes.

Most documentation assumes that the Taskbar lies on the bottom edge of the screen.

The Windows Media Player toolbar shows up only when the Media Player is playing something and its window has been minimized.

When Things Go Wrong

When you right-click the Taskbar and you don't see the Properties command on the shortcut menu, you're not clicking the proper part of the Taskbar.

When you cannot find the Taskbar, consider that it may be in auto-hide mode, reduced to a very thin strip, or clinging to the top, left, or right edge of the screen.

Gold Rush Nuggets

The Taskbar was introduced in Windows 95, replacing the job of the original Windows Task Manager. *See* Task Manager.

Digging Elsewhere

Desktop, Notification Area, Quick Launch Bar, Start Button and Menu, Toolbars, Windows

Text Editing

Despite its graphical nature, Windows includes a lot of text. Fortunately, all that text you type can be edited. Whether it's text in a text box, small or large, or text typed in the Notepad program, the text can be modified by using text-editing commands that are standard throughout Windows.

Text editing happens at the keyboard — specifically, with the alphabet, number, and symbol keys, along with the Shift key. Any key you press produces a character on the screen or in a text box or window — if the text box or window is selected and ready for typing input. (Looking really hard just doesn't cut it.)

The key to recognizing that a text box or window is ready to accept text is the blinking *insertion pointer,* or *cursor.* That vertical bar marks the position where new text appears as you type. It can also be manipulated by using special cursor movement keys on the keyboard.

Finally, all text in Windows can be selected with the mouse. The selected text is treated as a single block, and it can be deleted, copied, or moved.

Plain text   Selected text

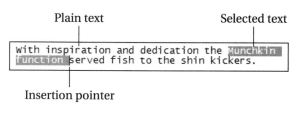

Insertion pointer

What to Do with It

Text editing is about typing stuff in Windows; basic stuff. The complex typing happens in a word processor, where text is not only typed but also formatted and made all pretty. But basic text editing, well, it's simply dealing with text.

Type or insert text

Text is entered into a text box or anywhere that text is typed in Windows by typing on the keyboard. Characters you type appear on the screen, in the selected text box or window.

Move the insertion pointer

The insertion pointer can be moved to any location where there's text. The easiest way to move the insertion pointer is by clicking the mouse; the insertion pointer hops to the mouse click's location.

You can also use the keyboard to move the insertion pointer hither and thither. Here are some keys and how they move the insertion pointer:

→	Moves right one character
←	Moves left one character
↑	Moves up to the preceding line (if any)
↓	Moves down to the next line (if any)

Ctrl+→	Moves right one word
Ctrl+←	Moves left one word
Home	Moves to the start of the line
End	Moves to the end of the line

Delete text

Two keys are used to remove text:

Backspace	Deletes the character to the left of the insertion pointer
Delete or Del	Deletes the character to the right of the insertion pointer

Select text

Text is selected by dragging the mouse over the text. Alternatively, you can press and hold the Shift key and then click the mouse button to select the text between the mouse-click location and the insertion pointer.

The keyboard can also be used to select text: Press and hold the Shift key while moving the insertion pointer. As the insertion pointer moves (while the Shift key is down), text is selected.

Selected text is treated as a block. You can delete the block with one of the delete keys, or you can copy or cut the block.

Copy or cut and then paste text

Any selected text in Windows can be copi cut, and any text box in Windows can be use pasting text. *See* Copy, Cut, and Paste Data.

Yes, the Copy, Cut, and Paste commands for all text in Windows, even in the tiniest boxes.

Watch Your Step!

Cursor movement keys on the numeric ke work only when the Num Lock is off (the Lock light is off).

In Windows, most basic text editing is single only, such as the text boxes found in a box. You cannot press the Enter key in s text box to start a new line of text; pressing is interpreted as clicking the OK button, confirms changes and closes the dialog bo.

When Things Go Wrong

Chances are good that when you type and see text appear where you're expecti Windows has moved its focus elsewhere. the mouse in the text box or window to e that what you're typing appears where looking.

Gold Rush Nuggets

The holy grail of computing is the computer that can understand plain English — you know, like on *Star Trek*. Mr. Spock would simply utter a task for the computer to do, and it would respond in its metallic female voice: "Working!" But I'll bet if there really is a 23rd century starship, they'll most likely still be using keyboards to type to the computer.

Digging Elsewhere

Cut, Copy, and Paste Data; *Dialog Box*; *Keyboard Shortcuts*

Themes

The theme of this entry is good versus evil. Or, maybe the theme is the 1950s or nature or the argument of fate against free will or the tendencies of feudal agrarian societies to more easily adapt to and flourish under the totalitarian state as opposed to the stagnation of post-industrial democracies. Then again, the theme here may be centered around *Star Trek,* in which case I'll have to fork over the $40 that some fanboy is asking for his nifty Klingon language font set.

On your computer, themes control the froufrou things you see: the text and fonts used by Windows, the style of window that's displayed, background images, sounds, and the mouse pointer. Each of those items individually can comprise or be used as a theme; or the whole kit and caboodle can be collectively changed by applying a preset theme.

In Windows Vista, several elements in Windows can have their own themes. They're all placed in the Personalization icon, found in the Control Panel; or, from the Control Panel Home, click Appearance and Personalization and then Personalization.

Personalization
icon

The Personalization window lists the hoard of things you can personalize in Windows:

Window Color and Appearance: Not only the window shape and color but also the fonts used by Windows.

Desktop Background: *See* Desktop.

Screen Saver: *See* Screen Saver.

Sounds*: See* Sounds.

Mouse Pointers: *See* Mouse.

Theme: Allows you to change multiple items at a time by applying a single theme.

Display Settings: Controls the screen resolution and colors, which I don't consider to be in the theme of the other themes, but the icon is in the Personalization window regardless.

What to Do with It

Let me be honest here: What you do with a theme is *play*. It's one of those opportunities in Windows where you can say that you're "making adjustments to the operating system" when what you're really doing is enjoying yourself.

Change the window color

The color of the window border is set by clicking the Window Color and Appearance item in the Personalization window. You can choose from preset hues or use the color mixer to select a new color.

Placing a check mark in the Enable Transparency box causes the windows to be semitransparent, which is a fancy visual effect that I find distracting.

Choose a window theme

When you want to get detailed, you can change the window theme, which involves more than just setting the border color. To do so, follow these steps:

1. Choose the Window Color and Appearance item in the Personalization window.

2. Click the link labeled Open Classic Appearance Properties for More Color Options.

3. Choose a preset color scheme from the Color Scheme drop-down list.

   The preview window shows you the over-all look of each selected color scheme.

4. Click OK to set the theme.

Create a custom theme

The Advanced button in the Appearance Settings dialog box allows you to customize each element of a window, by choosing color, size, and font options: Follow the steps from the preceding

section but click the Advanced button after you complete Step 3.

The Effects button in the Appearance Setting dialog box allows you to set certain graphical effects in windows, such as whether shadows appear under menus or windows display their contents when you drag them around the desktop.

To save your choices, as well as other display options, you can create your own desktop theme. Do this:

1. Click the Theme item in the Personalization window.

2. Click the Save As button.

3. Give the theme a name and, optionally, find a folder for the theme.

4. Click the Save button to save the theme.

Choose a custom or other theme

To use a theme you created, or another theme that comes with Windows, follow these steps:

1. Click the Theme item in the Personalization window.

2. Choose a preset theme from the Theme drop-down list, or use the Browse button to open a dialog box and hunt for a theme.

   Some of the theme's effects can be seen in the preview window.

3. Click the OK button to apply the theme.

Apply a new desktop background

See Desktop for information on setting the desktop background or wallpaper. The desktop background choice is kept as part of a theme, as covered in the preceding section.

Change screen savers

See Screen Saver for information on setting screen savers in Windows.

Choose a sound theme

Refer to the Sounds entry for information on setting a sound theme.

Select new mouse pointers

Choosing new mouse pointers is covered in the Mouse entry.

Watch Your Step!

I highly recommend using the Apply button in a dialog box to preview how your changes will affect Windows. When you don't see what you want, change the settings and click Apply again. (Clicking Apply is like clicking OK but not closing the dialog box. *See* Dialog Box.)

Changing any of the theme items affects only your account on the computer. Other accounts aren't changed.

When Things Go Wrong

When things go terribly wrong, such as when you (or some annoying young relative) choose the most obnoxious color combinations for your windows, you need to start the PC in Safe mode. (*See* Safe Mode.) Change the display settings back. Then restart the computer.

 As long as you save your theme, you can always restore it by using the Themes item in the Personalization window.

Gold Rush Nuggets

The Windows Plus package contains a host of various themes, including packages that come with custom window designs, sounds, and images.

There's also the issue of *skins,* which can be applied to change the overall look and appearance of Windows, by making it look like a Macintosh or giving windows a unique or unusual appearance. Search for **Windows skins** on the Internet for more information.

Digging Elsewhere

Desktop, Desktop Icons, Mouse, Screen Saver, Sounds

Time

Cs do many things well, but sadly keeping time is not one of them. Computers make lousy clocks. That's because so much goes on inside the computer that inevitably the clock lags behind. Not only that, but sometimes I'm guessing that the computer's clock gets utterly broken and that's when things seem to take an eternity to happen.

Your PC's clock is buried deep inside the console, maintained by a tiny battery which ensures that the time is kept even when the computer is unplugged and blindfolded. But that doesn't necessarily mean that the time is *accurate*.

To see the time, refer to the Notification Area on the Taskbar, where the time is often (although not always) displayed. *See* Notification Area.

Clicking the time display in the Notification Area displays a pop-up calendar and clock, plus any additional clocks you may have set.

The Sidebar can sport a clock of various fashions and styles right on the desktop. *See* Sidebar.

Time itself is controlled by using the Date and Time icon in the Control Panel; from the Control Panel Home, choose Clock, Language, and Region, and then click the Date and Time link. The *easiest* way to summon the Date and Time dialog box is to right-click the time display in the Notification Area and choose Adjust Date/Time from the pop-up menu.

Date and Time
icon

The clock plays a role in task scheduling. *See* Task Scheduler.

What to Do with It

The computer has a clock in order to prevent everything from happening at the same time. Seriously, the clock is used to time-stamp files, to set durations, and to remind you to get back to work.

Set the date and time

To correct the computer about the current date and time, do this:

1. Summon the Date and Time dialog box.

2. Click the Change Date and Time button.

3. Choose the current date from the calendar.

4. Check the current time.

5. Set the computer to the next minute (00 seconds).

   a. Double-click to select the hours and type a new value for hours.

   b. Double-click the value for minutes and type a new value.

   c. Double-click seconds and type **0**.

   d. Specify a.m. or p.m.

6. When the time gets to the top of the minute, click the OK button.

7. Close the Date and Time dialog box.

 Clue The idea is to set the computer's clock exactly. So, if the current time is 12:39:22, set the computer's clock to 12:40:00. Then, when the current time reaches 12:40:00, click the OK button to set the time exactly.

Set the time zone and daylight saving time

To pick which time zone the computer obeys, follow these steps:

1. Bring forth the Date and Time dialog box.

2. Click the Change Time Zone button.

3. Choose your time zone from the list.

4. Optionally, click to specify daylight saving time for your time zone.

5. Click OK, and then click OK to close the Date and Time dialog box.

Use the Internet to keep the time

The best way to help your computer keep track of time is to have it, every so often, connect with an Internet time server to coordinate the computer's internal clock to one of the government's accurate nuclear clocks. This is really simple to do:

1. Whip up the Date and Time dialog box.

2. Click the Internet Time tab.

3. Click the Change Settings button.

4. Ensure that a check mark is next to the Synchronize with an Internet Time Server option.

5. (Optional) Choose a time server from the drop-down list.

6. Click the Update Now button to test the server (and set the time).

7. Click OK, and then click OK again to close the Date and Time dialog box.

Use alternative clocks

Windows lets you toss up as many as two additional display clocks, which you can set to various time zones, just like on the wall of major newsrooms on TV and in film. Here's how the trick works:

1. In the Date and Time dialog box, click the Additional Clocks tab.

2. Put a check in the Show This Clock box.

3. Select a time zone for the clock.

4. Type a name for the clock.

5. Repeat Steps 2 through 4 for the second clock, if you want.

6. Click OK.

 Clue The alternative clocks appear in the time display, shown when you click the time in the Notification Area.

Watch Your Step!

Setting the time incorrectly goofs up some of the things a computer does that rely on date and time stamps. Scheduling, invoicing, and other mundane computer tasks are adversely affected when you set the clock, and specifically the date, incorrectly.

When you don't tell the computer to automatically adjust for daylight saving time, you must manually set your PC's clock to compensate for it.

When Things Go Wrong

Yes, the clock will be off slightly from time to time. The best way to prevent that is to use the Internet Time feature in Windows Vista. Otherwise, you have to manually adjust the clock.

If the time is consistently wrong, consider choosing another time server when you configure the Internet Time option for your computer.

The time may grow screwy when the PC's internal battery dies. This happens to older PCs more often than to new computers. You simply need to replace the battery.

Gold Rush Nuggets

Computers have always kept the time; a time ticker is required by the microprocessor. But early PCs lacked internal batteries to keep track of the current time. So when a computer user in the 1980s turned on a PC, the first thing to do was to set the date and time.

Computer clocks are internally set to GMT, or Greenwich mean time (also known as universal time). When the time is displayed, however, a certain number of hours are added or removed from the time, depending on the time zone and on daylight saving time rules.

Digging Elsewhere

Control Panel, Notification Area, Sidebar

Toolbars

It was long after the graphical user interface (GUI) became popular that menu bars quickly, and inexplicably, grew stalactites. Geologic formations may take centuries to form, but in the computer world, stalactite-like *toolbars* soon appeared immediately below menu bars, horning in on that vital real estate devoted to the creative part of the window. Despite the incursion, users welcomed toolbars. In fact, some programs lacked menus and simply had a series of buttons on a toolbar, each of which carried out a necessary command.

WHERE'S THE GOLD?

Toolbars cling to the edge of things. The typical toolbar is found just beneath the menu bar in an application window. Sometimes, you have more than one toolbar.

Separator

Toolbar handle   Toolbar buttons   Toolbar menu

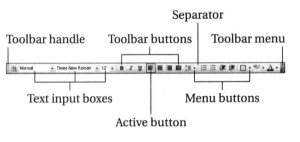

Text input boxes   Menu buttons

Active button

A toolbar can contain buttons, buttons with text, or just text. It can also sport drop-down lists, menus, and text input boxes.

Toolbar handle   Toolbar buttons

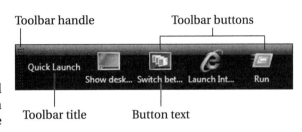

Toolbar title   Button text

On the left end of the toolbar, you find the toolbar's *handle*, which is used to move or rearrange the toolbar.

Toolbar handle   Show more button

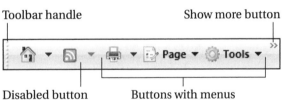

Disabled button   Buttons with menus

The right end of the toolbar may contain a Show More button, which displays buttons that don't appear on a narrow toolbar. The right end can also sport a toolbar menu, which appears as a downward-pointing triangle in the toolbar's lower right corner.

Toolbars can be fixed in their positions, either all the time or as a lock-down option. Most toolbars can also be freely moved, slid left or right, or rearranged from top to bottom. A toolbar can also be dragged off its docking spot, made to dock on any edge of the window or "float" away from an edge. A hovering toolbar is known as a *floating palette* window.

Active tool

Floating palette

Toolbars controlled on the View menu

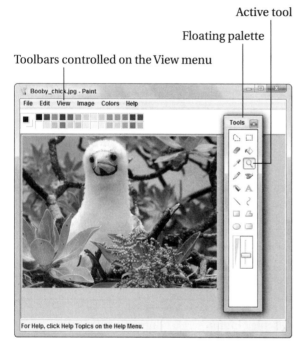

Toolbars are controlled from the application's View menu, although that's not a hard-and-fast rule. You can also right-click most toolbars to see their shortcut menus, which offer toolbar control or set various options, such as locking the toolbar.

What to Do with It

Most people don't mess with toolbars — on purpose. Only when you have a toolbar mishap does the desperate desire to fix things overwhelm you.

Move a toolbar

Most toolbars can be moved, slid left and right, or moved up or down. The key is to grab the toolbar's *handle* with the mouse and then drag the toolbar left or right or up or down.

 Clue

If you want to practice moving toolbars, use the WordPad program. Display the Toolbar and Format bar from the View menu. Then move the toolbars left, right, up, and down to help get the hang of things.

Moving a toolbar can be frustrating because it often involves other toolbars that move too, often in undesirable ways.

Move a toolbar too far and you create a floating palette! See the later section "Turn a floating palette back into a toolbar" to find out how to fix things.

Drag a toolbar to another edge of the window

Normally, toolbars dwell at the top of a window, but you can *dock* a toolbar to any edge of the window. Simply grab the toolbar's handle and drag the toolbar to any edge of the window.

As you drag the toolbar, you may see an outline representing the toolbar's position. When the toolbar gets close to the window's edge, the outline changes slightly. That's when you can let go of the mouse to release and dock the toolbar.

Resize a toolbar

Some toolbars can be resized or stretched. You can drag the right edge of the toolbar to the right to make the toolbar longer and show more buttons. Likewise, you can drag the toolbar's right edge leftward to make the toolbar narrow.

Some toolbars may attempt to show all their buttons as you resize the toolbar to be narrower. The buttons may juggle around or appear on two rows for a single toolbar. This is the case in some versions of Microsoft Word.

Create a floating palette

To transform a toolbar into its own window or floating palette, simply grab the toolbar by its handle and drag it into the middle of the window.

The floating palette window sits atop all other windows in the program, allowing you constant access to the toolbar's tools.

Turn a floating palette back into a toolbar

To transform a floating palette back into a toolbar, simply drag the palette window over to the edge of the application's window. The palette should dock back to the edge, just like a toolbar.

Add or remove buttons from the toolbar

Some toolbars can be customized, allowing you to add or remove buttons, create your own buttons or menus, and add pretty bits, like separator bars.

The first way to control a toolbar's buttons is to look for a toolbar menu. If it exists, the toolbar menu is found on the rightmost end of the toolbar, represented by a downward-pointing triangle. Buttons can be shown or hidden by using the menu or by choosing Customize or a similar command from the menu.

Show text for the toolbar buttons

Some toolbars have an option for showing text in addition to the toolbar buttons. This option can be found either on the toolbar's menu or by right-clicking the toolbar and choosing the appropriate text command from the pop-up menu.

Create a folder toolbar on the Taskbar

Windows lets you create folder toolbars on the Taskbar, which are toolbars that reference the icons stored in a folder. For example, you can have a folder full of shortcuts to programs, other folders, projects, or what-have-you. Here's how:

1. Create a special toolbar/palette folder.
   a. Open your User Account folder.
   b. From the toolbar's Organize button, choose New Folder.
   c. Name the folder **Toolbar**.
   d. Open the folder.

e. Copy into the folder the shortcuts to your favorite programs, folders, or files. (*See* Copy, Cut, and Paste Files.)

f. Close the folder window.

2. Right-click the Taskbar.

3. From the pop-up menu, choose Toolbars⇨New Toolbar.

4. Use the Choose a Folder dialog box to browse to the folder you created in Step 1.

5. Select the toolbar folder (that you created in Step 1) and click the Select Folder button.

A new toolbar appears on the Taskbar, one that lists your folder's contents as toolbar icons — similar to the Quick Launch bar.

6. Optionally, right-click the new toolbar to choose Show Text or Show Title to turn off those items.

7. Optionally, when you want to see bigger icons, right-click the new toolbar and choose View⇨Large Icons.

See Taskbar for more information on messing with the Taskbar.

Watch Your Step!

Moving toolbars is often an exercise in frustration. When a toolbar-locking command is available, I recommend that you use it; keep the toolbar (or toolbars) locked to avoid moving them around.

When Things Go Wrong

The Taskbar is the number-one toolbar and the number-one source of toolbar woe. In addition to the various toolbars' feats and abilities shown in this entry, the Taskbar can also be made thinner or temporarily hidden. *See* Taskbar for the details.

When you cannot redock a floating palette window, simply close the window. Then use the View menu to redisplay the original toolbar.

You cannot drag a folder toolbar from the Taskbar onto the desktop in Windows Vista. This was possible in previous versions of Windows, but can no longer be done.

Gold Rush Nuggets

Microsoft Word 2003 sported 19 toolbars, 2 customized toolbars (the Ruler and the status bar), and as many toolbars as a user could create himself. With all those toolbars visible, there's very little room left on the window for writing!

Digging Elsewhere

Menus, Quick Launch Bar, Taskbar

Uninstall Programs

At the end of the day, you may discover that those programs you once loved and used frequently are now gathering the electronic equivalent of dust. Or, maybe you're overwhelmed by a slew of programs preinstalled on your PC, things that the manufacturer was fooled into including for some special deal, from a company run by his brother-in-law, or maybe extra software installed in exchange for a trip to Puerto Vallarta. Whatever. There comes a time when you need to peel such software from your computer, by *uninstalling* programs.

WHERE'S THE GOLD?

Programs must be officially removed, or uninstalled. You can't just go around deleting software willy-nilly. The reason is that software often doesn't install itself in just one spot. And although it's called a computer program, you may have several program files and dozens of nonprogram files to remove, to fully uninstall.

There are two ways to officially and properly remove a program:

The Control Panel's Programs and Features window is the first place you should look to remove a program. You can visit that window by opening the Control Panel's Programs and Features icon, or from the Control Panel Home, click the link Uninstall a Program link (by the Programs icon).

You can also access the Programs and Features window from the Disk Cleanup program. *See* Disk Cleanup.

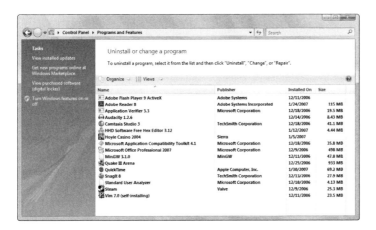

The second way to uninstall a program is by running its Uninstall or Remove command directly. This command is typically found in the All Programs menu, somewhere near the command to run the program itself. This isn't true for all programs.

What to Do with It

You can uninstall any program on your PC, from software purchased in the store to stuff obtained on the Internet. The primary reason for doing so is to increase disk capacity. Honestly, when disk space isn't an issue, there really isn't any need to remove old programs. Otherwise, the following sections describe what to do.

Remove a program

Say that you no longer use a game that occupies an exceedingly large chunk of hard drive space. Here's how to remove it:

1. Open the Control Panels' Programs and Features window.

2. Select the program to remove.

3. Click the Uninstall button on the toolbar.

Clicking the Uninstall button runs the program's associated Uninstall program. What happens next depends on the program; continue to follow the directions on the screen.

The Change button can be used to modify certain programs, but only when they offer that feature. One such program is Microsoft Office,

where the Uninstall program can be used to remove Office *and* to install various features.

The Repair button allows some programs to be fixed. This works by either reinstalling the program or running a special file checking-and-repair utility.

See how often a program has been used

As a tip, Windows lets you know how often you use various programs. To view that information, and potentially remove programs you seldom use, follow these steps:

1. Open the Control Panel's Programs and Features window.

2. From the Views toolbar button's menu, choose Details.

   Locate the Used column and see whether a given program is run rarely, occasionally, or frequently. When you cannot find the Used column, continue with these steps:

3. Right-click any column heading.

4. From the pop-up menu, choose the More command.

   The Choose Details dialog box appears.

5. Click to place a check mark by the Used item in the scrolling list.

6. Click OK.

Remove Windows features

The Programs and Features window lists only software you've installed in Windows. It doesn't list Windows programs and features by themselves. To remove those features, such as a game, do this:

1. Open the Control Panel's Programs and Features window.

2. On the left side of the window, click the link Turn Windows Features On or Off.

3. In the Windows Features dialog box, locate a feature to remove and then remove its check mark.

4. Click OK.

Windows updates aren't listed in the Programs and Features window. *See* Updates for details.

Watch Your Step!

The Administrator account must remove software installed for all the PC's users.

You cannot remove a program that you're using. Quit the program, and then try uninstalling it again.

Some games may uninstall, by removing all their program files but leaving data files. Those files are okay to delete; they're left on the computer in case you reinstall the game again so that you don't lose your old settings.

When Things Go Wrong

Some older programs, and programs not officially following Windows specifications, may not show up in the Programs and Features window. You have to refer to that program's documentation for official removal instructions.

For various reasons, some programs may not fully uninstall, or the installation program may halt with a slew of errors. Refer to the developer's Web site for assistance, although I typically just let the situation be.

Gold Rush Nuggets

Back in the days of DOS, programs were uninstalled by simply deleting them.

Early versions of Windows either lacked uninstall programs or had them of such weak quality that they didn't work. This led to a boon of third-party uninstall utilities. These are largely irrelevant today.

Digging Elsewhere

Delete, Disk Cleanup, Programs, Updates

Updates

Automatic Updates or Windows Updates are handy tools that modify or improve Windows Vista, by fixing problems or bugs that crop up or fine-tuning features that need more work or have been shown to be a security risk. Done right, updates happen automatically as you use the computer or are connected to the Internet. Rarely, if ever, are the updates anything to concern yourself over.

WHERE'S THE GOLD?

Windows Updates happen automatically. Well, they happen automatically when you configure them that way. But the gold itself is buried in the Control Panel, under the Windows Update icon. Opening that icon displays the Windows Update window. Or, you can view the window from the Control Panel Home by clicking the Check for Updates link, found under the Security heading.

The Windows Update window lists information regarding pending updates, plus links to change the update settings.

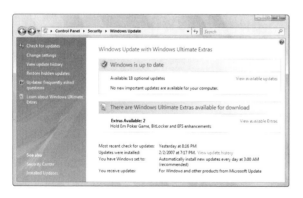

Another way to get to the Windows Update window is to choose the Windows Update command from the All Programs menu. *See* All Programs Menu.

What to Do with It

My preference is to use the updates, which ensures that Windows is current and stuffed with the necessary security precautions. I recommend having updates happen automatically, especially when your computer is on a high-speed Internet connection.

Activate automatic updates

To ensure that your computer's operating system is up-to-date and secure, turn on Automatic Updates this way:

1. Summon the Windows Update window.

2. Click the link on the left, Change Settings.

3. Choose the top setting, Install Updates Automatically (Recommended).

4. Set a schedule for the updates.

5. Click OK.

The second option allows updates to be downloaded, but you're prompted to install them. I find that annoying, mostly because I end up clicking OK when prompted to install the updates anyway.

I recommend against the third and fourth options because they promote bad computer security, which is almost as heinous as the gum disease known as gingivitis.

Manually update Windows

You can pull a *manual* update, a quick check to ensure that you have all you need to keep your PC's operating system current. To do so, in the Windows Update window, click the link on the left, Check for Updates. Windows ventures out to the Internet, looking for new updates that are available on the Microsoft mothership.

Review installed updates

Look what they've done to my PC, Ma!

To review the updates that have been installed on your computer, follow these steps:

1. Open the Windows Update window.

2. On the left side of the window, choose View Update History.

   The View Update History window appears, listing all the updates installed on your PC.

Eureka
Double-click an update to get a more detailed description of what the update did.

3. Click the OK button when you're done.

You can also see the View Update History window whenever a bubble pops up from the Notification Area, alerting you to installed updates. Click the bubble to view the Update History window.

Windows installed new updates   x
Your computer was restarted to finish installing updates. Click to see which updates were installed.

Remove an update

If an update leads to woe or you're directed to remove an update for whatever reason, you're given a notice, generally through e-mail. The message indicates which update to remove and references the update by a code that starts with the letters *KB*. You then obey these directions:

1. Open the Windows Update window.

2. In the lower left area, choose the Installed Updates link.

3. Click to select the update to remove.

Clue
Use a *KB* number, which is your clue to which update is the vile one.

4. Click the Uninstall button on the toolbar.

5. Click the Yes button to confirm.

6. Obey any additional directions, such as restarting Windows.

Each update listed in the Installed Updates window references more than one individual update. You can cross-reference which updates do what by using their KB number and reviewing the updates as described in the section "Review installed updates," earlier in this entry.

View available updates

Windows Update may not be so automatic when it comes to some types of updates. For example, noncritical updates or (dare I say it?) games can also be updated. The only way to find out whether such updates are available is to follow these steps:

1. Open the Windows Update window.

2. Near the upper right corner, click the View Available Updates link.

A list of potential updates, plus "extras," appears.

3. Choose the updates you want; click to put a check mark in the box.

4. Click the Install button.

Sit back and watch as the files are downloaded from the Microsoft mothership on the Internet.

5. Heed any further directions, such as restarting Windows.

Update other software

As with your operating system, you may entertain the thought of updating other software you own. How you perform the update varies, depending on the program; some applications may have an update command to run or a separate program, or the updates may be automatic.

The best way to confirm that updates for your programs are available is to refer to the manufacturer's Web site. Or, use the Help menu to look for an Update command or information about updating in the online Help system.

Watch Your Step!

Some updates require that Windows restart. When you activate automatic updates, you may discover that Windows has restarted the computer without your presence. That seems unsettling, but Windows is just doing what you asked it to.

Updating windows affects all users on the same computer.

If you have more than one PC, each one must be updated individually.

Yes, you occasionally must restart the computer to install updates. If you see a tiny shield icon over the Start button menu's power button, your PC is due for a restart to install new updates.

Windows Update icon

The shield on the power button indicates updates need to be installed.

When Things Go Wrong

The Windows Update service doesn't work when you have an illegal copy of Windows installed. This may not be your fault because an unscrupulous computer dealer may have swindled you out of your legitimate copy of Windows Vista. The only solution, unfortunately, is to buy a legitimate copy of Windows Vista and use its Product ID to register with Microsoft.

Some updates may prove to be incompatible with your PC. If so, you notice strange new behavior after the update is installed. To help resolve the problem, run the update troubleshooter:

1. Choose Help and Support from the Start button's menu.

2. In the search box, type **troubleshoot updates**.

3. Choose the search result item Troubleshoot Problems with Installing Updates.

   You may have to scroll down.

4. Review the various solutions offered.

Gold Rush Nuggets

The KB number refers to a specific article in Microsoft's online knowledgebase. The article describes the what's and why's behind the update. KB stands for Knowledge Base.

Some notorious Windows XP updates did more damage than good, leading computer gurus such as myself to recommend against automatic updates. Those problems have been addressed, so I've changed my tune: Automatic updates are now recommended.

Digging Elsewhere

Device Manager, Uninstall Programs

User Account Control (UAC)

The most obvious evidence of Windows Vista security is the UAC, or User Account Control, whic[h] pops up whenever you attempt to do something that might affect your computer system. Th[e] idea is that the UAC alerts you to a potential security risk. If your current activity involves seein[g] a UAC, such as modifying a Windows setting or installing new software, the UAC's appearance [is] accepted. But it's those times when the UAC appears unexpectedly that you need to take care. When i[n] doubt, just click Cancel.

WHERE'S THE GOLD?

Wherever the UAC is buried, it keeps popping out of its coffin and confronting you as you use Windows. The notion is security, but the degree varies. A UAC warning can mean anything from "Something disastrous was just prevented" to "The change you're about to make affects all users on this computer." It takes a good eye to spot the difference between these different warning levels.

There are several levels of UAC prompts:

The most serious UAC is color-coded red with a red alert shield. This warning indicates that an application has been blocked and cannot run. At a lesser level, the red shield warning may ask whether you want to continue with a potentially questionable activity.

The blue-green UAC with the gold shield indicates that administrator approval is required in order to continue, implying that the change being made affects all users on the computer. As long as you're the one doing the change and the change wasn't unexpected, it's okay to continue.

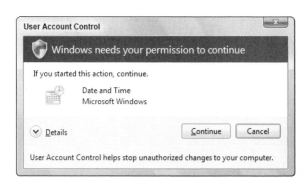

The orange UAC with the red exclamation point shield indicates an "untrusted" application is attempting to run on the computer. This typically happens for older programs that are unsigned or lack the proper credentials that come with newer applications (those customized for Windows Vista).

Other security warnings may appear when you download and install software from the Internet. Again, as long as you are the one downloading the program and the program named in the warning is the one you're downloading, things are okay.

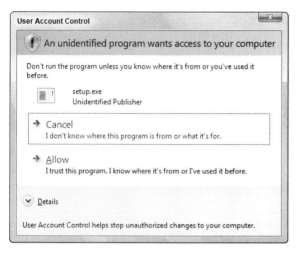

A similar orange UAC appears when you attempt to run a program from a Web page, such as running the Foxit Reader program to view a PDF file.

When you're using a Standard account, the UAC warning that's displayed might include a login prompt for administrator-level access. This happens when you attempt rather low-level security things that may affect other users on the computer. Rather than switch users, you can merely type the administrator password (or choose one of several Administrator accounts) and then proceed with the change.

UAC warnings associated with specific actions in Windows are often labeled by a shield icon. Whenever you see that tiny shield icon, such as on a button in a dialog box or beside a link in a window, administrator-level approval is required in order to continue.

What to Do with It

The UAC is an immediate-action item. It stops everything in the computer and demands your input. It's serious. You should be serious about it as well.

Deal with a UAC

The worst way to deal with a UAC is to figure that it's just routine and then choose the option that allows you to continue. After all, your dear friend Winifred would never send you a computer virus as an e-mail attachment now, would she?

The best way to deal with a UAC is to pause and consider the following questions:

✗ Am I doing something now that would cause this UAC to appear?

✗ Is the UAC related to something I just clicked?

✗ Is the security level of the UAC expected for this operation?

When the answer is Yes, feel free to proceed. But when a UAC seems to pop up out of nowhere, such as a UAC to install software while you're browsing the Internet and not downloading software, the answer is Don't Allow, Deny, Don't Install, or Cancel.

Disable UAC warnings

The UAC prompts exist for security reasons. For those who utterly disregard security, you can disable the prompts thusly:

1. Pop up the Start button menu.

2. Click your account picture in the menu's upper right corner.

3. In the User Accounts window, click the link Turn User Account Control On or Off.

4. Remove the check mark by Use User Account Control (UAC) to Help Protect Your Computer.

5. Click OK.

6. Click the Restart Now button to restart Windows so that the changes can take effect.

You can reenable the UAC warnings by repeating these steps, but in Step 4, add the check mark.

Watch Your Step!

Disabling the warnings leaves your PC vulnerable to takeover by malicious programs. I would say that it's a good idea only when your computer is *not* on the Internet and *not* being used by anyone other than yourself.

 You can easily get into the habit of clicking the Continue or Allow buttons when you see a UAC. Although it's against human nature, which is to form habits, please consider the importance of the warning. Most viruses and nasty computer programs profligate because of *social engineering*. That is, they fool you into doing something you normally would question, such as open an unknown e-mail attachment or click a Download button when you haven't requested any information to be downloaded.

When Things Go Wrong

There are two problems with the UAC warnings. Both are related to human nature. First, you can too easily get used to clicking OK or Allow. It's habit forming. The UAC colors, especially red, should alarm you. But you must be alert and not fall into the habit of thinking "It's okay" when it might not be okay. Second, humans tend to be too trusting, especially when a message that's received, which looks like a friend sent it, tells you to ignore the UAC warning. That's bad. Don't be a fool; check with the "friend" before you do anything. You'll probably find out that no friend sent you that message or perhaps that person really isn't your friend anyway.

Gold Rush Nuggets

Despite ridicule from many Microsoft critics, the UAC warnings shouldn't come up often as you use your computer. Only when you're doing administrator-level tasks, actions that can change how everyone uses the computer, do the warnings crop up a lot. Aside from that, during normal computer operation, you rarely see a UAC.

Digging Elsewhere

Administrator, Firewall, User Accounts, Windows Defender

User Accounts

Every account on your PC has a home, and the home for all those homes is User Accounts. That's where you can examine and change information about your own account — the picture, password, account name, and so on — or, if you're a snooty administrator and your PC is burdened with more than one user, you can change information about other accounts.

WHERE'S THE GOLD?

User Accounts dwells in the Control Panel. You can swim there by opening the User Accounts icon or, from the Control Panel Home, open User Accounts and Family Safety, and then click User Accounts.

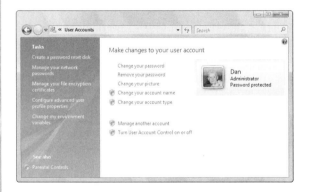

The easiest way to get to the User Accounts window is to pop up the Start menu and click your account's icon in the upper right area of the menu.

What to Do with It

You use the User Accounts window to manage your account, by changing various basic information, such as the password, account name, and image. From terrible and awesome administrator-level accounts, you can manage other accounts in the system. Woe be to he who chooses to abuse such power!

The following sections assume that you have the User Accounts window open and ready for action on your computer screen. (For information on changing or removing your password, *see* Passwords.)

Change the account image

I suppose that the most common thing to do with your account is to change the image. After all, you aren't really a silly flower, are you? And, how the heck can you identify yourself with a chess piece? Get real!

You can use any image on your computer for the account image. The graphics file formats preferred for the image are BMP, GIF, JPG, and PNG. For example, you can create an image in Windows Paint and use it. Or, you can use an image imported from a digital camera or scanner.

I recommend resizing a large image. Using graphics software, make the image about 300 pixels square. That's larger than Windows needs, but the image will be reduced (and made square if it's not), so the closer you can get to what Windows needs, the better the image looks.

To change the image, heed these steps:

1. In the User Accounts window, click the Change Your Picture link.

   A new window appears, listing your current picture plus all the silly pictures Windows offers.

2. Choose an image from those displayed, in which case you're done, or click the Browse link for more pictures.

3. Use the Open dialog box to hunt down the picture file you want.

   The Open dialog box displays the contents of your account's Pictures folder. From there, you can browse for the image you want. *See* Open for details.

4. Click Open to open the image you want.

Change the account name

Suppose that you were drunk the night you installed Windows. Or, perhaps you didn't recognize that Death Maven really isn't as cool of an account name as you once believed. Rest assured, you can change your Windows account name:

1. In the User Accounts window, click Change Your Account Name.

2. Enter an administrator password if you're asked (only administrator-level accounts have access to change an account name).

3. Type your new account name.

4. Click the Change Name button.

Change the account type

It's possible to change between Administrator and Standard User accounts. *See* Administrator for more information.

Add a new account

Each user on the computer should have his own account, which helps keep information, files, e-mail, favorites, and other stuff separate and secure. Even when you're the only user on the PC, having both Administrator and Standard accounts is the preferred mode of operation.

To create a new account, log in as an administrator and follow these steps:

1. In the User Accounts window, click Manage Another Account.

2. Click the Create a New Account link.

3. Input the user name.

4. Choose the account level: Administrator or Standard.

5. Click the Create Account button.

Remove a user's account

Cleaning up unused accounts saves a wee sliver of disk space, although it's probably not something you'll do every day. Obviously, you should do this by using an Administrator account:

1. Click the Manage Another Account link in the User Accounts window.

2. Click to select the account you want to banish.

3. Click the Delete the Account link.

4. Click Delete Files.

5. Click Delete Account.

Optionally, you can choose Keep Files in Step 4, but that means you intend to examine the user's files for things to salvage. That sounds like a pain, so have an intern do it instead.

Disable a user's account

User accounts can be disabled, which can be better for the short term than fully deleting the thing. To disable an account, obey these steps:

1. Bring up the Run dialog box.

   Pressing the Win+R key combination does this quickly; otherwise, *see* Run.

2. Type **compmgmt.msc** into the box and click OK.

   The Computer Management console appears.

3. Choose Local Users and Groups from the left side of the window.

4. Open the Users folder in the center of the window.

5. Right-click the account to disable and choose Properties from the shortcut menu.

6. On the General tab, click to put a check mark by Account Is Disabled.

7. Click OK.

8. Close the Computer Management window.

A disabled account doesn't appear in the list of accounts when you first log in to Windows or when you're switching users.

To enable the account, simply remove the check mark in Step 6. (These steps are also used to activate the secret Administrator account; *see* Administrator.)

Watch Your Step!

Administrator access is required in order to mess with other accounts on the computer. *See* Administrator.

You cannot restore an account after it has been deleted.

Changing an account name doesn't change the folder names used in Windows. The original name continues to be used for the User Profile folder. Changing the account name affects only the login name.

You cannot change the Guest account.

Account names should be short and descriptive. Specifically, an account name must be 20 characters or fewer and cannot include any of the following characters:

" * , / : ; ? @ [\ ] | + < = >

Periods and spaces are okay, although a user name cannot be all spaces or all periods.

When Things Go Wrong

Windows doesn't let you use a TIF graphics file for your account image. Likewise, specific image formats, such as Photoshop, aren't allowed. You must convert the image to BMP, JPG, GIF, or PNG. Most graphics programs allow images to be saved or exported in those formats.

You must enable the Guest account in order to demote a user to Guest account level. *See* Guest.

Gold Rush Nuggets

All accounts are based on the main hard drive in the Users folder. The pathname is `C:\Users`. Each account has a folder named after the original account name. That folder is the same as the User Profile folder; *see* User Profile Folder.

Digging Elsewhere

Administrator, Control Panel, Guest, Login and Log Off, Passwords, Standard User, User Profile Folder

User Profile Folder

I f your home is your castle, then the castle you have on your computer is officially known as the User Profile folder. I prefer to call it my *account* folder or, to borrow the Unix phrase, the *Home* folder. It's the main folder where your user account can store all the information you create and collect with your computer. It's a home base of operations, your own little (or not so little) cubbyhole on the PC's main hard drive, just for your stuff.

WHERE'S THE GOLD?

The User Profile folder is perhaps the easiest folder to access in Windows. As the main folder for your account, it should be! The tricky part is that the folder is given the same name as your account. So, if your account is named Sales 2F98B, the folder is named `Sales 2F98B`. On my computer, the folder is named `Dan`.

You can access the folder from the desktop, if the folder's icon appears there. (*See* Desktop Icons.)

The folder can also be accessed from the Start button menu, at the top of the right column, although it may not appear there, either. (*See* Start Button and Menu.)

From any Windows Explorer window (press Win+E to summon one), you can view your User Profile folder by choosing its name from the menu displayed by clicking the leftmost triangle on the Address bar. (*See* Address Bar.)

After the User Profile folder is opened, it reveals a host of folders and perhaps file icons. These folders were created by Windows when your account was initially set up. The idea is to use the folders to help keep your stuff organized.

Here's a rundown of the folders you may see:

Contacts: A location for contact information, primarily from Windows Mail, although other address book and database programs may use this folder.

Desktop: The true location where items on the desktop are stored. *See* Desktop.

Documents: The main folder for storing documents, files, and other stuff that just doesn't fit anywhere else.

Downloads: A location for programs downloaded from the Internet.

Favorites: The folder where Internet Explorer keeps your favorites (bookmarks).

Links: A folder full of shortcuts to other folders. The contents of this folder appear in the Windows Explorer navigation pane, at the top, under Favorite Links.

Music: A general place for music and audio files, used by Windows Media Player and other audio and musical applications.

Pictures: The folder where most graphics and imaging programs prefer to put graphics files, photographs, and other pictures.

Saved Games: The folder where all your player data and records from Windows games are stored. Soon, other game manufacturers will use this folder as well.

Searches: The folder where Windows saves any searches you performed, and where preset searches are saved.

Videos: The place for storing and saving any video files you create or download from the Internet. Also, the place where video-creation software saves files.

What to Do with It

The User Profile folder itself isn't really a place where you want to save your files. It's in the folder's subfolders where you want to save your files. In fact, the various Save As dialog boxes you use to save files are geared to choose specific subfolders from your User Profile folder, such as the Pictures folder for saving graphics.

Make your own, custom subfolder

I'm an organizational nut, so I prefer to have as many specific folders as possible in my User Profile folder.

For example, I created a prog folder, in which I put my programming files. I also have a Themes folder for my various customized themes (sounds and display, for example; *see* Themes). I also cannot live without my Misc folder, which I often call Sto or Junk, which has obvious uses. Here's how to create such a folder yourself:

1. Open your User Profile folder.

2. Click the Organize button on the toolbar.

3. From the Organize menu, choose New Folder.

   The new folder is created, and its name, New Folder, is highlighted and ready to be renamed.

4. Type a name for the folder, such as Junk or Sto; press Enter to lock in the new name.

See also Folders, especially for information on how to customize your folder to make it look more like the folders that Windows provides.

Encrypt the User Profile folder

For an extra layer of security, you can direct Windows to encrypt the contents of the User Profile folder. This prevents other users on the computer from casually plowing through your User Profile folder and its contents. *See* Encryption for details.

Only Administrator accounts can browse through other User Profile folders. Encrypting your account doesn't prevent this type of access. *See also* BitLocker.

Back up the User Profile folder

The User Profile folder is where all your computer information is stored. Unlike previous versions of Windows, *everything* that makes your account on the PC unique is kept in one location. Therefore, to back up all your stuff, all you need to back up is the User Profile folder and all its subfolders. For more information, *see* Backup.

Watch Your Step!

I don't recommend saving anything directly in the User Profile folder. Instead, use one of the subfolders for the stuff you save. When the preset folders don't seem to match what you're saving, create a new folder for those items.

Each user on the computer has her own User Profile folder. Other users' folders are protected, and access is restricted to their contents.

Clue The User Profile folder also sports various hidden subfolders. These folders are hidden to help restrict their access, although some of the stuff in those hidden folders is intriguing, it's nothing you really want to mess with. *See* Hidden Files and Folders for information on displaying the hidden User Profile folders.

When Things Go Wrong

When your User Profile folder's size grows larger than 4GB, or more information than can fit on a single DVD, you have to use the Windows Backup program to back up the folder as opposed to a simple file-copy operation.

Sometimes, when organizing files, you may choose to group or stack the icons in the User Profile folder. This has the effect of using the Windows Search command on the folder. To return to the normal way of viewing things, reopen the User Profile folder by following the directions offered earlier in this entry.

Gold Rush Nuggets

Each user on the computer has her own User Profile folder. These folders are usually found on drive C, in the Users folder. The pathname to your User Account Folder is often `C:\Users\` followed by your account name.

Digging Elsewhere

Computer, Folders, Public Folder, User Accounts, Windows Explorer

Web Page Cache

The most important thing to know about the Web page cache is that *cache* is pronounced "cash." It's a storage place. When you browse the Web, various elements from each Web page (graphics, mostly) are saved on your computer. When those elements are saved, the Web pages you visit load faster the next time you visit. That's because information can be fetched from the cache rather than have to be transferred at a much slower speed over the Internet. The place where that information is stored is the *Web page cache,* but it may also be known as Internet Cache or Temporary Internet Files.

WHERE'S THE GOLD?

Windows enjoys hiding the Web page cache just as pirates once enjoyed hiding their cache of weapons or swag o' rum! But, honestly, the Web page cache is a function of the Web browser software, not of Windows. So, specifically, the Web page cache belongs to Internet Explorer.

The Web page cache controls can be found on the General tab of the Internet Options dialog box. Clicking the Delete button on that tab displays the Delete Browsing History dialog box, from which you can remove various things you picked up while surfing the Web, including the Web page cache. (*See* AutoComplete.)

Physically, the cache is stored in a special folder located in the hidden AppData subfolder, in your User Profile folder.

What to Do with It

The Web page cache operates pretty much by itself. You don't need to set its size, as was done in some early Web browsers. Windows manages

things for you. But there are still a few cache things you can manage.

Empty the cache

Purging the cache isn't a routine activity, although it can be necessary at times — for example, to ensure that you're seeing the latest version of a Web page or for security reasons or to free up disk space. Here's how to empty the Web page cache:

1. Open the Internet Properties dialog box.

   You can open the Internet Options icon in the Control Panel or in Internet Explorer click the Tools button on the toolbar and choose Internet Options from the menu.

2. Click the General tab, if necessary.

3. Click the Delete button.

   The Delete Browsing History dialog box appears.

4. Click the Delete Files button.

5. Click the Yes button in the Delete Files dialog box to confirm.

To ensure that you're viewing the most recent version of a Web page, use the Refresh command after emptying the cache and loading the Web page. *See* Refresh.

Empty the cache with Disk Cleanup

Another place to delete the Web page cache is from the Disk Cleanup window. *See* Disk Cleanup.

Watch Your Step!

There's nothing truly serious to look out for when emptying the cache. Some Web pages may load slower than they once did, which is about the only downside.

Yes, the cache will fill up again — and quickly. But if your problem is that the PC is low on disk space, the solution is to add another hard drive and not keep repeatedly emptying the Web page cache.

When Things Go Wrong

Generally speaking, nothing should go wrong. If the steps in this section don't work, the cache is probably empty.

Gold Rush Nuggets

It was once popular to dig through the cache to look for material that otherwise could not be downloaded from the Internet, such as movies and music files. Although downloading such items directly was not possible, computer nerds routinely got copies of those treasures by finding their cached files and moving them to another folder. Sadly, this trick doesn't work anymore; most media content on the Internet is *streamed,* not downloaded to your computer in a complete chunk.

To see how much space will be freed by emptying the Web page cache, use the Disk Cleanup utility. The total amount of disk space used is listed by the Temporary Internet Files option.

Digging Elsewhere

AutoComplete, Disk Cleanup, Internet Explorer

Welcome Center

The welcome wagon waiting to warm you when you first start Windows is the Windows Welcome Center. A virtual candy dish and list of shortcuts, it's probably something you'll dismiss right away, eager to get into Windows Vista to do work or play a game or get online and do whatever it is that you enjoy doing while online.

The Welcome Center starts automatically when Windows starts. That's because of the check box in the lower left corner of the window, by the command Run at Startup. Removing the check mark turns off the automatic Welcome Center.

To reactivate the Welcome Center, open the Control Panel's Welcome Center icon, or from the Control Panel Home, click the link Get Started with Windows, beneath the System and Maintenance heading.

The Welcome Center provides handy links to popular Windows activities, including some "offers" from Microsoft. Better than the offers are the extras you can get through the Update service, such as a nifty Poker game for some versions of Windows Vista. *See* Updates.

One thing that's truly useful to new Windows Vista users is the Welcome Center's What's New in Windows Vista icon. Clicking that icon merely lists a host of features in the top part of the Welcome Center window, which pretty much sums up the entire Welcome Center experience.

Windows

Windows is the name of the PC's computer operating system, but it's also the name of a graphical element found on the screen. In fact, next to the icon, a *window* is the most common thing you see on the screen. Icons themselves open to reveal windows.

WHERE'S THE GOLD?

Never mind what's in (or through) the window; what's important to know lies on and near the window's border — the window's *frame,* if you're into construction. As a Windows user, it behooves you to know Windows nomenclature:

Border	Corner	Scrollbar
Close button	Maximize/Restore button	Title bar
Contents	Menu bar	Toolbar
Control menu	Minimize button	

An *active window* is the window you're using, the one in which activity is focused. Only one window is the active window, usually the top-most window on the desktop. The active window is colored differently from non-active windows.

A special type of window is a dialog box, which looks like a window but is better suited for specific purposes. *See* Dialog Box.

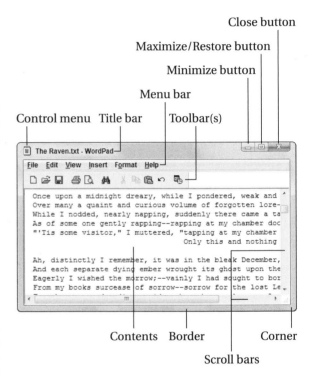

Close button
Maximize/Restore button
Minimize button
Menu bar
Control menu   Title bar   Toolbar(s)

Contents   Border   Corner
Scroll bars

What to Do with It

Windows are truly flexible things. Moving, resizing, arranging, and working with windows are perhaps the most basic tasks you do on your computer.

Move a window

A window's location is commonly changed by dragging the window's title bar with the mouse. The window can be dragged to any location on the screen or, more accurately, anywhere you can drag the mouse.

Resize a window

A window can be made larger or smaller by "grabbing" its edge and dragging the mouse. Dragging a window border extends or reduces the window's size in one direction; dragging a window corner extends or reduces the window in two directions at once.

The key to knowing when you can resize a window is when the mouse pointer changes to a this-way-that-way arrow. Dragging the mouse in either direction, as indicated by the arrow, resizes the window.

Some windows have a minimum set size beyond which the window cannot be made smaller. The size depends on the window's contents.

Windows can be manually enlarged to be greater than the screen size, although such windows are difficult to manipulate and doing such a thing must be reserved for times of intense intoxication.

Maximize a window

A *maximized* window is one that fills the entire desktop, corner to corner, edge to edge. To maximize a window, click the Maximize button.

The Maximize button changes to the Restore button when a window is maximized.

| Maximize
button | Restore
button | Minimize
button | Close
button |

You can also maximize a window by double-clicking the title bar.

Minimize a window

Shrinking a window and transforming it into a button on the Taskbar is referred to as *minimizing* the window. To do that, click the window's Minimize button.

Minimizing is one way to set a window aside. Rather than close the program or close its window, you simply minimize it, where it can be restored later when needed.

Restore a window

You have two ways to restore a window: To return a maximized window to its previous size and location, click the window's Restore button.

To return a window that has been minimized to a button on the Taskbar, click that window's button on the Taskbar.

Close a window

To close a window, dismissing it from the desktop and potentially closing the program that the window belongs to, click the window's Close button.

Clue You can also close a window by pressing the Alt+F4 key combination. Some, but not all, programs use the more logical Ctrl+W key combination to close a window.

Scroll window contents

A window displays only so much information. Indeed, it's a graphical *window* through which you view a larger document or image. To see more of the image, you enlarge the window or use the scroll bars to adjust what you see.

Documents or images that are wider than the window's dimensions sport a horizontal scroll bar.

Documents or images taller than the window harbor a vertical scroll bar.

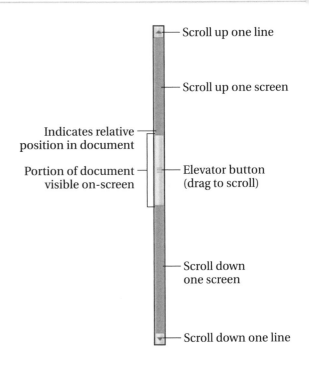

No matter its orientation, the scroll bar works the same way. Use the mouse to scroll the image in the window up or down in various degrees, or use the *elevator button* to specifically position the window contents.

The keyboard can also be used to scroll window content. The Page Up (PgUp) and Page Down (PgDn) keys, Home and End keys, as well as the standard arrow keys can scroll an image.

A mouse with a wheel button can be used to scroll an image. The wheel button itself can be pressed to "pan and scan" an image by dragging the mouse when the button is pressed, although this feature may not work with all windows.

Arrange multiple windows

To avoid having many windows on the desktop get out of hand, you can use the Taskbar's shortcut menu to quickly arrange the windows. Right-click a blank part of the Taskbar, and then choose one of these commands to arrange the windows on the desktop:

Cascade Windows: All windows are resized and arranged in a cascading pattern from the upper left corner of the desktop.

Show Windows Stacked: All open windows are arranged horizontally, each stacked atop the other.

Show Windows Side By Side: All open windows are arranged vertically, side by side.

Show the Desktop. All windows are minimized to reveal the desktop. You can also use the Win+D or Win+M key combination to reveal the desktop or minimize all open windows.

Switch between windows

To switch to another window, click that window — if it's visible. Otherwise, you can click the window's button on the Taskbar.

 Clue You can also use the Alt+Tab or Alt+Win key combinations to switch between windows. *See* Multitasking.

Use the Control menu

Clicking the teensy icon in a window's upper left corner reveals the Control menu, which can also be used to manipulate the window and to provide access to some specific system commands (when available).

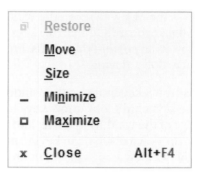

The Control menu provides shortcuts to common window-manipulation commands, although I confess that using the mouse to choose the Move and Resize commands is confusing; I recommend using the moving and resizing techniques mentioned earlier in this entry.

The Control menu can also be displayed by pressing the Alt+spacebar keyboard shortcut or, when a window is minimized, by right-clicking its Taskbar button.

Use the keyboard to manipulate a window

The Control menu comes in most handy when you need to use the keyboard to manipulate a window, such as when a window has slid off the screen or whenever the mouse is unavailable.

Press Ctrl+spacebar to activate the Control menu. Then choose one of these options:

Restore: Press the R key to restore the window.

Move: Press the M key to move the window, and then use the keyboard's four arrow keys to move the window in any of four directions. Press Enter when you're done moving.

Size: Press the S key to resize the window. Press one of the keyboard's four arrow keys to choose which edge of the window to move, and then use either the up-down or left-right keys to move that edge of the window in or out. Press Enter when you're done.

Minimize: Press the N key to minimize the window.

Maximize: Press the X key to maximize the window.

Close: Press the C key to close the window.

Change a window's look

You can adjust the appearance of windows, from the Aero transparent curvy look to the traditional solid and square Windows of years past. Here's a quick way to do that:

1. Open the Control Panel.
2. Open the Personalization icon; from the Control Panel Home, choose Appearance and Personalization, and then click the Change the Theme link (under Personalization).

The Theme Settings dialog box shows up.

3. Choose a preset theme from the Theme list.
4. Click OK; optionally, close the Control Panel window.

See also Themes for more information.

Watch Your Step!

The Minimize, Maximize/Restore, and Close buttons may subtly alter their appearance depending on whether a window is maximized or which window theme is being used, and even within certain programs.

Changing a window's size affects the size of any new windows created in that program. But this rule applies to only manually resized windows, not to windows you maximize. In other words:

Clue If you want windows to be larger all the time, resize them manually; do not use Maximize.

A window's size is remembered the next time you start the same program that created the window.

Closing a window is the same as quitting a program. Don't fret: When your data hasn't been saved, you're warned before the window closes.

When Things Go Wrong

If a window slides off the screen or you're otherwise unable to manipulate the window by using the mouse, you have to use the keyboard to rescue everything. First, refer to the earlier section "Use the keyboard to manipulate a window"; then try to move the window back to the desktop, and then resize the window so that you can access any of its edges with the mouse.

Windows cannot be moved or resized when they're maximized.

A maximized window doesn't overlap the Taskbar, unless the Taskbar is configured to appear behind windows. *See* Taskbar.

Gold Rush Nuggets

The first version of Windows, released in 1985, did not feature overlapping windows but, rather, *tiled* windows. All windows on the screen fit together like puzzle pieces; resizing or moving a window rearranged other windows.

Digging Elsewhere

Dialog Box, Icons, Menus, Taskbar, Toolbars

Windows Defender

The Windows Defender program is designed to help you fight the scourge of *spyware,* or those nasty programs that claim squatters' rights inside your computer, interfere with the things you do, betray your PC's power to the Internet, and generally upset everyone.

WHERE'S THE GOLD?

The Windows Defender program is relatively easy to find: From the Start button menu, choose All Programs⇨Windows Defender.

You can also open the Windows Defender icon in the Control Panel to see Windows Defender; from the Control Panel Home, choose Security and then Windows Defender.

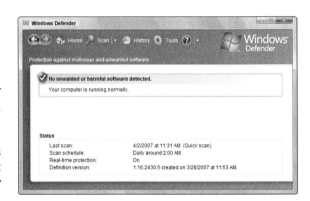

Windows
Defender
icon

The main window in Windows Defender should assure you right away that your computer is spyware-free, or at least working to get that way.

What to Do with It

Windows Defender runs automatically; there's really nothing else you need to do, unless you suspect that your computer has a problem that Windows Defender isn't dealing with.

Scan for nasty programs

To perform a manual scan for spyware in your computer, do this:

1. Start Windows Explorer.

2. Click the Scan button on the toolbar.

3. Sit back and watch.

Windows Defender reviews files on your computer, looking for telltale signs of spyware. If anything unsavory is found, Windows Defender deals with it automatically.

To do a more detailed spyware scan, click the Scan menu button to the right of the Scan toolbar button and choose Full Scan from the menu. Yes, that method takes a bit longer, but the operation is more thorough.

Review quarantined items

When Windows Defender finds a bit o' spyware that it cannot deal with, it puts the file or thingy in *quarantine*. Basically, the computer is safe, but the file itself still exists; Windows was either unable to remove the file or unsure about removing the file and what effect it would have.

To review quarantined items, click the Tools button on the Windows Defender toolbar. Then click Quarantined Items. A window lists any quarantined files. You can click to select them and then remove them individually or click the Remove All button to rid your computer of them.

When you see an item in the quarantine list that you really need — something that Windows Defender has accidentally placed in quarantine — click to select that item and then click the Restore button.

Use the Software Explorer

One great tool that I find highly useful in Windows Defender is Software Explorer: Click the Tools button on the Windows Defender toolbar, and then choose Software Explorer.

The Software Explorer window lists the programs running in your computer. The list should be "clean" and have nothing you don't recognize. That's because chances are good that an unrecognized program may be spyware or a Trojan horse that could be compromising your PC's security.

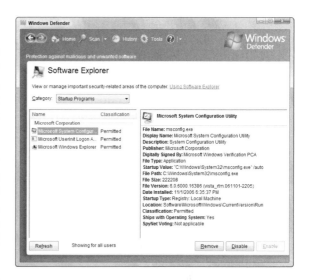

Be sure to choose the various types of programs from the Category menu button: Startup Programs, Currently Running Programs, Network Connected Programs, and Winsock Service Programs (Internet programs).

How can you identify a nasty program? Legitimate programs should have *Permitted* by their names in the Classification column. They also show detailed data on the right side of the window.

To attempt to stop a questionable program, click to highlight it and then click the Disable button. If that fixes the problem, click the Remove button to get rid of the program.

Check the Windows Defender history

To ensure that Windows Defender is doing a good job, you can review its history. Click the History button on the toolbar to see a list of items that piqued the computer's curiosity. Click to select an item to see more information.

Disable Windows Defender

If you choose to use another anti-spyware program, such as Spy Sweeper or any of the tools offered by Norton, you can disable Windows Defender. Here's how:

1. Open Windows Defender.

2. Click the Tools button.

3. Choose Options.

4. Remove the check mark by the option Automatically Scan My Computer (Recommended).

5. Click the Save button.

To reenable Windows Defender, repeat these steps but add the check mark in Step 4.

Watch Your Step!

Windows Defender does not stop computer viruses! *See* Antivirus.

Windows Defender does not provide firewall protection! *See* Firewall.

One main reason that people's computers become infected with spyware is that folks *invite* it into their computers. Spyware is usually attached to some "free" program or helpful utility — for example, a slate of graphical characters to add to your e-mail or a "shopping buddy" or similar online helper. These programs are advertised as marketing tools and may even claim to save you money. They don't. And, some of them are a *bear* to remove. Windows Vista makes it easy to deal with these problems, thanks to Windows Defender, but you can do most of the job by simply being aware of what you do on the Internet.

When Things Go Wrong

Windows Defender should be able to deal with most known spyware issues, although I recommend that you continue to keep Windows up-to-date. *See* Updates.

I often confirm that a specific program or freebie on the Internet is a virus by doing an Internet search. Type the name of the suspected program and the word *spyware* into a search engine. Then review the results to confirm whether the program is nasty. Do this *before* you decide to download the program.

Gold Rush Nuggets

Spyware is merely one member of a larger category of nasty programs called *malware* — or evil software. Other nasty programs include viruses, worms, and Trojan horses. Antivirus software helps you fight those bad guys.

Spyware got its name from the first slew of programs that "helped" you shop on the Internet. These programs claimed to innocently monitor where you go on the Internet to customize marketing material to you. Whether that purpose was legitimate or not, who knows, but in some of the worst cases, spyware prevented users from visiting specific Web pages and instead redirected the poor users to the spyware home page — where even more nasty programs were installed on their computers!

Digging Elsewhere

Problem Reports and Solutions, Safe Mode

Windows Explorer

Two programs named Explorer come with Windows. The one that most people are familiar with is Internet Explorer, which is used on the Internet to browse the World Wide Web. Another program is used just as often (if not more often): Windows Explorer.

Windows Explorer is the program that produces the window you see whenever you open a disk drive or folder icon in Windows. The window lists the contents of the PC's storage system.

To summon Windows Explorer, you merely need to open a folder or location listed on the right side of the Start button menu, open a folder or disk icon on the desktop, or manually run Windows Explorer from the Start menu: Choose All Programs⇨Accessories⇨Windows Explorer.

The keyboard shortcut to summon a Windows Explorer window is Win+E.

Most of the work in Windows Explorer is done by using the toolbar and its buttons:

Organize: The Organize button contains common file commands and commands that control the window's look.

Views: The Views button displays a menu that controls how icons are displayed in the window. *See* Icons.

Other buttons: The toolbar sports other buttons that come and go depending on which icon is selected in the window.

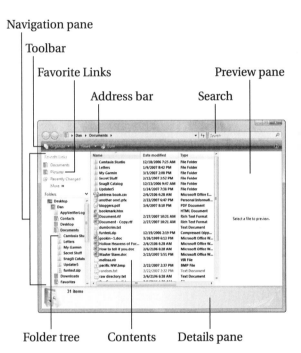

Navigation pane

Toolbar

Favorite Links

Address bar

Preview pane

Search

Folder tree   Contents   Details pane

What to Do with It

The Windows Explorer window is designed to help you accomplish the common tasks of working with files and folders and keeping the stuff you store on your computer organized.

Change the view

The icons in the Windows Explorer window can appear in a number of ways, each of which is chosen from the toolbar's Views button menu. Here are your options:

Extra Large Icons: Icons appear *huge,* using a 270-x-270-pixel grid. Although you can see the icons from space, the practical uses for icons this big seem limited.

Large Icons: Icons are displayed in a 96-x-96-pixel grid.

Medium Icons: This more traditional option for icons is 48 x 48 pixels.

Small Icons: Icons are shown in the smallest size.

List: Small icons are shown, but in a multicolumn list rather than in a grid. This view can come in handy for selecting similar icon types.

Details: Icons are displayed in a small resolution but in a table that also lists various information about the icons.

Tiles: Icons are displayed in a medium resolution but with additional information to the side.

You can also change the view between each of the menu options by simply clicking the Views button on the toolbar.

Clue Right-clicking in the window displays a pop-up menu with multiple viewing and icon-organizing options.

Set columns in Details view

Details view shows a bit more information about each icon in a window, more than any other view. Plus, the header row in Details view offers a few tricks and treats for manipulating how files are displayed.

Column-sorting triangle

Drag mouse here to resize columns

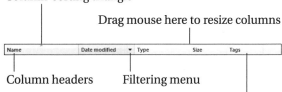

Column headers   Filtering menu

Drag headers from left to right to change order

Sorting icons: To sort icons, click a header. Clicking the Name header sorts the icons by name.

Clue A tiny triangle appears in the column that's used to sort the icons. When the triangle points upward, icons are sorted from A to Z, from smallest to largest, from oldest to newest. To reverse the sort, click the same column heading; the triangle points downward to indicate the reverse sort.

To sort by type and then by name, click the Type heading and then click the name heading.

Filtering icons: Pointing the mouse at any header displays the Filtering menu triangle. Click that triangle to display a menu full of options for further sorting the icons.

Changing column width: To change the column width, point the mouse between two columns and drag left or right. Double-clicking between columns adjusts the column width to match the size of the widest item in that column.

Rearranging columns: To change the column order, drag a heading with the mouse to the left or right.

Adding and removing columns: The columns you see are controlled by a menu and a dialog box. To see the menu, right-click any column header. Adding or removing a check mark from a menu item displays or removes the named header. Choosing the More menu item displays the Choose Details dialog box, from which you can select from a whole swath of headers or rearrange the header order.

Open an icon

To open an icon, double-click it by using the mouse. Opening a program icon runs the program. Opening a folder or disk drive icon displays the contents of that folder or disk drive. Opening a file icon attempts to load that file into the program that created it.

 Look on the toolbar for special Open or Edit command buttons. These buttons may display drop-down menus offering options for opening the file.

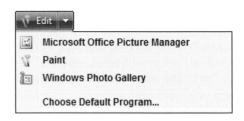

Browse to another location

As with its cousin Internet Explorer, Windows Explorer lets you browse to and fro through your PC's disk system. Here are your helpers:

Folders: Open a folder to display that folder's contents.

Address bar: Use the Address bar, and the Forward and Backward buttons, to navigate to various folders. *See* Address Bar.

Favorite Links: Choose another location from the Favorite Links area of the Navigation pane.

Folder tree: Use the folder tree in the Navigation pane to find and visit specific folders directly.

Hide or show various parts of the window

Controlling what's visible and invisible in the Windows Explorer window is handled by the Organize button on the toolbar. Using that button's Layout submenu, you can choose whether to display the Navigation pane, Details pane, or Preview pane. You can also conjure up the hidden menu bar, as covered in the next section.

Each of the panes can be resized by pointing the mouse on the border between the pane and the rest of the window. Drag the mouse in or out to change the pane's size.

To hide the folder tree in the Navigation pane, click the downward-pointing chevron next to the word *Folders*. This reduces the size of the folder tree and allows you to see more Favorite Links.

Display the hidden menu bar

If you're more comfortable using the traditional Windows Explorer menu, the one you were fond of as a kid, follow these steps:

1. Click the Organize button on the toolbar.

2. Choose Layout⇨Menu Bar.

Repeat these steps to hide the menu bar again.

 You can always access the menu bar by pressing the F10 key.

Use the Favorite Links

Windows lets you keep some of your favorite folders, disk drives, and network locations handy in the Favorite Links portion of the Navigation pane.

To visit a link, click it.

To add a link, drag the folder, disk drive, or network icon to the Favorite Links area.

To remove a link, right-click the link and choose Remove Link from the pop-up menu.

 The links themselves are shortcuts kept in the Links folder inside your User Profile folder.

Summon a new folder window

Often when managing files, you need to open a second Windows Explorer window, one from which, or to which, you're copying or moving files or comparing information.

To open a new Windows Explorer window, you must start the Windows Explorer program again: From the Start button menu, choose All Programs⇨Accessories⇨Windows Explorer.

Open a folder in a new window

Windows Explorer is configured to open folders in the same window, which helps reduce clutter but often slows you down when managing files. To direct Windows to open each folder in its own window, follow these steps:

1. Click the Organize button on the toolbar.

2. Choose Folder and Search Options from the Organize button's menu.

3. In the Folder Options dialog box, on the General tab, choose the Open Each Folder in Its Own Window option.

4. Click OK.

Only folders that you open are displayed in a new window. When you choose a folder from the Address bar, Favorite Links area, or folder tree, that folder opens in the same window.

To have folders open in the same window, repeat these steps but in Step 3 choose the Open Each Folder in the Same Window option.

Watch Your Step!

Some special windows displayed by Windows Explorer lack some of the features you find in a standard folder window or file window. For example, the Control Panel and Games windows lack some of the layout and display options.

Windows warns you when you try to browse to a folder to which you don't have access.

Opening a Compressed Folder looks like opening any other folder on the screen, although it's not the same. *See* Compressed Folders.

When Things Go Wrong

Windows Explorer can be configured to open icons with only one click, which is more Web-like but not like the way Windows normally works. To change this setting, follow these steps:

1. In Windows Explorer, choose Folder and Search Options from the toolbar's Organize button's menu.

2. In the Folder Options dialog box, on the General tab, choose the option labeled Double-Click to Open an Item (Single-Click to Select).

3. Click OK.

Gold Rush Nuggets

The direct ancestor of Windows Explorer is the old Windows File Manager. You'll see in the figure that the folder tree and icon list haven't changed much in 15 years. Well, yeah, the graphics are better.

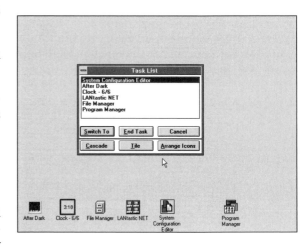

Digging Elsewhere

Address Bar, Files, Folders, Icons, Select Files

Windows Mail

When my 93-year-old grandmother easily figured out how to use e-mail, I realized that my career in writing about e-mail for beginners was nearing its sunset. That's good for everyone, and it's also good for me. Rather than bore you with simple details about Windows Mail, I can concentrate on describing some of the more useful and unknown things it can do. Sending e-mail? Well, that's the simple stuff.

Windows Mail is the e-mail program that comes with Windows Vista. It's essentially a do-over of the old Outlook Express program, which gained a bad name for being susceptible to computer viruses and other nasty programs. If you're familiar with Outlook Express, learning Windows Mail is nothing.

WHERE'S THE GOLD?

You start Windows Mail by popping up the Start button menu. From the All Programs menu, choose Windows Mail, or you may be lucky enough to find Windows Mail on the Start button menu itself. (*See* Start Button and Menu.)

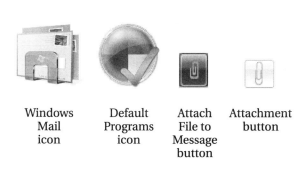

| Windows Mail icon | Default Programs icon | Attach File to Message button | Attachment button |

You can also manually run Windows Mail by typing **winmail** into the Run dialog box and pressing Enter.

The Windows Mail window looks like any standard e-mail program. The window sports useful toolbars plus various panels or panes for listing important e-mail things. Anyone who's been using e-mail for even a little while should be familiar with the Windows Mail interface.

Menu bar   Inbox

Folder list   Toolbar

Preview pane

What to Do with It

Sending, receiving, composing, and organizing e-mail are basic computer activities, akin to using a mouse or typing a letter. They're not really that difficult. Therefore, the following tasks are things you might not expect or useful things out of the ordinary.

Configure Windows to prefer your e-mail program

When you click a link on a Web page to send e-mail, you want to ensure that Windows opens the proper e-mail program, allowing you to use your favorite program and not some stupid program that Windows believes to be your favorite. Here's how to confirm that setup:

1. Open the Default Programs icon in the Control Panel, or from the Control Panel Home, choose Programs and then Default Programs.

2. Choose Set Your Default Programs.

3. Choose your e-mail program from the left side of the window.

4. Choose Set This Program As Default.

5. Click OK and close the other window you opened.

Display or hide parts of the Windows Mail window

The secret to playing hide-and-seek in Windows Mail is to know how to use the View⇨Layout command. In the Window Layout Properties window that appears, you can select which parts of the Windows Mail window show up and which remain hidden.

Note that unlike in Outlook Express, you have no way to display your contacts list in Windows Mail. *See* Contacts.

Attach a file

Next to writing e-mail messages, folks just love sending file attachments — particularly, pictures. Windows Mail lets you attach any file to a message, or multiple files, if you want. Here's how it works:

1. Compose your message as you normally do.

2. Click the Attach File to Message button on the toolbar.

   The menu command is Insert⇨File Attachment.

3. Use the Open dialog box to track down the file.

   See Open.

4. Click the Open button after choosing the file you want to attach.

5. Send the message.

The attachments are listed in the Attach area of the message headings.

Eureka

When sending more than a few attachments, consider putting them all into a compressed folder. Then send the single compressed folder rather than the multiple attachments. *See* Compressed Folders.

Save an attachment

When an attachment comes in on a message, you can follow these steps:

1. Click the honking Attachment button in the Preview pane's upper right corner.

2. From the Attachment menu, choose Save Attachments.

   Some attachments, you can view right away: images (JPG, GIF, PNG), movies (MOV, MPG, WMV), and audio files (WAV, MP3). Just about everything else should be saved first to disk.

3. In the Save Attachments dialog box, check the folder (at the bottom of the window). If it's not right, use the Browse button to choose a better, more appropriate folder.

4. Click the Save button to save the attachment to disk.

Don't forget about the attachment! You have to open a folder later to view the attachment, run the program, or do whatever with it.

Merely opening a file attachment does not save it to disk. Sure, that's okay for those silly pictures and movies that Uncle John sends you. But to save something, you need to heed these steps.

Forward a message

There are two ways to forward a message. The first is obvious: You read something you want to share with someone else, press Ctrl+F (the Forward keyboard shortcut), fill in the To field, maybe add your own text, and then click the Send button. Of course, this method is perhaps the crudest way of forwarding a message.

When I forward a message, I go to the body of the original and click the mouse in there, press Ctrl+A to select the message text, and then press Ctrl+C to copy it all. Then I start a new message and press Ctrl+V to paste in the body. The result is often cleaner than forwarding the message directly. *See* Copy, Cut, and Paste Data for details.

Use the Blind Carbon Copy (BCC)

The Blind Carbon Copy, or BCC, field can be used when sending a message to people who don't want everyone in creation to see their e-mail addresses. In fact, unless you want to look like a total computer newbie, or *noob,* put everyone's name in the BCC field whenever you send out a mass e-mail message.

To display the BCC field, choose View⊃All Headers from the menu.

Display missing pictures

Some e-mail messages contain embedded graphics, which normally don't show up in Windows Mail, as a security precaution. (Instead, you see a box with a red X in it.)

To show the picture, click just below the message header, where it says "Some pictures have been blocked to help prevent the sender from identifying your computer. Click here to download pictures." Clicking in that area displays the pictures.

To control whether pictures are blocked, obey these steps in Windows Mail:

1. Choose Tools⇨Options.

2. In the Options dialog box, click the Security tab.

3. In the Download Images section, remove the check mark by the option Block Images and Other External Content in HTML E-mail.

4. Click OK.

Compose a plain text message

Sure, it's fun to mess around with fancy formatting, text, and graphics in an e-mail message. You may even be one of those who are fond of a row of tiny, animated figures at the bottom of your electronic epistles. Then again, that stuff may not look right on other computer systems.

Serious e-mail is text only, or plain text. Businesspeople don't add bouncy, happy pirates or hearts that pucker to their online correspondence. Likewise, when you want to be taken seriously, you should avoid the e-mail froufrou and stick with serious, plain, good old-fashioned text messages.

To send a message in plain text, choose Format⇨Plain Text after you conjure up the New Message window. That's it.

Add a contact

The quickest way to build up your Contacts list is to add new contacts as you receive e-mail from them. The secret is to choose Tools⇨Add Sender to Contacts (or Tools⇨Add to Contacts) when reading the message.

For more information on your e-mail contacts, *see* Contacts.

Search through e-mail

The Windows Search command is used to hunt down specific text in an e-mail message. *See* Search.

Watch Your Step!

Avoid sending huge e-mail attachments. When sending anything larger than 5MB, consider sending a query e-mail first, asking whether the recipient can handle such a large message. Some ISPs limit e-mail inboxes to 5MB, although 10MB is more the average.

I never send e-mail attachments larger than 10MB. Instead, I burn the attachments to a CD, put the disc in a special mailer, and then send it through postal mail.

When Things Go Wrong

Windows Mail blocks certain e-mail attachments, and for good reason. Certain types of files can only do harm to your computer; these files might contain viruses. Yes, even when the message appears to be from someone you know or trust, a blocked e-mail attachment should stay blocked; do not attempt to open it!

E-mail sending and receiving problems are generally caused by some type of bad configuration of Windows Mail. Choose Tools⇨Accounts, and then select your Mail account in the Internet Accounts window. Click the Properties button and review your e-mail account settings. You might consider phoning up your ISP to confirm that the settings are correct.

Some links may not work in an e-mail message because Windows assumes that the links are part of a *phishing* scam. In other words, the link may claim that it goes to your bank when in reality it goes somewhere else, and Windows just doesn't want you to take that risk.

Gold Rush Nuggets

E-mail is one of the most ancient types of computer programs, even predating the Internet. It's said that the first e-mail message was sent in 1965. Computer pioneer Roy Tomlinson thought of using the @ symbol to separate e-mail user names from machine names in 1971.

Windows Mail is basically an updated version of the old Outlook Express e-mail program that once came with some versions of Windows. Outlook Express is not the same as the Outlook information organizer that comes with Microsoft Office. Your Windows Vista e-mail program may in fact be Outlook and not Windows Mail, in which case the information in this entry doesn't apply.

Digging Elsewhere

Contacts, Internet Explorer

Windows Media Center

The Windows Media Center brings your PC into the 21st century, creating a hub for not only traditional computer media — videos and music — but also other types of entertainment, such as television. In fact, yes, that's it: The Media Center is essentially a muscled-up version of the traditional Windows Media Player, but with the ability to let you mess with television and FM radio on your computer.

The Windows Media Center is designed to be the throbbing heart of the media PC, a great idea but one that has been very slow to be adopted. In fact, the guy at the computer store told me that everyone who comes in to buy a new PC is very impressed with the typical Windows media PC, yet very few folks buy the thing. Cost may be a factor, or it just may be too early for consumers to make the switch.

To get the most from the Windows Media Center, you need a PC with a TV tuner installed or attached. Oh, and if you have an FM radio receiver in your PC, you can listen to FM radio — but not AM. That's probably because AM radio is mostly conservative talk and Microsoft is a liberal company.

Windows Media Center is started from the All Programs menu on the Start button menu. The Media Center grows to fill the entire screen with an appealing and easy-to-use interface. As with the Media Player, if you're desperate to watch TV on your computer, you'll figure out how to do so in no time. Consider, as an alternative, using any software that may have come with your PC's TV tuner; it might be better and less complicated than the Media Center.

Windows Media Player

The Windows Media Player is the universal software tool for viewing or listening to media files in Windows. Using the player, you can listen to music, watch videos, or view other media files either directly or while you're doing something else with your computer.

Now, obviously, some people feel that the Windows Media Player seriously warrants its own, full chapter in any Windows book. I disagree. Although the Windows Media Player is a full, rich program and could stand to consume several pages of instructions, the truth is that the thing is pretty easy to figure out. I suppose the motivation to rip and burn your own CD music is just far too compelling to require someone to tediously wade through instructions on the topic. It's most likely the same reason why there are no instruction manuals for finding porn on the Internet.

Supposing that you're a parent or close relative of some teenager or 20-something who deftly uses the Windows Media Player or one of its better competitors, here's a rundown on how things go:

You can use Media Player to view media files — specifically, music, audio, and video files. These files can be stored on the computer or on a CD or DVD or found on the Internet. Media Player can appear inside a Web page window to play media content for you.

After inserting a music CD, you can opt to either play the music in Media Player or *rip* the music from the CD and store it on the computer. To rip the music, you click the big Rip button atop the Media Center window.

After music is on your computer, you can organize it into something called a playlist. The *playlist* is simply a group of songs, favorites, driving music, party music, or however you want to organize your own tunes.

Playlists can be burned onto a CD-R to create your own music discs or copied to portable music devices. To do so, click the Burn button atop the Media Player's window.

You can also use the Media Player to purchase music online, although in its current incarnation, I find this process awkward and not as efficient as, say, the iTunes online music store.

See also Windows Media Center.

WordPad

Microsoft enticed early adopters into buying Windows by tossing in a bunch of free goodies. For example, two graphical programs were included for free with the first version of Windows: Paint, which at the time was a pretty snazzy graphics tool, and Write, which was a graphical word processor rivaling many of the text-based word processors of its day. Both programs are still included with Windows. Paint is still Paint, but the Write word processor has become WordPad.

To run WordPad, you pop up the Start button menu and choose All Programs⇨Accessories⇨WordPad. The program bursts on the screen, showing a bunch of toolbars for formatting and other fun, plus a big, open space in which you can compose your thoughts.

WordPad comes with two main toolbars. A standard toolbar (with the silly name Toolbar) provides access to file, print (including print preview), copy and paste, undo, and time/date commands. A formatting toolbar provides shortcuts to character- and paragraph-formatting tools.

You can use the Ruler toolbar to set tabs and paragraph indents. To set a tab, click in the Ruler.

The toolbars and Ruler are controlled from the View menu.

Although WordPad provides the basic tools for word processing (including Find and Replace and the ability to insert and play with graphics), it lacks a few things that you would expect from modern word processors. Chief among those things that are lacking is a spell checker.

WordPad is also limited in its ability to open and save certain types of files. In Windows Vista, WordPad can work with only plain text or Rich Text Format (RTF) files. In previous versions of Windows, WordPad could also read and write the Microsoft Word DOC file format. This is no longer true in Windows Vista.

WordPad was originally named Windows Write, and even I sometimes refer to it as Write even though the name changed ages ago. Interestingly enough, the program filename for WordPad is still WRITE.EXE.

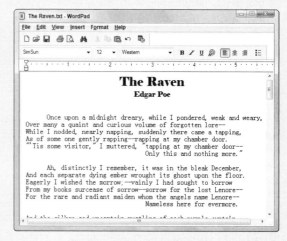

Index

Numbers & Symbols

2725